DIALOGUE OF CIVILIZATIONS
William Jones and the Orientalists

DIALOGUE OF CIVILIZATIONS

William Jones and the Orientalists

by

Mohandas Moses & Achala Moulik

ARYAN BOOKS INTERNATIONAL

New Delhi

DIALOGUE OF CIVILIATIONS

ISBN: 978-81-7305-363-4

First Published in **2009** by:
ARYAN BOOKS INTERNATIONAL
Pooja Apartments, 4B, Ansari Road, New Delhi - 110 002 (India)
Tel.: 23287589, 23255799; Fax: 91-11-23270385
E-mail: aryanbooks@vsnl.com

Computer Typeset and Printed in India at
ABI Prints & Publishing Co., New Delhi

Preface

The dialogue of civilizations began when man became a sapient being.

This book attempts to study the phenomenon of civilizations, their interactions, their impact on each other, their conflicts and clashes. The dialogue of civilization is not a new phenomenon; many have contributed to it. The reason we have set William Jones as the central figure is because through his work and researches he inaugurated a movement in Western Europe that came to be known as Orientalism and which spread to France and Germany where it became a special subject of interest. That this movement was inaugurated by an Englishman in the heyday of imperialism is remarkable enough. His ideals, work and legacy are set against the background of British administrative policies and European attitudes to India. The intent of this book is also to communicate at least a hint of the richness of the life of William Jones, his personality, the development of Indian studies against the setting of his time, and the epochal contribution he made by revealing India's contribution to human civilization to the world. His brilliant scholarship no less than his generosity and vision began a dialogue of civilization that is still continuing. This book describes how his legacy profoundly affected European response to Asian culture.

Russia developed Orientalism and Indology quite independent of Western Europe. Her contact with Indian civilization was propelled by scholars and artists of the eighteenth century who appeared on the scene about the same time as William Jones. Russian Orientalism had a different flavour from that of Western Europe. Her scholars and Indologists did not have to reconcile the grandeur of Indian civilization with the imperatives of imperialism.

The mind, William Jones wrote in the outline of his *Tract on Education*, cannot develop without absorbing the wisdom of other civilizations. A person's education cannot be complete by depending on the wisdom of one's own civilization alone. The wisdom of other cultures and their achievements is essential for self-improvement and understanding. Acquiring proficiency in languages therefore is an essential instrument for entry into other civilizations. With such understanding comes the good of mankind. William Jones believed that exchange of ideas and knowledge are the basis of dialogues between civilizations. Here we have in essence the Charter of UNESCO, written two centuries before it was declared as a policy of international organizations.

The idea of this book began in the summer of 1983 when my husband Mohandas Moses and I were visiting Calcutta. After his official discussions, Mohan and I went to the Asiatic Society to see the library. There he came across a copy of Warren Hastings' letter to Sir William Jones that was the beginning of a new chapter in the cultural history of the world. "Next year will the bicentenary of the establishment of the Asiatic Society," he reflected pensively. "I wonder if I can write a book on Sir William Jones in a year."

He could not. He had just been appointed Managing Director of the Karnataka Power Corporation and the state was reeling under an acute power crisis. He, an economist by training, plunged into the work of providing energy to Karnataka by expediting work on the various power projects of the state with the eager cooperation of his engineer colleagues. His remarkable achievements in this field are still remembered with admiration. But Mohan did not forget William Jones. Wherever he went on tours he carried books and notes on the subject and worked in the evenings. At home in the evenings he made notes from a heap of books.

Three years later he had completed writing half the book when he was selected to head the Food Corporation of India in New Delhi. There too a crisis was looming – the worst drought of the century of 1987-88. There too he earned high praise from the Union government for the manner in which he handled the drought and provided food security. In between various crises he wrote the book on the discovery of Indian civilization by Western scholars. Inspired by this, and goaded by Mohan, I began writing a novel on this period. In 1991 I joined the Archaeological Survey of India and realized the immense legacy of William Jones and Oriental scholars. We spent many hours in the Central Archaeological Library browsing through books and then adjourned to the tea lounge of the India International Centre to discuss our finds. These were some of the happiest days of our lives. Mohan hoped to complete writing his book after his retirement in 1994.

After serving as Union Secretary in several ministries Mohan was appointed as the Advisor to the Governor of Jammu and Kashmir by the Government of India in 1994. Militancy was at its violent height. With courage and determination the new Advisor entrusted with crucial development sectors decided to help in rebuilding the shattered infrastructure of this abandoned paradise. Among his many concerns was the rehabilitation of the wounded – in body and mind. This interest in the body-brain-mind had begun when he was Union Welfare Secretary. Now in Kashmir the interest became an obsession. He began writing *Last Frontiers of the Mind – Challenges of the Digital Age* which was completed in 2003, and his memoirs of Jammu-Kashmir-Ladakh in *Rajatarangini Revisited.*

On a December morning in 2003 Mohan passed away without a warning. *Last Frontiers of the Mind* was published by Prentice Hall of India in July 2005. I incorporated *Rajatarangini Revisited* in *A Stranger In Paradise,* my biography of Mohan, that was published by Har-Anand in March 2008.

It had been Mohan's wish all along that I should collaborate on the book on William Jones and write certain chapters. Yet he kept advicing me to write on other subjects. I had, therefore, written my own books. In the monsoon of 2005 I began to put together Mohan's manuscript of *Dialogue of Civilizations – William Jones and the Orientalists.* I worked on this book for nearly two years and handed the completed typescript to Mr Vikas Arya of Aryan Books International in July 2007 at the tea lounge of India International Centre.

Achala Moulik

Acknowledgement

Many persons have helped in the publication of the book.

I thank Dr. B.R. Mani, Joint Director General of the Archaeological Survey of India who has helped us to access valuable research material on the subject and given suggestions and advice on various ocassions. Dr Arundhati Banerjee of the ASI has given her assistance whenever required. I thank Professor Maheshwari Prasad of Benaras Hindu University for providing copies of old publications. I am grateful to Shri C.B. Patil of the ASI for providing me with illustrations of Oriental scholars and Dr Halakatti of the ASI who made available old publications for reference. I thank Shri S. Ramamoorti, IAS (Retd), former Chief Secretary of Maharashtra, Mohan's friend, who gave me suggestions about the book.

I thank the officials of the Asiatic Society, Calcutta, the officials of the Central Archaeological Library, New Delhi for their assistance. I also thank the staff of the Library of the Russian Center for Science and Culture, New Delhi, for their courtesy and assistance, and Smt. Hamsa Kalyani for her help.

I thank Mr Vikas Arya, Managing Director of Aryan Books International for his warm support for publication of the book.

I can never adequately thank Miss J. Jacintha who helped me to classify the material and notes with cheerful devotion through the dark monsoon of 2005.

Contents

Part III
British Attitudes to India

Part IV
Sir William Jones (1746-94)

Part V
European Indology

Part VI
Oriental Scholars and Dialogues in Civilization

List of Publications

PUBLICATIONS OF MOHANDAS MOSES

Last Frontiers of the Mind – Challenges of the Digital Age, Prentice Hall of India, 2005.

Rajatarangini Revisited – Kashmir Memoirs, Har Anand Publications, 2008.

PUBLICATIONS OF ACHALA MOULIK

1. *Silhouettes of Russian Literature*, Mysore University, 1976.
2. *Immortals of Italian Literature*, Vikas, 1988.
3. *El Dorado Revisited – A Cultural History of Spain*, India Book House, 1982 and Palgrave/Macmillan, 1983 & 1988.
4. *Pageant of Karnataka*, Govt. of Karnataka, 1983.
5. *World Heritage Monuments of India*, Archaeological Survey of India Publications, 1994.
6. *India – Monuments and Sites*, ICOMOS-UNESCO Publication, 1996.
7. *Our Bengal*, Writers Workshop, 1979.
8. *Kings, Queens and Lovers*, India Book House, 1978 & UBSPD, 1996.
9. *Camellians for Caroline* (Novel), Harlequins, 1985, Translated into French, Swedish and Finnish.
10. *Seasons in Paradise* (Short stories), IBH, 1980.
11. *The Conquerors* (Novel), UBS Publishers, 1995.
12. *Earth is But a Star* (Novel), UBS Publishers, 1997.
13. *Literary Titans of the Milennium*, UBS Publishers, 1999.
14. *Captors of Time: Monument of the Millennium*, UBS Publishers, 2000.
15. *Dream Journey*, UBS Publishers, 2003.
16. *Once upon a time* (Poems), Writers Workshop, 2006.
17. *Script for Sound and Light of Hampi*, Ministry of Tourism and Culture.
18. *Monuments of India*, Archaeological Survey of India Publication, 2008.
19. *Pushkin's Last Poem – A Play*, National Book Trust of India.
20. *A Stranger in Paradise – Story of an Extraordinary Civil Servant*, Har Anand Publications Pvt. Ltd., 2008.

21. *India's Contribution to Conservation of Angkor Vat* (Edited), Archaeological Survey of India Publication, 1995.
22. Translated 'Seemabaddho' from Bengali to English as 'Company Limited', Orient Longmans, 1977.

Part I

Dialogue Between Civilizations

1
The Crossroads of Civilizations

"These fragments have I shored against my ruin."

Ruskin wrote that great nations write their autobiographies in three manuscripts – the book of their deeds, the book of their words and the book of their art. The *summum bonum* of these is civilization. The book of their deeds describes the events that shape their history, the book of their words reflects their thoughts and beliefs while their art represents their creativity and their world of imagination. Civilization is what grows out of, and beyond, the everyday struggle for existence. The qualities of thoughts and sentiments aspire for perfection through science, philosophy, myths, music, art and finally spirituality. This process of creativity and harmony, enquiry and exploration of the material and the non-material world received patronage of the ruler because he was enriched by the process.

The original meaning of civilization came from the Latin word 'civitas' or city. It is in small cities usually located on the banks of rivers, or atop a hill, or on the shores of a protected bay that civilization began. Civilization grows out of energy and ambition, bursts of creativity, a need for identity, answers to the riddle of existence, and finally the quest for permanence not merely in present time and space but beyond. Every civilization strives to leave behind the evidence of its existence. Every ruler wants to extol not only the glory of the Almighty but his own transient passage through the temporal world. Towards this purpose he erects monuments, commissions ballads and sagas, paintings and sculptures. The thirst for immortality ensures the continuum of civilization.

The historian H.A.L. Fischer opens his book *History of Europe* by declaring, "We Europeans are the children of Hellas." Indeed every great civilization leaves behind a legacy, even those that are given the misnomer "dead civilizations."

No civilization has ever existed in isolation. Patient archaeology yields discoveries of ancient contacts between different civilizations. Pottery shards, jewellery, seals, figurines, fossilized foodgrains and plants resembling each other have been found in diverse excavation sites. Obviously there were contacts and communications that no chronicle recorded. Sailors, traders, travellers, and pilgrims may have exchanged notes and ideas, inspirations and techniques not made known to rulers and soldiers.

Few explanations are available however to explain the factors which lead to the rise of a civilization, sometimes simultaneously, in different parts of the world. The great civilizations of Egypt, Mesopotamia, China and the Indus Valley of India grew around four great rivers about 3000 BC. When the Hellenic world burst into splendour in the 6th century BC, there was a similar flowering of Chinese and Indian culture during this time. The glories of the Roman Empire existed with similar resurgence in China, India, and the Levant. There was an efflorescence of literature, art and architecture between the sixth and eighth century AD in India, in Umayyad Damascas, Abbasid Baghdad, in Carolingian France, and again at the turn of the second millennium of the Christian era and in the 12th and 16th centuries in Western Europe, in Muscovy, in Persia, China and India. In fact the 'new' civilization of 12th century Europe was an amalgam of Graeco-Roman-Byzantine-Moorish-Frankish-Gothic forms and ideas.

Historian Arnold Toynbee identifies contacts between civilizations both in space and time. For space he gives the example of geographic areas where civilizations encounter each other such as ancient Syria encompassing the North Arabian steppe and the Mediterranean Sea, Southern Anatolia and the Armenian plateau, the Oxus-Jaxartes basin, the Tigris-Euphrates basin, the Nile basin, Iranian plateau and the Hindu Kush, the Eurasian Steppe in the area around Caspian Sea, Aral Sea and Lake Balkash. In these centres, says Toynbee, many religions and associated cultures met such as Mahayana Buddhism, Zorastrianism, Hellenism, Christianity, and Islam. These areas, he observes, have the capacity for 'round-abouts of traffic' of various cultures. The Oxus-Jaxartes basin served this purpose because within its boundaries the Syriac, Indic, Iranic, Babylonic, Sinic, Hellenic forms met and fused. While the Mediterranean was the scene of conflicts between rival Phoenicians, Achaemenians, Greeks, Romans, Arabs, it also gave these races the opportunity to know each other, test their strengths and weaknesses, their products and creeds. With wars and conflicts came the slow penetration of new ideas and skills.

Minoan civilization based in Crete was inherited by the city-states of Sparta, Athens, Ithaca, Thessalonika and spread to Asia Minor and North Africa, and to the shores of the Black Sea and thence to Russia. After the wisdom of Socrates, Plato, Aristotle, the glories of the Periclean Age and the exuberance of Alexander, Greek civilization was exhausted. She was defeated by Roman legions. Rome adopted Greek culture, imparting it a new vigour but with less elegance. Greek influence was also pervasive in Asia Minor, the Levant, Bactria and Syria. When Rome fell to decadence and 'barbarian' invasions, the sinews of her culture was taken over by the Goths, Vandals and Franks. The Frankish warrior-king Charlemagne, who called himself the Holy Roman Emperor, sought to recreate the Roman world in his capital at Aachen (or Aix la Chapelle).

Toynbee calls this continuum as 'reintegration' or 'resumption of the universal state'. The other examples he cites are: the Abbasids continuing the Umayyad state which in turn was the legatee of the Persian empire that grew out of the Babylonian-Sumerian polity. The Ottoman Empire grew out of the Byzantine Commonwealth which arose out of the Roman empire which had in turn accepted the mantle of Athens. Similarly, the Moghul Empire adopted the framework of the earlier Hindu Gupta empire that was in turn the legatee of Asoka's imperium. In other words, there is never a break with the past that is an integral part of the present and the future.

Some historians have been baffled by the swift and sudden transformation of rough desert Arabs of the sixth century into the splendid Arab empire of the eighth and ninth centuries that overran the classical world and challenged established beliefs and customs. But as Toynbee points out in *A Study of History*, the Arabs and Jews had been ruled by the Romans for centuries and had ample opportunities to study Roman forms of warfare and governance. These were adopted when Mohammed welded them into a cohesive unit. Damascus and Baghdad, Cairo and Cordoba became centres of a civilization that was built on the foundations of the Sumerian-

Persian-Greek-Roman world. And it was in Moorish Spain that the works of classical philosophers, mathematicians, and scientists were studied and preserved. While the North European tribes ransacked the Graeco-Roman world, the Moors of Europe were paving the way for the Italian renaissance.

Charlemagne (crowned the Holy Roman Emperor by Pope Pius II in the pious hope that the Germanic ruler would defend the Church) was fascinated by stories of the Muslim Orient. He sent an embassy to the court of Haroon-al-Rashid at Baghdad, then the most splendid city of the world. They exchanged craftsmen who learned the art of illuminating books, binding with leather and studding with gems. Greek texts found their way from Byzantium to Baghdad and to Aachen. An elephant was sent by the Caliph to the Emperor; when it perished from the cold in Saxony, the tusks were extracted to make ivory chessmen. Water clocks fashioned by Arab chronometrists replaced the Roman sundial. Sartorial innovations were also made; short tunics were replaced by long robes and caps by eastern turbans.

Even before the Crusades the exchange of crafts and skills, ideas and theories between the Saracen world and Western Europe and Spain reached a exuberant culmination in Gothic art. Hindu fables and numerals were carried by Arabs to Spain, Italy, France and Germany. The fantastic features of Gothic art arose from these traditions. Arab architectural concepts were adopted by the Franks and Goths. While Crusaders slaughtered 'infidels', they borrowed Persian literary motifs of chivalry and courtly love. The Ottoman-Turkish tulip became the pride of Koekenhoff and Ming-Chinese blue and white porcelain became the symbol of Delft.

There was a peaceful and continuous dialogue of civilization then between the countries in South and East Asia in early first millennium of the Christian era. India did not engage in wars of conquest in East Asia; pilgrims and merchants carried Hindu and Buddhist religion, art forms, legends and myths to Burma, Thailand, Cambodia, Laos, Korea, China and eventually Japan. While adopting Indian cultural and religious traditions, each of these countries evolved their own distinct civilizations made richer by diverse streams.

Archaeological discoveries have sometimes revived ancient fashions. The excavations of Pompeii and Herculaneum affected eighteenth-century European sartorial fashions and coiffures, as well as furnishing and architecture. 'Discovery' of the paintings of Ajanta had similar effects in India.

Paradoxically, great civilizations are established on military victories. Greek victory over the Persian army at the battle of Thermopyle provided an impetus for Greek expansion in politics and ideas: Roman victory over the Greeks made her the heir of Athens: Frankish victory at Ronscevalle halted the Moorish advance and paved the way the consolidation of the Carolingian realm: the Arab conquest of Spain created the culture of Western Islam as well as the easternization of Spain: Haroon al Rashid's territorial expansion, the Ottoman conquest of Constantinople, and British conquest of India created new political and cultural entities. Each of these victories over an older and richer civilization paved the way for the evolution of a new culture out of the old. While the Mediterranean world shuddered at the 'infidel' Moor and the 'barbarian' Goth and Vandal, these newcomers brought vitality to decadent and static civilizations. As the invaders and immigrants settled down they brought order, new skills and created a new ethos. This process of assimilation is the function of civilization.

There can therefore be no 'death' or 'end 'of a civilization. It is a continuum, of borrowing and adapting, made possible by the insatiable curiosity of the human mind, and the thirst for expanding not only territories but the intellectual horizons and visions. This expansion confers upon the lender and the borrower an assurance and certitude. Out of the welter of cross-fertilization of cultures emerges stability and a new order.

2

William Jones and the Dialogue of Civilizations

In a comparison between Francis of Assisi and the great emperor Frederick II of Germany and Sicily, the historian Will Durant has said that when the names of emperors and conquerors have succumbed to the dust of history, people will continue to remember those who enriched civilization with their vision and compassion.

The same could be said in a comparison between the British conquerors on one hand and the British scholars and visionaries who came to India and made contributions that outlive empires. Today, when founders of the British Indian Empire are subjected to objective scrutiny sans jingoistic emotions, the Britons who emerge from the dust and debris of historical controversies are those who brought with them the enlightenment of the West and who in turn made the ancient heritage of India known to the West. While Robert Clive and others of his tribe have been relegated to the darker chapters of British-Indian imperial history, the name of William Jones continues to evoke respect and gratitude.

Empire building had some favourable, if unintended, side effects. Just as Napoleon Bonaparte's misadventure in Egypt led to more enduring achievements in the decoding of the Rosetta Stone and the evolution of Egyptology, so Sir William Jones played a crucial role in the encouragement of both Oriental studies and the formulation of British policies of the eighteenth and nineteenth-centuries.

Jones' writings on Indian civilization caught the imagination and interest of nineteenth-century European scholars and intellectuals that led to systematic study and research on the subject. In collaboration with Warren Hastings, he founded the Asiatic Society of Bengal that commenced and facilitated the study

William Jones

of Indian history, culture and social organizations; this laid the foundations for the re-discovery of India.

Political events influenced the development of interest in the world outside Europe and Britain. In the era following the Treaty of Vienna there was warm support for the principle of national self-determination and demand for Parliamentary reforms. In India, enlightened British rulers strove to bring to India Western laws and ideas of governance.

William Jones was not only a scholar, he was also part of the nascent British Raj in Bengal. His connection with both Leadenhall Street (the headquarters of the East India Company) and Westminster brought him into contact with the ruling elite who often consulted him on matters of governance and legal administration.

Both settings, Calcutta and London, were full of pageantry and colour whose echoes and shadows may still be glimpsed in what was the first capital of the British-Indian empire.

In fact Jones played a significant role in formulating British attitude to India and Indians. His accomplishments would have made him a celebrity in the enlightened society of eighteenth century England; he was an erudite scholar who knew twenty-eight languages and made numerous great discoveries in Indian languages. He understood the uses and imperatives of power though he would never exercise that power for his own ends. While he continued to be a part of the Raj, he recognized the need to understand the country that had been conquered. In the period after the Battle of Plassey, there had been social intercourse and even camaraderie between Indians and the Company officers. William Jones realized that to govern India well and to be enriched by India in non-material terms, the British rulers must also understand the wellsprings of Indian civilization. He saw no contradiction or dichotomy in this. Indeed this duality – of attraction for Indians and Indian civilization while supporting colonial rule – remained the attitude of many liberal Britons in India well into the early twentieth century.

There is a tendency in the writings on Jones for authors to concentrate on his scholarly propensities at the expense of Jones the man, to think of him in terms of Browning's scholar – a solitary scholar-hermit, a man who devoted a lifetime to the declension of a word – is to do him gross injustice. The Georgian era in

England was a gregarious age of coffee houses, clubs, and country houses and Jones was very much a creature of his time. A man – who knew twenty-eight languages, who could profess the sentiments of Tom Paine and yet secure a high public office, who was the leading scholar of his time and who yet could make a foray into the disorderly world of Georgian politics, who could be friends with Hastings after having been a close associate of his inveterate foe, Burke, who could be a member of Johnson's Literary Club, who could choose as his emblem the Hindu god Ganesa, and yet retain John Shore, the Evangelical Governor-General as his friend and biographer, who could have a pet tortoise which he called Othello – was a man whose depth and range were greater than pastel prose portraits have been able to convey.

One has to be wary when turning on the bright lights of biography to avoid investing episodes in the life of the subject with more significance than is due. The schoolboy Jones who had started writing poetry was undoubtedly attracted by the verbal music of the *Tempest*. But what makes the choice prophetic is the fact that the *Tempest* contains a clear warning against the dangers of colonialism. For the native Caliban the isle was 'full of sounds and sweet airs that give delight and hurts not.' But even for the learned Prospero it was a desert and for the newcomers Ferdinand and his friends it was 'full of devils'. The play epitomizes the cultural opacity that the colonists so often displayed in the Oriental environment, discarding all that was alien as bizarre or valueless. This was a drawback of even the educated element. The outstanding example of this later day Prospero was Macaulay who in his usual tones of stentorian confidence was to declare that little of India's literature or history was of any value.

Sir William Jones commenced the understanding and appreciation of Indian civilization. In the eighteenth century it was only a small band of men like William Jones who realized the cultural treasures the East contained and sought to commemorate them in the West.

In March 1774, Johnson wrote a prophetic letter to Warren Hastings hoping that, "a mind comprehensive like yours will find leisure, amidst the care of your important station to inquire into many subjects of which the European world thinks not all and thinks with deficient intelligence .... I shall hope that he who had once intended to increase the learning of his country by the introduction of the Persian language will examine the traditions and histories of the East and that he will survey the remains of its ancient edifices and trace the vestiges of its ruined cities and that on his return we shall know the arts and opinions of a race of men from whom very little has hitherto been derived".

Only fragments of India's cultural heritage were known to Europeans before the work of William Jones. The recognition of this cultural heritage to the extent that British prejudice admitted its merit, justified the preservation of the Indian Constitution and profoundly supported the conservative view of India.

William Jones did not appear in India, puzzled and disaffected, full of British prejudices against the people and culture of the land. He wrote: "It gave me inexpressible pleasure to find myself in the midst of so noble an amphitheater almost encircled by the vast regions of Asia, which has ever been esteemed the nurse of sciences, the scene of glorious actions, fertile in the products of human genius, abounding in natural wonders and untimely diversified in the forms of religion and Government, in the laws, manners, customs and languages as well as in the features and complexion of men." However, he also held the view that Asiatic despotism had blighted the progress of Eastern nations and that the free institutions of the West had made continued cultural achievements possible.

In tone and sentiment this was the attitude of a tolerant scholar and conservative. He wanted to preserve the values of Indian culture for the whole world. He studied hard to master Sanskrit and transmit the literature and learning of India to the West. In the effort he rediscovered great works of poetry and drama, and translated them for European readers; he uncovered neglected treatises on science, philosophy and history; he enquired into the profound theology of the Hindus; he wrote a remarkable tract on Hindu and Muslim law; and most importantly he was, with Warren Hastings, the founder of the Asiatic Society of Bengal which in turn paved the way for rediscovery of India both within and outside India.

Arberry, a biographer of Sir William Jones, states that he used "essentially medieval criteria in evaluating culture. He organized his own knowledge (and viewed Indian learning) largely in a medieval framework, the liberal acts and higher faculties, law, medicine, philosophy and theology. He had not adopted the nineteenth century emphasis on science, engineering and the social sciences as the hallmark of progress. To William Jones, as to ancient and medieval thinkers, virtue was the purpose of intellectual endeavour." Man had three faculties, viz., memory, the study of facts which gave rise to history; ratiocination, which was the basis of science and philosophy; and imagination which was the presence of art. These three faculties were designed to encourage virtue, for whether in European or Oriental society, virtue was man's goal. Thus, in judging India's cultural heritage, William Jones tended to approve any intellectual or artistic effort and sought to demonstrate how this effort encouraged freedom and hence virtue.

As he looked initially at Indian intellectual work in 1784, Jones concluded that European superiority lay in ratiocination, Indian in imagination. He had not supposed that Indians would have achieved much in rhetoric because the prevalent despotism had precluded "the idea of popular eloquence". He found "Indian drama and poetry of the highest order" and "Indian architecture sublime". The poetry he found "lively and elegant", the epics "were magnificent", the Vedas abounded in "noble speculation in metaphysics". As he went deeper into Indian thought he said, "If their numerable works on Grammar, logic, rhetoric, music, all of which are extent and accessible are generally known, it would be found that they had yet higher pretensions to the praise of a fertile and inventive genius." Indian work in science he found to be more impressive than he supposed and by 1794, the year of his death, he declared that Indians actually understood in general the principles of gravitation from the earliest times. About the high level of Indian philosophy, he wrote that no one could consider writing a history of philosophy without considering many Indian works. And he added, "One correct version of any celebrated Hindu book would be of greater value than all the dissertations or essays that would be composed on the same subject." (This is in sharp contrast to what Macaulay had to say seven decades later.) He warned Protestant missionaries of the danger of considering Indian theology and ethics as vastly inferior to Christianity and asked them to respect the religious institutions of India.

* * * * *

3

Contacts between Asia and Europe

Contact between Asia and Europe began early in the history of recorded civilization. To assess the impact of such contacts – commercial, cultural, political, religious – it would be necessary to examine the essential features of Asian and European civilizations.

Is there such a concept such as 'Asian civilization'? Asian civilizations are more diverse than European civilizations. One has to see the Persian Sassanian Empire and empires in T'ang China and Gupta India to appreciate the difference. Is Asia a geographical expression? Her political frontiers have not always corresponded to her cultural frontiers. Graeco-Roman influences created different Asian cultures; Syria, Asia Minor, Afghanistan, and Punjab were at certain points of time more 'European' than other parts of Asia. Conversely, peoples from Central Asia such as the Turkic and Magyar tribes, Tartars and Huns overran parts of Central Europe and Russia, and carried their native influences with them.

Where does Asia begin, territorially? On the Bosphorus? Or in Constantinople, where the Orient and Occident met in the great Byzantine Empire? Or is it in Russia, called (by Maurice Paleologue) the most Asian of European nations? The Roman Herodotus thought so; he called the River Don 'the terminus of Asia and Europe'.

Historians such as Samuel Huntingdon who refer to the clash of civilizations between Oriental Islam and Occidental Christianity overlook the fact that Christianity began in the same place – the Middle East – where Islam also began. The first converts to Christianity were not Romans, Greeks, Franks and Nordics who later imparted to Christianity a western flavour but Syrians, Copts, Arabs and Jews. Early Christianity comprised many features of

Asian religions until these were outlawed by the Church. One was the belief in reincarnation of the soul held by early Christians until banned by Emperor Constantine. He saw in the theory of karma a freedom of the individual soul to evolve towards liberation or salvation that the church felt should be its sole prerogative.

While religion defines a civilization so does economics and commerce, the social modes of production defined by Karl Marx. Asian societies have been agrarian, hierarchical, and often despotic. Peasants have tilled the fields, warriors have fought for more lands, rulers have governed or misgoverned with impunity. Feudal society in Europe was no different until the fourteenth century. Then a commercial revolution in Florence, Venice, and Germany eroded European feudalism. Luther's Reformation did the rest. This renaissance of the spirit and society drew inspiration from an older European tradition that had slumbered through fifteen centuries until it awoke and made Europeans return to the forgotten political and intellectual heritage of Greece.

The city states of ancient Greece bred adventurers and explorers, conquerors and travellers as the two great Greek epics indicate. It is unlikely that a single episode such as the abduction of a queen could have led to such a protracted and sanguinary encounter as is depicted in the Iliad. The invasion of the richer and more developed Troy sprang from an impulse for trade and territorial expansion. In the Bronze Age of the second millennium BC, Troy's possession and monopoly of the ingredients required for production of bronze impelled the Greeks to conquer Troy. Ulysses' encounter with dragons and demons is a traveller's tale. Sparta and Athens, Ithaca and Iona were too arid and infertile to provide the bounty required for a growing population and were also too small to contain the restless energies, the insatiable curiosity and the growing hunger for land and wealth of the Greeks. The impetus for commerce beyond the Aegean Sea produced navigators, shipbuilders, merchants, and eventually military adventurers. A new mercantile class that was neither peasant nor prince, neither plebian nor patrician, grew in wealth and power, and inevitably questioned the authority of the ruling class. Out of this development grew a new social and political ideology – of democracy and the rule of law. (This process was repeated in sixteenth-century Europe when the rise of the guilds and the merchant class put an end to the feudal structure of society, stimulated territorial expansion, the search for markets beyond their borders and conquest of richer lands.) This affluent and educated class produced philosophers, mathematicians, astronomers, poets and scholars who questioned established creeds and sought answers about the phenomenal as well as the spiritual world.

Asia produced its own merchant classes who were older than the Hellenic ones. Ancient cities of the Indus Valley had maritime commerce with cities of Mesopotamia, Africa and China in two millennia before the Christian era. In the first and second centuries AD, Indian merchants, priests, artists and soldiers went eastward to colonize Eastern Asia. Bali, Java, Sumatra, Kambhuja (Cambodia), Thailand, the Malayan archipelago bear witness to India's commercial, cultural and religious presence. While Hindu traders on the eastern coast were engaged in commerce and cultural exchange, the imperial Kushanas, Guptas, and the rulers of Kashmir maintained contacts with Hellenic Asia Minor and the pre-Islamic West Asia. The Silk Route to Rome was a flourishing centre of trade and exchange of ideas.

A question often asked is why India did not develop the Hellenic outlook. Western historians such as Charles Fitzgerald have explained it away by commenting on the resilience of the Indian spirit, of their reluctance to look outward, the resistance to new ideas, even though they may adopt new styles of art and architecture. They feel that Hinduism exerted an overwhelming influence over Indian minds and they felt no need to question or explore the thoughts of other civilizations. In other words, despite their maritime commerce, and their overseas colonies, their tolerance and assimilation, Indians remained inward looking. This attitude is put down to the Indian contempt for the material and visible world. Such an outlook produced a static society. European historians have not explained how a static society went on producing great literature, great philosophy, and great art whose influence spread far beyond her frontiers.

China, says Fitzgerald, appears to have followed a similar resistance to change despite her vast landmass, the invasions and migrations of different races, maritime and overland trade. She was always a self-contained, homogenous entity, whose certitude and pride kept strangers at the gate. China welcomed Buddhism only as a corollary to Confucianism and adapted the new creed to her own needs.

Western cultural historians say that Indian and Chinese civilizations were largely untouched by Western influences until the eighteenth century. When the contact came, first through trade and then through wars of conquest, these two great and ancient civilizations felt the full impact of the challenge posed by the West. However, the initial clash of cultures eventually gave rise to a dialogue.

4

Interaction of Cultures within Asia

There had been early voyages from India to towns on the Persian Gulf and Arabian Sea and to the Mediterranean port of Alexandria; the interaction had been more of commerce than culture but evidence of these contacts can be found both in the excavated sites of the Indus Valley as well as those in West Asia. Ancient Sumer and ancient India traded in timber and metals; ships from both countries crossed the Arabian Sea carrying merchandise. The Sinologist Professor Goodrich found evidence to suggest that China and India had links from the first millennium BC.

Just as Christianity played a role in European expansion, Buddhism was a driving force in the travels of Indians to East Asia. Emperor Asoka had initiated Buddhist missionary activities when he sent his son and daughter to Sri Lanka to propagate Buddhism to which he had been dramatically converted. The impetus continued into the second century when Buddhism was still flourishing in India.

The transmission of Buddhism from the land of its origin – India – to her eastern neighbours created an interaction of civilizations which were very different from one another but which forged bonds through Buddhism. In AD 67 two Indian Buddhist monks, Kasyapa Matanga and Dharmaraksha, carried Gautama Buddha's message to the imperial Chinese court. In the second century BC Chang Kien, a Chinese diplomat, found that Chinese products were being sold in the markets of Central Asia. Indian Buddhists who visited China to spread their faith also contributed to this cultural exchange. The Kashmiri prince Gunavarman established an order of Buddhist nuns in Nanking. Another prince Kumarajiva who had been taken as hostage to China in AD 401 spent his ten year incarceration in translating the Buddhist classic *The Lotus of the Good Law* into Chinese. Hindu scholars such as

Paramartha travelled to China by sea in AD 546 and translated seventy works into Chinese. Earlier a Parthian prince had translated Buddhist texts into Chinese.

The Chinese pilgrim Fa-Hsien came to India in the fourth century, travelling across 'drifting sands' (probably Taklamakan desert) to Kara Shahr, Khotan, Kashgar and Darel, then outposts of Indian culture, and to the cities of North India. It is to Fa-Hsien that we owe considerable amount of information of fourth century India.

The seventh century saw a quickening of this cultural cross-pollination. This is when Hiuen-Tsang, Wang Hiuen-tsi, and I-tsing visited India. Chinese scholar-pilgrims carried Buddhist texts, scrolls and sculpture from India. Hiuen-Tsang brought images of Buddha in gold, silver and sandal wood. It is believed that the Chinese pagoda is inspired from the tower built by Kanishka at Peshawar. The art historian J.H. Lindsay observes that Chinese art from the fifth to the eighth century was influenced by Gupta and Gandhara styles. The travel-chronicles of both men describe the opulence, order, tranquility, and administration of justice of the realms they visited. The empire of Chandragupta II is vividly described. This was a period of intense cultural exchange between India and China, thanks to the pilgrims who came to worship and study in the land of Lord Buddha, and take back texts on Buddhism. The great Chinese author Wu-cheng-en's classic '*Monkey*' is a unique work, half allegory, half travelogue (with a little tongue-in-cheek) that was inspired by Buddhist tradition.

Chinese pilgrims carried the message of Buddha to her eastern neighbours – Korea and Japan. While Buddhism had to compete with Confucianism in China, its progress in Korea and Japan was swifter. Prince Shotuku Taishi of Japan introduced Buddhism to Japan in early seventh century. Japan was transformed by the new faith that influenced art, painting, and outlook though the essential tenet of Buddhism – *ahimsa* or non-violence – was never accepted as a practice either in China or Japan. Nevertheless, Buddhism was one major factor of cultural interaction in Asia, from Afghanistan to Japan, and shaped the literature and art of this region. Tibetan Buddhism and Lamaism travelled to Mongolia.

Buddhist concepts and practices took new names and new forms; the *dhyana* (meditation) of India became *zen* in Japan, the Buddhist female Bodhisattva Maitreyi became Kwanon in Japan but the message of compassion and the eight-fold path for attaining

Nirvana remained. In fact the pragmatic approach to existence propounded by Buddha was more acceptable to the Chinese and Japanese than the Indians.

Buddhist pilgrims had earlier carried Buddha's teachings to Srilanka as well as Burma. During the Gupta period monuments both Hindu and Buddhists were built at Thatun (which had trade relations with Amravati), Pegu and Prome. Burma was the meeting point between Chinese culture and Indian religion. Merchants went to Java from Gujarat as well as the eastern kingdom of Kalinga and colonized the island. Migrations and colonization of Sumatra and Java occurred in the reigns of Pallava and Pala dynasties of India. It was under the fresh impetus of Buddhism that the Shailendra kings began the construction of the massive Buddhists monuments at Borobudur that shows the influence of Gupta art. Famous Hindu shrines were built at Prambanan dedicated to the Hindu trinity. Javanese literature flourished in the thirteenth century; many of the literary works were taken from the two great Sanskrit epics.

Indian merchants, scholars, and priests began exploratory journeys eastwards in the first and second centuries AD. While the movement of Central Asian tribes disrupted the overland silk route, the Arab victory over the Chinese in the year 751 closed free travel between India and China. As elsewhere, trade and religion went together. The same impulse for expansion that seized the ancient Greeks and intensified during the Crusades also touched Indian movement eastwards.

It is in times of cohesion and order that Indian expansion overseas took place. Commerce and culture went together. Hindu merchants and priests who sailed from Tamralipta went to Suvarna Bhoomi which is present day Thailand, Sumatra, Cambodia and to Palembang before the Christian era. The extension of Indian influence was through peaceful permeation and not through the force of arms. Merchants and missionaries rather than soldiers were transmitters of Indian heritage. The fact that these societies were simple tribal ones gave greater attraction for a highly developed culture that had much to offer in material and spiritual fields.

While Cambodia had ethnic links with China, their civilization was influenced by India. Their greatest king Jayavarman-II was a Hindu and had relations with Java. His successor Yasovarman built a new capital at Angkor which he named Yashodarapura. The Khmer kings of Cambodia adopted Buddhism and reached their apogee under Suryavarman-II when the great temple of Angkor Vat was built. The temple city of Angkor Vat is the largest temple in the world whose sculptures, bas reliefs and soaring *sikharas* or spires are influenced by Chola architectural styles. Suryavarman II was deeply influenced by Indian civilization. Borobodur and Angkor Vat are the material remains of the dialogue of civilizations that began two millennia ago.

Hindu influence pervaded the region that lay between her and China – Burma, Thailand, Cambodia, Java, Sumatra, Bali, the Malay Peninsula and Vietnam. It was later replaced by Buddhism. Siam, deeply influenced by Hindu traditions and culture, later embraced the Buddhist religion. The culture of Cambodia was a mixture of Mahayana Buddhism and Brahmanical customs and rituals. Brahmin priests were employed in the royal courts to conduct ceremonies and cast horoscopes.

The cultural and religious evolution of Sri Lanka, Burma, Thailand and Cambodia is an instance of the dialogue of civilizations. Indian cultural traditions played a large part in shaping the social, political, artistic and religious traditions of the countries that lay between the Arabian Sea and the Pacific Ocean. Both the Devanagari and Pali alphabets were adopted by these peoples and the names are variations of Sanskrit words. Indian myths and legends, beliefs and traditions have fashioned the architecture, sculpture, music, dance forms, religious ceremonies, social customs of this region. Hinduism and Buddhism struck deep roots into these societies because it was by a process of assimilation rather than by wars or conquest or coercion.

The cultural and commercial interaction came suddenly to a halt in the eighth century. It was as if an era of chaos had settled over all the centres of civilization; in India the imperial Guptas lost control as the 'White Huns' invaded North India; the Tang dynasty in China had to contend with incursions from Mongolia; Persia fell before the Arabs; northern tribes filled the vacuum left by the Roman imperium. It is only in West Asia that a new force – Islam – rose. This would soon be a challenge to older civilizations and the catalyst for a new order.

When the Yuan or Mongol dynasty of Gengis Khan was overthrown by a Ming solider of fortune in the fourteenth century,

China once more withdrew to herself, partly to consolidate the new regime, while Portugal, after a century of exploratory navigations, found a sea route to the East. Two centuries earlier the militant Crusaders had seen the military might as well as the material splendour of the Arab empire. When they found the land route to middle Asia blocked by Arabs, there began a search for a sea route to India. The Spice Route ushered in a new era of European colonialism.

Defending imperialism, historians of the early twentieth century attributed this search for spices, textiles and markets as an expression of their adventurous spirit, their scientific temper, their thirst for knowledge and other apologia for what was frankly an aggressive and aquisitive mercantile spirit. One even went on to say that Europe was in a resurgent spirit after having been threatened by barbarian Asiatic hordes for two millennia – Persians, Huns, Saracens and Mongols. This historian lauds the courage and perseverance that Europe resisted Asiatics and their influence while preserving its pristine identity. He omits to mention the Germanic tribes that obliterated for several centuries all traces of the classical world. He thought that while it is laudatory for Europeans to resist Asian influences, the resistance of Asia to Western influence was a sign of their 'static' society! Fortunately historians of later decades have been more objective about European colonialism, its motive force, its effects, and the dialogue of civilizations that commenced amidst wars and betrayals.

5

Early Cultural and Commercial Exchanges between East and West

Western historians have called Asian civilizations 'static' on the ground that they have been largely impervious to Western influences. Nor have they – with the exception of the ancient Persians under Cyrus and Darius and the thirteenth-century nomadic and militant Mongols under Gengiz Khan and Kublai Khan – been particularly eager to explore or conquer European territories. The principal reason may be that the major Asian civilizations had extensive territories of their own. Further, the major Asian civilizations had physical barriers that inhibited outward expansion – the formidable Hindu Kush ranges near India, the Central Asian mountains and daunting deserts around China. Until the rise of Islam, these barriers had for centuries protected China and India from invasions and allowed them to develop their own civilizations over several millennia. The ingredients of their civilizations were strongly flavoured by religion and as such there was a natural resistance to influences that posed a danger to the established religion and customs.

Western influences came nevertheless. Alexander of Macedon's invasion of Punjab and Sindh led to the establishment of Greek dynasties in Punjab. Greek presence is visible in early tracts on medicine and astronomy and the impress of the Hellenistic style is obvious in Gandharan sculptures. Gandhara was an outpost of Hellenism; Greeks studied at the University of Taxila and there were Indians who read Greek literature and spoke Greek. The massive Greek-style temples of Avantipur and Martand in Kashmir are Hellenic in inspiration.

The Macedonian invasion had another effect; it served to awaken Indian rulers to the danger of future armies. Chandragupta

Maurya consolidated his empire to meet such a threat. Colonies established by Alexander under his general Seleucus in Bactria and Asia Minor continued to exist side by side with the Mauryan empire, with courteous exchanges of gifts, scholars and the occasional philosopher. When Diodotus, governor of Greek Bactria and the Parthian Arsaces overthrew Seleucid suzerainty and established their own independent kingdoms, they occupied Mauryan Gandhara. The coins of this period embossed with the head of Demetrius are in Greek style and Greek letters. Later the coins resembling those of India were inscribed in both Brahmi and Kharoshti script. One of the pillars of an Indo-Greek temple mentions that Heliodorus who came as an ambassador from King Antialcidas became a worshipper of Vishnu. By the second century BC, Greeks settled around the Indian frontier had become Indianised and adopted Hinduism. Another Indo-Greek king Menander ruled Punjab and embraced Buddhism.

Though the Mauryan Emperors of North India had close connections with the Greek colonies in Asia Minor, cultural exchange was more with the Iranian empire. Zoroastrian Taxila, then an Iranian satrapy, and Hindu Pataliputra were in close touch. Emperor Chandragupta visited this city and his grandson, Emperor Asoka, drew inspiration from the stone pillars of Persepolis for recording his edicts as well as the bell-capitals. The concept of *vihara*s carved from rock may have been borrowed from the tombs of Achaemenian rulers. While the form may have been derived from outside, Indian artists and artisans gave their creations a different spirit.

Gandharan culture flourished in north-west India and in present day Afghanistan; this produced a school of art that is a fusion of Greek and Buddhist traditions. Hellenic form and style, depiction of clothes, facial expression, Corinthian pillars, bas relief, and representation of Olympian deities coexist with Buddhist fervour and simplicity.

Both Indian and Western historians have been puzzled by the fact that while Greek and Roman chronicles by historians such as Herodotus, Megasthenes, Strabo and Pliny are full of reference to India and information on ancient India, no Indian chronicle recorded India's contact with the Western world in the early years of the Christian era. A civilization that could produce two massive epics, particularly the *Mahabharata*, could surely have composed a saga or two on the aliens who came to trade with them! Nowhere do we find references to Plato or Pericles, Homer or Aristotle. There are however references to the presence of Greek or Ionian generals and merchants by the term 'Yavanas'. A great deal of information of this period comes from the text *Questions of Milinda* by the Buddhist philosopher Nagasena who recorded his conversations and dialogues with the great king. Interestingly, the text is in the form of a dialogue between Socrates and Plato.

The first century AD was a period of interaction of cultures as well as a period of turmoil caused by migration of the Kushanas from Central Asia to India and Asia Minor. Their chief Kadphises marched on Gandhara and overthrew the last Greek ruler Hermaeus. They conquered territories held by other Greek, Parthian and Scythian chiefs, occupied West, Central and North India up to Kashmir. The most famous of the Kushana rulers was Kanishka who made Peshawar his capital. His realm was a cosmopolitan one with Greek, Zoroastrian, Buddhist, and Hindu subjects. The Roman Empire sought the friendship of the Kushana rulers to facilitate the silk trade. Their caravans could safely traverse the Silk Road. A Roman sea captain who visited India in the first century AD saw the brisk trade in various commodities such as silk, spice, and slave girls in return for Roman gold coins and Greek wines and recorded this in his chronicle *Periplus Maris Erythrae*. Kanishka's conversion to Buddhism stimulated other influences to flow into India. Greek, Roman and Syrian ideas of art and sculpture mingle with the brisk and unrefined Central Asian spirit in Kushana culture.

In his *History of India*, Vincent Smith describes Kushana culture as "when nascent Christianity met full grown Buddhism in the academies and markets of Asia and Egypt while both religions were exposed to the influences of surrounding paganism in many forms ... and of the countless works of art that gave expression to the forms of polytheism. The ancient religion of Persia contributed to the ferment of human thought, excited by improved facilities for international communications and by the incessant clash of rival civilizations."

The Egyptian city of Alexandria stood at the confluence of Hindu-Buddhist civilization and the new creed of Christianity whose first home was in Syria and Egypt. Indians visited Alexandria where Clement of Alexandria learned about Buddhism. There are similarities in the doctrines of Gnostic philosophy and Mahayana Buddhism, as well as the accounts regarding the birth of Christ and Buddha.

China's first recorded contact with Europe is significantly a commercial one. It was in the first century BC when the Han emperor Wu-ti, striving to consolidate his realm, sent his commander Chang Ch'ien to Central Asia to report on the political conditions there. The emperor felt that the vast frontiers of China could best be guarded by tribes friendly to his realm. He sent gifts to these people through envoys and embassies. The gift most prized was silk which the nomadic people sent further west to the Levant and eventually Rome. Imperial Rome, especially its patrician women, stepped up the demand for Chinese silk. A Roman ambassador was sent to China by Marcus Aurelius in 168 BC. There was no political significance in this; the mission was a purely commercial one to secure a steady supply of silk. In return China imported few European goods and those too only of little value for the Chinese people.

The impulse which prompted Greeks and Romans to trade and conquer were absent in India, China and Japan. They had no need of more territories. They did not require spice or silk or exotic fruits. The need of Indians for material goods was met by their own produce. Asian economies were self-sufficient whereas trade with Egypt and Asia had always been important to Europe. Rome's territorial expansion was as much for commerce as it was for military glory and political power. Roman galleons patrolled the Mediterranean and Red Seas, the Persian Gulf and the Indian Ocean to safeguard the shipment of grain and other essentials. Studying the pattern of the monsoon winds, Roman ships sailed to South Indian shores and did a brisk trade in various commodities – silk, ivory, pepper, ginger, cinnamon, cloves, medicinal herbs and perfumes. Rome sent commodities to India that were not essential – corals, pearls, copper and glass that interested only the wealthier classes. Persia, India and China produced commodities that had become essential for Romans, especially the patricians. Fruits, rice, sugar, and cotton were in great demand.

The balance of trade was adverse. In order to meet the growing demand for exports from the Orient, gold was exported, resulting in loss of bullion and gold reserves. The Roman Senate heard angry protests against the high-born Roman ladies whose mania for silk was draining away Roman gold. (Large quantities of Roman gold coins have been found during excavations on the south-eastern coast of India, at Arkimedu and Kaveripatnam, which were centres of silk production during this time.) This was one of the causes of the economic crisis of the Roman Empire. Excessive imports, adverse balance of trade, loss of bullion, inflation and lack of production paved way for rapid economic decline.

The demand for silk remained steady even after the Western Roman Empire had fallen before the northern 'barbarian' tribes leading to the transfer of the capital to the city on the Bosphorus that came to be called Constantinople. The Byzantine Empire was even more addicted to luxuries than her Roman predecessor. But by the fifth century AD silk was produced within the Byzantine Empire and overland trade with China and India ceased. After a period of chaos, China became wealthy and powerful under the Tang dynasty in the seventh and eighth centuries. China's frontiers almost touched those of Byzantium. There was exchange of envoys and emissaries who gathered information.

The invasion of Rome by the Germanic tribes in the fourth and fifth centuries threw the Western empire into chaos; it would take three centuries to restore order under a very different cultural ethos. When trade on the overland Silk Route declined, India concentrated on her eastern neighbours.

In between the European and Asian civilizations lay a no-man's land from where there would be sudden bursts of military activity among the nomadic people. Avars and Sarmatian tribes had overrun Russia, Huns under Attila threatened the Roman empire, and in the thirteenth century rose the formidable Mongol empire stretching from China to Central Europe, from the Pacific Ocean to the Black Sea. The Great Khan of Cathay drew Europeans into his orbit – the Papal ambassador Giovanni de Piano Carpini, Franciscan friars such as Giovanni de Monte Corvino and William of Rubruck, the Venetian merchants Nicolo, Matteo and Marco Polo. The Christian emissaries met with little success but there was exchange of information about block printing, manufacture of gunpowder and noodles (that the Polos took back to their homeland to become Italian pasta). Europeans engaged in a mortal combat with Islam hoped to enlist the Mongols to their side. From the travellers who returned they also learned of the luxury and wealth of the Mongols in China, their postal system carried by swift ponies, their cabinet system of governance and the use of gunpowder.

These travellers' accounts fired the imagination of the Mediterranean states, in particular Portugal whose captains under the guidance of Henry the Navigator, had initiated exploratory trips around the bulge of Africa in the fourteenth century. The quest for an all-water route to Asia began under Manoel el Sabio, king of Portugal, who christened himself with an absurdly grandiose title, 'Lord of the Conquest, Navigation and Commerce of India, Ethiopia, Arabia and Persia.' On 7th July 1497, his captain Vasco da Gama set sail for India. The age of European colonialism began, an age of both clashes and encounters between different civilizations.

6

Clash and Confrontation

The European colonial age began in 1497 as a result of the Portuguese endeavour to wrest the spice trade from the Arabs. Voyages of exploration around the coast of Africa under the supervision of Prince Enriques the Navigator had begun earlier in the century at Sagres, on the south-west tip of Portugal. Here the skills of navigation and cartography had been developed to a high degree. The voyages of the Genoese captain Cristoforo Colombo to the New World sponsored by the Spanish monarchs had renewed Portuguese interest. Spain was acquiring domains across the Atlantic; she already had matrimonial alliances with the Holy Roman Empire that had brought her Burgundy and the Netherlands. The Portuguese king expedited the building of ships and the journey east.

Vasco da Gama landed at Calicut on the south-west coast of India in May 1498. Had India been united under a strong sovereign, his voyage would have been an insignificant episode centred around the purchase of spices. Unfortunately even within the small territory of Malabar coast of Kerala there existed rivalries and feuds between the different kings. The ruler of Calicut, the Samudra-Raja or king of the seas (later shortened to Zamorin by the Portuguese) was rich and powerful; his Arab allies had built caravelles or swift ships for him. The Raja of Cochin envied the Zamorin's commercial success and alliance with the Arab traders and wanted it for himself. Further north was the splendid Vijayanagar kingdom that stretched from the Vindhya mountains to the Deccan, and spanned the territory between the Arabian Sea and the Bay of Bengal. Though the capital at Hampi was well protected by seven rings of fortifications, the kings of this powerful realm had uneasy relations with the Muslim kingdom that stood to her north at Bijapur. The stage was set for a third party to play havoc. Invaders from the north-west had always found easy access not because they were stronger or better equipped but because there was always a group to betray the existing ruler. Cochin was soon to open the door to the Portuguese in return for defeating Calicut while Vijaynagar would lend assistance to the Portuguese to defeat Adil Shah of Bijapur and capture Goa.

Affonso de Albuquerque established Portuguese rule in Goa in 1510 and gained monopoly of the spice trade that had hitherto been held under Arab control. Portuguese territory extended to Daman and Diu and then further east up to the straits of Malacca. The prospect of trade with China was alluring; the Portuguese soon established a base at Macao.

Portuguese colonialism was prompted by the quest for Oriental spices and infidel souls. Commerce and crusading zeal went together. To attain success in both objectives the Portuguese displayed cruelty and intolerance. They were not inhibited by considerations of either ethics or humanity. Subjugation of the infidel or heathen was considered a sacred duty while amassing wealth from the spice trade was a patriotic one. Even the slave trade was justified as bringing them into contact with Christian teaching. Thousands perished on the slave ships from the shores of Senegal, Nigeria and Ghana to their destinations in Europe and the Americas. Portugal was enriched by the trade with India and her Oriental empire. Lisbon became one of the richest cities of Europe. Portugal experienced a renaissance of her own, quite independent of the Italian one, when poets, painters, architects, as well as explorers and priests created a culture that made these years her golden century. On the voyage to India, Luis Camoens, inspired by ideas of the Orient, composed the epic poem *Os Lusiads* which became the national poem of Portugal. Outward expansion brought to Portugal, as it brought to contemporaneous Spain, a new vitality and creativity.

Indian response was withdrawal. High caste Hindus in Portuguese territory moved elsewhere since they refused to be converted and therefore stood in danger of being persecuted as heretics. Others embraced Christianity in form if not in spirit. There was considerable inter-mingling between the Portuguese soldiers and officials with Indian women. Albuquerque encouraged mixed marriages with the intention of creating a new race of mixed blood which would live in India to safeguard Portuguese rule. Though Goa, Daman and Diu remained pockets of Portuguese culture, the rest of India remained largely untouched by the Lusitanian ethos. This is difficult to understand since India had eagerly embraced and assimilated alien influences from earliest times. Nor was India the only society to remain impervious to Portuguese influence; other far eastern nations also resisted these influences.

Western historians have sought explanations for this and have offered various theories. One is that Asian civilizations were too deeply rooted in their customs, traditions and religions to be affected by an alien creed. For all the success of Muslim conquests in India, the sporadic persecution, imposition of the jizya tax for those who refused conversion, the allurement of office and favour, and their more or less continual rule for almost a millennium, the success of Islam as a religion was not significant. It remained a minority religion though in other spheres such as architecture, painting, literature, language, music, dress, cuisine, Islamic influence was evident. As the cultural history of Asia would show, in the eighteenth century Western influence was considerable in certain aspects of life only. In other words, Indian society adopted what it wished to adopt; she resisted coercion. The dialogue of civilization could only be on her terms.

Japan provides a different picture in the dialogue of civilization. From the early years of the Christian era, Chinese civilization came to Japan who adopted Chinese writing, architecture, religion, art, customs, courtesies and system of governance. China was already a great and ancient civilization. Her influence was all-pervading. In the seventh century Buddhism, travelling from India via China and Korea, went to Japan where Prince Shotuku Taishi made it the state religion. Buddhism was eagerly and reverently accepted not so much because of its inherent attractions as a way of life but because it had already been accepted and practiced in China for several centuries. China waged no wars of conquest; statesmen, scholars, priests, artists and craftsmen came to Japan with their ideas and skills and fashioned a new civilization. This was possible because Japan was just emerging from tribal culture and animism. Chinese influence flourished on this fallow and fertile soil.

The first imperial capital was at Nara. By then there was already the formation of a national consciousness, facilitated by Japan's geographic position as an island. Though Chinese culture and Buddhism gained ascendancy, Japan's older cultural forms and ways mingled with the new influences. The old feudal codes of the Samurais and the Shinto creed began to reassert themselves. By the Kyoto period in the eleventh century, Japan had evolved her own national outlook and civilization through a process of absorption and adaption. The failure of the Mongol invasion under Kublai Khan (when a 'divine wind' or *kamikaze* was said to have destroyed the formidable armada) gave Japan a new confidence. By the time the first Europeans arrived, the Japanese were undergoing a time of turmoil and wars between feudal lords.

Internal dissension and disunity, whether in India, Visigothic Spain or feudal Japan, has always proved a blessing for the potential invader or explorer. Though the Emperor remained the titular head, Japanese warlords squabbled among themselves. Caught in their internecine strife, the feudal barons thought that a foreign connection would benefit them against the other. Portuguese ships carrying weapons was an appealing prospect. Baron Nobunaga took the initiative in inviting the Portuguese to the port in his fiefdom. He treated the Jesuit missionaries who came in the Portuguese ships with deference. Japan was eager to learn and adopt European influence in the sixteenth century. How a free and sovereign Japan modernized herself, particularly after the Meiji Restoration while retaining her traditional culture up to the mid-twentieth century, is another instance of the dialogue of civilization.

7
India's Seashore of Humanity

India began her dialogue with other civilizations in pre-historic times.

Rabindranath Tagore, the great Indian poet, educationist, nationalist and humanist called India the seashore of humanity. In brisk cadence he wrote,

Here came Aryans, Non-Aryans,
Dravids, and Mongols;
Tribes of Moghuls, and Huns
Scythians, and Pathans,
In one body they merged.

and –

They came to take and will stay to give
But they will never leave
*This seashore of humanity.**

This then was the message of India over five millennia of known history. The intermingling of many racial strains is written in the genetic code of her people, in their varied aptitudes and gifts. In India there was no clash of civilizations. In the midst of invasions and turmoil there was a continual and enriching dialogue.

Echoing Rabindranath Tagore, Lord Meston observes, "There was therefore very little clash between India's own ancient culture and the alien culture imported from the West; no violent conflict of ideas or methods: no forcible replacement of one social stream by another. The more fitting metaphor would be that of a new stream of thought and practice flowing into the sea of Indian traditions and life. The movement of western civilization into India has been a slow and peaceful penetration." *(Modern India and the West – A Study of The Interaction of their Civilizations)*

---

* Authors' translation.

A German anthropologist, Baron von Eichstedt stated that there are no Aryan and Dravidian races and that these are only the names of linguistic groups. He describes waves of migrations from Africa and Melanesia, and from the Iranian plateau. Common 'Aryan' place names, language and sacred books have been found in India, Iran, Asia Minor, in the Hittite capital of Boghaz Keui, the Upper Euphrates and ancient Chaldea. Migrants from the Swat valley and modern day Baluchistan settled in the fertile Doab – the land between the two rivers, Ganga and Jamuna. The Indus Valley civilization is now considered a far wider area than the boundaries earlier envisaged, thanks to the excavations which show extended territories to the south and to the west. Examination of skeletal remains indicates that the inhabitants of the Indus Valley were of mixed racial strains, though preponderantly Mediterranean and Sumerian. In Biblical and pre-Biblical times the west coast of India traded with Mesopotamia and Palestine; timber from the west-coast forests is said to have built the Temple of Solomon in Jerusalem. Steles have been found in the ancient sites of Ur, Nineveh and Chaldea indicating trade with Indus Valley towns.

Semetic tribes settled in the north and west, Afro-Arab merchants sailed across the sea and traded in spices with the Malabar coast, acquiring families and homes away from homes. Greeks bequeathed their Hellenic ideas in art and architecture, their colour and stature in the Punjab while Polynesians came to Banga, Anga and Kalinga (modern Bengal and Orissa); in turn merchant princes from these eastern parts went to Laos, Cambodia, Thailand, Sumatra and Java with Buddhist and Hindu thoughts and art. Huns and Scythians came, conquered and were conquered in turn by the bounty of the land. The Kushanas embraced Buddhism and made sacred Mathura the second capital of their Indian empire. Zoroastrians fleeing persecution settled near Dwaraka, Lord Krishna's capital. The fierce Pathans and the intrepid Moghuls charging down through arid mountain lands settled in the fertile Indo-Gangetic valley.

Each invasion brought assimilation; plundering hordes invigorated the vanquished with a strange resistance and those who came to take left behind their unwitting gifts. Sometimes Indians met persecution with a spurious docility and a quiet obduracy that bided for time and opportunity for renewal. Invaders mistook this for acquiescence and servility until they were absorbed in the complex amplitude of Indian ways.

India's complex historical background provides a clue to her cultural identity. India is not one country, but many countries, inhabited not by a homogenous people (if there are such people at all) but by a fusion of many racial strains. What Socrates said of Greece might be said even more of India – that it is a name of a culture, not a race. Indeed there is no coherent race-pattern in India.

On this was superimposed from recorded times some traces of foreign influence. But generally speaking it may be said that the religious and social systems, the literature and art of Hinduism, "were to use a popular neologism, the product of an 'ideology' which owed very little to outside contributions. It is this 'self-determined civilization' which has made India what English writers have called a cosmos in itself and French writers call *un monde particulier* and it is owing to it that there is a fundamental unity between men who had no common knowledge and who were socially atomized and politically divided but who had common sympathies founded on same religion, social institutions and to some extent intellectual appetencies." (Sir A. Lyal – *Asiatic Studies in Religions and Art*, 1884).

Indian culture has an essential unity largely because of the continuity of land surface and the use of Sanskrit which was the lingua franca of the sub-continent very much as Latin unified medieval Europe before the emergence of modern nation-states. Sanskrit was the language of the philosopher-sage Sankaracharya of Kerala as well as the language of the poet-historian Kalhana of Kashmir. Through Sanskrit Hinduism prevailed over the whole sub-continent and produced general uniformity of culture even though there was no uniformity of race. Religion was interwoven with the Hindu system of law. Art and literature that are mirrors of a civilization and reflect the aesthetic sensibility of her people drew their inspiration from Hinduism. The joint family, the village community, the caste system – all in different ways preserved the unity of culture.

Hindu civilization maintained its vitality under Muslim rule and never became a Muslim country. Both Muslims and Hindus gave and received from each other cultural inspiration that produced a synthesis. The Pathans and Mughals became Indianised and ceased to be an alien people. Akbar and Jahangir patronized Hindu poets. Dara Shikoh, eldest son of Shah Jahan, was in close touch with the exponents of Hindu philosophy and had the *Upanishads* translated into Persian.

When a great empire declines, whether in Athens, Rome, Damascus, Constantinople, London, Paris or Petersburg, the soil is prepared for a new age and a new ethos. The strength and sagacity of Akbar gave way to decadence in his successors; the empire weakened and the people were generally the "tools and slaves of power, little more than revenue paying units with no rights against the State. The administration seems to have been a huge money making machine for the benefit of the ruling classes. Invasions wrecked institutions, agriculture and stability." Sir A. Lyall writes in *Asiatic Studies in Religions and Art:*

> It was an era of chaos unprecedented even in the annals of Asiatic history, an era such as only follows the break-up of a wide spreading empire which has so carefully knocked out and cut away all internal and local stays and ties that its fall when it comes is a ruinous crash and leaves a vast territory in a state of political disillusion.

Sir Thomas Roe used somewhat exaggerated language when he said that the people lived as "fishes in the sea – the great ones eat up the little ones. The great rob the lesser and the King robs them all". One may pause here to reflect that English colonists substituted one form of exploitation for another. It was not just a question of degree. Burke cast the proper light when he pointed out that exploitation by the local ruler who has to continue is quite different from exploitation by the colonists with no permanent stakes.

By the very nature of its mercantile code, European colonialism in Asia was different from other conquests. The European merchants and soldiers had homes of their own, – perhaps not as opulent as in India – where living was harsh, but homes to which they wished to return, plumped by profits from this alien land. They had no intention of being absorbed into the complex Indian social structure nor did they wish to impose their ethos on Indians.

> It must always be difficult to distinguish between changes imposed by an alien government upon a subject people and the free acceptance by the people of the standards brought by the alien government. In law and justice for example there are certain tenets of British

> jurisprudence, certain offences in the penal code to which Indian opinion is not wholly reconciled but the great bulk of both civil and criminal law which the British Government has enacted commands the general intellectual assent of the people, the more so as their indigenous family law has been respected and preserved. In many regions of art and literature, India has paid western culture the compliment of imitation for instance in the poetry of Toru Dutt and Mrs. Naidu. Music remains a striking exception; to the Indian ear European music has little attraction as Indian music with its 'melody untouched by harmony' and its subtle cross rhythm and quarter tones has for the ordinary European. But in 'nation building services and education India has met them with zealous approval'.

(*Modern India and the West – A Study of the Interaction of their Civilizations*. Edited by L.S.S.O'Malley. Foreword by Lord Meston)

Lord Meston goes on to say that education has been the chief instrument for bringing Western influence into Indian life. There has been a continuous debate and discussion, both amicable and acrimonious, on the sagacity of the British Government in replacing the old indigenous systems of teaching by definitely Western methods and particularly in giving the English language prominence at the secondary stage and dominance at the university stage as a medium of instruction. Time alone will judge its wisdom and efficacy. But the facts today are clear. The Orthodox view is that British policy has inhibited the spontaneous flowering of the intellectual genius of the people. In the field of scientific development "this criticism would not apply, if only because no scientific vocabulary exists in any of the Indian languages." But in other intellectual realms – literature, history, philosophy – the teaching of English has "deflected the Indian mind from the traditional lines of culture which an advanced vernacular education might have encouraged."

This is one side of the scenario. It is also true that the widespread knowledge of English and the use of the English language has enabled the Indian mind to turn to new concepts: 'freedom of speech and pen, criticism of authority, the questioning of accepted dogmas, the insistence on the rights of man as opposed to his duties.' Introduction of English as the medium of instruction gave a new dimension to the Indian outlook: skepticism and rationalism, a subtle resistance to authoritarianism, and a demand for representative government.

The authors feel that language is both a vehicle of ideas and on a deeper level the mirror of civilizations. As the German philosopher Fredrich observed, "He who acquires a new language acquires a new soul." One wonders to what extent the super-linguist William Jones was aware of this. It is possible that he was less aware of this than Macaulay.

After two and half centuries since India came into contact with Western virtues and vices, its rich creativity, as well as its formidable powers of destruction, one has to ponder on how the basic tenets of the two civilizations will blend and be reconciled. Will India, in its customary fashion, slowly assimilate and adopt Western ideas and concepts to suit its own native genius or will India be transformed? The answer lies in a bit of both.

The viewpoint of a Frenchman, Amaury de Riencourt, in his *Soul of India* gives another insight into the question of clash and dialogue of civilizations.

> There was an awakening of India's head and heart when India was firmly under British rule. This was sparked by contact between European culture and India's ossified civilization was quickened by the fact. European culture was already in full development and had generated the industrial revolution. Incidentally this took place in an Anglo-Indian atmosphere and expressed itself in relatively new linguistic mediums. English replaced Persian as the universal language of India (as Persian had replaced Sanskrit) and the vernacular developed an entire group of autonomous literatures in various provinces.
>
> The first British proconsuls felt romantically attracted by an alien culture that they did not understand and encouraged its renewal rather than its modernization. Warren Hastings founded the Calcutta Madrasa in 1781. William Jones, the great Orientalist founded the Asiatic Society in 1784. The Resident of Benaras Jonathan Duncan started a Sanskrit College there in 1792. But as British rule spread and became more and more secure the British began to lose interest in an alien culture that they had hardly began to understand. Charles Grant, a Company civil servant, first touched upon the idea of establishing a new educational network to teach English and impart European culture to Indians on the ground that the old culture was responsible for India's evident decadence. Christian missionaries followed up his suggestions and established educational institutions. Every tentative effort made subsequently by Anglo Indian governments to encourage strictly Indian learning was

discouraged by enlightened Indians; chief among them was Ram Mohan Roy whose eloquent protest against establishment of a Sanskrit college in Calcutta remains a classic. Referring to this decision in a petition to the Governor-General Lord Amherst he pointed out that 'the Sanskrit system of education would be the best calculated to keep this country in darkness if such had been the policy of the British legislature. But if the improvement of the native population is the object of the Government, it will consequently promote a more liberal and enlightened system of instruction embracing mathematics, natural philosophy, chemistry and anatomy'.

Late in the eighteenth century around the time of the French Revolution, Anquetil Duperron translated the *Upanishads* from a French translation and from then on the most spectacular salvage operation known to history was underway; nothing less than the total recuperation of mankind's past wisdom entailing a colossal broadening of man's collective memory. A large part of two movements grew simultaneously; one part contrasted in extricating dead ruins from the sands or the jungles in deciphering dead languages and scripts which no living man could read. But the other and most fruitful part consisted in attempting to understand those civilizations that were still alive though immensely old and crippled with cultural arthritis. It was the fascination of large portions of the human race still living and abiding by their old religions and cultural traditions going back to the remotest antiquity, apparently indifferent to the impact of the West and totally lacking in a corresponding curiosity about European culture. This was the profound impact of the East on the West. European minds could not rest till the secrets of these uncanny ways of life and thought had been brought to light.

With prophetic insight Anquetil Duperron pointed out that Kant's idealism had many points in common with the *Upanishads*. Germans began to discover their national authority from Indian thought. But in the early days most of the spadework was done by the British overlords themselves. Conscious of the vastness and mysterious character of their new domain they had determined that they would explore the cultural depths of India in order to secure their political rule. William Jones, Charles Wilkins, Thomas Colebrooke, Nathaniel Halhed and the Asiatic Society of Bengal all worked tirelessly at this culture.

Many more British scholars followed in their wake. But then a curious reaction began to take shape in Britain. The imperial mistress was fast increasing the India domain, but with it grew a fear of the sight of the intellectual monuments of a defeated civilization, fear for her political supremacy and her cultural superiority. From this reaction sprang the increasing un-enlightened outlook of the "missionary attitude" and a closing of the mind and a gradual elimination of the former cultural understanding in favour of an imposition of political and economic supremacy. Domination always produces a degree of incomprehension and British dominion was to survive in India. The great quarrel between the Anglicists and the Orientalists had to be won by the former – which it was around 1835. Macaulay hammered the last nail in the Orientalist's coffin by denying the usefulness of any attempt at understanding Indian culture and deciding that English was to become the medium through which Indians would receive the benefits of modern knowledge.

The Germans took up where the British left off. Politically unconnected with the Orient and with a far superior philosophic approach, the Germans were to prove the greatest Indianists of all – just as the French remained the greatest Sinologists.

They were quite conscious of the switch when the German poet Henrich Heine pointed out with irony, 'the Portuguese, the Dutch and the English have been for a long time, year after year, shipping home the treasures of India in their big vessels. The Germans have all along been left to watch it. Today Schlegel, Bopp, Humboldt etc are our East India sailors. Bonn and Munich will be good factories' Behind this lay the historic bitterness of Germany which goes a long way to explain their modern history. It was a strange but profoundly significant co-incidence that Johann Godfried von Herder's famous *Ideas on the Philosophy of History* should have been published in 1784, the very year of the foundation of Calcutta's Asiatic Society.

8

Orientalism and the Western World

Not all would accept the theory that the encounter between the Orient and the West produced a dialogue of civilization. The eminent academic Edward Said's book *Orientalism* published in 1978 declares that, "Orientalism is a western projection onto and will to govern over the Orient." After the Romanticism of the eighteenth century, Orientalism became a more serious subject. It was no longer an exploration into the mysterious unknown; it was a part of the inexorable quest for territorial expansion, markets and raw materials for burgeoning industries. Orientalism, Said says, "had accomplished its self metamorphosis from a scholarly discourse to an imperial institution." Said accepts that Orientalism produced scholars sympathetic to Asia and her culture, that these scholars dabbled "in esoteric subjects such as Sanskrit grammar, Phoenician numismatics and Arabic Poetry."

This is an over-simplification of Oriental scholarship. William Jones delved into the depths of Sanskrit culture: the *Rig Veda*, other *Vedas*, *Upanishads*, *Bhagavad Gita*, *Manusmriti*, *Silpashastra*, *Nitishastra*, *Advaita*, Caraka's medical texts, and *Surya Siddhanta* (astronomy). The study of Sanskrit was the basis for understanding of the Orient by the Occident. Max Mueller observed Sanskrit was essential "to discover the first germs of the language (Sanskrit), the religion and mythology of our forefathers." Nor can A. Keith's observation that "Kavya literature contains some of the greatest poetry of the world" be construed as an esoteric pursuit.

However, the advancement of knowledge which Oriental studies produced, he felt, was a means of extending imperial power. European scholarship about Asia "was a conscious handmaiden of power and subordination. Explorers, missionaries, archaeologists, linguists were all part of a colonial enterprise ... every instance of European curiosity about the East from Flaubert to Marx, was part of a grand design to exploit and remake what westerners saw as a passive, rich, but ultimately contemptible 'Oriental' sphere." (Christopher Hitchens – *Where the Twain Should Have Met*).

Here again is a simplification of the situation. It is no coincidence that early Orientalism evolved simultaneously with the Enlightened Movement. The convergence of these two schools of thought enriched each other and led to closer scrutiny of the concepts of citizenship, governance, and justice. Far from being a handmaiden of imperialism, the votaries of 'Orientalism' advocated the preservation of native customs and laws against the onslaught of alien (Western) practices.

Eventually, as will be discussed later, Orientalism became the catalyst for nationalism in the later colonial period. 'Discovery' of ancient manuscripts and texts, monuments and sites gave the nationalists the historical continuity and cultural identity so essential for the struggle for nationhood.

An interesting side effect of Orientalism was that concepts such as 'Aryan' or "Indo-European' as opposed to Semites or non-Aryans served political purposes in Germany and elsewhere.

It is true that the East was regarded as "a source of inexhaustible riches" by Clive and "a career" by Macaulay. Karl Marx commented that England was "causing a social revolution in Hindustan" but it was motivated "by the vilest interests". But even Marx the abuser of imperialism observed that a social revolution brought about by external agents was desirable.

Edward Said also hinted that there was truth in what Marx had said about Orientals: "They cannot represent themselves; they must be represented." In the end Said declared, "Orientalism overrode the Orient." Components of Oriental literature or philosophy was used against them, texts were quoted out of context to disparage Oriental culture. "The closeness between politics and Orientalism, or to put it more circumspectly, the great likelihood that ideas about the Orient drawn from Orientalism can be put to political use, is an important yet extremely sensitive truth. ... It necessarily provokes unrest in one's conscience about cultural, racial, or historical generalization, their uses, value, degree of objectivity, and fundamental intent. More than anything else, the political and cultural circumstances in which western Orientalism has flourished draw attention to the debased position of the Orient or the Oriental as an object of study." In fact Said felt that there was an unholy alliance between the Enlightenment and Imperialism, between Orientalism and colonialism.

Edward Said went on to say,

> From the last decades of the eighteenth century and for at least a century and a half, Britain and France dominated Orientalism as a discipline. The great philological discoveries in comparative grammar made by William Jones, Franz Bopp, Jakob Grimm, and others were originally indebted to manuscripts brought from the East to Paris and London. Almost without exception, every Orientalist began his career as a philologist, and the revolution in philology that produced Bopp, Sacy, Burnouf, and their students was a comparative science based on the premise that languages belonged to families of which the Indo-European and the Semetic are two great instances. From the outset, then, Orientalism carried forward two traits – (1) a newly found scientific self-consciousness based on the linguistic importance of the Orient to Europe and (2) a proclivity to divide, sub-divide and re-divide its subject matter without ever changing its mind about the Orient as being always the same, unchanging, uniform, and radically peculiar object.
>
> Friedrich Schlegel who learned his Sanskrit in Paris, illustrates these traits together. Although by the time he published his *Uber die Sprache und Weisheit der Indier* in 1808, Schlegel renounced his Orientalism, he still held that Sanskrit and Persian on the one hand and Greek and German on the other had more affinities with each other than with the Semetic, Chinese, American or African languages. Moreover, the Indo-European family was artistically simple and satisfactory in a way the Semetic for one, was not. Such abstractions as this did not trouble Schlegel, for whom nations, races, minds and peoples as things one could talk about passionately – in the ever-narrowing perspective of populism first adumbrated by Herder – held a lifelong fascination. Yet nowhere does Schlegel talk about the living contemporary Orient. When he said in 1800, 'it is in the Orient that we must look for the highest Romanticism,' he meant the Orient of the *Sakuntala*, the *Zend-Avesta* and the *Upanishads*.

Said continued to say that as colonialism extended so too did Orientalism extended to China, Japan, and Sumer.

Said derided the idea held by western Orientalists that

> the regeneration of Europe by Asia" – was a very influential Romantic idea. Friedrich Schlegel and Novalis, for example, urged upon their countrymen and upon Europeans in general a detailed study of

> India because they said, "it was Indian culture and religion that could defeat the materialism and mechanism (and republicanism) of Occidental culture. And from this defeat would arise a new revitalized Europe; the Biblical imagery of death, rebirth and redemption is evident in this prescription. Moreover, the Romantic Orientalist project was not merely a specific instance of a general tendency; it was a powerful shaper of the tendency itself as Raymond Schwab so convincingly argued in *La Renaissance Orientale*. But what mattered was not Asia so much as Asia's use to modern Europe. Thus anyone who, like Schlegel or Bopp mastered an Oriental language was a spiritual hero, a knight errant bringing back to Europe a sense of the holy mission it had now lost."

Said believes that the modern Orientalist

> was in his view, a hero rescuing the Orient from the obscurity, alienation, and strangeness which he himself had properly distinguished. His research reconstructed the Orient's lost languages, mores, even mentalities. ...The specific Orientalist techniques – lexicography, grammar, translation, cultural decoding, restored, fleshed out, reasserted the values both of an ancient classical Orient and of the traditional disciplines of philology, history, rhetoric and doctrinal polemic.

The authors feel that Edward Said's views do not do justice to the process that started three millennia ago when the Mediterranean world began its explorations of the societies that lived beyond its geographical boundaries. In his condemnation of Orientalism as a handmaiden of imperialism Said overlooks the contribution made by German Orientalists. In scope and depth, German scholars on Asia and particularly India, have carried the mantle of William Jones even more brilliantly than his British successors. In fact the predominant branch of Indology throughout the 19th and 20th century was the contribution of German scholars. The profound and gifted German Indologists who analyzed, critiqued, and translated ancient Sanskrit texts and tracts worked without any imperialist motives. However wistful Heine might have been of the British Empire in India, Germany had no plans for Asian colonies during the late eighteenth and early nineteenth centuries.The Prussian Kaiser's *drang nach osten* (march to the east) came much later; before that every major German university had a department of Indology and Berlin was often referred to as the Benaras of Europe.

Friedrich Schlegel

The subtle connection between the pursuit of knowledge and political pursuit is not restricted to Orientalists and Imperialists.The quest for knowledge has usually been accompanied by a quest for power. Knowledge - whether intellectual, social or political - confers power on the possessor. The priesthood of ancient societies exerted immense power by virtue of their command over religious texts and rites, the educated classes have exercised authority on the same ground. Nowhere has ignorance brought power.

Said does not mention the predicament faced by Orientalists such as William Jones and Warren Hastings. The period between 1784-1794 was a time of intense intellectual and political concerns. While expanding British territory in India, Hastings commissioned Wilkins to translate the Bhagavad Gita. Apart from praising the work as the greatest work of spiritualism, Hastings wanted to underline the civilizational greatness of India in order to persuade London to allow India to be governed by her own laws. Similarly, William Jones was caught in the dilemma of understanding and promoting Indian civilization while promoting effective governance by the British.

Edward Said's views may have been formed by the West's attitude to Islamic societies from the time of the Crusades. He ruefully observes of how the clash between Christendom and Islam led to abusive descriptions of the 'Saracens' along with depiction of their sensuality, fatalism and cruelty. (But then the Arabs spared no words in describing the uncouth infidel.) Notwithstanding what the propagandists said on both sides, the inter-action of the two people did produce a syncretic culture and adoption of ideas and technology. The contribution of Arab philosophers such as Averroes and Avicenna have been acknowledged by Christian artists and scholars. Rafael's famous painting 'School of Athens' shows Averroes sitting with Greek philosophers. Dante's contempt for the Muslim infidel in the high tide of medieval poetry should not be used to condemn Orientalism.

The attitude of European scholars to Islamic-Arab culture has certainly been different from western scholars of Indology.

Long before the East India Company scholars took up studies of ancient India and Sanskrit, Christian missionaries began studying Sanskrit texts. They realized that if they had to convert Hindus, they had to know the religion of the country. Warren Hastings' policy of spreading knowledge about India however was not a part of his imperialist purpose. In fact by making Indians aware of their heritage he unwittingly paved the way for a national consciousness that had been lacking in India. The new discipline of comparative philology gave Sanskrit an exalted position as the oldest of other Indo-European languages. Confronted with a civilization both ancient and sophisticated, European scholars made an effort to ascribe an 'Aryan' (by implication European) character to Vedic civilization. The fascination for Indology that spread from England to Germany (who was not a colonial power in the early nineteenth century) had little to do with imperialism. It was to do with the discovery of an older civilization – Hindu-Buddhist – that had a message of its own; of resilience before disasters, of humanity, of a search for ultimate reality.

The diehard imperialists such as Macaulay and Shore had little interest in Indology and believed in propagation of western knowledge to bolster their political agenda. They believed, absolutely erroneously as it turned out, that a westernized bureaucratic elite would be the best guarantee of sustaining British rule in India. In the end, despite their different motives and their completely different agendas both William Jones and Macaulay assisted in the resurgence of India.

Samuel Huntington has advanced the theory of clash of civilizations in an article of the same name in the summer issue of *Foreign Affairs* in 1993. His thesis is that after the dismemberment of the Soviet Union, the Cold War has been replaced by the clash and conflict of civilizations. Globalization would not unite nations he wrote, rejecting the 'end of history' ideas of his rival Francis Fukuyama. The Western world is not engaged now in a mortal battle with the Communist world but with more insidious adversaries – the Arabs, and the Chinese. According to Huntington "the fundamental source of conflict in this new world will not be primarily ideological or primarily economic. The great division among mankind and the dominating source of conflict will be cultural. Nation states will remain the most powerful actors in world affairs but the principal conflicts in global politics will occur between nations and groups of civilizations. The clash of civilizations will dominate global politics. The fault lines between civilizations will be the battle lines of the future."

Huntington went on to enlarge on this theme in his book of the same name in 1996 where he speaks about "civilization identities" that delineates eight major civilizations from one another. According to Said, this narrow and constricting definition undermines the very concept of 'civilization' which develops and progresses on inter-actions. Huntington's implicit message is that these "identities" are so different, their ethos so opposed, that there can only be conflicts between them.

Perhaps without realizing it, Edward Said, by denouncing European Orientalism as a handmaiden of imperialism has tacitly agreed with Samuel Huntington that there is a fundamental conflict of interest between the East and the West.

In the twenty-first century, the delineation between the different cultures and races is blurred; communication and economic interdependence has removed the once-clearly defined profile of a society or civilization. This process actually began with the onset of the colonial age when different hemispheres and different continents came into contact with each other. After the initial clash, mutual suspicion and misgivings, there commenced an imperceptible cross-fertilization of ideas and aspirations that transformed the ruled no less than the rulers.

There has never been clash between cultures; the clash has been, and still is, between power. Europe has seen some of the most bloody battles and ages of conflicts from the first millennium BC – between Sparta and Athens, Greece and Rome, between the two Germanic states of Prussia and Austria, Spain and England, and continuous warfare between England and France. All of them were products of European-Christian civilization. Faced with the specter of German militarism, republican France signed a military pact with an autocratic Tsarist Russia. Western capitalist powers were glad to have the assistance of communist Soviet Union in their common fight against Hitler. Unlike Russia, Germany was a part of western civilization but that did not prevent a world war. With the onset of the Cold War the United States and Britain assiduously sought (in the fifties and sixties) the political and military alliance of autocratic and feudal rulers of Islamic nations (Saudi Arabia, Iraq, Jordan, Iran, Turkey) to contain Soviet Russia and safeguard her oil supplies. Islam was not perceived as a threat then. Huntington's thesis springs not from cultural problems but because he sees threats to Anglo-American influence in Asia by the rise of Islam and a powerful China. The blasting of the Twin Towers by Arab terrorists in September 2001 temporarily lent credence to Huntington's theory. However, American academics such as Noam Chomsky, a Jew by birth, refuted this theory. The United States, he said, had Saudi Arabia, the most fundamentalist of Islamic states, as its staunchest ally, and Iraq had once been the US's ally in her struggle against Iran.

Civilizations are not self-contained homogenous entities. The more complex the culture, greater is the variety and diversity, with layers of influences. The dialogue between civilizations is a long and continuing process. It goes on in spite of hostilities and clashes.

Part II

British Rule in India in the Age of William Jones

Each age is an age that is dying or one that is coming to birth.

O' Shaughnessy

Men do not build themselves a new world out of the fruits of the earth, as vulgar superstitions believes, but out of the historical accomplishments of their declining civilization. They must in the course of their development begin by producing the material conditions of a new society and no effort of mind or will can free them from this destiny.

Karl Marx, 1847

9
The Prelude to Plassey

India has long been regarded by the West as a land of wonder. Pliny and Herodotus have extolled her natural beauty and wealth. Alexander of Macedon braved forbidding mountain passes and deserts to reach India. Accounts of India's wealth reached southern Europe through Arabs who were the cosmopolitan transmitters of information in the first millennium AD. Ibn-Batuta and Marco Polo travelled widely and carried back tales of the fabulous Orient. It would not be long before others came to explore. India was then a powerful polity; the Delhi Sultans and the Moghuls had made her a force to contend with. As such she commanded both awe and respect.

> The land of India – with its mighty rivers, fertile plains and forests, its gold towered temples and jeweled idols, palaces of marble and gem, its vast granaries and splendid markets – had always beckoned to those who lived beyond the high Himalayas, eking out a living from their arid plains. They came through forbidding passes and gorges; Caucasians, Scythians, Huns, Mongols and Pathans to encounter a civilization of lofty metaphysics and erotic madness, exacting logic and fearful superstitions, a thirst for renunciation and a chaotic greed. They were drawn too by whispered legends of fabled wealth, and they came, bringing with them challenge and innovation. Enriched and invigorated by these invaders, India however soon absorbed their separate identities and became a seashore of humanity – unvanquished. (*The Conquerors*, Achala Moulik).

The year 1492 was a watershed in world history. The discovery of a hitherto unknown continent by Columbus across a vast uncharted ocean produced a spirit of adventure not known since the Roman legions marched on their campaigns of conquest. Indian merchant princes had sailed "from the mouths of the Ganges to

Ceylon, from Ceylon to Java and from Java to China in ships manned by Indian crew." The ancient world had sent pilgrims and missionaries to other lands – Mahendra and Sanghamitra from India, Peter and Paul from Galillee, and Fa-Hien and Hiuen-Tsang from China. The medieval world had produced celebrated travellers – the Venetian Marco Polo, the Moroccan Ibn-Batuta, the Russian Afnasy Nikitin, Enriques the Portuguese navigator – but none of them had gone in search of new lands to conquer and subjugate. The *reconquista* of Granada in 1492 by the combined arms of Castile and Aragon ended seven centuries of Moorish rule in the Iberian peninsula and released energies to the *Conquistadores* to acquire an overseas empire. The Ottoman Turks were turned back from the gates of Vienna by Stepan Bathory. The breakdown of feudal societies in Europe, the rise of an assertive middle class, the intellectual and artistic ferment of the Renaissance, the turmoil in Europe due to Martin Luther's Protestant creed and by the Gutenberg printing press, created a new *zeit geist*. The spirit of maritime adventure coalesced with an aggressive commercial mood.

The age of European colonialism began not in Asia but in the New World. However, after the first orgies of plunder of Mayas, Aztecs and Incas, and the demographic disasters in South America caused by Spanish and Portuguese labour policies, it became clear that the exploitation of the New World would be more exacting. It entailed hard work and enterprise, of setting up the infrastructures of an *imperium*. The Europeans turned their attention to the fabled Orient, which had excited Caesars and Alexanders and where the opportunities for trade were more lucrative. In the late 16th century, the French traveller Bernier went back to Europe with accounts of India's wealth, while the arrival of Jesuit priests in the court of Akbar whetted the appetites of their royal compatriots. Silks, spices, saltpetre – and souls – all were to be had in this realm.

> A new crusade was begun by men in search of dreams – not only of silk, muslin, spices and gold – but of new lands to conquer. They saw a great land torn by fratricidal wars and ruinous campaigns. They were eager to trade and grasp the wealth of a wounded empire. These white, tawny haired men sailed across seven seas, waited patiently, building their clay forts, haggling with local merchants and cringing before the imperial courts for firmans and concessions. Their spheres of activity increased and their territorial

appetites swelled. To these men of Europe's crabbed and confined towns Hindoostan was a country rich in romance, a land of enchantment and wonder. She was a synonym for wealth and splendour, 'a country in which be diverse countries with a bewildering diversity of creeds, customs and ways of life, a home of curious creatures such as cannibals, elephants, crocodiles and snakes.' It was also a perpetual lure for expansion and enrichment. From sleepy Calcutta and steamy Madras they watched with veiled eyes the intrigues, local wars and invasions that left the realm bloodstained and shattered. They watched the imperial citadel fall apart to await another conquest.

Two outstanding men of ambition and audacity laid the foundations of the British empire. This empire brought many emissaries; traders who came to plunder and enrich themselves with the gold of India, soldiers to expand the boundaries of their domain, administrators to offer a new aspect of law and justice and missionaries to introduce a new religion.

Then there were the great scholars who came with wonder and humility to explore the vast and ancient civilization of India, and who awakened the Indians to pride in their great heritage. And by doing so they brought the challenge of western civilization and unwittingly opened the floodgates of self-esteem, pride and nationalism that would end their empire. (*The Conquerors*, Achala Moulik).

This is a chronicle of that encounter in the dialogue of civilizations.

10

Foundation Stones of the British Empire

It was a popular saying at one time that the British empire was created in a fit of absent-mindedness. This was one of the classic examples of an untruth poured into the mould of a catchy statement which managed to fasten itself to the imagination of successive generations. Even the most superficial examination demonstrates its patent falsity. The epigram could be interpreted in a deep Hegelian sense to mean that the zeitgeist was leading in some other direction. The sequence of events however from the collapse of the Moghul empire, accentuated by the third battle of Panipat, the consequent vacuum and chaos, the ascendancy of the British at Plassey and Buxar seem to point to a culmination where establishment of British rule in India became inevitable.

While Sir Thomas Roe gave congenial advice to the Company in its first struggle for trade – "without controversy it is an error to affect garrison and land wars in India" – it was a temporary strategy. The dream of an empire germinated in the minds of even the first Englishmen who came to India with the ostensible intention to trade. From the outset, the Company's privileges and possessions resembled an empire in miniature; these were steadily developed as foundations. They waited for opportunities for future expansion.

The Company's enterprises necessitated building of fortified palaces and troops. In 1668 Bombay was leased to the Company that acquired sovereign rights over the territory and its inhabitants. In 1687 the Company was permitted to establish a municipal constitution in Madras. By 1682 Sir Josiah Child was already speaking of a "sure English dominion in India for all time to come".

In his *Constitutional History,* Keith says little to suggest acquisition of dominion in the debut of the Company. "These men sailed the seas and faced death to trade, to earn an honest penny, not to conquer."

It is not to the infancy of the Company but the period of its adolescence and maturity that one has to turn for an answer to the question whether the empire was built up deliberately by the agents of the Company in consonance with the wishes of its directors.

As V.P. Menon observes in *Integration of Indian States*: "The British empire in India presents the curious phenomenon of having been built by the agents of the Company in India, at any rate during the initial stages, notwithstanding express directions to the contrary from their principles."

Guy Wint in his book *The British in Asia* states that:

> the empire was in fact the result of a more or less private enterprise of a small number of British expatriates. After the British navy opened the eastern seas in the eighteenth century (without which no empire could have been thought of) the British Government gave its more audacious subjects authority or license or encouragement to win in the East by whatever intrigue and the most economical use of a small white force they could seize and by their own devises hold.

It is incorrect to suppose that British expatriates alone built the empire, though some of that band, notably Robert Clive and Warren Hastings, did build on the foundations already purposefully laid in England. If the history of 18th century British India is examined in terms of its leading personalities, the theory of the British Empire in India as the unintended result of historical circumstances becomes even more implausible. For the India of the eighteenth century was characterized by a succession of masterful Englishmen who saw clearly the directions which the East India Company affairs and British rule in India should take. In the main they were domineering, self-confident men who on coming to India matured early, became cynical prematurely, undertook great responsibilities while still almost boys. If there was one quality these men lacked, it was absent-mindedness! They deliberately formulated policies; though men of action many of them articulated their intentions and shaped the nature of the British presence in India. Of these the greatest were without doubt Clive and Hastings.

From Clive's time onwards, British India never lacked minds seeing and planning far ahead. There was no trace, even momentary, of absent-mindedness in such rulers as Warren Hastings, Wellesley, Lord Hastings or Dalhousie. The mood and temper of British rule in India was shaped by the personalities of these remarkable men.

There has been much debate of how the British occupied Bengal. The historian Ram Gopal in his *A Corrected Account of the 1756-1765 Events* observed that,

> if the English servants of the East India Company had carried out the orders of the Court of Directors honestly and scrupulously there would have been no British empire in India. The events of 1756-65 tell a fascinating story of how blunders turned out to be the foundation stone of the empire. The fortification of Fort William in contravention of the Director's instructions, the provocation of Siraj-ud-doula by Drake led to the battle of Plassey. The Company's servants' indulgence in inland trade and fraudulent use of custom-free concession led to the quarrels with the Nawabs particularly the war with Mir Kasim ultimately led to grant of Dewani. Bribery, corruption, forgery, cheating and avarice on the part of the Company's servants to the consternation of Directors led to every new Nawab becoming more and more subservient to the British. This was the way that brick by brick the foundations of the British Empire were laid.

Only a few Indians saw the writing on the wall. "I was not looking at the private apartment of the queens. I was looking in the direction of the Europeans who were coming from beyond the seas to tear down thy curtains and destroy thine empire." This was the prophetic reply of Tegh Bahadur, ninth Guru of the Sikhs, when he was accused of staring from his prison window in the direction of the harem of the Great Mughal. The prophecy was now reaching fulfillment with the consolidation of the Company's power in Bengal.

Under the Act of 1784 the Company policy in India was subjected to British Governor-General and contained a clause forbidding the Governor-General and Council to make war or conclude a treaty likely to lead to war for the simple reason that to pursue schemes of conquest and territorial expansion were "measures repugnant to the wish, the honour and the policy of the nation".

> Wellesley openly repudiated the policy. He affirmed, I can declare my conscientious conviction that no greater blessing can be conferred

on the native inhabitants of India than the extension of British authority, influence and power.

To recreate the intellectual ambience of the past is a much more arduous enterprise than conjuring up a vanished city. For that in India we have to see the water colours of the Daniell brothers and the mezzotints of Zoffany. But for the British approach to Indian affairs of that time and the Indian reaction to it, a time machine or a mechanism of recall of much more complex construction is needed. It is not that the Englishmen of the eighteenth century were inarticulate; it was quite the contrary. In London itself there were thunderous diatribes of Burke, Sheridan and Fox and in counterpoint the muted magisterial tones of Pitt and the sober counting-house tenor of Dundas. In India there were still the stentorian echoes of Clive balanced by the more mature voice of Hastings and in the settlements of Madras and Bombay could be heard voices varying in stridency in relation to the strength or weakness of the British presence.

The Englishmen of the eighteenth century, whether in England or India, were great writers of letters, memoranda and reports. There were also persons who indulged in a considerable amount of introspection and self-analysis. Their diaries, their minutes, their lengthy letters to colleagues in India, their friends and patrons in England, their memoranda to the Court of Directors, Leadenhall Street, might appear prolix to us who live in an age where letter writing suffers because of the telephone, telegram and e-mail and where the distractions of the media have rendered diary writing for posterity, a lost art. Charnock, the archetypal trader-cum-pirate wrote surprisingly detailed reports to his masters in Leadenhall Street in which he attempted, usually unsuccessfully, to justify various courses of action he had adopted such as why the extension to the stockade at *baitakhana* was called for and why it was necessary for the British to make their commercial presence felt. Even Clive, the quintessential man of action, put down carefully reasoned in detail the pros and cons of direct rule and rule in the name of Nawab. His memorandum on why he chose the *Diwani* to the alternative of direct rule in Bengal is a classic of introspective analysis. We do not therefore suffer from any lack of material for calling up the dominant themes and approaches of the time.

It is only that there is a welter of voices, not a chorus but a periodic cacophony. By 1783, when William Jones appeared on the scene, the diffident trader of the days of Roe, the tentative traders of Surat, had given place to the very definite British presence at Fort William that fostered the aggressive colonist of the days of Charnock, the unscrupulous 'Nabob' Governor Pitt of Madras. The conqueror in the incarnations of Clive of Plassey and Munro of Buxar, to the ruler in the shape of Hastings, the evangelist John Shore, the proconsul of Wellesley, the reformer of Macaulay, the guardian of the Lawrences, were stereotypes which were still to appear. But the strands of all their approaches were implicit in the British-Indian situation of the 1780s. The explorer, the trader, the colonist, the conqueror, the evangelist, the imperialist, the reformer and the guardian were not roles which could be embodied in a single administrative persona. There were bound to be internal conflicts and these conflicts made themselves manifest in the 1780s. In a fashion typical of eighteenth century, the leading men of the period were setting down, albeit in a tentative and groping fashion, the justification for British intervention in Indian affairs.

The chief of these was Warren Hastings, that strong man full of contradictions, who more than any other Englishman, including Clive, was the architect of the British Empire in India in the eighteenth century. The English in India were by this time under Hastings committed to a role in government. Clive had adopted for *Diwani,* government in the name of shadow emperor who nominally continued to be the source of authority. Under Hastings *Diwani* was being shown more and more to be a farce and a sham and there was a growing awareness that the real rulers were the British. The vehicle through which British rule had to be conducted was a Company whose unequivocal policy was that of maximizing dividends. The inherent conflicts in this arrangement were being voiced by Burke.

In retrospect the patent absurdity of a commercial company, whether the United Fruit Company in Cuba or the East India Company in India trying to rule a country, especially a country as large and diverse as India, seems manifest but in the 1780s when the British were reluctant conquerors, Leadenhall Street was writing to Hastings in censorious tones to curb his territorial ambitions. This quite unsatisfactory arrangement was to continue for another seventy years. But in 1783 the only British presence in India was the East India Company. The Indians invested it with a personality and gave it the honorific of the Jehan Company

(Honourable Company) which was anglicised into John Company. Everything in and around Calcutta was done in the name of John Company; the Nawab at Murshidabad had ceased to play any effective role in the administration. At the same time, the British had not created any administrative structure, any machinery for the maintenance of law and order. In fact they were not aware of what laws were needed to be administered. To them the native administration of law appeared to be arbitrary subject to the wisdom of the caprice of the judges appointed by the Mughals. There did not appear to be any fixed courts of law. There appeared to be different systems of law for Hindus and Muslims and the severity or levity or punishments appeared to be subject to the whims of the individuals who served as Judges. Nor was there any fixed principle for collection of revenue.

To add to this stage of institutional chaos, the mechanism of Dual Rule had introduced an element of uncertainty as the Judges and the tax gatherers did not know whether to serve their erstwhile rulers or the British. The situation was further vitiated by the fact that the majority of Englishmen who came to India came with the avowed intention of "shaking the Pagoda tree", came with no motive in mind except private profit. As a result, in Bengal there was the *firman* of the Mughal emperor, the shadow Nawab at Murshidabad, the very real presence of the John Company and the cupidity and rascality of the servants of the East India Company. To compound the chaos, the John Company did not have at the outset any intention of playing an effective role in the administration of the country but was being drawn inexorably into the vacuum created by the collapse of the Mughal empire and the local administrations. Added to this was the territorial imperatives of British trade with India.

Dominating the scene was that seemingly diffident colossus Warren Hastings, who as time showed had sinews of steel and a tenacity of will and purpose rivaling that of Clive.

Though the idea of empire was slowly coming to birth, the various strands of the empire were to be found in microcosm in Calcutta of 1783. The concept of the White Man's Burden, the mission of civilizing India, the task of knitting the variegated cultural strains of the country into a grand tapestry, were all in the future; the Seeleys, the Macaulays, the Hebers and the Curzons were still to come.

11

Preliminary Skirmishes

The first step in the foundation of the British empire was taken when Queen Elizabeth I granted a Charter to the East India Company on 31st December 1599 under the historic title of "The Governor and Company of Merchant of London Trading into the East Indies."

The merchants in 1601 sent their first fleet to the Indies. Sailing from Torbay, the Company's ships reached the island of Sumatra and sailed thence to Java, capturing on the way a Portuguese vessel laden with calico and spices. This first voyage yielded a 'handsome profit'. Further expeditions followed to islands of the Indian Ocean but the possibility of trading in cloths and calicoes soon drew English adventurers to India itself. Permission was obtained for establishing 'factories' or trading posts at Ahmedabad and three other places. The Moghul Emperor confirmed these privileges with a *firman* in 1613.

The history of the Company as a force in Indian politics now began in earnest. To the Moghul court went Sir Thomas Roe in the character of the Royal Ambassador of England. The great sub-continent of India which was to fall swiftly and perceptibly into the hands of the Company is described by James Mill as "at that time the seat of one of the most extensive and splendid monarchies on the surface of the globe." Akbar, grandson of Babar the founder of the Mogul empire, ruled from 1556 to 1605 over the greater part of India and maintained complete religious toleration. Already the Moghuls, like previous rulers of the country, were in the process of becoming Indianised; they had ceased to regard themselves as strangers and had no home but India. Cultural forces had been at work for years to blend the rival traditions of race and religion into what was slowly becoming a synthesis of Indian character.

Akbar realized the value of this for the unity of India. He was the greatest political strategist of his age and came close to the ideal of the benevolent despot. He initiated vital reforms like prohibition of *sati* – the self immolation of Hindu widows – and of enslavement of prisoners captured in war.

Akbar died in 1605; no succeeding emperor was equal to him in power or character. The 17th century saw the building of Taj Mahal and the Peacock Throne but it was also an age of social disintegration. The one virtue of autocrats which is strength declined among the unrivalled luxuries of the Moghul Court. The Company made advances in their trading concessions during the reign of Shah Jahan. An open lamp had set fire to the silk veil of his favourite daughter Jahanara. Learning of this episode the English surgeon of an East India Company ship, Gabriel Boughton offered to treat her. When Jahanara was saved from disfigurement by Dr. Boughton, Shah Jahan gave the Company the right to trade in Bengal free of duty as a mark of gratitude.

The normally suspicious and cautious Emperor Aurangzeb never thought that the British would constitute a threat to the Mughal empire. In 1639 the Company obtained land at Madras. Oliver Cromwell abolished the East India Company in 1654 but found that the Dutch made such headway in India and Ceylon that he was obliged to restore the charter. Bombay held by Portugal since 1530 passed into English hands in 1662 as part of the dowry of Catherine of Portugal upon her marriage to Charles II of England. In 1668 it was leased to East India Company and the third great centre of British penetration was established at Calcutta in 1690. A clumsy and premature effort to seize political power was made in 1686, when a military expedition was sent against Aurangzeb but this was a complete failure. For the rest of the century the Company continued its activities to the trade passing through its factories. "Search any man", wrote Macaulay, "however sagacious, would have thought it possible that a trading company separated from India by fifteen thousand miles of sea and possessing only a few acres for the sake of commerce, would in less than a hundred years, spread its empire from Cape Comorin to the eternal snows of the Himalayas."

In the interregnum of chaos after Aurangzeb's death, the English addressed a petition to Emperor Farukshiyar in 1713 for a new trade *firman* which said "the request of the smallest particle of sand, John Russell, President of the English East India Company, with his reverence due from a slave amongst those that make their request to Your Throne which is a seat of obstacles"... Farukshiyar was treated by the staff surgeon of the East India Company, William Hamilton, who cured the decadent emperor of a tumor in the back. As fee he asked for a sizable grant of land on the Indian peninsula never before given to a foreign power; the thirty-seven villages contiguous to the factory at Calcutta which gave the English the command of the river for ten miles south of the river. The depredations of the East India Company awakened the Nawabs of Bengal, particularly Murshid Ali Khan to the dangers of encouraging British mercantile interest in Bengal.

The English had dropped their anchor at Sutanati Ghat on the bank of the Ganges in 1690 under the leadership of Job Charnock, who is regarded as the founder of the present city of Calcutta. He arrived on the eastern coast as Chief Agent of East India Company in 1686. Threatened by the Mughal Viceroy of Bengal, he moved twenty-seven miles to Sutanati – the site of what is now Calcutta and which became the capital of British India and the second city of the Empire. The establishment of Calcutta as the capital of British-Indian empire was largely the result of Charnock's persistence.

Little is known of Charnock's early life beyond the fact that he came to India after a long sojourn. Frequently at odds with Indian leaders and his superiors, Charnock was accused of mismanagement, theft and brutality to Indian prisoners. He was undoubtedly of questionable morality and was once recommended for dismissal. Job Charnock possessed the qualities of a pirate and a practical trader. Only such men would have braved the dangers of sea and would arrive to trade in the uncertainties of the seventeenth and eighteenth centuries.

In 1699 Murshid Kuli Khan, Nawab of Bengal, received valuable presents from the Company. In return the Nawab of Bengal accorded his thoughtless consent and ordered the zamindars of the three towns of Sutanati, Govindapur and Kalighat to transfer their titles and rights to the Company for a sum of one thousand rupees which the Company's men in Bengal regarded as the best money ever spent for so great a privilege.

Charnock was one of those combinations of romantic adventurers and hard-headed businessmen with which the history of East India Company abounds. He was a stubborn, persistent man, who when he was turned out of the settlement at Hughly, moved south and established his base at Sutanati, site of the present Calcutta. He chose the site well, because the river was wide and deep at this point. Strategically also it was a good selection because it was protected on one side by the Hooghly River and on the other by the salt lakes. The new site had unrestricted access to the sea as the Dutch and French settlements were located up-river. The Indian merchants migrating from the silted-up port of Satgaon had settled at Sutanati and adjoining areas. This contributed to the eventual commercial importance of the whole complex. At Sutanati once stood a great peepal tree where Job Charnock is said to have had his *baithakhana*, or sitting place, and where he and his companions smoking their hookahs, laid out the plans for the new settlement. The peepal tree no longer stands, but Sutanati became Dalhousie Square.

Charnock is reputed to have on one occasion cut with his sword a chain barrier across the harbour. On another occasion he is said to have terrorized the traders on the banks of the Hooghly by setting fire to their houses with a gigantic lens mounted on his boat. But the exploit which has endeared him to posterity and which inspired generations of writers from Jules Verne to John Masters, was the manner in which he acquired his wife. We will let Colonel Newell tell the story:

> His marriage was the result of as surprising and dramatic an adventure as any imagined in the wildest fiction. The tale runs that Charnock habitually made a nocturnal round of the Company's factory preceded by torchbearers and protected by an armed guard. One evening while so employed, he passed a burning ghat. The pyre was ready and a young widow was performing the last rites prior to committing suttee. She was tall, fair-skinned and beautiful. Charnock commanded his guards to rescue her and bring her to him.

Charnock was devoted to her and one of his daughters by her became the wife of Sir Charles Eyre; the other daughter married a member of the Salisbury family.

But Charnock with all his deeds of derring-do was nevertheless a bureaucratic type of brigand and an honest and conscientious servant of the East Indian Company. Proceedings were meticulously kept, as for instance this Consultation dated 28th

August 1690 which reads – "The Right Worshipful Agent Charnock, Francis Ellis, and Jeremiah Peachie resolved that such places be built as absolutely necessary, viz., a warehouse, dining room, a room to sort cloth in, a cook room and an apartment for the Company's servants. The Agent's house likewise Mr. Peachie's to be repaired, as also the Secretary's office."

The Directors of the East India Company, with their chronic disregard for the worth and achievements of their representatives in India, rewarded him with threatened dismissal, two supercessions, numerous censures and made his last years miserable. His monument, however, stands. It is not the ungainly mausoleum of Charnock of stone from far off Pallavaram which his son-in-law Charles Eyre put up in his memory. As for Wren, one can say of Charnock *si monumentum requires circumspice*. And the *baitakhana* where he and his companions sat and planned the new settlement became the heart of Calcutta.

Alexander Hamilton tells the story as to how instead of converting his wife to Christianity, Charnock was converted by her to the cult of *Panch Pir* or five saints – a sort of combination of Mohameddan and Hindu devotion emanating from Bihar. "The only part of Christianity that was remarkable in him was burying her decently and he built a tomb over her where all his life after her death he kept the anniversary day by sacrificing a cock on her tomb after the pagan manner." After long years of faithful service, having endured the bitterness of being superceded, wearied out by long delays and the deaf ears of his masters in England, living in an exhausting climate, weakened by constant fevers, far from the influences of his mother Church, it is surprising that old Job's declining years were spent in indolence and disorder.

Newell describes Charnock thus: "buried in a dreary open space frequently subjected to the depredations of hogs and other unwelcome intruders .... Tradition avers that he sleeps besides his dearly loved wife, the beautiful Hindu widow whom he so romantically and dramatically rescued from the flames of Suttee. His mausoleum constructed out of gneiss Pallavaram brought from Madras by his son in law Sir Charles Eyre still stands but the burial ground is now part of the sanctified grounds of St. Johns Church."

It is strange that Kipling who in other cases was only too willing to praise the achievement of men of action with a streak of rascality in them should have withheld his just dues to Job Charnock, the founder of Calcutta. Early British India was full of such colourful characters as Philip Francis, James Hickey, George Thomas, David Ochterlony, Walter Reinhart who contrasted oddly with scholars and serious statesmen.

The Company built Fort William and Queen Anne's Church during the reigns of King William III and Queen Anne. They conducted a brisk trade in broadcloth muslin, copper, lead and zinc not only with Indian merchants but also with the older Portuguese and Armenian settlements.

The 18th century saw the dissolution of Moghul power. After the death of Aurangzeb, the governors of provinces became independent, soldiers of fortune carved out kingdoms for themselves, local potentates usurped power. The country was swept by invasions – outside and within. In 1739, Nadir Shah of Persia captured Delhi and massacred its inhabitants. During 1748 to 1762 there were repeated Afghan invasions. Inland territories periodically were laid waste. Ahmed Shah Durrani defeated the Marathas at Panipat but had to return to his own dominions leaving the Maratha chiefs the strongest force in India to grapple with new enemies. While the armies of the Moghuls and the Marathas had been concentrated on the northern plains, the British merchants had made themselves virtual masters of Bengal.

As the Moghul empire began to swiftly disintegrate, far-sighted Englishmen saw the possibilities of establishing a new empire on the ruins of the old one – as the Goths and Vandals had built the Holy Roman Empire on the ruins of the empire of Caesar's. Whereas in Rome the race of Caesar's had shifted to Constantinople, in eighteenth century India there were effete and glittering royal puppets to be manipulated and used for the Company's purpose. The Nawab became the mouthpiece of the *Nabob.* However, the future rulers had a ready-made infrastructure of governance designed by the Moghuls.

Calcutta expanded and prospered. From Fort William Calcutta was to grow into an imperial city second in importance to London in the late eighteenth and nineteenth century. The transformation of Calcutta runs parallel to the British role during these eras. From the status as freebooters they moved into the great pantheon of the heaven-born Indian Civil Service. The main theatres of action were located on the eastern side of India. It was there, between

Madras and Pondicherry, that the battle for trade and ultimately for India was fought between the British and the French. It was Calcutta, on the Bay of Bengal with China to trade with round the Malay Straits and the whole of the fertile and heavily populated Punjab to draw on that managed to gain for itself the role of a premier city.

It was in Calcutta that the most legendary *Nabobs* were made, conjuring images of portly figures reclining in luxury among a crowd of turbaned retainers attended by parrots, pet leopards, *Bibis* and pale brown progeny. Around Chowringhee were the pillared white mansions of the *Nabobs* that can be seen even today in their ruined glory. Fortunes were made by jute and indigo merchants. But this is to anticipate.

> Nawab Murshid Kuli Khan was disquieted by the spectacle of the Company's burgeoning wealth, and forbade Indians to trade with the English. His commands were overruled by the Mughal emperor Farukshayar. The commercial spirit of the Company was not to be suppressed. Pleased by lavish gifts from the English the next Nawab Alivardi Khan accorded more concessions to the Company. 'The English' he said 'are like bees. Press them gently to extract honey but do not get stung'. The bees however soon became eagles that could not be dislodged as Alivardi's grandson, Siraj-ud-doula discovered. Lacking the astuteness of his grandfather the imperious young Nawab fell headlong into conflict with the devious and calculating Colonel Robert Clive of the East India Company in Bengal. Siraj-ud-doula's imperiousness made enemies of his own courtiers as well. Some of these disgruntled men joined Robert Clive in a conspiracy to depose the Nawab. The overthrow of Siraj became an urgent necessity for the British as he was having his army trained by the French who also nursed imperial dreams. (*The Conquerors*, Achala Moulik)

The genius of the Frenchman, Joseph Francois Dupleix came to India in 1730 and conceived of a European empire in India. He knew he must destroy his European rivals. French mercenaries were lured by Indian princes. The growing French presence in South India threatened the British settlement at Madras. The riverine port of Chandanagar was acquired by the French soon after. The tactics of Dupleix was imitated by Clive with greater success.

In the eighteenth century the British eclipsed all their European rivals. The great power of Spain began to decay after 1648 with Philip IV who was last but one of the Spanish Hapsburgs. France was in turmoil; a long series of wars with Britain and Prussia added to the discontent of the middle classes. Austria and Prussia were concerned with European politics. The British Empire had extended to North America. It was only after the loss of the American colonies in 1780 that Britain turned in earnest to India where the East India Company grew from a trading enterprise to a territorial overlord. The initial economic motive became a desire for political power.

12

Clive the Conqueror

Of the two outstanding British figures in 18th century India, Clive comes out in colours of red and gold against a background of murky darkness. The stodgy portrait of him by Blackmuir does him no justice. Restless, ambitious, arrogant, self-opinionated, Clive was an early guerilla leader, diplomatist, plunderer, and reformer. His was a classic East India Company career, the stuff of that school-boy stories are made of. Joining the Company's service as a clerk, instead of as a solider, Clive arrived in Madras in 1744 at the age of seventeen. Obviously unsuited to the existence of a clerk, he was given to fits of depression and despair in the heat and loneliness of Madras. He thought of ending his life and played Russian roulette with his revolver. When the pistol misfired he came to the conclusion that fate had better things in store for him. He was present during the French capture of Madras in 1746; blackening his face he escaped to Fort St. David in the garb of a *Dubash*. He bore the ennui of the Writer's desk for six years. Then fate took a hand. Clive acquitted himself with dash and heroism in the English siege of Pondicherry in 1748. When the British force at the siege of Arcot in 1751 needed a leader he readily volunteered, scored a dramatic victory and never returned to the counting house. Instead he went from victory to victory.

During his stay in Madras he married Mary Mascaleyn in the church of St. Mary in the fort compound where Charnock had his daughter baptized.

Meanwhile, the French erected defences around their principal factory at Chandanagar and the Dutch did the same at Chinsura. Both places were on the river Hooghly upstream of the British settlement at Fort William in Calcutta. In 1743, the English set to work on building a moat around the northern part of Calcutta which came to be known as the 'Maratha ditch'. The Nawab however had no intention of allowing the Europeans to become too strong and when he had finally settled matters with the Marathas, the English and the French asked his permission to increase their defences, the Nawab replied, "you are merchants, what need have you of a fortress? Being under my protection you have no enemies to fear." But it was not the Nawab or the Marathas the Europeans feared. They feared each other.

With an unerring political instinct Robert Clive, 'the heaven born General' (of Pitt's acclaim), saw the potential of an empire for Britain in the Moghul empire which had a well established system of revenue and administration available for use by a successor government. Clive was one of the most restless and ambitious men that ever lived and would have drawn Madras under his command if possible. He was already aware that the three Presidencies should be under one rule and that this should be Bengal which he described as "an inexhaustible fund of Riches".

In the prelude to the betrayal of Siraj-ud-doula, Clive drew up double agreements – one of white paper that was genuine and the other in red paper which was fictitious. Watson's signature was forged by Clive. Under the terms of the red paper Amirchand – or Omichand as the British called him – was to get L 200,000 while under the white paper he was to get nothing.

At the battle of Plassey or Palashi (Palashi in Bengali means the field of the *Palash* trees), Clive halted his force in a large mango grove; he did not expect to win against the might of the Nawab's army which had been trained by the Frenchman General St. Frais. He had said earlier, "We must give them the best fight we can during the day and at night sling our muskets over our shoulders and march back to Calcutta. We cannot win against the impressive cavalry, the heavy artillery and the officers under command of General de St. Frais." However, Clive had taken the precaution of winning over the commander-in-chief of the Nawab's army, Mir Jafar, who held back the army at the crucial juncture. The only general loyal to the Nawab, Mohanlal, regrouped the forces and led a desperate charge against the Company's army. General Mohanlal fell in the reckless charge and the mighty army of Bengal retreated. Young Siraj-ud-doula implored Mir Jafar for aid and advice but finding neither, escaped, while the victorious army of the East India Company marched towards his capital at Murshidabad on the 28th of June 1757. The traitor Mir Jafar came forward to congratulate Clive who informed him that he, Mir Jafar, was now the Nawab of Bengal.

The battle was a turning point in the destinies of two nations – Britain and India. Like Montgomery at El Alamein two centuries later, Clive took his title from this victory. But the battle of Plassey was no feat of arms. The casualties were relatively small on both sides and the outcome of the battle was a foregone conclusion. Plassey has been called "not a battle but a transaction" in which the compradors of Bengal sold the Nawab to the English.

Clive had turned from clerk to guerilla fighter to manipulator. After Plassey, Clive appeared in another role – that of a man who would not hesitate to sacrifice principles to attain his objectives. Without a qualm he forged the signature of his superior Admiral Watson on a bogus treaty in which a substantial reward of L 200,000 was promised to a financier of the times, Amirchand, for his help in the intrigues which ultimately led to the defeat of the Nawab Siraj-ud-doula of Bengal at Plassey. After the outcome of Plassey, Clive's aide "Seratton said to him in the Indostan language 'Omichand, the red paper is a trick. You are to have nothing'. These words overpowered him like a blast of suplhur. He sunk back fainting and would have fallen to the ground had not one of his attendants caught him in his arms". The merchant Amirchand was carried back home "where he remained many hours in stupid melancholy".

This account of the scene at the house of the banker, Jagat Seth, may be apocryphal. Macaulay joins the chorus and wrote that Amirchand lost his reason but the history of the times tells us that Amirchand lived to serve Clive in other ways. What is likely is that Amirchand concealed his outrage and thought it prudent to co-operate with Clive, the now de facto ruler of Bengal. Amirchand even left L 2000 to the Foundling Hospital in London – perhaps to indicate to his English colleagues of his magnanimous nature!

The episode gives Macaulay occasion for thin-sounding moralizing. However, it is clear from Macaulay's essay on Clive that he was attracted to the personality of this overbearing, headstrong, unscrupulous man. To all these qualities Clive added one more in his last visit to India: Hypocrisy.

During his earlier career Clive had set the pattern for 'shaking the pagoda tree.' The spoils of Plassey brought him L 400,000. To this by a convenient fiction he added the revenues from one of the richest jagirs – the Twenty-four Parganas. Even battles in which he had not fought had brought him riches!

The Company became Zamindar of the Twenty-four Parganas comprising of eight hundred and eighty square miles to the south of Calcutta. The revenue of the Parganas amounted to L 150,000. Clive received L 234,000. Later on when he was being tried in London he said he was "astonished at his moderation". In this matter at least "Clive was very easily astonished". He was firmly convinced that whatever personal advantage he collected was somehow different from and altogether holier than the gain seized by smaller men.

As the British historian Thomson observes, "A gold lust unequalled since the hysteria that took hold of the Spaniards of Cortes' and Pisarro's age filled the English mind. Bengal in particular was not to know peace until it had been bled white." Historian Garratt says, "We think his enormous greed provided an example against which his severity towards others (who took smaller amounts in ways he considered irregular) was entirely ineffective. For the monstrous financial immorality of British conduct in India for many years after this, Clive was largely responsible."

In his essay on Clive, Macaulay has summarized the process that developed from financial indebtedness and military dependence that made rulers of Bengal the helpless vassals of the British merchants.

> The servant of the Company obtained – not for their employers but for themselves – a monopoly of almost the whole of internal trade. They forced the natives to buy dear and sell cheap. Every servant of a British factor was armed with the power of his master and his master with all the power of the Company. Enormous fortunes were thus accumulated at Calcutta while thirty million human beings were reduced to the large extremity of wretchedness. They were accustomed to live under tyranny but never tyranny like this.

Clive returned to England in 1762. Aged only thirty-five, he had shown astounding prowess and spirit in both war and peace. He bought a palace in Kensington that had fireplaces built by the celebrated Adam and an extensive estate in Shropshire with gardens laid out by Capability Brown. Macaulay says of him that, "this warrior who had been content in India with the uniform of a soldier supplemented his wardrobe with two hundred shirts of the finest linen." The *condottiero* had become the *Nabob.*

But destiny had still left him with one more and quite uncharacteristic role to play. The Directors of the East India Company had become increasingly alarmed by the cupidity of their merchants in India. A thorough cleaning-up, they felt, was called for. And for these Augean stables they chose a most improbable Hercules – Clive. It is a measure of the many-sided genius of Clive that this *Nabob* of *Nabobs*, this arch intriguer should have played the role of administrative reformer with consummate success! On landing in Calcutta he declaimed in words which ring with all the sincerity of a good actor: "To what low depths has the reputation of the Company fallen!" Clive's task was to stop flow of gold into pockets of Company's servants; as the English traders cynically remarked, "the poacher has turned gamekeeper. By sheer force of personality, brazen effrontery and the self-exculpation of a truly egotistical and self-obsessed man, he made the miscreants of Calcutta forget his own dubious antecedents. He had unambiguously written in April 1764, "The trade in salt, betel and tobacco being one cause of the present disputes I hope these articles will be restored to the Nawab and your servants absolutely forbid to trade in them." Clive also promised "he would not engage in any kind of trade himself". Yet within a month of his arrival in Calcutta he entered into a partnership with some of his colleagues in the Select Committee for "the purpose of dealing in salt, betel nuts and tobacco".

But discontent against this skilful adventurer was spread through the Company's directorate and also Parliament. His conduct fostered this discontent. He had become perhaps the king's richest subject.

There began now the "sharing of the Pagoda tree". 'Pagodas' were coins used in South India and the term 'Pagoda Tree' is strictly speaking more applicable to Madras where during the last fifty years of the eighteenth century the Company's servants were in every way baser as well as more venal than in Bengal.

The trouble was that the majority of the Company's servants in Bengal were keen to engage in private trade and plunder. For Clive the Company's well-being and profit were, if not paramount, at least as important as his own. As early as July he was asking the Directors in London to send "capable young men for the civil service". A month later he suggested that it would be worth the Directors' while to attract good professional soldiers into their service in India "for to be assured there are very few in your service at present: the best are killed or dead (of illness or fever)".

The Moghul emperor granted the British the right of the *Diwani* or the right of revenue collection in Bengal. This legitimatised the British presence and absorbed it firmly into the Indian tradition.

The Company's disassociation from actual administration was also necessary from a purely physical point of view. There were not enough Englishmen to take over the running of the country even if they wanted to. In particular, there was a shortage of the right kind of Englishmen. The clash between the Company's interest and the private interest of its employees had created the predicament in Bengal.

13

Shaking the Pagoda Tree

Clive's political aims from which Hastings was to differ strongly were set out in his final direction to the Calcutta Board on 16th January 1767. This states:

> The first point in Politics which I offer to consideration is the form of Government. We are sensible that with the Acquisition of the Dewanee the power belonging to the Soubah of these Provinces is totally vested in the East India Company. Nothing remains to him but the Name and Shadow of Authority. This Name, however, this Shadow, is indispensably necessary and we should seek to venerate; every Mark of Distinction and respect must be shown to him and he himself encouraged to show his Resentment upon the least want of Respect from other nations. Under the Sanction of Soubah every encroachment that may be attempted by foreign powers can effectively be crushed without any Interposition of our own authority and all real Grievances complained by them can through the same channel be examined and redressed. Be it therefore always remembered that there is a Soubah, that we have allotted him a Stipend which must be regularly paid in support of his Dignity and that though the revenues belong to the Company, the territorial jurisdiction must still rest in the Chiefs of the country acting under him and his Presidency in Conjunction.

This was Clive's famous 'dual system.' An element of sham runs through all administrations everywhere – but the Indian government has often almost seemed to have preferred that fiction should occupy the public attention while in fact (a very different fact) it got the actual ruling done.

After the battles of Plassey in 1757 and Buxar in 1765, the Company had ceased to be a mere trading organization and according to Garratt and Thomson, had become in fact "the most formidable commercial republic known in the world since the destruction of Carthage."

Entering on his second period of power, Clive became eloquent on the subject of corruption in Calcutta. "One of the most wicked Places in the Universe, corruption, licentiousness and want of Principle seem to have possessed the minds of all the Civil Servants by frequent bad Examples, they have grown callous, Rapacious and luxurious beyond conception and the Incapacity and Inequity of some and the use of others". Of Clive's dual system Hastings was scornful and called it "a Pageant of our own and a mere Idol".

One of the most astonishing historical statements was made by Clive before the select Parliamentary committee in 1772 when he ended in the rhetorical outburst: "Mr. Chairman, at this moment I stand astonished at my own moderation." What is remarkable is that after all this furore, Prime Minister Pitt called Clive 'the heaven born General'. Military did much as they pleased. Though Clive was commander-in-chief as well as civilian Governor, his sympathies were plainly with the civil power.

Clive has been called "a malcontent, a brooding bully and an outsider" who if he had pursued his natural bent on his native shores, would have landed in a lock-up whereas on the wilder shores of India, he found a natural theatre for his undoubted military genius, his talent for seizing the main chance, his willingness to risk all on the throw of a dice. While he was the quintessential man of action, the classic condottiero, he also had the good fortune that on the most of the important passages of his life, his private interest and that of the long-term British imperial interest happened to coincide. If there had been a conflict, there is no doubt that Clive would have sacrificed the interest either of the British people or the East India Company without a qualm. He was a lone wolf, as most of the early colonists were, a solo player, playing his own private symphony, of the school of Job Charnock. The fact that his private interest supervened is exemplified in the notorious case of Clive's *jaghir*.

Not surprising therefore that the loner pursuing his own devices, was the archetypal colonist and imperialist. Whether it was Charnock or Clive or Hastings – they all conformed to this type. But Clive was astute enough to realize that he was playing a role for posterity and at every stage of his career he recorded the reasons for his actions.

The metamorphosis from the trader to the *conquistadore* is seen by the first obsequious attitude displayed by the letter of the East

India Company to Emperor Farukshiyar and the subsequent arrogance of Clive after the battle of Plassey and the arbitrary conduct of Hastings. The cold cynicism of Clive's dual system which was an institutionalized sham in disguising the Company's power were all part of the chicanery and hypocrisy that characterized Clive. He remained aloof from the Indians unless they served his purpose such as Sayyid Mohamed Resa Khan.

In his book, *The Transition in Bengal*, Abdul Majed Khan observes that there was some continuity and overlapping of functions between British and Moghul administrations than generally perceived. Company servants like Clive seemed to the populace more of a Moghul noble than an alien administrator. Instead of the British taking over the local administration with the intention of removing corruption, the traditional style of administration continued under Resa Khan, who resisted efforts of the East India Company officers who tried to increase the revenues for the Company and of course their own incomes. As later with Nanda Kumar, so with Sayid Mohammed Resa Khan, the Company brought trumped up charges against him and put him on trial. He had committed the unpardonable act of trying to check the plunder of the Company officials. Despite the pressure on Hastings to have him convicted, Resa Khan had to be acquitted and reinstated as Naib Nasim of Murshidabad.

Resa Khan had no illusions about the growing power of the British. In his book *Consideration on Indian Affairs,* W. Bolts may have been right when he says that "if the youngest Writer in our service had been sent with the authority of the Company to Shah Alum, it was certain that His Majesty would have granted away the reminder of his empire". But it was also true that the Moghul grant was necessary, however it was obtained. This was despite the invasions of Nadir Shah and Ahmed Shah Durrani which had left the person of the Emperor a mere shell.

In more normal times the Company was represented in the Bengal Subedhar's court by native *vakils* or agents usually Hindu. Only on very rare and important occasions did the Nawab himself grant interviews to the *vakils*. This was only natural as the military aristocrats of the imperial or provincial courts did not hold merchants in any high regard; they were treated as subjects, useful but not to be fraternized with, nor treated as social equals. The Nawabs long maintained a virtual monopoly in salt, betel nut, opium and saltpetre. The presence of an English company in Bengal, however, considerable its trade could not disturb the picture of Bengal as a Moghul *subah*. If Moghul titles such as Sabut Jang or Dilawar Jang were bestowed on the 'firinghis' like Colonel Clive, Admiral Watson, Major Kilpatrick, it was a mark of condescension by the local rulers and a sign of their acceptance of these upstart foreign traders.

The conspirators at Murshidabad before Plassey secretly appreciated the nature of the English power which they were calling to their assistance. Curious though it may appear, the Nawab did not appear to have understood that the Company was not an individual but an impersonal and a corporate body of merchants. When Clive was about to go home in early 1760, Mir Jafar sent with him seven packets of curiosities to his ally, Clive's master in London and with them a letter addressed as though to some individual chief or ruler. The letter in Warren Hastings's translation reads as follows: "The lights of my eyes, dearer than my life, the Nabob Zobdut ul Mulk Mayanodowla Sabut Jang Bahadur (Clive) is departing for his own country – a separation from him is most afflicting to me. If you dispatch him speedily to these parts and grant me the happiness of seeing him again, it will be a real obligation."

When Clive set sail once more for England in 1770 he felt that his mission was successful and he could write patronizingly to Warren Hastings. He had all through his life been driven by demons of despair which were not successful in destroying him when he attempted suicide in Madras in 1732. Forty-one years later, the demons were successful; Clive died by his own hand in 1773.

14

The East India Company

"I have known merchants with the sentiments and abilities of great statesmen and I have seen persons in the situation of Statesmen with a character and conceptions of pedlars" – Burke

The East India Company was unique. Never in the history of the world has a group of adventurous merchants shaped an epoch and formed an empire. It is worth looking at the phenomenon of its growth and development.

C.H. Philips in his *The East India Company* gives a vivid picture:

> The East India House was the home of the grandest society of merchants in the Universe. It was situated on the south side of the busy thoroughfare of Leadenhall Street in the city of London. A splendid new building went up in 1726 from which the Company functioned for the rest of its days. A coat of arms over its front door embellished with the motto 'Auspicio Regis et Senatus Angliae' which has a fine imperial ring. The earlier motto was 'Deus Indicat' – or God Points the Way. It was a plain four story stone building serviceable but not beautiful although it had a narrow frontage of only seventy feet it extended backward over three hundred feet and contained a spacious hall, a garden and a courtyard, rooms for the Directors and offices for the Clerks as well as several large warehouses in the rear. Most of the offices including the important office of Examiner of Indian Correspondence were on the upper floors. This part of the building was gloomy and dingy and intersected with long corridors and dark staircases. Charles Lamb who served for thirty three years as a Clerk in the Accountant's Department wrote of 'the labyrinthine passages and light excluding pent up offices where candles for one half of the year supplied the place of the sunlight'.
>
> Down to 1784 the home Government of the Company had consisted of the proprietors of India Stock and the twenty four Directors. Any person who brought shares in the capital stock of the Company was

> nominated a Proprietor and was permitted to attend the meetings of the General Court of Proprietors.
>
> One contemporary writer maliciously described the General Court as 'a popular senate', no distinction as to citizenship – the Englishmen, the Frenchmen, the American – no difference as to religion – the Jew, the Turk, the Pagan: no impediment as to sex – the old women of both sexes (Alexander: *East India Magazine*). However, the General Court drew its strength from two main sources: the banking, shipping and commercial interest of the City of London which had invested money in the Company's concerns. Secondly the retired Anglo Indians or Nabobs who acquired India stock either as a convenient form of investment in yielding a assured dividend of 8% or as a means by which they could gain influence, a directorship, power and patronage in the company.
>
> The most important function of the proprietors was to elect the twenty four directors who formed the executive body of the Company in England – the election of whom was done every year on the second Wednesday in April.

This eighteenth-century institution provides a unique example of an empire founded by buccaneer-traders and expanded by condottieros who were in turn followed by colonial administrators and missionaries. The ships in which they came to India from 1748 to 1772 – the famous 'East Indiamen' were mostly of one size – 499 tonnes – for the very simple reason that all craft of 500 tonnes and more were compelled by law to carry a Chaplain. The merchants had no pretensions to either a civilizing mission or of a sacred trust. The Company was only interested in book-keeping, warehouses, collection of customs, rents and taxes. They had come to make money and they made it.

The extent of influence of East India Company patronage in English political life was undoubtedly exaggerated by contemporaries. But Writer-ships and Cadet-ships were useful as bargaining counters for a seat in Parliament, and along with church livings and university fellowships, formed part of the complex structure of the political life of that time and were so regarded by responsible politicians. The ability of the *Nabobs* to get elected aroused in the ruling class "the most potent mixture of feeling envy and alarm". (C.H. Philips, East *India Company*).

The trade with India had considerable effect on the industrial life of Britain. "Very soon after Plassey", writes Mr. Brook Adams, "the Bengal plunder began to arrive in London and the effect appears to have been instantaneous, for all the authorities agreeing that the industrial revolution, the event which has dwarfed the nineteenth century from all antecedent time began in the year 1760 ... possibly since the world began, no investment has ever yielded the profit reaped from the Indian plunder, because for nearly fifty years England stood without a competitor."

Clive appears to have attempted to check the rapacity of his subordinates to some extent but as Thompson and Garatt make clear in their *Rise and Fulfillment of British Rule*: "Clive's enormous greed provided an example against which his severity towards others was entirely ineffective. For the monstrous financial immorality of British conduct in India for many a year after this Clive was largely responsible."

The same authorities have recorded that about the gold lust that took hold of the English mind. But it was the great eighteenth-century statesman Edmund Burke who in his one of his memorable speeches summed in these words the conquest of Bengal and the consequences to its inhabitants: "The Asiatic conquerors soon abated of their ferocity because they made the conquered country their own ... every rupee of profit made by an Englishman is loss forever to India.".

Such was the situation of Bengal at the mercy of these "birds of prey and passage" who overran the country after the battle of Plassey. Lord Clive denounced the corruption of which he was the father. Nothing else could be expected of a Company whose governing body exhibited according to Macaulay "all the trickery and corruption of a Grampound election." Profit and power were the natural objects of its shareholders and among them Lord Clive "laid out a hundred thousand pounds in purchase of stock which he then divided among nominal proprietors whom he brought down in his train to every discussion and every ballot".

Empire building had begun in earnest.

From the ruler of Bengal the British extracted a concession freeing them from payment of inland revenue duties payable on conveyance of goods. Though normally this exemption applied only to the Company's goods it was claimed in practice by the servants of the Company who were doing a considerable trade on their own account. The revenue duties therefore acted in the manner of a tariff against Indian commerce. Indian trade declined while the Company and its servants made vast fortunes.

Made arrogant by their military successes, the Company rapidly extended its operations. Complaint or opposition was met with reprisal. The principal purchase originally was cloth which they sold in England, for this was before the decay of the Indian cotton industry and some years before the rise of the cloth trade in Lancashire. The Company forced Indian traders to sign contracts to deliver cloths at prices fixed by the Company. An English merchant William Bolts writing in 1772 tells of Indian weavers being flogged if they refused to sign contracts fixing prices at 15% to 40% below market rates.

A climax was reached when Mir Kasim the ruler of Bengal, decided to abolish all inland duties to save Indian merchants from ruin. The Company had demanded exemption on its own account and upheld the private claims of its servants in which even the highest officials were implicated. "They now," wrote James Mill, "insisted that it (the Government of Bengal) should impose duties on the good of all other traders and accused it of being guilty of a breach of peace against the English nation because it proposed to remit them". The quarrel ended in the usual way with the deposition of Mir Kasim and his replacement by a puppet heavily indebted to the Company and its servants for the cost of putting him on the throne.

In Britain the activities of the Company were not regarded with universal favour. Writing in 1776 Adam Smith, the father of Political Economy, and a cold clinical Scottish economist, anticipated Edmund Burke when he passed his judgement in these words upon the East India Company which by then had become the ruling power in Bengal:

> The Government of an exclusively Company of merchants is perhaps the worst of Government of any country whatever. It is in the interest of the East India Company, considered as sovereigns, that the Europeans goods carried to their Indian dominion should be sold there as cheaply as possible and that the Indian goods brought from there should be sold here as dear as possible. But the reverse is their interest as merchants. As sovereigns their interest is exactly the same with that of the country which they govern. As merchants their interest is directly opposite to that interest.

It is a very singular Government in which every member of the administration wishes to get out of the country and consequently to have done with Government as soon as he can and to whose interest the day after he has left it and carried his whole fortune with him, he is perfectly indifferent though the whole country was swallowed by an earthquake ... About the prosperity or ruin of the great empire in the Government of each that both gives him a share he seldom cares at all.

No other Governments ever were or from the nature of things ever could be so perfectly indifferent about the happiness or misery of their subjects, the improvement or waste of their dominions, the glory or disgrace of their administration as from irresistible moral causes, the greater part of the Proprietors of such a mercantile company are and necessarily must be. (*White Sahibs in India*, Reginald Reynolds)

A Select Committee of the House of Commons said:

numerous fleets of large ships loaded with the most valuable commodity of the East arriving in England in a constant and increasing succession, imposed upon the public eye and naturally gave rise to an opinion of the happy condition and growing opulence of a country whose surplus production occupied so vast a space in the commercial world. This export from India seemed to imply also a reciprocal supply by which the trading capital employed in those productions was continuously strengthened and enlarged. But the payment of a tribute and not a beneficial commerce to that country wore this specious and delusive appearance.

The proprietors of East India Company were not entirely blind to the danger caused to their own interest by the impoverishment of the country from which they drew their wealth. The act of 1769 was one of the many steps by which the interest of a chartered Company was gradually becoming merged in the commercial and political life of this country and as that process evolved the whole political weight of Britain, it was increasingly brought to bear on the development and maintenance of an empire on which British national prosperity was built. Many saw with misgiving this state participation in the spoils of India as well as the new power of corruption exercised in British political life by those who had made the fortunes in the East.

The actual collection of taxes was done through Indian officials who brought their right from the Company in auction. "Thus," wrote Harry Verelst after his retirement as Governor of Bengal, "were numberless harpies let loose to plunder, whom the spoil our miserable people enabled to complete the first year's payment."

Famine was the inevitable result. In 1770 the Calcutta Council of the East India Company recorded that "in the famine which has ensued the mortality and beggary exceed all description. About one third of the inhabitants have perished in the once plentiful province of Purneah and in other parts the misery is equal."

The poet Cowper was among those in England who watched the Company's activities with some misgivings. He wrote:

"The thieves at
home must hang;
but he that puts
into his over gorged
and bloated purse
the wealth of the
Indian provinces escapes."

The methods by which the Company consolidated its power and obtained its revenue were notorious for their severity. Professor Thompson tells us of Indian offenders against the Company's rules who were whipped to death in Calcutta in the eighteenth century by a Court which could not execute an Englishman without a royal warrant from England. According to Thompson, mutilation remained a common punishment and impalement was practiced in the last quarter of the century.

At the end of the eighteenth century, the administration of India was in Edward Thompson's words "a mass of corruption" in spite of higher salaries. Hastings was succeeded by Sir John Macpherson whose administration was described by his successor Cornwallis, as "a system of the dirtiest jobbing".

Cowper asked,

"Hast thou, though suckled at fair freedoms breast
Exported slavery to the conquered East
With Asiatic vices stored thy mind
But left their virtues and thine own behind."

The management of Company affairs was largely in the hands of its Directors who were elected by the proprietors of the Company and who were supervised by the British Government. After 1784 the chief concerns of the Company centred around patronage, commerce and stable governance in India.

Eventually the interests of Lanchashire succeeded John Company. With the huge fortunes they made in India, the Company's servants bought up on the 'rotten boroughs' of England and acquired influence in Parliament. Paul Penfield, the most famous of them who was employed by the Company at Madras, held no less than eight boroughs and his notoriety was immortalized by Edmund Burke in a terrible onslaught in the House of Commons. Writing in 1770 the Earl of Chatham observed that,

> there has been an influx of wealth into this country which has been attended with many fatal consequences because it has not been the regular natural product of labour and industry. The riches of Asia have been poured upon us and have brought with them not only Asiatic luxury, but also I fear Asiatic principles of Government. Without connections without any natural interest in the soil the importers of foreign gold have forced their way into Parliament by such a torrent of private corruption as no hereditary fortune could resist.

This was the protest of the aristocracy against the parvenu. But the main issue was not the conflict between the *Nabobs* and the aristocrats. It was the inevitable conflict between the interest of the Company and the rising industries of Northern England.

15

The Enigmatic Warren Hastings (1732-1818)

The life of Warren Hastings requires to be written by a dramatist rather than a historian. He was drawn by destiny into the maelstrom of events that accompanied the rise of British imperialism in India. Determined to expand his country's territories in India, he acted with a subtlety and astuteness that offered a contrast to the clumsy and rough methods of his countrymen in India. Pilloried, persecuted, and reviled, Hastings never wavered from his purpose. He withstood the calumny of his impeachment with a resilience (that Clive lacked) and died without bitterness. Britain had persecuted the man who had put the British Empire in India on a sure footing.

But for all this Hastings was not an unscrupulous condittiero like Cortes nor an avaricious soldier like Clive. Hastings had grand visions of an imperium, of recreating something like the Roman Empire whose laws and credo would echo around its domain. And like the Romans who absorbed the culture of her subject races, Hastings wanted the people of Britain to be enriched by the civilization of India. It is a strange paradox that the man who conquered India and sealed British imperial destiny was also a lover of India, her people and her customs. He respected Indian laws and institutions and yet he used an antiquated British law to arrange, along with the Elijah Impey, the judicial murder of Nanda Kumar. He put an end to the evils of Clive's 'Dual Policy' which was ruining the Indian peasantry and merchants, yet he put down the slightest sign of political resistance with ruthlessness. In an age of doubt and skepticism, Hastings had a certitude that one associates with Christian martyrs yet on a deeper level, Hastings was an intellectual schizophrenic, with a Janus-like mind that sought to reconcile the West to the East.

Warren Hastings

The portrait of Warren Hastings in the National Portrait Gallery in London shows a figure that reflects the chiaroscuoro of his personality – brooding yet determined, skeptical yet touched by ideals, pride in his achievements yet aware of their transience. He was neither Gleig's plaster saint nor the Machiavellian figure depicted by Macaulay. As Shakespeare had said earlier of Julius Caesar: "All the elements mixed in him."

Rawlinson in *Short History of India* writes:

> The dominions of Asia like the distant Roman provinces during the decline of that empire had been abandoned as lawful prey to every species of peculators, in so much that many servants of the Company after exhibiting such scenes of barbarity as can scarcely be paralleled in history of any country returned to England loaded with wealth; where entrenching themselves in borough or East India stock influence they set justice at defiance either in the cause of their Country or oppressed.

This was the situation when Hastings came to India.

Moncton-Jones in *Warren Hastings in Bengal* refers to the period 1772-1774 as a time "when the East India Company and its servants in Bengal wandered deeper and deeper into the night of disorder that seemed ... without hope of dawn." Hastings was the first of a line of Colonial administrator whose term as first Governor-General of Bengal consolidated British rule of that province and established patterns of British administration in India.

Warren Hastings was born in 1732 in the south of England to a family that had once possessed large estates but had lost them during Cromwell's rule due to their adherance to King Charles I. In 1715 the Hastings Manor House at Daylesford was sold and the family moved to the nearby village of Churchill. His mother, Hester, died a few days after his birth. His father Peniston remarried, went to Barbados, and left the little boy in the care his paternal grandfather. Young Warren was brought up on stories of the family's former eminence; he vowed to regain the family fortune and recover the Manor House. He attended the village school at Churchill until he was eight. When his uncle Howard Hastings saw the promise and aptitude of the little boy, he took charge of his education. Taking Warren to London he enrolled the boy at a good school at Newington. The school had Spartan discipline including sparse food; in later years Warren Hastings attributed his slight stature to the poor food given there! Soon after the boy was sent to Westminster, one of the best schools in England where he studied classics. Young Warren's bright mind absorbed the best of a classical education. The study of Homer and Aeschylus, Virgil and Cicero sharpened his mind and gave him a love of antiquity, which was to have a long-term effect not only on his career but that of India as well. It was his erudite and enlightened mind, which made him realize long before any other Englishmen, of the wealth of ancient Indian civilization. It is this background that set Warren Hastings apart from men like Clive. In the final examinations Hastings ranked first. Another classmate was the poet Cowper who in the dark years of Hastings' impeachment protested against the accusations made against him. Cowper could not believe that the man who was kind and generous could ever commit the crimes of which he had been accused by Burke and friends.

If his uncle had lived, Hastings would probably have gone to Oxford or Cambridge to pursue his natural bent in scholarship. But with the death of his uncle his formal education came to an end. Since he had no family or fortune, the offer of a position as a Writer or Clerk in East India Company was the best alternative. His teachers at Westminster offered to provide his scholarship so that the bright youth could continue his studies but the seventeen-year-old boy decided to go to India and earn his own living.

When Warren Hastings reached India in 1750 the Mughal Empire was in the stages of dissolution but the semblance of authority still remained. Nawab Allavardi Khan ruled Bengal though the East India Company was making inroads into the trade of Bengal. The East India Company was now the leading trading organization in India followed by the French and the Dutch.

However, it was not as a guerilla leader but as a trading agent in Murshidabad, trusted by his superiors in the East India Company as well as the Indians with whom he dealt, that Hastings first comes to notice. Posted as Collector for Kasimbazar, he was assigned the task of keeping accounts and supervising the warehousing of muslins, silks and saltpetre for export. As no Europeans lived there, Hastings mixed freely with the ordinary people of Bengal and came to know their customs and beliefs. During this period he acquired fluency in several Indian languages and his keen eye and remarkable mind absorbed the realities and potentials of the situation in India, particularly Bengal. He saw the perceptible change of British mood after the Battle of Plassey when from being a supplicant before the Moghul court the Company became in fact the sovereign power in Bengal.

The warfare and competition between the French and the British reached a point where Clive felt that a decisive blow had to be struck to settle British supremacy in Bengal. The Battle of Plassey and its aftermath have been described earlier. Seeing the developments in Calcutta, Hastings left Murshidabad and went to Fulta where a small group of English officers prepared for battle with the Nawab's army.

There he met a young widow, Marian Buchanan, whose husband Captain Buchanan had died in the 'Black Hole' of Calcutta. It is possible that the chivalrous young man of twenty-five felt compassion for the young woman and married her. She was a simple girl who flitted across history without leaving an imprint in Hastings' turbulent chronicle. Nor did this first brief marriage appear to have brought Hastings any happiness. He had two children by Marian – a daughter who died in infancy and a son George. Young Mrs. Hastings died soon after the birth of the little boy. Fearing that the climate of India might damage George's health, Hastings sent him to England to be cared for by a friend. The boy died at the age of eight. Hastings became solitary and taciturn and led an austere existence in Bengal. He matured early and with a high sense of responsibility. Unlike other officials and upstart *Nabobs*, Hastings developed a genuine feeling for India and its peoples and a deep curiosity to learn about them.

The contrast between him and the officials of the East India Company who indulged in luxury and debauchery was stark. Members of Warren Hastings's Council received annual salaries of 80,000 rupees. Even then they ran into financial difficulties as they lived extravagantly with a huge retinue of servants, palatial houses, innumerable coaches and parties every night where lavish food and drink was the order of the day. (*Britain and India –The Interaction of Two Peoples* by M.E. Chamberlain)

Along with his studious habits was Hastings' oddly Spartan life. "I eat sparingly," he wrote, "I never sup; and am generally abed by ten. I breakfast at six. I bathe in cold water daily." And in that age he practiced most eccentric of all, "total abstinence from wine from which I have already experienced benefit". Nor were his clothes appropriate to his station. He ordered only two suits a year and one frock coat "merely for fashion". He was almost happiest when pottering about the garden in the shabbiest of clothes. From his first arrival in India, he had been trying to acclimatize English plants, and as Governor-General we find him writing to England for "seeds of honeysuckle and sweet briar to be packed for voyage in small bottles with ground glass-stoppers." He eagerly brought rare Asian plants from the Himalayas and from the upland frontiers of Burma. He was fond of experimenting and was proud of a hybrid grain he produced which he called "barley wheat". Interested in animal husbandry, he describes how cows ran after him when they heard his voice and in a letter to Imhoff he confesses his devotion to his cows because of their "accomplishment and moral virtues". Calcutta society grumbled at Hastings' greater interest in Colonel de Boigne's conversation than in that of the richest merchant prince, but he preferred a life of quiet rectitude than the pursuit of gaudy dreams.

Hastings offered a sharp contrast to General Claude Martin who was in charge of the arsenals of the Nawab of Lucknow. He lived in great comfort with four concubines, a number of eunuchs and a host of slaves. His library was famous. He had collected 4000 volumes of Latin, French, Italian, English, Persian and Sanskrit works. In his gallery hung 150 paintings, including pictures by Zoffany, Danniell and Kelly. His house was "built on the bank of the river Goomty and boats passed under the room in which he lived. He had underground apartments even at the edge of the water, the most comfortable in the world in the hot weather and the most elegantly decorated. As the water rises he ascends; the lower storey is always flooded in the rains and the second generally; when the water subsides they are repaired and redecorated ... It would require a week at least to examine the contents of his house." (*Swords For Hire*)

In the second-half of the eighteenth century, at the time of the Industrial Revolution, Britain was a maritime and trading nation. Though she had colonized parts of North America in the seventeenth century, Britain became an imperial power only after the establishment of her domains in India. Nevertheless, trade remained the primary concern since India provided a vast market for her manufactured goods which swelled with the Industrial Revolution.

It was only after prolonged efforts by Warren Hastings to sweep the Augean Stables that order and propriety returned in some measure. Yet it was this man and not Clive who was tried at the hands of his countrymen for the very abuses that he had tried to stop.

As early as the sixteenth century, the Elizabethan poet Marlowe wrote:

Until the Persian fleet
And men of war
Sailing along the Oriental sea
Have fetched about the Indian continent
Even from Persepolis to Mexico
And then unto the straits of Gibraltar.

Hastings returned to England in 1765 but not in time to see his little son who had just passed away. He felt alone and homeless in England. During the sojourn in England he squandered all the money that he had made as a servant of the East India Company and in private trade. Warren Hastings lived for four years in England. He could not recover the family Manor House at Daylesford. However, he was generous to his relatives and offered financial assistance to them particularly to his sister. Since he had not been one of the East India Company officials to join the brigade of brigands, the senior members of the East India Company at London were not anxious to re-employ him. However, as events developed Hastings was offered a post with the Company at Madras. He set off for India in March 1769 on the ship *Duke of Grafton*.

The Company appointed Warren Hastings as Governor of Bengal in 1771 and he assumed the post in the following year. Warren Hastings summed up his task as "to reclaim men from dissipation, to revive a general spirit of industry, to lead the minds of men from gaudy dreams of sudden acquired wealth to a patient expectation of growing fortunes". As Hastings prepared to take up this heroic role, he received a long "intolerably patronizing and self approving" letter from Clive displaying the attitude of an elder statesman: "I wish your Government to be attended as mine was, with success to the Company and with the consciousness of having discharged every duty with firmness and fidelity." Hastings' courteous and guarded answer meant that he intended to keep his business to himself. Between him and Clive there was always intense dislike.

There were other differences as well. Unlike Clive, Hastings had been an outstanding scholar in his youth. When in his later years he was being hounded as an ogre by Burke, Hastings' boyhood friends remembered him as a serious student and a pleasant, good-natured boy.

On his second voyage to India, Hastings fell in love with Baroness Maria Imhoff, a German lady who was accompanying her husband, a portrait painter seeking his fortune in the land of the Rajahs and Nawabs. According to Sir James Stephenson, Hastings bought Maria from her husband for L 10,000. There was a ludicrous side to the affair as Baron and Baroness Inhoff lived together with Hastings in an amicable mènage a trois while the divorce proceedings were put through in far off Franconia. Hastings married Maria Imhoff in 1777. Though he was disappointed that Maria bore him no children, this unusual marriage was marked by a deep and unbroken affection between the two.

The second Mrs. Hastings was very attractive and had pleasing manners. She had the tact and charm that earned the approval of Calcutta society as well as the King and Queen of England when she was presented to them in London many years later. However, there were others who felt that she was extravagant and avaricious and liked to flaunt her power over the Governor-General. Supplicants often went to her to get favours as she had great influence over Hastings.

This steadfast relationship was not spared mockery. James Hicky in *Hicky's Gazette* wrote "a displaced civilian asking his friend the other day the readiest means of procuring a lucrative appointment was answered – 'pay your constant devoirs to Marian of Allypore or sell your self body and soul to Poolbundy' referring to Mrs. Warren Hastings." Detractors also made fun of her German accented English.

When Warren Hastings arrived in India the Moghul Empire was in the last throes. Though the decline had set in after Aurangzeb's death, the semblance of authority had remained. Prosperity of the realm continued until the time of Mirza Najat Khan like the dying flicker of a guttering candle. The imperial Moghul power was finally extinguished by the excesses of Gulam Kader Khan in 1788. Moghul power had actually ceased to be a political reality by 1756. But like the Roman Empire of the fifth century it retained its hold over the imagination of even those who were dismembering it and remained the legal source of authority until the Company's supremacy was finally established. Every fresh usurpation was legalized by a *firman* issued from Delhi. The Company after defeating Emperor Shah Alam relied on a *firman* from him to legalise its position!

Such a situation required proper administration of justice. Where justice was concerned, Hastings was an ardent believer in the maintenance of local laws. It was true that the Mughal judicial code had fallen into disrepute with the collapse of Moghul authority, leaving actual control of the Courts in the hands of individual rulers. This enlarged the ad hoc legal powers of the Zamindars in a manner that to the common people justice became a much abused word. But despite existing chaos Hastings maintained that the Company's motto should be "preservation not innovation". As he stated frequently, "A renewal of the laws and forms established of old in the country with no variations than such as is necessary to give them their due effect and such as the people understood". He was emphatic on the question of setting up of English Courts in India that was being discussed in the English Parliament. "If the Lord Chief Justice and his Judges should come up among with their institutions the Lord have mercy upon us." Adding as a further protest he observed, "they (the Indians) have been in possession of Laws which have continued unchanged since the remotest antiquity."

To lend weight to his arguments he invited ten of his *Pundits*, experts in ancient Hindu law to come to Calcutta to collate and summarise the traditional code. On completion of the task, the document produced was translated into both English and Persian and long extracts sent back to England with a comment: "the people of this country do not require our aid to usher them into a rule of conduct. Even the most injudicious or fanciful customs which ignorance or superstition may have introduced among them are perhaps preferable to any which could be substituted in their norm. They are interwoven with their religion and are therefore revered as a highest authority." Hastings reintroduced a measure of justice with the condition that the Council could take action in exceptional cases as the Supreme Court of Appeal. Around the same time he also launched on his first commercial and political reforms. In the midst of this Hastings was confronted by grave problems of internal security.

With the collapse of the Nawab's power robber bands known as dacoits began marauding villages and entire districts as there was an absence of effective policing. Hastings acted with Draconian severity; he issued orders that dacoits should be hanged summarily whether or not they were caught *in flagrante delicto*. Proof of previous activity would be enough to merit the rope and any village that offered shelter would be subjected to collective fine while their families would be rounded up and individual members sold as slaves. A great famine contributed to the chaos; starving peasants unable to pay their landlords swelled the ranks of the dacoits.

Bands of marauding *sanyasis* were particularly active in Malda in 1783. Hindu soldiers were unwilling to fight against the *sanyasis* who they regarded as holy men. This in an extreme form was the problem that was to become a central concern for Grant and his conception of British rule in India – the question of religious interference, of imposing on Indian social custom a pattern of law and order that conflicted with the beliefs of the people. Law and order, Grant argued in 1783, should take priority. When in later years, Grant and his friends argued for the necessity of intervening in the religious customs of India, they tended to argue on the ground that the religious and moral imperatives of the Christian faith compelled interference while their opponents maintained that political realities forbade such intervention.

One of Hastings' major contributions was the introduction of the Regulating Act of 1773. In 1770, the Tory Party led by Lord North, returned to power after a period of political wilderness. The party assumed the reins of government at a time when the name and prestige of the Company had touched rock bottom and popular detestation of the *Nabobs* was widespread. The Tories hoped to cash in on this unpopularity to bring the Company under the aegis of Westminster and its profits vested into the treasury. Only a year before the General Elections, the Company in an effort to allay fears in London, had analyzed its accounts and declared dividend of 12½%. Unable to meet its obligations, the Company turned to the Bank of England for a loan of half a million pound. Both the Bank and Lord North refused. The matter was referred to the House and a select committee was set up to inquire into the Company's finance. What emerged was that the Company was incapable of meeting its greatly increased commitment. Now that its Indian territorial position covered an area considerably greater than that of the British, its "administration teemed with inequities so rank as to smell to earth and heaven," observed Lord Statham.

What followed in the wake of the Committee's inquiry into the scandals was an outcry in the press, machinations of ministers and the Company's counter-machinations which resulted in the Regulation Act of 1773 – a compromise between the warring factions. At first sight this Act "for establishing Regulations for the better management of the affairs of the East India Company as well as in India" gave the appearance of being a sensible, practical document.

The Governor of Bengal, Bihar and Orissa was to become Governor-General, not only taking precedence over the Presidencies of Bombay and Madras but having a controlling voice in their policies to govern with aid of a Council. The Directors would continue to issue broad directives to the Governor-General and Governors but all such instructions would have to be submitted to the King, and Ministers' approval were to be obtained prior to dispatch of any instructions to India. In the same way any dispatch from India had to be shown to Ministers within fourteen days of arrival at Leadenhall Street.

Parallel with creation of the post of Governor-General, the Act's eighth clause provided for constitution of a Supreme Court of jurisdiction in Calcutta. The paramount authority of the sovereign was declared by the creation of a Supreme Court of Justice, establishing the Supreme Court Judicature at Fort William in Calcutta. It was to consist of a Chief Justice and three puisne judges; the original members were Sir Elijah Impey, Chief Justice, Robert Chanters of the Middle Temple, Stephen, Cesar and Lemaistre of the Inner Temple and John Hyde of Lincoln's Inn. The clauses also stated that "every officer of the Company and the Company itself were subject to this jurisdiction and powers of that Tribunal subject only to the appeal to the sovereign in Council".

Philip Francis and Charles Grant were friends and allies in their opposition to Hastings. In a letter he wrote in 1777 to Lord North, recommending sweeping changes, Francis wrote of "the able assistance" of Grant who had at this time incurred heavy debts through gambling and living far beyond his income. In his old age Lord Teingmouth warned his son who had gone to Bengal that "there were endless hours that were to be dozed away in listless idleness filled up with some occupation". Gambling was the most common way of occupying time. Even if an East India Company servant did not gamble, the standard of living was so high that a profitable private trade was necessary to keep out of trouble. Grant's early career typified the rivalry between the Commercial Resident and the Collector. Grant pointed out that the mis-treatment of the weavers by the Tax Collectors was losing him money. He would have agreed with a later civil servant Charles Trevelyan that "the laws of god are so happily adjusted that in benefiting the natives, we benefit ourselves." In many of these disputes the issue at stake, Grant was convinced, was the nature of the Company's government in Bengal. What had to be decided, he told the Dinajpur Collector, was whether the Company's role was a system of power or a system of law.

In their public speeches the Company officials could make the rafters ring with their passionate conviction. In their political careers they often displayed the crassest chicanery. This phenomenon went deeper than the glib modern phrase "double standards" which was part of a way of life. To get even a glimmer of the enigma that was Warren Hastings, it was necessary to understand this.

Ten years later when William Carey was on his way to India, he reflected the common opinion of his time by speaking of the "abominable East India Company" as an enemy of the progress of the people of India. A year or two later he noted that he had "no spirit for politics here, for whatever the East India Company may be in England, their servants and officers here are very different".

16

Administrator and Reformer

One of the first acts of Warren Hastings was to establish the system of government in consonance with the traditions of the people. In pursuance of this, he instituted an inquiry into the ancient language and literature and the legal system of the Hindus. This was in the tradition of earlier enlightened rulers of India such as Sher Shah, Emperor Akbar and his great-grandson Dhara Shikho who got scholars to translate Hindu scriptural texts into Persian which was then the official language of India. Hastings' policy encouraged European scholars to study Sanskrit and Indian classics that is narrated in later chapters. The interest in Indian civilization spread into other fields from literature into art. English connoisseurs like R. Johnson, banker of Warren Hastings, brought Mughal and Rajput paintings to England, which are now in the India Office. The earlier Englishmen adapted themselves to the customs of the country such as Colonel Kilpatrick resident at Hyderabad "who spoke Persian and wore Mughal costume and could hardly be distinguished from a Muslim noble". The *Nabobs* were thoroughly Oriental in their outlook. In the early nineteenth century the English novelist Thackeray immortalized the Company's civil servant of the Joseph Sedley type.

It was part of the Company's policy not to interfere with the religion or customs of the people. The money spent on education was devoted to the encouragement of the indigenous learning of the country. Warren Hastings endowed a Madrasah or Muslim College in Calcutta. Jonathan Duncan, the Brahminised Englishman, founded a Hindu college for teaching Sanskrit at Banaras where he was Resident. Customs such as *Sati*, infanticide and slavery were tolerated. In fact the Company acted as *Shastris* for temples and through that they derived substantial income from piligrim tax. Indian regiments had their gods of honour. In the early days Protestant missionaries were not admitted to British India. Nevertheless a few established their centres in areas outside the jurisdiction of the Company.

Seeing the state of lawlessness in Bengal, the Directors of the East India Company decided to set up a Supreme Court in Calcutta. The simultaneous arrival of the Members of the Supreme Court did not help to alleviate Hastings' gloom, strongly opposed as he was to the imposition of the British on the Indian code of law. Nor was he reassured by the fact that Court was to be independent of all local authority. Its principal task was "to keep control of the Company servants". The only consolation was that the Chief Justice was his old Westminster school friend. It was beneficial for Hastings as Sir Elijah Impey's friendship and loyalty was his great support in the next four years when he had to fight for survival as Governor-General.

The jurisdiction of the Court was a crucial factor in administering law and justice. It was plain that the clauses of the Regulating Act delineating the powers of the civil and judicial authority were urgently in need of revision. For instance the Court had jurisdiction over British subjects and all Company employees but the legal authority vested in the Governor prior to the Court's arrival had never been abrogated. Nor was it clear as to whether the Court's jurisdiction was limited to Calcutta or extended to the whole area of the provinces.

Acrimonious verbal battles were fought in public. But finally Hastings and Impey met and because of their long standing and sincere friendship worked out a solution, which was largely the Governor-General's brainchild. It was proposed that the Court's jurisdiction should be recognized as covering the inhabitants of all the provinces irrespective of race, creed and colour and that there should be fusion of Court and Council to form a superior court in direct control of all civil and Diwani Courts. Impey thought the proposal excellent and practical. The majority disagreed but as they had no alternative the draft plan was sent to Parliament for approval.

The Supreme Court decided to administer English law, the only law it knew and decided to apply it not only to all the English in Bengal but also to all Indians connected with them. In practice this meant those Indians in Calcutta and it led to such grave abuses as the hanging of Nanda Kumar for offences not recognized as capital in any Indian Code.

On 20th January 1776 Hastings sent to London a plan for the better administration of justice in the provinces of Bengal."The design of it," Hastings wrote to Lord North, "may be comprised in a few words. It is to extend the jurisdiction of the Supreme Court and the Supreme Court of Judicature to all parts of the provinces without any limitations to confirm the Courts which have been established on the principles of the ancient constitution of the Country by the names of Nurgamutt and Benami to invite the judges of the Supreme Court with members of the Council in the control of the latter and to give the Provincial Council a legal authority in the internal Government of the country and the collection of the public revenue." The chief feature was the proposed creation of the *Sadar Diwan Adalat* or Superior Civil Court to be composed of Governor-General and Council and the Chief Justice and the Judges of the Supreme Court of Judicature assisted by native officials. This Court was to receive appeals from the native Council and its decrees were to be final.

Writing to Lord Mansfield, Hastings says, "Your Lordship will find very little novelty in the plan. The design of it is to prevent innovations not to add to them and I sincerely believe that it shall be far compatible with the indispensable principle of English law, neither the laws, usages nor inclinations of the people will be injured by the introduction of it ... I have a pleasure in declaring that in all occasions which had been his aim in particular and in general that of the other Judges of the Supreme Court to support the authority of Government and temper the law of England with the laws, religious customs and manners of the natives. Your Lordship will hear a different report from my associates in the Council but I confidently rely on the facts on which our different opinions are founded for confirming my testimony".

"Subsequent to the introduction of the judicial system, the original law has been almost buried under volumes of regulations and ordinances rendered necessary to adapt it to our principles of rule." Fortescue who was officiating as judge at Benaras in 1816 said, "As to the Hindus, not one in a thousand of their pundits can read Persian much less Arabic and many of these persons would consider it defilement to pursue the books wherein alone the law can be found." This has reference to the Code of Criminal Law adopted from the Muslims.

It is a tragic irony that Hastings who believed that Indians should be judged by their own laws should have used an antiquated British law to destroy an adversary. The Nanda Kumar episode casts a grim shadow on Hastings' career.

The war between Hastings and the Triumvirate took on a new aspect. Nanda Kumar, who was no more venal than any other man in that seting was the instrument used by Francis and Grant to put Hastings in the wrong. Undoubtedly Hastings saw the execution as a means of instilling mortal fear in the hearts of those who were beginning to imagine that the Governor-General could be slandered with impunity. As a contemporary observed "The voices of a thousand informers were silenced in an incident. From that time whatever the difficulties Hastings might have to encounter he was never molested by accusations from the natives of India."

As far as the Triumvirate was concerned they made no efforts to save Nanda Kumar from the noose. He was more useful to their purposes dead since his execution could serve as a major charge as indeed it did in the impeachment of Hastings. There can be few examples in history of such a cold blooded and cynical betrayal. It was they as well as Hastings who should have been accused of judicial murder.

The next difference between the Governor-General and Supreme Court arose as to jurisdiction of Court over English and native offices of the Company employed in connection of revenue for corrupt or oppressive acts done by them in their official capacity. Section 14 of the Regulation Act gave jurisdiction to the Supreme Court. The third cause of quarrel was regarding the right of the Supreme Court to try action against the judicial officers of the Company for acts done in execution of what they believed to be their duty. This applied for instance to the "Patria Clause".

Macaulay writes,

> A reign of terror began, of terror heightened by mystery for event what was endured was less horrible than that which was anticipated. No man knew what was next to be expected from this strange Tribunal which came from beyond the black waters as the people of India view the mysterious sea with horror. It consisted of judges not one of whom was familiar with the usage of millions over whom they claimed boundless authority. Its records were kept in

> unknown character; its sentences were pronounced in unknown terms ... No Mahratta invasion has spread through the province such dismay as this inroad of English lawyers. All the injustice of former oppressors Asiatic and European appeared as a blessing when compared with the Justice of the Supreme Court.

Hastings saw peace between Supreme Court and the government as indispensable to his policy. While he fought for the independence of his government, Impey realized that the authority of the executors must be supported but Hyde and Lemaister seemed determined by the stretch of their judicial authority to undermine the government. Macaulay said of Impey, "No other such judge has dishonoured the English ermine since Jeffreys drank himself to death in the tower."

Pitts India Act of 1784 that succeeded Fox's India proposals and extensive parliamentary investigation, established dual control over Indian government which was to last until 1858. Under this system the East India Company appointed and trained the military and civil officials sent to India formulated the policies of this administration and supervised the results. A Board of Control comprised of ministers and soon headed by a President who was usually a Cabinet Minister supervised the East India Company in its work. The Board designated the highest officials in India, ultimately controlled matters of war and peace in India and obliged the Company on many occasions to accept its advice on political policy.

> Pitt's India Act relieved the Governor-General from the tutelage of his Council which became advisory only. Such scenes as those between Hastings and Francis were never to occur again in the Council Board. The Governor-General was made an autocrat in a land that understood autocracy but was himself subject to the ultimate control of the home Government through the Board of Control under a President of Cabinet rank. Its Indian legislation served India until the time of the mutiny. (G.M. Trevelyan, *History of England*)

Confusions arose in governance due to the time lag in correspondence. It took about a year before reply to any letter to England could be expected. Usually a crisis had passed or deepened for want of instructions and gave the need for initiative to the administrators. Sometimes disputes were settled by duels. When

Francis' offensive remarks became intolerable, Hastings challenged him to a duel in which the former was 'winged'. This became a minor scandal in Calcutta.

In this noisy dueling society, intellectuals like Warren Hastings was a rara avis.

17

Burke and the Indian Constitution

Burke was the main protagonist of the 'conservation' theory and was a vigorous advocate for the need to preserve the Indian Constitution. Burke's main point about the Indian political order was that India was "a concise polity possessing laws, institutions and traders worked out through centuries of effort, framed according to needs and representative of the principles of human order, that is the national law." India he said may have faults but "God forbid we should pass judgment upon a people who formed their laws and institutions prior to our insect origin of yesterday." He also stated, "provision was made for the administration of justice as if it were a province of Great Britain." Notwithstanding his liberal views on India, Burke was more concerned with expounding and justifying conservative principles than with defending the laws, customs and the outlook of India.

"Under the national law as the Conservatives visualized India, the legislators of the nation had framed the peaceful and orderly polity which survived to the present. The institution of caste was the capstone of this order whereby all individuals understood their places in the hierarchy and performed roles useful to the whole society. Peasants, scholars, craftsmen and princes were all part of a comprehensive scheme under which useful economic activity, exquisite craftsmanship and profound learning were produced under responsible political leadership. India was a polity of village republics which had survived centuries of changing empires and political dynasties. Princes came and went but the polity remained bolstered by the 'empire of opinion', which represented the customs, traditions and attitudes of the past and the present and this polity provided Indians with the means of their political and social existence." (A. Cobban in *Edmund Burke and the Revolt Against the Eighteenth Century*). This was a remarkable polity to conservatives.

Burke saw how the Indian polity had achieved remarkable things in the past but how in the present it was being "distorted and put out of frame by the barbarism of foreign conquests". He wanted to expose "these tactics of barbarism and despotism which had come with foreign conquest and were without warrant in the civilized world". He prosecuted Warren Hastings interminably as the example of all the evils threatening the Indian polity.

Britain, he observed, had come to India at a time of chaos and distress and could have brought order, peace and knowledge instead of violence and despotism and had introduced unhelpful British institutions. After Plassey, Burke declared, "provision was made for the administration of justice as if it were a province of Great Britain". That would not do. "The principles of the British constitution, not its practices, institutions and prejudices were applicable to India. India had to be governed according to Indian experience and tradition, lest the fabric of Indian society be destroyed." Burke's crusade against Warren Hastings was thus designed to protect Indian Constitution against the disastrous meddling of the West.

In all that he did Burke showed an inclination to take a philosophical view of political conditions. He was not ultimately concerned with administrative arrangements, political experiments and appropriate legislation. He was concerned with having political action correspond with the nature of the political order under God.

In defending the Indian Constitution, Burke was more concerned with expounding and justifying Conservative principles than with defending the laws, customs and civilization of India. He was not familiar with the literature and philosophy of India and did not understand India according to Indian concepts.

Edmund Burke's doctrine of Trusteeship sprang from a romantic conception of Indian civilization. His reverence for the past was based on scholarship and an intuitive understanding for the need to preserve past traditions that he perceived as the repository of civilization. But trusteeship in the hands of the East India Company was like trusting lambs in the care of tigers. What he said about India he would repeat when news reached London on the execution of the king of France during the French Revolution. Recanting after his initial support of the uprising against the oppressive *ancien regime*, Burke stressed the doctrine of Conservation without which there can be no continuity in civilization.

Burke succeeded in making plundering and misgovernment of India impossible on a large scale. After Burke, the British were obliged to establish a framed civil service, well enough paid to avoid graft and corruption and in its political polity, Britain had to recognize the needs and political characteristics of that country. But the attitude Burke bequeathed to the conservatives of the East India Company and British political life steadily declined in influence after Burke so that British Government in India gradually came to be conducted on British principles rather than Indian.

A. Cobban in *Edmund Burke and the Revolt Against the Eighteenth Century*, observes that England "having come to rule in India a civilization that was old when Western Europeans were only wandering savages, Burke demanded that she should respect the time honoured customs of this ancient people and conserve its proper and well established law". One cannot help wandering whether *Sati* and child marriage and other religious and social abuses came under the heading of proper laws which it was necessary to conserve.

Burke is chiefly remembered for his veneration of the traditional order which was already a capitalist order. He had no romantic yearning for a bygone feudal era though he insisted that the Christian religion was the indispensable basis for political stability and defended the hierarchical establishment. Burke believed that "no one generation has the right to destroy the agreed and inherited fabric of society. A country is not a mere physical locality he argued, but a community in time in which men are born". (*The Writings and Speeches of Edmund Burke*: Vol: V, India, Madras and Bengal 1774-1785. Edited by P.J. Marshall)

The imperial issue engaged Burke's attention for two decades. Like many Britons he had mixed feelings about the commercial activities of a chartered trading concern, the British East India Company, which had created an extensive empire. In the years from 1760s to the 1770s, when British power in India was being consolidated by Clive and Hastings, Burke opposed interference by the English Government in the Company's affairs as a violation of chartered rights. However, he learnt a great deal about the state of the Company's Government as the most active member of a select committee appointed in 1781 to investigate the administration of justice in India but it soon widened its field to that of a general inquiry. Burke concluded that the corrupt state of Indian Government could be remedied only if the vast powers which it possessed was neither in the hands of the Company nor of the Government. He drafted the East India Company Act in 1783 of which the Whig statesman Charles James Fox was the nominal author. The Act proposed that India should be governed by a Board of independent commissioners in London. After the defeat of the Bill, Burke's indignation came to centre on Hastings, the Governor-General of Bengal from 1772 to 1785.

British victories in India especially after the loss of the American colonies were welcomed in Britain until they were faced with evidence of grave conditions in India. Warren Hastings had reported on the decay of the trade, oppression of the people and the complete devastation he saw in every village on a tour to Benares. Hasting's enemies in the Bengal Council led by Burke's friend Philip Francis reported that a once rich and flourishing India was reduced to "begging and ruin". Parliament and the British aristocracy were faced with the rich Company officials, the *Nabobs* who flaunted their ill-gotten wealth. The British governing classes heard of the charges of corruption, financial scandals and misgovernment in India. The realization of the conditions in India led to the parliamentary investigations in the 1780s. Burke's denunciation sharpened British interest. A Committee of the House of Commons charged the East India Company "of grave wrongs, offensive military operations, the corrupt influence of the Company officials in the domestic and national quarrels of Indian states, the frequent violations of firmans and breaches of treaties, the speculation of local officials and the criminal relaxation of the East India Company directors."

Influenced mainly by Hastings' bitter foes, Burke chose him as the symbol of the evils to be cleansed. "Was there," Burke thundered, "ever heard or could it be conceived that a Governor would dare to heap up all the evil practices, all the cruelties, oppressions, extortions, corruptions, briberies of all the innocuous usurpers, degenerate robbers, thieves, cheats and jugglers that ever had office, from one end of Asia to another and consolidating all this mass of crimes and barbarous domination into one code, establish it as the whole duty of an English Governor."

During the 1780s most of Burke's energy was devoted to his crusade against the East India Company. England's Indian empire was indeed in Burke's view a proper White Man's burden, but he took strong exception to the way Parliament had allowed that burden to be exercised, with inadequate supervision or control by the chartered East India Company. He compiled such a mass of evidence of the Company's "dishonourable wishes, its corrupt and genocidal behaviour" that he was able almost single handed to persuade the House of Commons to impeach the chief architect and defender of the Company's policies, Warren Hastings, and thereby bring those policies into a glare of publicity unprecedented in British parliamentary history.

The British public gradually came to be aware that the wealth of the Nabobs was "not the result of patient industry or shrewd trading. It was the result of extortion and forcible extraction from a country which was not, what was at one time believed, a land of untold wealth but a poor and bleeding land staggering under pillage and oppression." The realization of the true state of affairs came from the formidable triumvirate of Burke, Fox and Sheridan. It was the age of rhetoric and these were the greatest orators of their time. But the dominant voice was of Burke and over the centuries one hears in his inimitable cadences the plea for sympathy with the Indian people and the denunciation of the evils of the East India Company rule – "wave upon wave".

It was at Burke's instigation that Hastings was impeached in 1787. He challenged Hastings' claims that it was impossible to apply western standards of legality and authority to government in the East. Burke appealed to the concept of the law of nature, the moral principles rooted in the Universal order of things to which all conditions and races of men were subject. The impeachment dragged on for eight years and ended with the acquittal of all charges. The proceedings resulted in an authoritative statement of the principle of responsible rule in imperial affairs. But it was regarded as an injustice to Hastings who despite questionable methods had the disinterested service of the Company and of the British name in India.

> The impeachment is the most conspicuous illustration of the failings to which Burke was liable throughout his political life. Burke's political position was sometimes marred by gross distortions and errors of judgment. His India speeches at times fall into a violence

> of emotions and abuse, lacking restraint and proportion. His reliance on the opinions of Sir Philip Francis one of Hastings most pertinacious enemies illustrates his inability to rationally and accurately judge personality. Burke's parliamentary activities were at times irresponsible and fatuous. In Indian affairs he did not escape the charge of personal interest. Throughout his career he was associated financially and politically with his brother Richard and putative kinsman William Burke – both doubtful characters known to be unsuccessfully speculating in East India stock. The Burkes' joint finances were always in a precarious condition and as Edmund was ever eager to forward his kinsmen's political fortunes it is understandable that he appeared in hostile eyes as hardly more than one of a clan of Irish adventurers." (Gleig, *Memoirs of Hastings*).

Unlike Warren Hastings who had spent his life and entire career in India, Burke had never been to India. Unlike Hastings he had no real feeling for Indian people. But he chose the Indian question as his issue and the trial of Warren Hastings as the theatre of his ideas. His motives were not entirely disinterested. His brother was the English agent of the Nawab of Arcot and Edmund Burke himself was initially the Nawab's Advocate in London. Then there was the strangely ambiguous figure of Charles Fox, the brilliant Parliamentarian, profligate and dissipated man who found in the disorderly affairs of the East India Company the weapon he needed to attack the Government of Pitt and who found in the arrangements in his Bill for the return of East India Company a plank for his parliamentary campaign but who again showed no real understanding of the practical complexities of trade and administration in India. The third member of this triumvirate, Richard Brindsley Sheridan the author of *The School for Scandal,* found in the trial a magnificent stage for his histrionic talents.

The antagonism to Hastings deprived his adversaries of a dispassionate approach and while using the state of affairs in Bengal for their rhetorical purposes, they did a disservice to the truth. Burke's unflawed and unrestrained rhetoric ignored the fact that the system within which Warren Hastings had to operate was not one of his own making. The evils which Burke was describing in his incomparable cadences were largely the result of government by an agency which was not meant for such a role at all. The East India Company had not assumed the White Man's Burden and was reluctant to shoulder responsibilities. The evil lay in entrusting governance of a country to a mercantile institution.

Burke did not realize the irony implicit in his criticism of a Government impervious to the tradition of the people it governed when the man who was the object of his diatribes knew Persian and Urdu, encouraged Indian studies, believed in the need for maintaining the integrity of Indian institutions and warned against interference with Indian tradition, religion and culture. Burke who had believed in institutions being the repository of culture failed to accord credit to Hastings who was striving to maintain Indian culture in the face of the Western onslaught. Burke failed to see through Francis' bias. He failed to realize that in fact he shared with Hastings a common concern: the distance over thousand of miles of ocean, lack of communications, and the imperative to take decisions without the luxury of consultations. Nor did Burke realize that during the major part of his tenure Hastings was not the master of his own house, and had to contend with the intrigues of his own council members, and was not always free to follow the policy he would have liked. All this led to the tragedy of Hastings' impeachment.

The question that arises – was the natural order in India one of good government and free trade? Could the British presence be limited to holding a benevolent umbrella of protection over a self-regulating and self-sufficient society? Was not Warren Hastings more perceptive when he wrote of the conflict between "the primary exigencies of the Company" and the "interests of the people". Indeed it was not the people of India who vilified Hastings; they were quick to acknowledge the benefits of the change that he had made.

Unfortunately the very concept of imperialism is based on the subjugation of one nation to another. The interest of the subject people would be promoted to the extent when it did not in any way affect the prosperity and power of the ruling nation. When the interests were in conflict as they often were, the rulers were obliged to protect their interests. Burke believed in Utopian imperialism and Hastings strove hard to reconcile the inherent conflicts and contradictions of imperialism.

18

Evaluation of Hastings

It is one of history's paradoxes that while it was due to Hastings that vast territories passed to the British, he was the negation of the Imperialist; he believed firmly that India rather than newcomers on the Indian scene were those whose interest deserved most of his services. Although a practicing Christian, he believed that it would be wrong to force a foreign faith on India's millions. "The most that can be expected from the most liberal and enlightened of all nations," he said was, "that which Providence has appointed to be guardian of their (Indians) civil rights is to protect these persons from wrong and to leave their religious creed to the Being who has so long endured it and who will in his own time reform it."

Warren Hastings was the first, the most abused and the least rewarded, of the rulers of India. He was not even given a knighthood. William Jones was given knighthood at the age of thirty-six. Ramsay Muir says, "For my part I count him the greatest Englishmen of the eighteenth century in an age prolific in great men."

Even Hastings' most resounding historian-critic Macaulay said of him, "It is not too much to say that if he had been taken from the head of affairs, the years 1780 and 1781 would have been as fatal to our power in Asia as to our power in America."

A practical and pragmatic administrator like Sir John Malcolm points out that Hastings' acquaintance with the languages and usages of the natives of India, added to the high qualities of his mind, gave him advantages without which he could hardly have saved the empire committed to its charge – but points out that both he and Clive were calumniated.

During the impeachment proceedings Hastings gave a forcible and vivid description of the growth of British power in India:

> The seed of this wonderful production was sowed by the hand of calamity. It was nourished by fortune and shaped by necessity. Its first existence was commercial, it obtained in its growth the sudden accession of military strength and territorial dominion to which its political adjunct was inevitable.

> From the vehemence and perseverance with which my immediate superiors laboured during the course of ten years to weaken my authority, to destroy my influence and to embarrass all my measures at a time when their affairs required the most powerful efforts to sustain them, which I alone by my office could direct ... I much fear that it is not understood as it ought to be how near the Company's existence has, on many occasions, vibrated on the edge of perdition.

Warren Hastings established a stable administration. He wrote to his friend John Stewart, "though I made a number of chops and changes I never called myself a reformer". But the people were quick to acknowledge the benefits of the change which he had made. Stewart continues:

> The general reaction was one of relief and gratitude. In spontaneous expression of opinion, in addresses sent to England during his impeachment when they had nothing to gain and nothing to hope from him, they declared he had laid the foundations of justice and the pillars of law; tyranny and oppression were not permitted and the people lived in ease and peace.

In the same spirit the closing words of the Muslim historian Riyasu Salati (1788) eulogized the English as "unrivalled in the laws for administration of justice, for the safety of their subjects, for the extermination of tyranny and for the protection of the weak ...."

The condition of other parts of the country before the inception of British rule had little to recommend them. The Northern Sircars were disorganized to such an extent that not only forms but also even resemblance of civil authority was lost. Further south, Sir Thomas Munro declared in 1801:

> A decade of Mughal government in Cudappah had been almost as destructive as so many years of war .... The Nizam's army and those of local chieftains plundered the countryside, murdered and robbed, no better than bandits. There were no governmental courts of justice, the village heads dealt with disputes among themselves. Even in Tanjore with its relative prosperity a court was established by the Rajah at the close of the eighteenth century at the suggestion of his

guardian, the Danish missionary Schwartz ... Along the west coast especially in the Malabar area there was trial by ordeal ...

By contrast conditions in Bengal were more settled, more peaceful and had semblance of a functioning legal system. For this Warren Hastings must take the credit.

The impeachment of Hastings represented to a large section of the British contemporary opinion as a protest against its methods rather than an attack on an individual. It may well be argued that in impeaching Hastings the enemies of the Company selected the least venal of its officials and then based their case against him on his less important misdemeanours.

The weight of historical evidence is probably against Sheridan's contention that "the British name had been dishonoured and rendered detested throughout India by the maladministration and crimes of the principal servant of the East India Company. Neither was Hastings the worst administrator nor the unique cause of the hatred which the Company inspired." Sheridan was exaggerating when he said, "Hastings had nothing great but his crimes."

The greatest paradox of Warren Hastings the empire builder was that in a process of Hegelian dialectics he set into motion a movement which in the midst of the conquest of India would lead eventually to the awakening of India to her own greatness, awareness of her heritage, and a growing recognition of her nationhood. This was through the establishment of the Asiatic Society and his patronage of the great British scholars who commenced the discipline of Indology.

The greatness of Warren Hastings was that in the midst of the Rohilla Wars, the Maratha Wars, the daily dissensions within the council, the continuous battle against the obduracy of Leadenhall Street and the complicated intrigues of Company administration, amidst all the realpolitik concerns, it was typical of Hastings that he could still find time and place to fashion a long term policy for English administration in India and to give concrete step to his idea that Company administration should not be grafted onto Indian society but that Indians should be governed using their own language, their own institutions and their own laws. This philosophy found practical expression in Halhed's two works – the *Gentoo Laws* and the *Bengali Grammar*.

Hastings had always been fascinated by India – her languages, folk tales, customs, inhabitants and institutions. Hastings financed from his own pocket a digest of Hindu law and founding of a Madrasa or college of Arabic studies in Calcutta and two expeditions to Tibet as early as 1781. He helped Wilkins financially with his Sanskrit studies and offered generous patronage for the translation of the *Bhagavad Gita*. Hastings' *Preface* to the English translation, which may still be seen at the Asiatic Society Library says of the *Gita*, 'the greatest work of scripture'. Almost his last act before leaving the country was his substantial backing for the formation of the Asiatic Society of Bengal. In fact he contributed so lavishly to the project that in 1783 he confessed his private debts were such that he was unable to draw a single penny of his salary for several months.

Hastings left India in February 1785. Throughout the voyage the sea had been comparatively calm. The former Governor-General spent much of his time on his apologia for relaxation – composing verses. He landed at Plymouth on 13th June. But far from finding the peace of retirement after a turbulent imperialist career he was hounded by his adversaries and critics who accused him of the very wrongs that he had sought to set right. He was tried before the House of Lords, impeached and finally acquitted in 1795. Hastings bore his ordeal with a grave dignity that impressed even his adversaries.

While we cannot agree with Gleig's portrayal of Hastings as a Christlike figure, his contributions were significant at a crucial juncture in Indian political history. The forces he set in motion by fostering Indian culture led to the Indian renaissance.

19

Later British Colonial Administrators

Warren Hastings was succeeded by Lord Cornwallis, who suffered a humiliating defeat at the hands of the American revolutionary army under George Washington at Yorktown in 1780. The battle marked the end of British dominance in the western hemisphere. Lord Cornwallis was reappointed Governor-General and returned to India in 1805 to establish "an upright and personal government" there as Pitt and the East India Company desired. A man of energy rather than intelligence, he did not possess either the intellect or the experience to deal with the growing British Empire in India. Tory statesmen wanted a Governor-General who would be honest and faithful to his party's interest in England. How they chose a man who could not deal with even the smaller theatre of the American colonies is a mystery. Their decision can only reflect their poor understanding of the Indian situation.

Cornwallis' task was to preserve the empire which had been damaged by corruption and concentrate on internal administrative reforms and not to wage costly wars. He had scanty knowledge about India and did not have the conservative Burke's admiration for the constitution and culture of India. His one-dimensional mind led him to believe his mission was to introduce British principles and British institutions to India for the benefit of Indians.

Cornwallis' significant measure in Anglicization of Indian administration was his reform of land tenure and land revenue. He believed that introduction of a British type of landlordism would ensure property and create a class of landlords loyal to the British. He introduced the Permanent Settlement that was regarded as a sincere means of fixing land revenue which was to be paid by the land-owners or zamindars. In actual practice this system put enormous and unfair burden on the peasants who bore the burden of the taxes and became dependant on the zamindars, who like the French landowners of the *ancien regime,* bled the peasants white. Forced to pay taxes beyond their capacity or their earnings, they were burdened with debts and often had to sell their land. Fertile lands lay fallow while the zamindar extorted what he could, to pay his British overlord and for his own pleasure. Bengal suffered for a century under this iniquitous arrangement. South India fared better since the *ryotwari* system protected the interests of the ryots or farmers. Cornwallis replaced the traditional Indian system of law with magistrates, judges and police trained in British practices. Transplanting British customs in an alien soil revealed the inherent contradictions of foreign rule.

Cornwallis was followed by another aristocrat with limited intelligence, the Marquess of Wellesley who discouraged 'fraternization with natives', banned Indians from invitations to the newly built Government House, frowned on social and matrimonial relations between Britons and Indians. However, he was responsible for the opening of the college at Fort William that taught Sanskrit to young Company civil servants. His brother Arthur Wellesley, the future Duke of Wellington, won territories for Britain in Mysore by defeating Tipu Sultan. Wellesley's Subsidiary Alliances was a cause of serious misgovernment. The Company army protected Indian rulers on their thrones and allowed every kind of misrule provided the Indian rajahs and nawabs remained allies of the Company. The Indian rulers had power without responsibility; the Indian people were crushed by taxes and oppression. The deterioration of agriculture, impoverishment of the peasantry, and the resultant economic stagnation which impoverished India had their genesis in these policies.

Wellesley's reign was not totally devoid of achievements. In 1800 he established a college at Calcutta where newly appointed inexperienced officials would be instructed in Indian languages, law and Company administration. The Company objected to Wellesley's college largely on account of expense but in 1806 with the encouragement of the British Government the Company established Haileybury College in England where British youths appointed to posts in Indian administration learnt and studied Indian languages, her laws, customs, Newtonian science, principles of moral conduct from Paley's *Moral and Political Philosophy*. The students were however not encouraged to become Indianized. As a consequence they did not possess the empathy for the land they ruled in the manner of some of their predecessors. They were told to conduct themselves in a manner that would demonstrate superiority of British military and political power as well the superiority of British character. And while they might learn much about India and its culture they would propagate British principles and introduce British institutions in administering India. By Anglicizing India and her people, the Company and London felt it would be easier to rule this complex land.

Unable to grasp the magnitude of his task, excited by his brother Arthur's victories over Tipu Sultan of Mysore, this Governor-General envisaged himself in the role of a Pro-consul of the Roman empire behaving with a thoughtless arrogance and hauteur which alienated possible allies.

The Marquess of Hastings who followed was no better. He became Governor-General of Bengal and Commander-in-Chief of forces in India through the influence of the Prince of Wales. Assuming office in 1813, he began the process of Indianization by increasing the powers of subordinate Indian Judges. He was a competent administrator but was recalled under a cloud and was sent off as Governor of Malta in 1824.

As the Company tentacles spread further into Indian territory, there was simmering discontent. The first of the organized stirring against British rule came with the Vellore mutiny on 6th July 1806 when Indian troops killed hundreds of British soldiers and officers. This was a shock to British power and produced a sudden awareness of how lightly based dominion in India might really be. The immediate explanation was the "whisker shaving affair". These were regulations issued by John Craddock, commander-in-chief of the Madras army who displeased with the unsoldierly appearance of the Sepoys in his Company issued regulations that they were all to cut their beards, wear a uniform style of head covering and remove the caste marks on their foreheads before appearing in parade. Bentinck and Craddock were recalled on the assumption that army regulations had been the cause of the outrage but this belief was soon challenged. Bentinck and Craddock were filled with resentment at what they considered to be an injustice. They contended that the real cause was not the Regulations but the activities of missionaries and evangelical chaplains that Charles Grant had sent to India.

Speaking about Britain's Indian empire, Sir John Malcolm instructed officers acting under his orders in Central India in 1821:

> Comprehending numerous tribes and nations, with all their various institutions and governments, may truly though metaphorically be viewed as a vast and ancient fabric, neither without shape nor beauty, but of which many parts are in a dilapidated state and all are more or less soiled and decayed; still it is a whole and connected in all its parts; the foundations are deep-laid and to the very summit arch rests upon arch. We are now its possessors and if we desire to preserve, while we improve it, we must make ourselves completely masters of the frame of the structure of its minutest ornaments and defects, nor must we remove the smallest stone till another is ready, suited to fill the vacant niche, otherwise we may bring ruin of our own heads and those of others, on the spot where we too eagerly sought to erect a monument of glory.

About Sir John Malcolm, his biographer Kaye says,

> I do not know an example out of the regions of romance in which so many remarkable qualities generally supposed to be antagonistic were combined in one person. It is no small thing to cope with a tiger in the jungle, it is no small thing to write up a elaborate state paper, it is no small thing to write the history of a nation, it is no small thing to issue a difficult negotiation at a foreign court, it is no small thing to lead an army to victory and I think that with truth it may be said that that he would do all these things with such brilliant success as Sir John Malcolm was a very remarkable man in a very remarkable age.

There were other brilliant and dedicated civil servants who ruled smaller areas. The most notable of them was Sir Thomas Munro who came as an East India Company cadet at the age of seventeen. In an age of growing British arrogance and alienation from Indians, the noble figure of Munro casts a bright glow on the grim Indian scene. He ushered in enlightened administration in the Madras Presidency, took initiative to reorganize revenue settlement, toured and surveyed the land with boundless energy. Munro strenuously rejected the idea that the natives are too corrupt to be trusted and argued:

> If they are trusted and properly paid they will respond just as the English did when their allowances were raised though not perhaps to a similar degree. Nor we cannot expect to find in a nation fallen under a foreign yoke the same pride and high principle as among

a free people ... foreign conquerors have treated the natives with violence and often with great cruelty. But none have treated them with so much scorn as we, none has stigmatized the people as a whole as unworthy of trust.

Though Munro insisted that power should be with district officers, he wanted Indian judges to be appointed to hear cases and wanted to recognize village panchayats and village committees to which he would give powers of petty courts to try small offences – just in fact the kind of power that these village courts were to be given more than a century later in the last phase. Thomas Munro held that "the advantage of knowing the country's languages is not merely that it will enable you to carry on public business but that by rendering you more intimately acquainted with people will enable you to think more favourably of them."

Following these tenets Elphinstone and his near contemporary Charles Metcalfe provided the kind of administration that would be the model for later generations of Indian civil servants.

However, the spirit of the times cannot be extinguished. While Lord Dalhousie established Universities in the Presidency towns and sought to spread the benefits of Western education to young Indians, create a class of Indians who would be natural allies of the British rulers, bring in a stern code of law and order, and put an end to the extravagances of Indian rulers through the Doctrine of Lapse, his governance in fact sowed the seeds of the nationalist movement. The Doctrine of Lapse spurred endangered Indian princes to revolt against Company rule. They found ready supporters among the soldiers of the Company whose mutiny in 1857 led to the first serious revolt against Company government. Twenty-five years later the Indian National Congress was formed and the freedom movement began.

* * * * *

Part III

British Attitudes to India

20
East Meets West

Ian Bruce Watson suggests in his *Foundations of the British Empire* that the clash of West with East, of modernity with traditions, lies at the core of Anglo-Indian relations during the seventeenth and eighteenth centuries and that out of this clash was formed the mood and temper of British imperialism.

This is a debatable point. The antagonism that grew between the two nations was not because of ideology or cultural differences but because of the political power of one, the economic exploitation of the other, the sense of superiority of one and the resentment against this of the other. Paradoxically, it was Britain's action in introducing Western education and institutions to India that led her intelligentsia to claim the rights and privileges enjoyed by the British people.

Historian Arnold Toynbee observes in his *The World and the West*:

> The estrangement between India and a western world which for India, had been represented by Great Britain, goes back behind the beginning of the Indian movement for independence in the 1890's and behind the tragic conflict in 1857. It goes back to the reforms in the British administration in India that was started in 1780's. The birth of estrangement from reform in the relations between Indians and the British people is one of the ironies of history and yet there is a genuine inner connection between the two events. In the eighteenth century the then newly installed British rulers of India were free and easy with their newly acquired Indian subjects in two senses. They were unscrupulous in using their political power to fleece them and oppress them, and at the same time they were uninhabited in their social relations with them. They hob-nobbed with their Indian subjects off duty. Besides meeting them at work on less agreeable terms the more intellectual British residents in India in the eighteenth century enjoyed capping Persian verses with

Indian colleagues; the more lively Indians enjoyed being initiated into English sports. Look at Zoffany's picture "Colonel Mordaunt's Cock-Match at Lucknow" painted in 1786. It tells at one glance that at that date Indians and Englishmen could be hail-fellow-well-met with one another. The British rulers of India in the first generation, behaved, in fact very much as their Hindu and Muslim predecessors had behaved. They were humanly corrupt and therefore not inhumanly aloof; and the British reformers of British rule, who were rightly determined to stamp out corruption and who were notably successful in this difficult undertaking deliberately stamped out familiarity as well, because they held that the British could not be induced to be super humanly upright and just in their dealings with their Indian subjects without being made to feel and behave as if they were tin gods set on pedestals high and dry above those Indian human beings down below.

21
Early Encounters

When the East India Company was granted its charter in 1599, the intentions of the thirty-nine gentlemen who founded the Company were purely commercial. Their motto was *Deus Indicat* and at the time of the founding of the Company, the Deity seemed to indicate only trade and not dominion. Thoughts of dominion would have appeared fool-hardly to Thomas Roe and John Hawkins, who were trying to establish their trading presence on the subcontinent and who were the Company's first emissaries to the court of the Moghuls. The first British Governor of the East India Company Sir Thomas Roe addressed Emperor Akbar with deep humility. In the earlier days of Britain's encounter with India, the traders were diffident and tentative in their approach. The British were content with their role as traders during the entire period of the seventeenth century and were grateful for the concessions that they received from the Moghul Emperor Aurangzeb by way of establishment of trading outposts at Surat, Masulipatnam, Madras and Cuddalore. But it was evident by the turn of the seventeenth century that the sun of the Moghul Empire was setting. Aurangzeb died in 1709 and from that date to 1767, when the Afghan invader Ahmed Shah Durrani captured and blinded the puppet Emperor Shah Alam, the history of the Moghuls was one of swift decline. It was also, incidentally, a period which saw a series of masterful Englishmen who realized the role that Britain could play in the vacuum left by the declining Moghul empire. These were men who had been sent in boyhood to the service of the East India Company and who met the complex challenge of their responsibilities and their new environment with verve and resourcefulness. Of them, the most outstanding were Robert Clive and Warren Hastings.

When the first British traders came to India in Surat, Madras, Bombay and Calcutta they stayed in their own settlements and did not venture out from there except when they moved from one factory to another. Usually they went with a caravan, which carried their merchandise. Sometimes the exigencies of commerce brought them into contact with local rulers before whom they did obeisance for reasons of diplomacy. Otherwise the life of these British colonies was entirely self-contained. As in the medieval Hanseatic League so here too the merchants and their retinue maintained discipline and a stern schedule with almost monastic austerity. Like the members of the Hanseatic League, the inmates of these trading colonies were not encouraged to fraternize with the local population. The people they meet regularly among the Indians were members of the merchant class – 'Shroffs' at Calcutta, 'Banias' in Surat or the 'Dubash' in Madras. The other class of Indians they interacted with was their servants. Exposure to a new society compelled the Europeans to reassess their outlook while the Indian merchants remained rooted in their traditional social norms.

As a result the East India Company servants were generally ignorant of Indian languages as they relied mainly on the Dubash or interpreters. Later on, the Directors of the Company encouraged Company servants to learn Indian languages when they realized the importance of direct communication with Indian merchants. Special benefits were given to those Company officials who acquired fluency in Indian languages; punitive measures such as the imposition of fines were taken against those who failed to learn the local language. The East India Company maintained language schools in their different settlements. However, since the Armenians and Portuguese had arrived earlier as traders, it was the hybridized version of these two languages that was in current use along the east coast of India. Consequently these languages became more important than the vernacular languages of India. Without the facility of language the social intercourse between the British Company servants and Indians was limited to traders and domestic servants. It is interesting to note that while Clive remained distant and arrogant in his dealings with Indians, his French contemporary Dupleix had friends among the local gentry such as Anandaranga Pillai. Consequently the early British settlements had no contact with the larger picture of Indian society and traditions nor did they aspire to anything more than profitable trade.

While the above conditions prevailed in Bengal and to some extent in Madras, the British were more courteous and circumspect in their dealings in Surat and Bombay on the west coast where other foreign merchants – the French, Portuguese and Dutch – flourished and offered competition to the British traders. As a result, the English merchant community moved on terms of equality with Indian merchants. They were careful to respect local religious and social customs. The earlier contacts of British Company officials with Indians was amicable. Indeed, as traders they could not afford to be either aloof or arrogant. They even adopted the sartorial fashions of the local people such as the 'banyan' and 'Moormen's trousure.' In Bengal however the English continued to wear the clothes that were meant for a cool temperate climate rather than the tropical conditions in which they found themselves.

The Company was firmly established in their settlements in Bombay, Madras and Calcutta by the first decade of the eighteenth century and had made their equations with Indian rulers. The perceptible disintegration of Moghul power enhanced their commercial and political strength. Emboldened by the weakness of the central authority in Delhi, the local rulers ignored Moghul rules of taxation and revenue and dealt with the English traders on terms most advantageous for them. Eventually the dissolution of an effective central authority weakened the local rulers as well because they had no one to turn to for protection when the avarice and arrogance of the Company traders reached new and sometimes intolerable levels. The Company's settlements located in their well-guarded forts gave them security and strength. With strength came a boldness that discarded moral constraints.

From the humility displayed by Sir Thomas Roe to the aggression shown by later traders, we see the changes in the power equation between the Company officials and Indian rulers. The change of attitude was brought about also by the growth of an industrial base that ushered in economic prosperity in Britain.

The employees of the Company acted as private traders and organized their activities with the assistance of Indian associates who found the alliance with the English traders a convenient way of taking advantage of the concessions and *firmans*. This appeared to be a mutually beneficial arrangement while the Indian polities could remain as a counter-balance to English ambitions. With the dissolution of Moghul authority the Indian merchants had to contend with the aggressive and arbitrary trade practices of the East India Company traders and officials.

The Company's attitude toward its servants was analogous to Thomas Pitt's towards his servant: "I employ the damnedest villain that ever was in the world and see him cheat me before my face but then he is a most dexterous indefatigable fellow in business which makes me such amends that can afford to bear with it."

As George D. Bearce has pointed out in *British Attitudes Towards India*, Britain was mainly a rural economy in the 1780s; her industries were chiefly centred around handicraft. British politics was dominated by a conservative aristocracy that zealously preserved its own rights and privileges. But the Industrial Revolution was ushering in social and economic changes to the agricultural society led by a land-owning aristocracy. There grew a vigorous middle class that now sought opportunities to attain wealth and power. Foreign colonies offered outlets for their energies and ambitions while the industrial base gave Britain the power necessary for territorial expansion and dominance. In the nineteenth century Britain forged ahead with establishment of new industries. Railways and ships facilitated communication and transport of goods, and promoted overseas trade. In a familiar cycle trade brought power which brought more prosperity.

By contrast India was a patchwork of various kingdoms; there was no national consciousness among the people who were bound more by the caste system and its corresponding rituals. But like politically fragmented Italy ('the geographical expression' as Metternich had declared contemptuously), India had a deeper unity based on Hinduism. By the end of the 17th century, coinciding with the decline of Moghul power and authority, India lost the political stability required for economic growth. Despite the wealth of the Mughal monarchy, the Nizam, and rulers of Rajputana, India remained a rural economy of cottage industries and handicrafts and was not prepared for the new age. India found her ancient and enduring cultural traditions, her social and political institutions threatened by the technical and organizational challenges of the West. Meanwhile, Britain forged ahead as an industrial power. Right up to mid-nineteenth century India lacked a vigorous middle class that could provide the political leadership and technical knowledge that is a *sine qua non* for progress. While India remained bound by her ancient customs, Britain was being transformed by economic and political power. India acquiesced before the armed might of a nation. It was not a new phenomenon; a vigorous nascent power had often gained ascendancy over an older and non-combative society.

These fundamental differences made it difficult for Britain to understand the political and social institutions of India. They regarded with disdain of what they perceived as a medieval and autocratic society; they were unable to understand the turbulence India had experienced through eight centuries of invasions and the resultant political and intellectual predicaments of her people. These conflicts became intensified with the arrival of British power in India. The industrial revolution and the growing aspirations of Britain's professional and working classes led to an intellectual ferment that was reflected in turn by their attitude to India.

From the indiscriminate "shaking of the Pagoda tree" to the concept of "the white man's burden", there is a change in perception – of a sense of responsibility – towards India and her peoples. There were changes also in the relationship between the Indians and the British that was not entirely determined by political considerations. A powerful colonial administrator like Hastings had respect and understanding of India's cultural past.

Strangely enough, the social relations between the affluent Indians and the Company servants in the period preceding and following the Battle of Plassey were cordial and sometimes close. This was an era of uninhibited intermingling, when neither winning souls for Christ nor carrying the white man's burden agitated the minds of the European men who came to make their fortunes. For a brief time the two people met in camaraderie. The Company officers visited Hindu temples, offered animal sacrifices. A Kali temple frequented by the Company officers was called 'Firinghi kalibari' or Foreigner's Kali temple. They were often invited to the homes of rich merchants where they consorted with nautch girls, smoked the hookah, and occasionally married Indian women. James Hickey had his Jemdanee, Kilpatrick his Hyderabadi princess, David Ochterlony looked after his many wives. (Charles Metcalfe, Resident of Delhi a generation later, kept his Sikh wife hidden from public view). Many European soldiers of fortune such as George Thomas, Count de Boigne, Claude Martin, Colonel Mordaunt served as military advisors to Nawabs and Rajas, organized *mushairas* and *nautches*. William Fraser, the Resident at

Delhi, busied himself with conservation of Moghul monuments and wrote Persian poetry. Several contemporary paintings by John Zoffany, Tilly Kettle, and Charles Smith depict scenes of inter-racial conviviality.

This free interaction was halted with the arrival of British women in the famous "fishing fleets." Gradually the English population began to live in the stockade atmosphere of British settlements that came to be called white towns.

With this grew a sense of alienation and indifference to the Indian situation. One can contrast Hastings, Munro and Malcolm with later colonial administrators who did not have knowledge of Indian languages nor empathy for her predicaments. With the progress of the Industrial Revolution in England, India came to be viewed as a source of raw material for British industries as well as a market for her products. India became a partner in Britain's industrial prosperity against her own volition.

However, along with the clash and the conflict of two nations, a new relation was forged between Britain and India through the efforts of enlightened administrators and dedicated scholars who realized that the interaction between the two nations could be mutually advantageous. While recognizing their differences, Britons and Indians tried to bridge the gap. William Jones tried to introduce an understanding of Indian culture with Europe. Philosophers such as Burke and John Stuart Mill, literary figures such as Scott and Thackeray had sympathy for India's plight and shaped a different response to the Indian scene.

Indians such as Ram Mohan Roy saw that the contact with Britain and the West could be turned to India's advantage. He promoted the study of Western science and philosophy and sought to encourage Indian understanding of Western ideas and institutions. British appreciation of Indian society and culture and Indian respect for modern thought made the British Empire in India a place for the cross fertilization of two very different civilizations.

The attitude of the British in the seventeenth and eighteenth centuries to the Indian cultural and religious milieu was in striking contrast to the Portuguese who unlike the British concentrated their hold on Goa as the key to the control of the Malabar coast. Unlike the British the Portuguese did not hesitate to interfere in Indian customs, traditions and practice of religion. In Goa the

Portuguese attempted to close down the Hindu temple. The intolerant Portuguese attitude was exemplified by their introduction of the Inquisition into Goa.

Albuquerque occupied Goa in 1510 and the experience of Portuguese colonization in India was an object lesson in contrast to the British approach in India in the seventeenth and eighteenth centuries. The Portuguese brought with them a mind-set of intolerance. As Perceival Spear succinctly puts it, "They carried their culture with them." As a matter of policy, Albuquerque encouraged mixed marriages in order to "rear a population possessing Portuguese blood and imbued with Portuguese Catholic culture who would be committed by race and taste to the Portuguese settlements and so form a permanent self-perpetuating garrison". This mingling of blood did not however result in the developing of a sympathetic understanding of Indian culture and customs. The Portuguese occupied Goa for four hundred and fifty-one years – from 1510 to 1961– and though their intolerance mellowed over time, the cultural and intellectual exchange that marked British colonization of India was by and large absent. They were deeply impregnated with the idea that no faith need be kept with an infidel. It was from this period that the word *feringi* or *farangi* – derived from the word 'Frank' – acquired the opprobrium of which the echoes may still be heard today.

22

Chaos and Camaraderie

The consolidation of British power in India from the time of Clive and Hastings produced not order but chaos in India. As the central Mughal authority disintegrated, the power of local rulers was unchecked and the East India Company acted in an arbitrary manner. The merchants of the East India Company in whose name the British ruled in India were neither prepared nor competent to discharge the responsibility of governing India effectively. Company officials under the weak supervision of the Directors in London were attracted to the plunder that seemed to be there for the taking. In general, corruption, oppressive taxation, and economic exploitation characterized Company rule in India.

The rise of British power in India raised the problem of order; the Company realized that by becoming the defacto authority in Bengal and Bihar, they also had to keep order if they were to function effectively as rulers and traders. This remained a constant problem in the hundred years from the Battle of Plassey in 1757 to the outbreak of the conflict of 1857.

The British public was becoming increasingly aware of events in India in the 1780s. They exulted in the victories of Clive and Eyre Coote at Plassey and Assaye. But when they saw the returning *Nabobs*, with their luxurious houses in Kensington, their sumptuous coaches, their flamboyant clothes and their country estates with gardens laid out by Capability Brown, they became envious of these parvenus; with this envy came the increasing recognition that this new-found wealth was being taken from a poor and oppressed people. The protest and the quiet voice of conscience grew into a murmur and the murmur came to be in time magnified into the thunderous diatribes of Burke, Fox and Sheridan.

The motivations of this formidable trio were various. For Fox, the great Whig politician, the attack on the East India Company served as the focus for his attack on the government of Lord North. For Sheridan the playwright, it was a drama in red and gold and with an actor's sincerity he threw himself wholeheartedly into the role. For Burke, who was a great crusader for upholding traditions, the oppression of a nation by his own compatriots roused him to express the indignation of a Justinian in eloquent terms.

Adam Smith, the economist and advocate of economic *laissez faire*, devoted considerable space in the analysis concerning the Mercantilists and a company of merchants that could assume political power and the advantages that accompanied this power in India. He observed in his *Wealth of Nations* that the role of a ruler is to secure the welfare of his subjects while a mercantile Company could only be interested in making profits. There was therefore an inherent contradiction in the roles; the effect of this undesirable situation, Smith observed, was reflected in the conditions of Bengal where famine, want, mortality, tyranny, starvation, depopulation ravaged the people. Smith found the situation morally reprehensible. To Karl Marx the political philosopher, the Company's misrule was synonymous with the unbridled exploitation on which early capitalism was built.

In his novel, *The Surgeons Daughter*, Walter Scott observed that the Company officials 'left their conscience behind at the Cape of Good Hope and forgot to collect it on the return voyage.' A more accurate picture probably was that they brought with them to India the prevailing social and political mores of England. It would be unfair to be unduly censorious of this bygone age which was so productive in other ways. The iniquities of eighteenth century British India are to be seen so easily because of the rawness of the times and the flamboyance of the protagonists. The times were also less hypocritical. The 'birds of prey and passage' excoriated in lasting phrase by Edmund Burke are still with us. The plumage is different, that is all.

Perceival Spear describes the scene:

> The English lived out their lives in eighteenth century India in the setting of the Mughal Empire. This provided as it were the framework in which public life, commercial and political, was carried out. The empire is generally thought of as in decline during this time and this is broadly true. But like some flowers and creepers in autumn there was a last fever of growth at the extremities when decay had already begun to offset the roots. Thus while imperial power was

> declining in the north and west it was extending in the south during the first and third part of the century.
>
> The Mughal Empire was thus a major political factor for the early traders. It provided the political atmosphere that men breathed. So potent was it that the essentially Hindu nature of Indian society was not realised till the century was well advanced. Europeans were not in general aware of the riches of Sanskrit or the treasures of Indian philosophy till the later years of the century in the days of Warren Hastings and Sir William Jones.

Taken as a whole British-Indian relations were much less inhibited in the eighteenth century than in the nineteenth. The rough and ready ethos of the trading milieu was an important factor. Though in the 1780s the Company was to assume the *Diwani*, the Company's servants had still to adjust themselves to their new role as rulers. They regarded themselves primarily as traders and they could not afford to distance themselves from the native population. Once British position as the paramount power was established, it was natural to regard India as a trading outpost. After that there was greater segregation when the British population lived in well guarded cantonment areas.

The atmosphere of mutual understanding which prevailed in the third quarter of the eighteenth century between 1760 to 1785 coincided with the rule of Warren Hastings. This period was called the 'Brahminising' period by Sir John Seeley. During this era, British scholars such as John Forbes, Colonel Palmer and William Jones called the tune. Hastings saw the direction that British rule was taking and improvised policy as he went along. He realized that it was not possible to prepare a blueprint of action. Munro, Malcolm and Elphinstone belonged to this school of reconciliation and understanding.

"I jabber in Sanskrit every day with Pundits," William Jones confided to Warren Hastings. "My principal amusement is Botany and conversation with Pundits." William Jones wrote to Sir John Shore, "I am glad Jayadeva's *Geeta Govinda* pleases you." (June 1789) "I have more Brahmin teachers than I can find time to hear" (August 1787). To Sir John Macpherson, William Jones wrote in November 1786, "by rising before the sun I allot one hour every day to Sanskrit and I am charmed into knowing so beautiful a sister as Latin and Greek" (November 1786). William Jones wrote to Lord Cornwallis, "The Hindu and the Mohammedan Laws are locked up for the most part in two very different languages – Sanskrit and Arabic – which few Europeans will ever learn because neither of them will lead to any advantage in worldly pursuits." "If temperance and composure of mind will avail I shall be well but I would rather be a valetudirian all my life than live unexplored the Sanskrit mind which I have just opened," Williams Jones confided to Charles Chapman.

"The hills and woods abound with uncommon plants and animals. Indeed the eastern peninsula must be a new world to the philosopher," William Jones wrote to Patrick Russell in September 1786. So great was the enthusiasm of Sir William Jones for everything Indian that a contemporary wrote that: "He was led by his enthusiasm from the banks of Ilysium to the stream of the Ganges." William Jones and Warren Hastings were the first of the brilliant cluster of Britons who were drawn by the appeal of India's ancient civilization.

There were numerous European adventurers such as George Thomas, Claude Martin, General Perron, Colonel Skinner, Comte de Boigne who adopted Indian customs and attitudes while their royal Indian masters adopted Western ways. This exchange occasionally helped to break down the social and racial barriers. The more refined and educated servants of the East India Company felt the impact of Indian literature such as Colebrooke, Wilkins and Halhed. This period in India coincided with the era of Enlightenment in France, Germany and England and reached its pinnacle during the period of Warren Hastings.

The third quarter of the eighteenth century from 1750 to 1785 saw a series of significant changes in the Indian political scene that had serious repercussions on the history of race relations. There was a gradual transformation from the secluded if not always elegant life of the early factories to the cosmopolitanism of later Calcutta. After the wars of conquest in Bengal and Karnatak, the British realized the need to strengthen the political base rather than the sole pursuit of commercial interests. The English "developed from the pettifogging traders quarrelling in their seats in church to imperial swashbucklers and large scale extortionists".

The social scenario began to alter with changes in the political equations in the last decade of the eighteenth century. The nature of social relations underwent a perceptible change with extension of British territory and power. While the earliest Englishmen were traders, their later role as soldiers and administrators made them distance themselves from the local population. Instead of the earlier curiosity and camaraderie, they developed an attitude of condescension and contempt for everything Indian. Indian civilization was regarded as inferior to their own.

The insecurity produced by the Napoleonic wars, the rise of British power in Europe and in India after the battle of Waterloo brought about a change in the social as well as political atmosphere that eventually led to an unworded antagonism between the two peoples. Even in the midst of this estrangement eminent Britons such as Sir Thomas Munro and Colonel Todd ploughed a lonely social furrow. Some Settlement Officers were thrown back on the society of Indians and did not adopt the arrogance of their compatriots. As Perceival Spear says, "The designs of the English became more imperial and their attitude more haughty and aloof." The earlier Englishmen had disapproved of Hindu superstition and Muslim bigotry while admiring Hindu philosophy and mythology. With the consolidation of British power in India, the curiosity and respect turned into contempt for a conquered people. The amicable relations and mutual understanding prevailing in the time of Warren Hastings never again reappeared.

23
Alienation

In the last decade of the eighteenth century, there developed a mood of alienation between the two people. One can compare the empathy towards Indians of Hastings, Thomas Munro, John Malcolm, Charles Metcalfe and Elphinstone, to the lack of understanding displayed by Cornwallis and Wellesley. There was no widespread awareness in 1783 of the depth, richness and variety of the culture of India. It was generally assumed that India was an Islamic country since it was ruled by Muslim nawabs. The average Englishman thought Indian languages were 'Moorish'. It took great scholars such as Jones, Halhed, Wilkins and Colebrooke to make known the ancient heritage of India that existed long before the Muslim invasions.

Lord Cornwallis accelerated the process of estrangement, motivated by what he regarded as a high ideal – and that was to improve the character of the Company officials. He felt that fraternization of the Company officials with the local population led to indiscipline and undesirable interaction. He believed Indian ability and character to be inferior to the superiority of ordinary Englishmen. Through the Permanent Settlement, he created a new land-owning aristocracy and also excluded Indians from higher administrative posts, which were now occupied by men who were administrative ancestors of the later 'Steel Frame' of the Indian Civil Service. In their keenness to maintain discipline and distance, rulers like Cornwallis lost touch with the local people. For instance, the abolition of the Nisamat Courts in 1790, and their place taken by civil courts presided by Europeans aided by Indian assessors, placed the administration of justice in the hands of those not acquainted with local rules and customs. "The belief of Lord Cornwallis in English permanence and excellence was only equaled by his distrust of Indian ability." (T.G. George, *The Briton in India)*

Sir John Shore who followed Lord Cornwallis as Governor-General was a man of narrow and rigid views. "Shore has many strong prejudices and a universal one against the natives of India," wrote Colonel Palmer to Hastings in 1786. Unfortunately, the attitude of men like John Shore who had little sympathy or understanding for local people prevailed. They created a race of conscientious civil servants who were dispassionate but who had no empathy for the vast country with its complex time-honoured traditions.

The dialogue in civilization begun by Warren Hastings and the Company scholars was terminated for the time being by Thomas Babbington Macaulay with his *Minute on Education*. Only three months in India, he had no conception of India's past achievements in philosophy, literature, mathematics, law and art and could not therefore gauge her potential. All he believed was that everything Indian was contemptible and everything Western was worth emulating. While introduction of English as the official language of governance created other problems it nevertheless opened India to western knowledge and promoted the dialogue between civilizations that Hastings and his friends had so assiduously fostered.

Nowhere is the contempt for India more blatant than in Macaulay's malicious caricature of the Bengali character. "There is a Castilian proverb which could apply here – men, women, earth, water and Bengali." And, "there never perhaps existed a people so thoroughly fitted for a foreign yoke". One can compare this attitude to William Jones' 'pundit hunting' at Krishnagar.

Macaulay's essay on Clive reveals the ideas of ordinary Englishmen regarding Indian conditions; the justification of every act of immorality by maligning the character of Indians. "The truth seems to have been that he (Clive) considered Oriental politics a game in which nothing was unfair." Macaulay tries to defend the conduct of his compatriots in India by blaming the low standards of morality then prevalent! "During this period the business of the servant of the Company was simply to wring out of the natives a hundred thousand pounds as speedily as possible ... that he might return home before his constitution had suffered from the heat, to marry a Peer's daughter, to buy rotten boroughs and give balls in Mayfair." On Warren Hastings' Macaulay muses –

> There remains proof that he had remitted more than a 180,000 pounds through the Dutch East India Company and more than 40,000 pounds through the English East India Company.

A few of Macaulay's compatriots found his complacent arrogance difficult to digest; the sophisticated Lord Melbourne, a leading politician of the early 19th century, said of him 'I wish I was as sure of anything as Macaulay is sure of everything.'

The historian Vincent Smith says that,

> In his habit of making sweeping statements he (Macaulay) wrote 'Nearly all the notable men of that age lived vicious lives stained by gross sensuality and insatiable greed.'

Continuing in the same vein Dr. Johnson, another pronouncer of grandiloquent statements said, "I am clear that the best plan for the Government of India is a despotic governor, if it he be a good man, it is evidently the best government and supposing him to be a bad man, it is better to have one plunderer than many. A government whose power is checked let others plunder, the less there will be for himself, so he restrains them." (Boswell's *Life of Johnson*) There appears to be some truth in this in describing the period of Clive and Hastings.

24

Charles Grant and the Struggle to Save Indian Souls

When in later years, Charles Grant and his friends argued for the necessity of intervening in the religious customs of India, they tended to argue on the ground that the religious and moral imperatives of the Christian faith compelled interference while their opponents maintained that political realities forbade such intervention.

Ten years later when William Carey was on his way to India, he reflected the common opinion of his time by speaking of the "abominable East India Company" as an enemy of the progress of the people of India. A year or two later he noted that he had "no spirit for politics here, for whatever the East India Company may be in England, their servants and officers here are very different."

Grant's lengthy paper "A Proposal For Establishment of a Protestant Mission in Bengal and Bihar" (1787) led to an awakening of interest by British churches in the 'Evangelist of India.' The basic intention of the proposal was to win "the patronage of the Government for mission work in India". His argument was that confronted by the task of governing a people in "as depraved as they were blind and as wretched as they were betrayed", the British had to create conditions that made good administration possible. Later on neither Cornwallis nor Pitt were convinced of this. Their attitude had an effect on Evangelical clergymen and laymen. For instance, William Wilberforce supported missionary activity though his chief concern was the abolition of slave trade.

Grant produced an influential tract in 1792 – "Observation of the State of Society Among the Asiatic Subject of Great Britain". What made the *Observations* significant was that it attempted to find "a sanction for British rule in India through a comparative evaluation of the merits of the two civilizations that were confronting each other".

Many of the great administrators at the end of the eighteenth and beginning of the nineteenth century did not look upon the British rule in India as permanent. In 1777 Warren Hastings declared in a memorable passage, "The dominion exercised by the British Empire in India is fraught with many radical and incurable defects ... all that the wisest institutions can effect in such a system can only be to improve the advantages of a temporary position and to protract that decay which sooner or later must end."

Fifty years later Sir John Malcolm in the process of bringing great areas of Central India under British control expressed very similar sentiments because like Hastings he had a sense that India was so essentially alien that British rule would always be extraneous to the life of the people. Grant on the other hand considered British rule permanent. Apart from the fact that Grant was writing after a period of settled government and Hastings before, more important was their different attitudes towards Indian civilization. Hastings had a warm regard for the customs of India and he sought in his own striking phrase to create a system for "reconciling the people of England to the native of Hindustan". On the other hand, the fundamental argument with Grant's observation was that British rule can never be reconciled to India "until the native of Hindustan was radically altered". Grant's observation was that "abandoned selfishness was the distinguishing mark of Hindu character. Throughout the country human nature exhibited itself in a very degraded and humiliating state". Grant gave graphic descriptions of "the idols worshipped by the people of the cruel and licentious Gods and especially the skull draped images of Kali."

Perceival Spear has referred to the "hard boiled" and the "sentimental schools of thought on India". The hard boiled school which was made up of merchants and traders connected with the Company both in India and Great Britain saw the relationship between England and India in economic terms. Most of them would have agreed with Grant's evaluation of Hinduism. However, many of them would have thought it none of their business to bring about any change. The real opponents to Grant's views were the increasing number of people who finding in Indian culture a deep and appealing wisdom argued that the Indian people had a way of life that was valid for them, however, different from Western civilization.

One of Grant's early contemporaries in the Company's service said that the central core of Hinduism "the universal religion ... no other than the religion of the heart". (Grose, *A Voyage to the East Indies With An Account Of The Mughal Government And of the Mahometan, Gentoo and Parsee Religions*, 1772). Seratton who had helped Grant get his first appointment in the Company in 1793 had found that the Hindus accepted "those truths which formed the harmony of the universe and believed in one Supreme God whom they served through charity and good work." Even Shore who later gave complete approval to Grant's views, as a young man had thought the "religion of the Hindus was pure deism with a wonderful resemblance to the doctrines of Plato".

Other writers praised the institutions and material civilization of India. Just before Grant wrote the *Observations* a writer called Crafurd in *Sketches Relating to the Historical Learning and Manners of the Hindoos* (1790) wrote that India, not Egypt or Greece, was the home of the arts and the sciences and that the Hindoos were 'a polished and civilized nation.' William Hodges who travelled in India in the 1780s advised his countrymen not to despise Hindu architecture and sculpture simply because it did not conform to Greek rules of beauty. There were, he suggested, other canons of taste than those of the western world. (*Travellers in India During the Years 1780 –83*). One of the writers of this school of thought whom Grant found especially annoying was the Glasgow historian Reverend William Robertson who thought that Hindu law which regarded as cruel and barbarous was worthy to be ranked 'with systems of jurisprudence in nations most highly civilized'. Robertson also praised the caste system as 'a marvelous instrument for ordering and adjusting society'. (*An Historical Acquisition Regarding the Knowledge the Ancients Had of India*)

The most serious challenge to Grant's view of Hindu society came from the writings of the first English Indologist William Jones who had an established reputation as an Oriental scholar even before he went to India. While other scholars had been aware of the greatness and antiquity of Indian culture, their accounts had been based on fragmentary knowledge and very often on poor scholarship. Jones however spoke with the authority of personal knowledge of Sanskrit texts. As his biographer John Shore said, he presented his findings with "discrimination and rapture". Grant was aware of Jones' ardent enthusiasm for Indian studies; on a visit to Malda in 1785, Jones' "variety and depth of learning" had filled Grant with "the shame of being unlearned". It was probably the encounter with Jones, which led Grant, as a footnote to the *'Observations'* show, to read most of the works that had been published in English on India.

Although Jones did not rhapsodize over Hinduism as a religious system, his works give a clear indication that Jones was aware of its great antiquity, the wealth and variety of its literature and the profundity of its philosophical texts. As Grant realized, they provided ready source for those who wished to show that India had no need to import religious doctrines from the West. To counter this use of the great scholar's researches, Grant argued that there was nothing in Jones' work to justify the conclusion that was being drawn from them about missionaries. (Charles Grant, *Observations on the State of Asia)*

Grant wanted the introduction not only of Christianity but all Western learning. He assigned priority to the need for introduction of the English language in India as a means of assimilating the conquered people. Many of the troubles of the British in India, he believed, could have been avoided if English had been adopted as the language of administration from the beginning of the Company's territorial administration. He argued that English would not only improve the Company's administrative efficiency but through its use Indians would inevitably learn the arts, philosophy and religion of the governing race and the "fabric of error would be silently undermined. English education would affect upper classes but would also percolate to the present that through his knowledge of western science would improve agriculture". Or, "Idolatry with all its rabble of impure deities ... its false principles and corrupt practices would fall and the people risen in the scale of human beings would live in peace, comfort and justice under British rule" or "Once the Hindus had been shown the truth, Grant asserted, "they would abandon their ancient falsehoods and accept the new revelations, which should lead to a new order of Society."

For Grant the issues were simple. Were the people of India to be communicated "the divine principles which have raised in the state of being" or were they "to be left in error and ignorance".

Though Grant's proposal that the Company should officially sponsor missionary work in India was decisively rejected by the English Parliament and the Company's own administration, his general attitude towards the character of the people of India and his view of the nature of obligations of British rule become almost unquestioned assumptions. The triumph of the ideas contained in the *Observations* was what Max Muller had in mind in 1882 when he deplored the fact that young civil servants went out to India convinced that the people they would rule were "not amenable to the recognized principles of self respect, uprightness and veracity ... Never restrained in the dealings by any regard for truth, never to be trusted on their word".

"Risky people like missionaries who were educational and social reformers as well were not allowed by the Company to go to India," as J.W. Kaye, the eminent nineteenth-century historian of India, put it. "India was a close preserve in the hands of the East India Company. To go there without a license from the Company was to become a poacher and to incur the risk of being ignonimously sent home. A man without a covenant was in the Company's estimation a dangerous one; doubly dangerous such a one with a Bible. Reform of any sort was bad for business. Alas for the Company, the age of Reform was upon them whether they wanted it or not."

In all this one wonders whether it was Christian fervour that prompted Grant and made the British Government finally accept his views or was it because it provided them with a moral justification for British rule in India?

Observing the campaign in his old age, Warren Hastings sadly concluded that the attitude to India, which Grant championed, had triumphed over his own. In a letter that he wrote to the then Governor-General, Marquis of Hastings, he said: "Our Indian subjects having been represented as sunk in grossest brutality ... it is therefore said that we possess the power, so it is our duty to reform them, nay to coerce them, into goodness by introducing our faith among them."

About a proposal for erecting a monument to Grant, a proprietor said it should not be East India House where there was already a statue of Warren Hastings "for how could Charles Grant look Warren Hastings in the face or Warren Hastings, Charles Grant?".

But the spirit of the rulers in 1860 would have been more congenial to Grant than Hastings. What prevailed in the ensuing era of British bureaucracy was Grant's attitude to India and his interpretation of British rule rather than that of Hastings who sought to reconcile imperialism with the coexistence of two cultures.

Charles Grant saw India as an inferior nation and his own as immensely superior. His attitude was based on ignorance and prejudice – the ideal soil for a clash of civilizations.

25

The Evolution of Anglo-Indian Mythology

An important figure in the propagation of the myth of Western superiority was James Mill. Born on 6th April 1773, Mill was a philosopher, historian, economist, and prominent representative of philosophical radicalism. He was father of a famous son, John Stuart Mill, who wrote the celebrated *On Liberty*. The older Mill was Jeremy Bentham's chief companion and ally. His article on government had considerable influence on public opinion in the 1820s and helped prepare the ground for the passage of the first Reform Bill (which enlarged the franchise) by Parliament in 1832.

Two years after publication of Mill's *History of British India*, he was appointed an official in India House of London in 1819 and despite his drastic criticisms of British rule in India in *History*, he rose gradually through the ranks until he was appointed head of Examiners Office in 1830. *History of British India*, his magnum opus, was the first full narrative of the British conquest of India. Applying his own political theory to the growth of Hindu civilization, he severely criticized successive stages of the conquest and administration of British India as Hindu traditions became overshadowed by European interests and policies. The work itself and the author's official connection with India during the last seventeen years of his life influenced attitudes and policies of the East India Company in India.

The Indian empire, its economic impact on Britain, and the inevitable repercussions on India occupied a prominent place in Utilitarian thought. British perceptions of India in the nineteenth century were obfuscated by reports of those who had not really understood India. Though the people of India were regarded as one concerned with both the material and spiritual aspects of life,

Indian history was depicted as static and concerned only with spiritual matters. Indologists, pre-eminently the nineteenth century German, Max Muller, relied heavily on the Sanskritic tradition and saw Indian society as an idyllic village culture emphasizing qualities of passivity, meditation and other-worldliness. In sharp contrast was the approach of the British historian James Mill and the Utilitarians who condemned Indian culture as irrational and inimical to human progress. (It is interesting that neither Max Muller nor James Mill had actually come into contact with Indian life, like Edmund Burke fifty years earlier but both Burke and Mill had considerable influence on British rule in India.) Mill's chief contribution was that he divided Indian history into the three main eras into Hindu, Muslim and British periods.

In his Preface to Mill's *History of British India,* the eminent scholar Horace Wilson had remarked on

> the unrelenting pertinacity into which Mill labours to establish the barbarism of the Hindus ... with very imperfect knowledge, with materials exceedingly defective, with an implicit faith in all testimony hostile to Hindu pretensions, he has elaborated a portrait of the Hindus which has no resemblance whatever to the original and which almost outrage humanity. As he represents them the Hindus are not only on par with the least civilized nations of the Old and New World, but they are plunged without exception in the lowest depths of immorality and crime. Considered merely in a literary capacity, the description of the Hindus in the *History of British India* is open to censure for its obvious unfairness and injustice. But the effects which it is likely to exercise on the connection between the people of England and the people of India it is chargeable with more than literary demerit; its tendency is evil, it is calculated to destroy all sympathy between the rulers and the ruled, to pre-occupy the minds of those who issue annually from Great Britain to monopolize the posts of honour and power in Hindustan with an unfounded aversion towards those over whom they exercise power.

Wilson was of the opinion that "a harsh illiberal spirit has of late years prevailed in the conduct and councils of the rising service in India which owes its origin to the impressions imbibed in early life from the history of Mr. Mill".

Mill, the self-proclaimed rationalist, marinated in prejudice. This fact was no accident nor can Mill be given individual responsibility for what was in fact a process inherent in the growth of imperialism. Mill was an outstanding example of an inevitable phenomenon – the arrogance of the conqueror, an arrogance based on misinformation, an arrogance that was an armour against self-reproach.

The steady growth of race prejudice as a psychological concomitant of imperialism can best be realized by compiling the observations of the earlier English commentators with the obiter dicta of the present day. Thus, Ovinghor writing in 1696 commends the honesty of the East India Company's Hindu servants. Warren Hastings found the Hindus "gentle and benevolent, more susceptible of gratitude for kindness shown them, and less prompted to vengeance for wrongs inflicted than any people on the face of the earth." Hastings no doubt had reason to be grateful for this fact. Elphinstone, the brilliant Resident at Poona found the villagers everywhere "amiable, affectionate to their families and to their neighbours and to all but the Government honest and sincere."

Bishop Heber's tribute of praise was even stronger. He was an unusual missionary. He must have come with the intention of bringing the Gospel to India but was so impressed by the gentle and comely 'pagan' people that he lost some of his proselytizing zeal. A devout Christian, he refrained from making any derogatory comments about Hinduism. Heber's *Journal of a Voyage Through the United Provinces* describes with keen eyes the boat sailing through the Ganges, of the bishop spending his time learning Hindustani and reading Saadi's *Gulistan*. When the boat anchored in Saugar Roads near the Island of Saugar he described "a perfectly flat and swampy shore with scattered tall trees, dark like fires and jungle about the height of a young coppice wood, of a very fresh and vivid green. With a large glass I could distinguish something like deer grazing or lying around amid the swampy grass". Heber describes the encroachment of sea that drove away deer and tiger and recalls instances of tigers swimming from the coast for a considerable distance. He describes the coffee coloured water of the river around the marshy inlets and half-burnt corpses floating past, the fruit boats coming near their barge rowed by "small slender men, extremely black, selling shaddocks, plantains, coconuts." Bishop Heber was struck by the "vast width and rapidity of the water flowing and many large vessels going towards the sea." He describes the English hotel at Fulta and says that accidents are frequent and that the Brahmins had prophesied that the river would rise and drown all Calcutta.

Prejudice had reached formidable proportions by the time Mill wrote his *History of British India.* Max Muller points out that Mill was chiefly guided by Dubois, a French missionary, and certain other selected authorities - "All of them neither very competent or very unprejudiced judges". Mill became the fashion among subsequent British historians of attributing almost all Hindu habits and practices to some mean or despicable motive and discussing all Hindu culture with contempt. Thus, for instance, of the Hindus' alleged propensity for litigation he writes, "As often as courage fails them in seeking more daring ratification to their hatred and revenge, their malignity finds a vent in the channel of litigation."

Mill was probably the first English writer to propagate the impression that Hindus were by their nature dishonest and untruthful. In fact Mill's horrifying portrayal of the Hindus would lead one to ask how such a degraded race survived at all! Even Hindu music to which no political significance can be attached is discussed by Mill in a single paragraph with a remark that "all Europeans even those who are most disposed to eulogize the attainment of the Hindus unite in describing the music of the people as unpleasant and void of both expression and art".

James Mill's utilitarian evaluation of Indian society was even darker than Grant's. Lord William Bentinck, friend of Grant and Mill, explained why he had abolished *Sati.* He was seeking, he said, to free the Indian people from "the primitive rudeness and ignorance" of their own culture since this led them to observe customs "opposed to true happiness and repugnant to the best feelings that Providence had planted in the human breast". Sir Henry Maine said Britain's right to be in India was based on the "principle of progress which we Englishmen are communicating to India ... we received it and we are passing it on". This illustrates the cultural gulf present between the Indian people and those who were their interpreters to the British public. Mill's attitude became the criterion of orthodoxy in future English writers.

By the end of the nineteenth century, the British in India had for the most part given up the attempt to understand the people over whom they ruled. G.W. Stevens who held that a Westerner would never understand the Hindu mind was quite clear that

British rule was indispensable. Yet he realized that "the new generation of Anglo-Indians is deplorably ignorant of the native languages and that after a dozen years in the country the average British administrator could not converse with a peasant or read his language". Flora Annie Steel, wife of a civil servant living in India, observed, "Of the life, character, habits and thoughts of the peasantry, always concealed by the Orientals from those in authority over them the knowledge grows more and more extinct every year. Statistics accumulate and knowledge decays. The longer we rule over India the less we know of it."

There is the sharpest contrast between the speeches of Burke in the eighteenth century and Macaulay in the nineteenth century though each represented liberal thought in his own generation. The people of India had become in the jargon of Macaulay – "A race debased by three thousand years of despotism and priest-craft." And the very speech in which the words occur was made to a half empty House of Commons which was laying down the whole future of India in the Chartered Act of 1833 – "a circumstance which may surprise those who are not aware that on a Wednesday and with an Indian question on the paper, Cicero replying to Hortensius would hardly draw a quorum".

26
Upholding Indian Traditions

"Sir William Jones and William Robertson represented the western impulse to understand both the culture of the past and the other areas of the world. This was a characteristic tendency of European scholars and historians manifest in the first coherent translation of Beowulf and the salvaging of the Elgin marbles as well as in the preservation of Indian literary and philosophical texts." (*British Attitude Towards India – 1784-1858* by G.D. Bierce)

As scholars and historians they tried to overcome these established prejudices. They did not display the contempt that imperialism generated towards non-Western people, an attitude with which they justified the politics of British finance. They were prepared, indeed eager, to find great merit in the new civilization that they were encountering and hoped that their endeavours would help advance cross-fertilization of cultures. They had a firm belief in the necessity to preserve the civilizational achievements of India which had made such outstanding contributions and which were prerequisites to the future development of India. The political order, social improvement and cultural achievement of India, they insisted, could not continue unless this development was founded on the tradition and laws of the country. Sir William Jones and William Robertson thereupon encouraged their own countrymen to treat India according to this conservative theory of progress. They helped to generate a deep and abiding interest in Indian culture both among Indians and Britons. Warren Hastings believed that Indian culture was to be promoted as a way of meeting Indians likely "to acquiesce in British dominion".

The later modifications of this attitude were coloured by men like Burke who followed a path of expedient conservatism. The attitude of these men was shaped by their backgrounds. Loyalty to Britain and the Christian faith, as well as education in Western science and their professed respect for western concepts of liberty made them look upon India with inherent prejudice. Whatever served the cause of imperialism was to be preserved. And this entailed promoting British interest or conserving British interest at the expense of India. The concern of imperial statesmen was to strengthen British power; the Indian Constitution and the inner stability of India did not concern them. Conservatism itself was under fire from men like Jeremy Bentham and Tom Paine who were dissatisfied with prescriptive rights and prescriptive contributions into hereditary institutions, monopolistic corporations, established churches and a static closed structure. Paine hoped to spread his democratic ideology and establish representative government in Europe, Asia, and Africa.

The role of Conservatives after Burke was to try to educate the British public into some respect for Hindu culture and institutions, and delay and modify the inevitable and inexorable changes that come with a new age. The writings of James Cummings are a characteristic example of the function of Conservatism.

James Cummings was a Clerk in charge of judicial and revenue affairs in the Board of Control in 1793. Though he never went there, Cummings acquired extensive knowledge of India and wrote an important treatise on internal administration in India where he described British type courts and revenue administration. Cummings was distressed by British administration in India and the elaborate system of regulations that were disrupting the Indian Constitutions that had taken many centuries of Indian experience to develop. He wrote, "The British had become so intoxicated by their victories in India, that young Anglo-Indian officials tried to impose British ideas of jurisprudence and political economy and administration of justice on an alien country." He observed that the conservative respect for Indian culture persisted without much public support. Many Anglo-Indians and Oriental scholars continued to study and preserve the literature of India.

Sir Thomas Munro, who later became Governor of Madras, told the House of Commons in 1813 that Britain would greatly benefit from the cultural exchange with India. For years he supported Oriental scholars like H.H.Wilson. Munro sought direct government assistance to promote Oriental studies in India.

Great administrators such as Munro and Malcolm saw the dangers of sudden break with cultural and religious sentiments.

They were realists as well the voices of Enlightenment. In his *Political History of India from 1784 to 1823* John Malcolm wrote: "All that Government can do is by maintaining the internal peace of the country and by adapting its principles to the various feelings, habits and character of its inhabitants give time for the slow operation of the desired improvement with a constant impression that every attempt to accelerate this end will be attended with danger of its defeat". His words summed up the balanced and enlightened views of the last representatives of the age of reason.

Between 1784 to 1843 the British Parliament displayed little interest in Indian affairs. India was a kind of 'dinner bell' which cleared the House of Commons. From 1784 to 1813 Parliament passed no real significant legislation relating to the East India Company or India. The Charter Act of 1793 slightly altered the commercial system of India. Other Acts introduced British style courts in Calcutta, Madras and Bombay. There were no serious debates on the purposes of British rule in India. Nor did members of Parliament reveal any real understanding of the country. The British Government felt that the commercial interests of Britain were being taken care of by the East India Company.

Indeed it was the East India Company that nursed mercantile and imperial ambitions. As a chartered Company possessing an exclusive trade to India and China, they had an important financial stake in continuance of trade and empire. Under Pitt's tutelage and sobered by the impeachment of Hastings, the Company assumed the image – somewhat erroneous – of a responsible public Corporation which promoted both British and Indian interest. It took a bloody uprising in 1857 to put an end to this untenable rolc.

27
Educating Indians

The first educational attempt of Warren Hastings and the East India Company in the direction of reviving Sanskrit and Arabic studies faded with the Company's policy which encouraged the study of English and which was taught in the mission colleges particularly in Serampore. The study of English led to the popularization of Western knowledge. Under the inspiration of Macaulay, a decision was taken in 1835 to promote English education in India as a measure of government policy. This soon after became an avowed objective of the British Government.

K.M. Panikkar in his book *Asia and Western Dominance* observes that education itself was "largely an emasculating process in India. Its origin was not the indigenous system but the needs of the East India Company." Speaking of India a century ago, Sir Claude Hill said: "A prime necessity at that time was the furnishing of Clerks capable of doing the work in a manner which would be satisfactory to the English Board of Directors." A more grandiloquent contemporary sponsor of this policy, Macaulay, explained himself in words which every educated Indian remembers "we must at present do our best to form a class who may be interpreters between us and the millions we govern: a class of persons Indian in blood and colour but English in taste, in opinions, in morals and intellect".

"The ultimate effect of this policy," observes Panikkar , "was the creation of a class of unemployed intellectuals which originally formed the nucleus of the national movement. While the primary education of millions was neglected a denationalized minority was brought into being for which secondary schools and colleges were provided and here the culture and prejudices of the ruling race fostered. The control of the press and the framing of enlightened literati completed the process."

"The English language is the basis of this educational system and while the literature of its own country is forgotten the Indian schoolboy is fed on Shakespeare and taught to glory in British military achievements." Ronald Ross writes, "Mr. Brailsford has drawn a mordant picture of a class of children with enlarged spleens struggling to learn by rote a table of the Plantagenet kings."

The prophetic words of Elphinstone have proved to be true: "We have dried up the fountains of native talent, and that from the nature of our conquest not only all encouragements to the acquirement of knowledge is withdrawn but even the actual learning of the nation is likely to be lost and the productions of former genius to be forgotten."

India did not share the technological changes that were taking place in the western European world after the Renaissance. In Europe, the Gutenberg Press was established in 1468 ushering in an intellectual revolution. The first Bible was printed in 1470. Portuguese travellers brought a printing press to India in 1556. In 1578 a sixteen-page tract called *Doctrina Christa In Lingua Malabar-Tamil* was printed in Quilon. This was the first book printed in any Indian script. Bengal took two hundred years after this to publish her first book. Unlike parts of south and west India, missionary activities in Bengal were curtailed.

While efforts were on to westernize Indians, Wellesley's plan for Fort William College became a symbol of the nature of government he believed necessary for India. "The College must stand or the college must fall," he pronounced. He wanted prospective British civil servants to learn about India but he did not anticipate other consequences. Young Britons would go out to India at the age of fifteen or sixteen to complete their education and they would become part of India, not representatives of the culture and civilization of Great Britain. Grant also opposed this, on the ground that civil servants would not have to send their sons homes to be educated and in this way a hereditary class of civil servants would be created, divorced from English life and self-perpetuating. Henry Dundas also saw the danger of colonization in Wellesley's scheme. Another fear of Dundas was that the literary and philosophical men Wellesley might collect at the College might very easily become breeding ground for Jacobinism.

In the dispatch of 1798, mention was made of one of the principle dangers threatening the British connection with India – the fear that civil servants might undergo "an assimilation to Eastern opinions". Grant feared what his friend John Shore once called "the deplorable infatuation with Indian life that lead young men to become Indianized forgetting the customs, manners and state of society in England".

The spread of Western knowledge was not forced upon Indians. Indeed progressive Indian thinkers and social reformers wanted Western style education to be introduced to India. With the establishment of the four universities in the major cities of India – Calcutta, Madras, Bombay and Allahabad – the demand for Western education gained momentum from 1854. This also opened opportunities to the Christian missionary to pursue the spread of Christianity.

The weakness of this system is that the chasm widened between the English educated classes and those educated in the traditional manner. Those educated in the Western tradition became somewhat alienated from the others.

The enduring benefit of Macaulay's policy was that the educated elite of India was brought into contact with the mainstream of western culture. Western education laid the foundations for modernization of India. It is a dramatic paradox that while British administration was aimed at suppressing any attempts and aspirations of self-rule by Indians, and the creation of a buffer class of westernized Indians sympathetic to the British Raj, in actual fact ideas of national self-determination emanating from Europe struck roots in young Indian minds. The other unintended benefit was that for the first time after the tenth century, when Sanskrit had been the lingua franca of India, the widespread use of English provided a common linguistic bond between the peoples of India and expedited the consciousness of a nation-State.

Western education also enabled Indians to share in the intellectual achievements of the European Enlightenment. The greatest good of the greatest number had become an acceptable formula in a country to which an exclusive Whig oligarchy had given prosperity, security and an empire spread over the four corners of the world.

Despite the introduction of Western education, often through missionary schools and colleges, and the efforts of the missionary themselves at proselytization, India did not become Christian. The efforts and achievements of the Orientalists instead strengthened Hinduism and led to its emergence as a world religion. They represented eighteenth century enlightenment and were also free from missionary motives. This was entirely due to the Western scholars who rediscovered ancient Indian heritage both for the benefit of the Indians and for the West. This was the outstanding, indeed the epochal, achievement of William Jones.

Jones' belief that it was unwise to tamper with Indian customs was not the result of commercial considerations of the above type but was the result of Burke's philosophy which respected traditions and customs that were autochthonous and integral to the life of the people. William Jones believed that a ham-handed Western approach could do great harm. In the extreme case we have the pre-Bentinck approach to *Sati*. In the 1780s therefore there was the commercial approach of the East India Company which felt that "reform was bad for business". At the other end of the spectrum, scholars such as William Jones, Halhed and Wilkins believed that customs and institutions consecrated by traditions and integrally woven into the lives of the people should not be tampered with. All this changed with Carey, Marshman and finally Bentinck.

Missionaries concentrated on education and on the translation and printing of the Bible into as many Indian languages as possible. Often the language had not been properly written down before so the missionaries prepared the first grammars and dictionaries. While educating Indians they also hoped to convert them. What happened instead was a flowering of Indian nationalism and vernacular literature. Despite Victorian evangelical optimism, relatively few Indians became converted to Christianity. But there is no doubt at all of the value of missionary achievements in education and in social reform particularly of the lives of Indian women.

This unintended phenomenon is illustrated by the painting by Robert Hume depicting William Carey and his chief pundit Mruthunjay. Although the East Indian Company gave official permission only in 1813, some missionaries had already gone to India illegally. Most famous of these was William Carey, the first English missionary in India who arrived in India in 1793 sent by the Baptist Mission Society.

As the industrial revolution progressed men such as Macaulay and Trevelyan felt that Western style progress can be induced but their reformist zeal sprang from contempt for Indian civilization. The early Victorians like Macaulay and Trevelyan found the careful opinions of "old India hands" like Munro and Malcolm an anachronism.

By 1835 Munro and Malcolm were no longer on the scene and reform was the order of the day. Once English became the official language, 'progress' and 'improvement' was hurried on by legislation. The British were by now impatient of opinions like Malcolm's that "great and beneficial alterations in policy to be complete must be produced within the society itself; they cannot be the mere fabrications of its superiors or of a few who deemed themselves enlightened".

We have therefore a wide spectrum of attitudes and perceptions of Britons about the Indian scene from the seventeenth to the nineteenth century, from those who respected and understood India to those who had contempt. With Macaulay the wheel comes full circle on 7th March 1835 when English became the official language of India and eventually the medium of instruction for higher education.

After the emergence of the British as the dominating power in Bengal, the missionaries got a free hand. Though their proselytizing activities were restricted they made a landmark control to the cultural evolution of India, especially William Carey and his colleagues in the Danish colony at Serampore. The publication of *Bengali Grammar* ushered in printing in Bengal. This was followed by the establishment of printing presses both for religious and secular works.

Warren Hastings had resisted the free easy press of James Hickey, the founder-editor of India's first newspaper, *The Calcutta Gazette,* for his scurrilous invectives against Mrs Hastings. "The sword crossed the pen and the battle was on. Hastings was helpless. He could not stop the wheels of time."

28

Attitudes to the Indian Empire: Guilt and Atonement

Both guilt and atonement played a role in the British attitude to her Indian empire.

It has long been part of the apologetics of modern imperialism to invoke the analogy and the precedent of the Roman Empire and comparing the Romans in Greece to the British in India. It has been strenuously argued that Rome and Britain were both in a position to confer peace and order, law and justice on the peoples they conquered. While Dalhousie like the Roman Lucullus vigorously propounded an aggressive and expanding imperialism, so Cobden and Bright like Cato and Scipio were averse to this national aggrandizement and its attending responsibility. Romans, as a Mediterranean people in contact with related cultures, were better able than the British to assimilate their subjects and to bring them, regardless of their race or colour, into the ambit of a common citizenship. Though the British were less successful in this, they were on the other hand more enlightened than the Romans in their perceptions of liberty of subjects and rule of law.

Both had convinced themselves that they had more to give than receive and adopted a Messianic posture in their self-imposed civilizing mission. This singular posture of political condescension could assume absurd proportions though they were in no way comparable to the bigotry of Spanish conquistadores described by an Englishman as "reckless, ruthless as like intoxicated".

The Romans and Britons were dissimilar in one important respect. The liberal traditions of eighteenth century England, the humanism of post-Renaissance Christianity was absent in an authoritarian pagan Rome. As a result Britons covertly carried a sense of guilt and desire for atonement which could not be stifled even by the grandeur of imperialism that reached its pinnacle during the time of Viceroy Curzon.

There was a divergence of attitude of the British to their own empire. The British Empire was of course *sui generis*. It still seems incredible that a handful of Englishmen could rule an alien and ancient civilization of many millions over a vast subcontinent for over a century "with a mixture of motives and methods, principles and policies that baffles analysis and defies explanation". And yet Thomas Munro could write as early as 1818 to the Marquess of Hastings: "Foreign conquerors have treated the natives with great violence and often with great cruelty. But none has treated them with so much scorn as we." Macaulay proclaimed in 1833 that the Indian Empire "the strangest of all political anomalies resembled no other in history and found itself by a separate class of political phenomena so that its growth and decay were regulated by unknown laws".

Anticipating the predicament, Charles James Fox had advised: "Is a Governor in India to consult Puffendorf and Grotius? But I will tell you what he is to consult; the laws of nature – not the statutes to be found in those books nor in any books – but those laws which had to be found in Europe, Africa and Asia that are found amongst all mankind, those principles of equity and humanity implanted in our hearts which have their existence in the feelings of mankind that are capable of judging."

The Utilitarian plea comes in handy as an ex post facto justification. Professor Eric Stokes in *English Utilitarians in India* argues that Utilitarianism is not just a convenient device of imperialist self-defence on meeting its end. It was actually "the deliberate policy of a gifted and eccentric middle class in those formative years before the Crown took over from the Company full responsibility for the Government of the Indian sub-continent. It can therefore all the more easily be filled into the Whig–Imperialist model used by hacks to celebrate, not merely justify, the record of the British rule in Asia. The British not only transmitted to an alien Asiatic people the spirit of the European Renaissance and of the Reformation and the Enlightenment, they not only extended an aristocratic establishment from an island to a global empire, they also exported the age of reform from liberal England, the virtues of public probity and state philanthropy and the magic carpet of collectivism in harmony with private enterprise to an under developed continent in its pre-industrial state of nature."

The authoritarian element in British Utilitarianism easily lent itself to imperial ends as well as imperial theories of self-justification. Utilitarianism has lent itself to diverse interpretations and uses. It has been invoked on behalf of authority as well as freedom. The young Bentham was an advocate of enlightened despotism and never became a sincere democrat. The elder Mill believed that happiness and not liberty was the end of government. He formulated in its extreme form the absurd doctrine of "Oriental despotism" which provided a theoretical justification for British imperialism in India. His son's passionate concern for liberty led him to assert that it was immoral for one people to govern another. At the same time, James Mill's *History of India* made John Stuart Mill withhold the generosity of his liberal ideas in the case of India on the ground that these could not be applied to the conditions prevalent in Asia.

The conflict and antagonism arose due to the differences in attitude of the two peoples – the Hindus who guarded their spiritual and cultural traditions from foreign contamination and the British who stood socially aloof from the Indians. The distance between rulers and ruled added to a sense of alienation that seemed to grow with the passage of time. Those who chose to cross this seemingly insurmountable barrier did so only by losing their own identity and alienation from their own people. Yet in the end the results of the interaction of Indians and Britons were epochal and enduring.

A unique political and cultural cross-pollination took place. India facilitated the industrial revolution in England by acting as the market and source of raw material for English goods. England unwittingly ushered in the Indian renaissance by bringing India into the mainstream of the nineteenth century liberal thought. The results of the British encounter in India proved to be deeper and more far reaching than the consequences of the French and Portuguese empires in Asia or even the Roman empire.

Mid-Victorian Radicals were deeply concerned about the consequence of empire. Cobden saw no advantage in this vast Indian empire for the ruler or the ruled. Bright saw the empire as an expensive luxury; the cost of governing India, he felt, outweighed the benefits of markets and cheap raw material. The

Radicals provided one element in British imperialism in India that was muted but never wholly discarded. The concept of atonement lingered on until the empire came to its end under the auspices of Clement Atlee.

Other elements came to the foremost of the time and that was the desire to maintain the rule of law and to spread the Pax Britannica, and a genuine concern for good governance. These sentiments were expressed with a Biblical cadence and in a somewhat grandiose manner by Earl of May in Ajmer to the Princes and Chiefs of Rajputana in 1869: "That justice and order shall prevail, that everyman's prosperity shall be secured, that the traveler shall come and go in safety, that the cultivator shall enjoy the fruits of his labours, and the trader the products of his commerce, that you shall make roads and undertake the construction of those works of irrigation, ... that you shall encourage the education and provide relief to the sick."

There was also an underlying sense of racial superiority, a belief held but not always expressed explicitly, that the English were elected and divinely appointed to bear the white man's burden. This was proclaimed most clearly by Disraeli for whom "the colonies possessed intrinsic and not instrumental value."

As the nineteenth century progressed and the Prussian Empire expanded, the British caught the contagion of pride in military power, deification of discipline, requirement of submission before authority. Ironically and inevitably it was this imperial attitude that sowed the seeds of revolt in Bengal, Punjab and Maharashtra; it would not be long before organized attempts were made to overthrow British rule. In other parts of India there grew a spirit of opposition that gathered momentum and culminated in Gandhi's non-cooperation movement.

Diverse and often opposing elements shaped the mood of the British Empire. There was the imperative of a peaceful order such as the Buddhist Emperor Asoka had introduced and which had also been the aim of the Roman Empire. There was a Brahmanical touch in the racial exclusiveness and a feeling of racial destiny later translated as 'white man's burden'. With the rise of other European empires, especially the Kaiser's, there was an emphasis on military glory and discipline. The final phase was voiced by the liberal-radical elements who saw empires as unethical and exploitative and who offered atonement and expiation for the damage done.

There were also four main schools of thought – the Burkean doctrine of imperial trusteeship; the Utilitarian theory of state activity that was propounded by Bentham but also by the two Mills; the Platonic conception of a ruling elite that could act as wise guardians and the Evangelicals who wished to spread the gospel so as to elevate the character and save the souls of even perversely unwilling people; finally there was the Peter Pan theory of India as J.A. Spender called it – the East is regarded as unchanging and Orientals are considered no better than children.

The interactions between the four doctrines were too subtle and complex to be reduced to any simple scheme for stable relationship. Each doctrine bolstered the expansionist policies of Britain. Trusteeship appealed to the British Parliament, Utilitarianism to the imperial government, Guardianship to the civil service, and Evangelism to missionaries and non-official bodies. Burke provided a moral code, Bentham a socio-economic programme, Plato a veneer of classical philosophy and Wilberforce a spiritual garb and sanction for social and political change.

29

Thomas Babbington Macaulay – Dialogue or Clash of Civilizations?

While Clive and Hastings formulated imperialist policies for governing India, Macaulay contributed to a different kind of imperialism. Clive, Cornwallis and Wellesley believed in colonial rule in its crassest form. While consolidating the British territories in India, Hastings also sought to make it more humane. He felt that having established the empire India could be held by a policy of reconciliation by respecting Indian institutions, traditions and culture. Each one of them followed policies in pursuance of their ideas.

Macaulay did not have to face the frustrations of William Jones; his rise for a man of no rank or fortune was unusually quick for his time. Macaulay took his promotion quietly and paid little or no heed to the hard words that attended his success. He kept his happiness in his own hand and would never permit it to depend on the goodwill or the forbearance of others. But unlike William Jones Macaulay had during his lifetime to pay the price in terms of vituperative attacks in the press. However, it must be said the attacks were as extravagantly boisterous as Macaulay's attacks on others. He got as good as he gave and was paid back in his own coin.

As in the time of William Jones the voyage to India took six months. During this long journey passengers of a scholarly bent like William Jones had ample time for study and cogitation. They carried chests of book as William Jones had done which was a virtual miniature portable library. Like William Jones, Macaulay drew up his scheme of study for the voyage. Macaulay records in his diary on 4th January 1834: "The programme I design for the voyage is Richardson, Voltaire's works, Gibbon, Sismondi's *History of the French, The Orlando* in Italian, *Don Quixote* in Spanish, Homer in Greek, Horace in Latin." In passing he mentions, "I must also have some books on Jurisprudence and some to initiate me in Persian and Hindustanee." Macaulay records of his voyage; "During the voyage I read with keen and increasing enjoyment. I devoured Greek, Latin, Spanish, Italian, French and English, Folios, Quartos, Octaves." There are no indications of Persian or Hindustani reading in this list. About his voyage to India, he says, "I became too mere a bookworm in India and on my voyage home."

"After all the best rule in all parts of the world as in London itself is to be independent of other men's minds. My power of finding amusements without companions was pretty well tried on my voyage. I read insatiably, the *Iliad* and *Odyssey*, Virgil etc." The scholarly traveller of those days travelled not with a book-bag like the Somerset Maugham character but with an entire library. The seven volumes of Voltaire and the seven thick folios were especially intimidating. This is yet another aspect of leisurely sea voyage which needs emphasis. In Macaulay's case it could not be said that his shipboard reading was a preparation for India as the only book which dealt with India was that of James Mill who was certainly not the best of guides, contemptuous as he was of Indian culture and literature as evidenced by his supercilious remarks on William Jones.

But where Jones looked forward to arrival in what he considered a fascinating country or what to others was discomfort and disappointment, there were still others of less scholarly bent who used the journey for marinating in their prejudices which by the time they reached Calcutta or Bombay or Madras had become obsessions and solidified hatreds of men such as Philip Francis, Colonel Monson and General Clavering who could barely be civil to Hastings when they met.

Macaulay appeared on the Indian scene in 1836 at about the same time as Lord Dalhousie, another fervent believer in the benefit of British imperialism. Before arriving in India Macaulay had already been influenced by the writings of James Mill whom he admired, and James Mill finding in him a compliant disciple who would translate his ideas into policies, sponsored Macaulay for appointment in India. After reading Mill's *History of British*

India, Macaulay was convinced that what India needed was the imposition of Western civilization on India. It is open to debate whether Macaulay did indeed wish to promote progress in India or whether he formulated a policy that he felt best designed to assist in long term British occupation of India. He may have believed like the ancient Romans that complete integration of India with Britain by imposition of British culture Indians would cease to have a separate identity. Without this identity the potential danger of rebellion against and opposition to British rule would disappear. He gave a speech in the House of Commons on 10th July 1833 stating "that by good Government we may educate our subjects in the capacity for better Government ... that they may in some future age demand European institutions ... to have found a great people sunk in the lowest debts of slavery and superstition to have so ruled them as to have made them desirous and capable of all the privileges of citizens would be a title to glory all our own".

Macaulay saw this as a much more certain victory and a more enduring one than the victories attained by a force of arms and subjugation. He went on to say: "These triumphs are the pacific triumphs of reason over barbarism: that empire is the imperishable empire of our arts and our morals, of our literature and our laws." We learn from Owen Dudley Edward's book on Macaulay that Daniel Defoe's *Robinson Crusoe* influenced Macaulay in his childhood and he believed that a savage cum slave could be tutored to rise to European standards. This facile belief stemmed from Macaulay's utter lack of knowledge and information on Indian civilization despite the pioneering work done generations earlier by William Jones and his contemporaries. Macaulay also seems to have been unaware of the historical fact that the Roman conquests of Germany and Central Europe did not secure peace for Rome. Indeed it is the Germanic tribes who overthrew Roman rule in Europe. Nor did Pax Romana prevent the Germanic tribes from invading and sacking Rome between the fourth and seventh centuries. Nor would he ever acknowledge that the 'barbarians' brought egalitarianism and a fresh vitality to the Roman Empire. In October 1836, Macaulay wrote to his brother Zachary, "We shall also get rid indirectly of everything that can properly be called slavery in India." He was alluding to the Indian Penal Code which he had been drafting.

It must however be said to the credit of Macaulay that he did not indulge only in denigrating Indian civilization. In the Roman fashion he wanted to introduce British laws to India. He worked towards this end by drafting the Indian Penal Code and the Code of Criminal Procedure. He did this with the belief that Indian subjects should be accorded full legal protection and should ultimately win full citizenship after Western education and prosperity entitled them to these benefits. In these efforts Macaulay received support and encouragement from the Governor-General Lord William Bentinck whom Macaulay came to regard as the "greatest man I have ever known". Macaulay also contributed to the establishment of a free press in India. He was genuinely motivated by the belief that if all barriers between the ruled and the rulers are removed by bringing about social equality between them, there would be no cause for discord. In this he was guided by the principles of David Hume and Zachary Macaulay. He did not believe in immediate representative government as propounded by his mentor James Mill.

"Macaulay had no illusions as to the sordid origins and atrocious character of the East India Company," writes Penderel Moon. The Company's servants were 'intelligent, daring and eager to be rich represented the strength of the civilization without its mercy.' Against their irresistible strength the people of Bengal were helpless. The only protection they could find was in the moderation, the clemency, the enlarged policy of the conquerors. That protection, Macaulay believed, was found at a later date through the eloquence of Burke and the enlightenment of the British parliament. Macaulay should have given greater credit to Hastings who had sought to temper the greed and violence of the Company officials before Burke and his companions became aware of them.

Macaulay's views are reflected in his famous arguments in the *Minute on Indian Education* "calling for absolute priority for cultural anglicisation of India." He had virtually no sympathy with the position of persons interested in Indian culture and antiquity, whose furtherance he saw as "likely to maintain the obstacles in the way of Indian advancement". He regarded the evangelical faith as a necessary requirement in human advancement. In a letter to Zachary he said, "The Hindoo religion is so extravagantly absurd that it is impossible to teach a boy astronomy, geography, natural history without completely destroying the hold which religion has on his mind. But the Mahometan religion belongs to a better family. It has very much in common with Christianity and even where it is most absurd it is reasonable when compared with Hinduism." (Samuel Huntington has obviously not read Macaulay.)

Macaulay combined a strange mixture of cultural imperialism advocating imposition of Western civilization, the principles of Utilitarianism as well as the need eventually to introduce representative government and civil liberties, and also free press for Indians through education.

In a way Macaulay reversed the trends initiated by Warren Hastings and William Jones who believed in the preservation of Indian culture. In his book *Western Culture in Eastern Lands*, the Hungarian Indologist Arminius Vambery regretted that Macaulay who was prejudiced against Indian civilization won victory over Hastings, William Jones and Elphinstone and spurred Lord William Bentinck's resolution that "the Government shall undertake to spread the knowledge of the West to India."

Macaulay had strong views on the imperial civil service. The question before the House of Commons was the process by which the functionaries such as Judges and Collectors in India should be selected. There had been talk of giving the Governor-General unlimited power of appointing whom he chose. Macaulay opposed this on the ground that by giving this power to distribute Residencies, seats in the Council, seats in the Revenue Board "upon men without the least acquaintance with the character or habits of the natives and with only such knowledge of the language of the natives as would enable them to call for another bottle of pale ale or desire their attendant to pull the punkah faster".

Sir Charles Woods proposed that admissions to the civil service of India should be distributed according to the results of an open competitive examination. In his speech on this he said, "The ablest man who governed India was Warren Hastings and was he not in the first rank at Westminster? The ablest civil servant I knew in India was Sir Charles Metcalf and was he not of the first standing at Eton?". He ended by saying that "but the general rule is, beyond all doubt that men who have been first in the competition of the schools have been first in the competition of the world".

From the early days of the Company the only requisite qualifications for appointment had been the rudiments of commercial knowledge but Lord Wellesley in 1800 realised that a much higher standard of education and training was necessary if the officers of the Indian Civil Service were to carry out their administrative duties efficiently. Accordingly in 1800 he established a residential institution at Calcutta under the name of the College of Fort William that all future candidates and those who had been in the country for less than three years, were to attend for a period of three years. Its curriculum was very comprehensive and included a study of Indian history, law, religions, ethnology, Oriental languages, ethics, civil jurisprudence, international law and general history. Eminent Orientalists served as professors; H.T. Colebrooke for Sanskrit and Hindu law, Francis Gladwin for Persian, Captain Charles Steward for Persian and Arabic and the famous missionary William Carey for Bengali. One important aspect of training was to cultivate a thorough mastery of the Oriental languages. The institution produced very distinguished civilians like Metcalfe, Bayley, Scott, Elphinstone and others but it was not destined to have a long life. The Directors of the East India Company found Wellesley's scheme too costly and grandiose. They only agreed to continue this College as a School for Oriental Studies. It continued in an attenuated form till 1835 as a residential college.

A galaxy of distinguished scholars and civil servants were a product of this age of and contributed richly to the dialogue between civilizations. These were William Jones, John Shore, Robert Orme (pre William Jones), Francis Gladwin (Persian), Sir Charles Wilkins, Jonathan Duncan, Henry Thomas Colebrooke, Elphinstone, John Leyden, James Prinsep, Sir William Macnaughten, Sir William Muir, Sir William Irskine, Sir Henry Miers Elliot, Sir Alfred Lyall, Sir Edward Clive Bayley, M.S. Howell, H.G. Keene, A.N. Wollaston, Sir George Greerson, Sir William Hunter, and Alan Octavian Hume. (*The Indian Civil service and some extra departmental activities of its Members – Bengal Past and Present*) Jan-Dec 44 - Vol.

Macaulay's way of life would have been deemed solitary by others, but it was not solitary to him. While he had a volume in his hands, "he would never be without a quaint companion to laugh with or laugh at and adversary to stimulate his combativeness, a counselor to suggest wise or lofty thoughts and a friend with whom to share them. When he opened for the tenth or fifteenth time some history or memoir or romance every incident and almost every sentence of which he had by heart – his feeling was precisely that which we experienced when we meet an old comrade whom we like all the better because we know the exact lines on which his talk will run. There was no society in London so agreeable that Macaulay would have preferred it at breakfast or at dinner to the company of Sterne or Fielding or Horace Walpole or Boswell. That invincible love of reading which Gibbon declared that he would not exchange for all the treasures of India was with Macaulay a main element in one of the happiest lives it has ever fallen to the lot of a biographer to record."

Macaulay spent his time in Calcutta reading Thucydides, Xenophon, Plautus four times, Lucretius twice, Catullus, Silvius, Italicus, Livy, Tacitus, Ovid, Sophocles and Homer. So immersed was he in the role of a Roman Pro-consul that he read these books of antiquity as if they were guides and shunned all books that could have enlightened him on Indian civilization!

Nor could he look at India without comparisons to his homeland. In a series of journal letters addressed to his sister Margaret there are comparisons to English countryside and landscape: "The people whom we met were as few as in the islands of Scotland." About a journey from Madras to Arcot he notes: "We came to a mountain pass which reminded me strongly of Borrodaile, near Derwentwater." His reflections on Tippu Sultan's palace is "the palace is in the condition of Tintern Abbey and Melrose Abbey". During the ascent to Nilgiris he likened the scenery to the "vegetation of Windsor Forest or Blenheim spread over the mountains of Cumberland". During his journey he met the Maharaja of Mysore who insisted on showing him his entire wardrobe and his picture gallery. Macaulay observes, "He has six or seven coloured English prints not much inferior to what I have seen in the sanded parlour of a country-inn. But the bijou of his gallery of which he is as vain as the Grand Duke can be of Venus or Lord Carlisle of the three Maries is a head of the Duke of Wellington which has most certainly been on a signpost in England. Yet after all the Rajah was by no means the greatest fool whom I found at Mysore."

The harking back to English scenes and landscapes is not unnatural. Nor should it be regarded as lack of empathy. One should not forget that these were initial impressions recorded in 1834 when Macaulay had just landed in India when he beheld landscapes with eyes homesick for Cumberland and Derwentwater.

One should also not forget that in his letters to his sister Margaret he was resorting to the objective correlative, adopting shorthand which enabled his reader to evoke the images which he wished to create by relating to shared and familiar landscapes. While this may have been a species of shorthand, it also shows that Macaulay from the outset preferred to look at Indians through English eyes and think of India in English terms and interpret India in English categories. Whether there was waning of this tendency with the passage of years needs to be verified from his further writing from and on India. There was a definite contrast between the tenor and nature of Macaulay's first impressions and that of William Jones. Where William Jones was soaking in the sights and sounds of India, Macaulay writing from Ootacamund says, "As soon as I reach Calcutta I intend to read Herodotus again."

His frequent letters to his sister Margaret ends on a sad note when the last letter reached England Margaret was no longer in the land of the living. It frequently happened that the addressee was gone before the letter reached him or the statesman whose patronage was sought might have been fallen out of power, favour which existed might have evaporated during the journey of the letter. England and India were not only two worlds in space. They were also two worlds in time.

Yet this same man could be a Justinian too. Macaulay was assailed by a ferocious attack by the Press for his advocacy of the Act known as the Black Act which withdrew for British subjects resident in the provinces their so called privilege of bringing civil appeals before the Supreme Court in Calcutta. The change embodied in the Act was one of little practical moment (such cases were to be tried by the Sudder Court which was manned by the Company's Judges) but it excited considerable opposition. Macaulay records,

> In my opinion the chief reason for preferring the Sudder Court is that it is the Court we have provided to administer justice in the last resort to the vast body of the people. If it is not fit for that purpose it might be made. If it is fit to administer justice to the great body of the people why should we exempt a mere handful of settlers from its jurisdiction?... If we give our own countrymen an appeal to the King's Courts in cases where the others are forced to be content with the Company's Courts we do in fact cry down

> the Company's Courts. We proclaim to the Indian people that there are two sorts of justice – a coarse one which we think good enough for them, and another of superior quality which we keep to ourselves. If we take pains to show that we distrust our highest courts how can we expect that the natives of the country will place confidence in them?... We know that India cannot have a free Government. But she may have the next best thing – a firm and impartial despotism.

The historian Trevelyan writes of Macaulay;

> It is fortunate for India that a man with the taste and training of Macaulay came to her shores as one vested with authority: and that he came at the moment when he did: for that moment was the very turning point of her intellectual progress. All educational action had been at a standstill for sometime back on account of an irreconcilable difference of opinion in the Committee of Public Instruction which was divided five against five on either side of a controversy vital, inevitable admitting of neither postponement nor compromise and conducted by both parties with a pertinacity and warmth which does nothing but honourable for those concerned. Half of the members were for maintaining the old scheme of encouraging Oriental learning by means of stipends paid to students in Sanskrit, Persian and Arabic and by liberal grants for publication of works in these languages. The other half were in favour of teaching the elements of knowledge in the vernacular tongues, and the higher branches in English. On his arrival Macaulay was appointed President of the Committee. But he declined to take any active part in the proceedings until the government had finally pronounced on the question at issue. Later in January 1835 the Advocates of the two systems then whom ten abler men could not be found in the service, laid their opinions before the Supreme Council. On the second of February Macaulay as a member of the Council produced a Minute in which he adopted and defended the views of the English section in the Committee.

Macaulay's query "how stands the case?" and the following hurrah passage is brimming over with the pride and certitude of the conqueror.

> We have to educate the people who cannot at present be educated by means of their mother tongue. We must teach them some foreign language. The claims of our own language it is hardly necessary for us to recapitulate. It stands pre-eminent even among the languages of the West. It abounds with works of imagination not inferior to the noblest which Greece has bequeathed us, with morals

> of every species of eloquence, with historical compositions which merely considered as narratives have seldom been surpassed and which considered as vehicles of ethical and spiritual instruction have never been equaled; with just a lively representation of human life and human nature with the most profound speculation of metaphysics, morals, government, jurisprudence and trade: with full and correct information respecting every experimental science which tends to preserve health to increase the comfort or to expand the intellect of man. Whoever knows that language has a ready access to all the vast intellectual wealth which all the wisest nations of earth have created and hoarded in the course of ninety generations. It may safely be said that the literature extant in that language is of far greater value than all the literature which three hundred years ago was extant in all the languages of the world together. Nor is this all. In India English is the language spoken by the ruling class. It is the language spoken by the higher class of natives at the seats of Government. It is likely to become the language of commerce throughout the seas of the East. It is the language of the two great European communities which are rising one in the South Africa, the other in Australasia, communities which are every year becoming more important and more closely connected with our Indian Empire. Whether we look at the intrinsic value of our literature or at the particular situation of this country, we shall see the strongest reason to think that of all foreign tongues the English tongue would be that which would be the most useful to our native subjects.
>
> The question now before us is simply whether, when it is in our power to teach this language we shall teach languages, in which there is, by universal confession there are no books on any subject which deserve to be compared to our own: whether when we can teach systems which by universal confession whenever they differ from those of Europe differ for the worse and whether when we can patronize sound philosophy and true history we shall countenance at the public expense, medical doctrines which would disgrace an English furrier, astronomy which would move laughter in the girls in an English boarding school, history abounding with Kings thirty feet high and reigns thirty thousand years long and geography made up of seas of treacle and seas of butter.

Macaulay's contempt for anything non-Western is borne out in a remark he made during a discussion on the propriety of printing books of Oriental science "that the Saracens a thousand years ago cultivated mathematical science is hardly a reason for translating Arabic treatises on mathematics into English".

Another derisive comment he made with racist overtones is regarding the performance of a play by pupils of a Calcutta college – "I can conceive of nothing more grotesque than the scene from the Merchant of Venice with Portia represented by a little black boy."

In a supercilious comment Macaulay said, "Russia has gradually emerged from the ignorance in which it was sunk and has taken its place among the civilized countries ... there is no reason to hope that this vast empire which in the time of our grandfathers was probably behind the Punjab, may be in the time of our grandchildren be pressing to close on France and Britain in the career of improvement ... The languages of Western Europe civilized Russia. I cannot doubt that they will do for the Hindoo what they have done for the Tartar."

Trevelyan says that "the Minute which in its original shape is long enough for an article in a quarterly review and as businesslike was a report of a Royal Commission set the question at rest at once and for ever. On the seventh of March 1835 Lord William Bentinck decided that the great object of the British Empire ought to be the promotion of European literature and science among the natives of India. Two of the Orientalists retired from the Committee of Public Instructions; several new members both English and native were appointed."

He had allies in the Indian camp; but for different reasons. The Indians who supported Macaulay and Bentinck such as Ram Mohan Roy did so not to shackle India to the West but to liberate India from the fetters of superstitions, obscurantism and oppression that had accumulated like an impenetrable crust over the pristine values of Hinduism.

The historian Rawlinson describes Ram Mohan Roy as the greatest Indian of his age and the prophet of the new India. A wealthy aristocrat, he held a government appointment and came into contact with Western thought. Roy believed that India could progress only through Western education. A gifted linguist, he learnt Greek and Hebrew so that he could read the Bible in the original. In the true Hindu fashion he absorbed all that was beneficial in Christianity and adopted Christian tenets to the new sect which he founded. He was the first Indian to realize that religious literature and rituals alone would not suffice for society in the age of science and technology and that to be part of the mainstream of civilization India needed to be modernized without losing her soul.

If Ram Mohan Roy was the mind of resurgent India, says Rawlinson, its heart was the mystic Ramakrishna Paramahamsa and the energy of his disciple Vivekananda who also purified Hindu practices and rituals by returning to its source – the *Vedantas*. Yet so simple were the teachings that one did not have to be a Sanskrit scholar to understand them. The stories and teachings were published in Bengali and other Indian languages. The challenge posed by Christian missionaries receded; India remained largely Hindu. The movement begun by these two men spread to all parts of the world. The Ramakrishna Missions, established in many European and American cities, brought the message of Hinduism and won converts to a religion derided by Macaulay and his ilk.

Out of these mingling of many streams of thought came the Indian renaissance that was never envisaged by Macaulay but which was lit by the eclectic spirit of William Jones.

30
The Nationalist Response

In 1910 the British Prime Minister Ramsay Macdonald said, "Efficiency is not better than self government. The Report on Indian Constitutional reform combined a theory of political liberalism and a doctrine of active state intervention." The wheel had come full circle. The triumphant Utilitarianism of the exponents of a theory of enlightened despotism in the early decades of the nineteenth century had now returned under the guise of a new conception of state socialism. This was used together with the exigencies of war, the Burkean conception of trusteeship adapted to the interests of minorities, as well as the inability of the Platonic guardians to grow up and face the facts of life around them, to delay the consummation that had been envisaged by Munro, Elphinstone and even by Macaulay. In the end it had to come.

Paradoxically the theories propounded for safeguarding imperialism led in fact to the nationalist response. In the early decades of the nineteenth century Metcalfe had written: "all India is at all times looking for our downfall". Bentham at the same time referred to Ram Mohan Roy as his "intensely admired and beloved collaborator in the service of mankind".

Many Indian nationalists declared that Occidentals could only understand the language of force and the concreteness of organised violence. Paine's powerful attack on Burke was widely read – man had no property in man, the authority of the dead could not be invoked against the rights and freedom of the living and no nation had the divine right to rule another.

In 1930 the Congress party adopted a resolution in favour of 'Poorna Swaraj' or complete independence "which spoke the language of pain with detachment and calm dignity of Gandhi." Gokhale cited Gladstone's dictum "it is only liberty which helps men to gain liberty." Gandhi said only individuals could be trustees not nations: "The State represents violence in a concentrated and organised form. The individual is a soul but as the State is a soulless machine, it cannot be weaned from violence to which it owes its very existence." As for guardianship, observed Gandhi, "there is no room for patronage among equals ... Imperial domination must be replaced by partnership on equal terms." As to evangelical Christians, Gandhi said, "They have distanced India from Christianity and placed a barrier between Christian, Hindu or Muslim...The Christian imperialists had much to learn from Indian religious thought and ethics." Gandhi's appeal to Etonians was not to follow slavishly in the step of empire builders such as Wellesley, Metcalfe, Canning, Elgin, Dufferin, Lansdowne, Curzon and Irwin who had appealed for a partnership similar to Greece and Rome. Gandhi challenged all the assumptions underlying trusteeship, guardianship, utilitarianism and evangelicalism.

Theories boomerang with dramatic irony. In the eighteenth century the Whigs were taken aback in astonishment when they found that the revolting American colonies had adopted Whig ideals as their official creed. The imperialists in the early twentieth century found to their deep distress that their policies had generated a triumphant nationalism.

It cannot however be denied that the imperialists had brought to Indian society a vitality and vigour lacking since the declining days of Mughal India. They had unintentionally initiated the inexorable political awakening of the masses and the emergence of a new middle class. By the very application of their doctrines, trustees, guardians, Utilitarians and evangelicals brought about their own downfall leaving behind them "scattered traces of their thought and vocabulary".

Unlike the Romans whose certitude in their policies amounted to hubris the humanism of the Renaissance and Enlightenment led the Britons to question the ethics of their imperial mission. The imperialists made every effort to justify the empire. Indeed the paternal element in British Utilitarianism easily lent itself to the imperial purpose. Liberalism could be modified to co-exist at home with benevolent despotism abroad. This resulted in a desire to maintain rule of law, good government, carry the white man's burden and encourage pride in military power. At the turn of the twentieth century it looked as if this order would continue. It had however outlived its time.

31

Conflicts and Cross-Pollination of Cultures

By the eighteenth century various factors had made France and Britain look beyond her own boundaries for expansion and trade. The Reformation and Enlightenment had freed the European mind from static medieval dogmas; in the intellectual ferment thus generated the old concepts of right and wrong, of morality and ethics were being questioned. Wealth and luxury frowned upon by the early Church fathers had become a cherished objective during the Renaissance when the pleasures of this earthly life were extolled. Finally the discovery of the western hemisphere, voyages of the Iberian navigators who circumnavigated the world had removed fear of unknown seas and territories from the European mind.

By the early nineteenth century Britain was the paramount power. The phantom Moghul court received perfunctory lip service. Apart from the four Presidencies where direct British rule had been imposed, scattered throughout the royal courts of India were the British Residents who governed in the name of the Governor-General. The idea of an empire, the *imperium* of Roman times, attracted men who had received a classical education at Oxford or Cambridge and had no doubt read Cicero's ideas on the subject. The urge to introduce Pax Britannica to India as the Romans had imposed Lex Romana on their territories gained momentum. Moreover, they were aware that they had injected a new vitality in their territories that the effete Moghuls had failed to do in the eighteenth century.

The Roman Empire, which was the aspiration of British administrators in India, was a European phenomenon, operating mainly in European territories that were inhabited by barbarians who were easily absorbed in the fold of Lex Romana. When the Roman legions went into the non-Western world such as Palestine and Egypt they faced resistance. Similarly, Indian religious and cultural ideas were easily assimilated in East Asia – Thailand, Cambodia, Laos, Java, Sumatra, Vietnam and even China and Japan – because no conflicts were generated through imposition of authority or the imperatives of commerce.

Historians like Raghavan Iyer have held that if the British had settled in India as the alien Manchus had settled in China, their ideas would have taken deeper roots and they in turn would have been Indianized. In the 1780s, in the India of Hastings and William Jones, this might have been possible as Indo-British relations stood at the crossroads. But Cornwallis and Wellesley took the relations on a different path from what Hastings and Jones had envisaged. Hastings saw the direction which British rule was taking and did not wish to impose a blueprint. But this intermingling was obviously what Cornwallis and Wellesley abhorred.

Imperialism must start with an ideological battle. When governing an alien nation, the rulers must appear superior to the ruled. How else can they impose their will on a subject race? Foreign domination begins on this fundamental premise. An elaborate justification – political, social, cultural – for foreign rule is therefore an essential requisite to impose alien rule. In the nineteenth century the Utilitarians under Bentham propagated the theory that Orientals were suited for despotic rule since they had no experience of representative government. The doctrines of democracy and social justice that agitated the British liberals at home were clearly not for export to India and other Asian countries. Such theories were comfortable alibis and precluded the application of doctrinaire approaches. There developed instead a paternalistic attitude, culminating in the idea of the White Man's Burden.

Spender contrasts the attitude of the nineteenth century Indian civil servant trained at Haileybury to the East India Company official or trader of the eighteenth. The former were aloof and upright in their own light while the latter fraternized and shook the pagoda tree. In the vacuum created by dissolution of Moghul power, a band of enterprising and avaricious traders assisted by an equally avaricious and arbitrary band of Indian bureaucrats assumed power. And yet at this time there was no discord, despite Hastings' attempt to curb corruption. The disharmony between the two peoples came in the more ordered years of the nineteenth and twentieth centuries. The British civil servants then were caught in the conflict between duty to Britain and their duty to the Indian people. In the eighteenth century the conflict was a less serious one – between the claims of commerce and the dictates of the Company directors. In the eighteenth century the barriers of colour, creed and race had not been erected. With the advent of the missionaries and memsahibs barriers were erected.

Hastings had frowned upon the advent of missionaries to India. He felt they were a destabilizing force and created tensions by offending the Hindu faith in the process of proselytizing. The remarkable fact is that despite the exertions of the Evangelical Governor-General, the Clapham Sect and the Baptists missionaries, and Macaulay's immoderate diatribes against Hindu gods, India did not become Christian. In a typical Toynbean challenge and response phenomenon, Bengal and later India, reacted to Christian monotheism by returning to the monotheism of the Upanishads. The simplicity of Vedic society urged Hindus to start social reforms. Paradoxically, the Baptist Missionary press at Serampore turned out publication of works long forgotten and stimulated new literary efforts. The Bible unwittingly ushered in the Bengali renaissance!

The political philosopher Jowett believed that there must be a bond between the ruler and the ruled. It was not a particularly novel theory; the tragedy of Sita in the epic *Ramayana* sprang from her husband Rama's sense of duty to the meanest of his subjects. Jowett felt that once this bond was established the path of governance would be smooth. It is possible that this invisible bond and relationship of trust could not be established between the British rulers and the Indian people. This is, to quote Marx, the inherent contradiction of imperialism.

Seeing the trends of a nascent nationalism, Charles Metcalfe, the young Resident at Delhi, stated that all of India waited for the downfall of the British Empire. Had he seen Lord Canning's 'cloud no bigger than a man's hand' darken the horizon as a prelude to the bloody conflict of 1857? Or did he realize, living in the shadow of the Moghul court, that all empires must eventually end? Elphinstone, Resident at the court of the Peshwa at Poona, had observed: "After all India is a country of complex contradictions where the single Hindi word Kaal means both yesterday and tomorrow."

The other extreme in British attitudes is expressed in the book *The India We Left* by Lord Trevelyan, great-nephew of Charles Edward Trevelyan, who served in India at the very end of the Raj. Pragmatic, realistic, unromantic, this attitude looked at the facts and got the work done.

> We the last generation served India to the best of our ability, without any missionary spirit or feeling of dedication or devotion to a cause. We served India because it was our job and because we enjoyed it. Our Indian friends seemed to consider us sympathetic without being patronizing. We had little use for Englishmen who ceased to be English and tried from the best of motives to become Indian in outlook and habits. We believed we could best serve our own country and India by remaining ourselves. When Indian and British interest conflicted we took the view which we thought right for India. We were convinced that the British had brought great benefits to India but at the end it was time for us to leave. India was our life. That life was in part harsh and unattractive and cut us off from our own country. But it was in the main rewarding. We were content we had chosen it. Romantics and realists, visionaries and pragmatists, theorists and grass-root-wallahs, traders and statesmen – the British Raj was founded on them all.

* * * * *

Part IV

Sir William Jones (1746-94)

It is paradoxical but true that it is because of Macaulay that I write in English and communicate with other Indians in English. But it is because of William Jones that I know India. Macaulay introduced Indians to the culture and philosophy of the West but William Jones awakened Indians to their great heritage and introduced the world to the civilization of India.

Mohandas Moses

32

Tribute to Sir William Jones

William Jones may be considered as the greatest gift of Britain to India. Seldom has one man, coming from a very different civilization done so much for the understanding of another civilization. Jones' contribution was all the more extra-ordinary because at that time India was to the British a land that had been subjugated and exploited, oppressed and denigrated in the most offensive terms. At this juncture there appeared on the scene a man who was neither a rebel nor an outsider but a member of the Establishment sent by the British Government to be a judge in the Supreme Court, a brilliant and admired member of the intelligentsia comprising of Dr. Johnson, Edmund Burke, Oliver Goldsmith, a friend of aristocrats, son-in-law of a Bishop of the Church of England. He did not come to India to start a dialogue of civilization; his sole purpose was to save enough money to retire comfortably in the country with his beloved and accomplished wife and perhaps enter Parliament or continue with his Oriental studies with periodic forays to London.

India changed all that. With the vision of a great mind he realized very early the grandeur that lay beneath the poverty and despair, the superstitions and decadence, and the sullen servility of the defeated. Like a dedicated archaeologist he was determined to unearth the treasure of Indian civilization and make it known to the West.

He was already a renowned linguist and Oriental scholar; he had translated Persian works. The London literati called him Oriental Jones. The redoubtable Dr. Samuel Johnson had called him 'the most enlightened of men.' He did not require further accolades. So why did he have this all consuming desire to transmit the knowledge of India to Britain and the world? Was it motivated by a scholar's generosity? Or was it a *beau geste* of a member of the ruling class to a conquered people?

The first hint of his attitude can be gleaned by his action when he took charge as a judge in the Supreme Court of Calcutta. He made it clear almost on the first address to the jury that he wanted justice to be done, no matter who were the litigants. In order to administer justice to the Indian people he needed to know their laws and customs; he began to study Sanskrit and delve into ancient manuscripts, to understand and interpret the laws of Manu. Hence his dogged pursuit of compiling the ancient laws of the Hindus as well as the Muslims – the Digest that cost him his life. He wanted to be a new Justinian, certainly, but while the Byzantine Emperor gave laws to his own people, William Jones wanted justice for an unhappy alien race whose rights were being trampled upon by his own government and the East India Company that employed him. His study of Sanskrit and the rediscovery of ancient Indian literature revealed to the Western world India's splendid achievements. It was as momentous as the rediscovery of the classical world by Europeans in the fifteenth century. Europe could no longer look upon India as a barbarous land where they had brought civilization. And as in Europe, this rediscovery led to a renaissance within India. As the nineteenth century progressed William Jones' pioneering work began to gain momentum; Indians became aware of their national heritage. From this recognition sprang the demand for national self-determination.

William Jones, like many great men, was ahead of his time. His liberal views had delayed his appointment as a judge in India because neither Tories nor Whigs felt comfortable with his liberal ideas. Had he been appointed earlier and had been able to work with Warren Hastings, a great deal more would have been accomplished. Both were men of vision and foresight. Jones' plea for legal reforms was not taken up by men like Burke and Pitt who, while shouting themselves hoarse over about the welfare of Indians, did nothing to expedite the proposals that could have reformed the judiciary in India. In India his suggestions for improvements were blocked by petty men of limited intelligence such as Macpherson, Cornwallis and to some extent John Shore. William Jones, the best Englishman in India, was overlooked for appointment as Chief Justice; the post was given to a corrupt and indolent man who would 'cooperate' with the East India Company.

However, as Frederick Engels observed nothing can stop an idea once its time has come. It was in the very age of a callous colonialism that Europe produced men of wisdom and humanism. Jones saw two centuries before other Westerners that if the East and West were to enrich each other, it would have to be not through commerce but through exchange of ideas, mutual respect for each other's culture and traditions. He showed through his own conduct that 'to win hearts and minds' one had to set impeccable ethical standards.

The UNESCO charter speaks of building the defences of peace in the minds of men. It is as if we hear the voice of Sir William Jones speaking to the world across two troubled centuries. Empires have disappeared but the voice of a great man still echoes around us and shows the way for peace and harmony in a world torn by strife.

There have been many tributes to William Jones but two of them are particularly noteworthy. At the bicentenary birth anniversary of Sir William Jones, S.N. Mukherjee offered this homage: "The eternal mind of ancient Hellas clad in the toga of Imperial Rome and aligning itself with the spirit of eighteenth century Europe came to our country in the personality of Sir William Jones and acted as the golden wand which made us shake away the sleep of the ages."

Sir John Shore, Governor-General of India and biographer of William Jones, sums up the genius of Sir William Jones:

> In the short space of forty seven years, by the exertion of rare intellectual talents he acquired a knowledge of arts, sciences and languages which has seldom been equaled and perhaps never surpassed. If he did not attain the critical proficiency of a Parson or Parr in Grecian literature, yet his knowledge of it was most extensive and profound, and entitled him to a high rank in the first class of scholars, whilst as a philologist he could boast a universality in which he had no rival. His skill in the idioms of India, Persia and Arabia has never been equaled by any European; and his compositions on Oriental subjects display a taste which we seldom find in the writings of those who had preceded him in these tracts of literature.

F.W. Thomas, Professor, Boden Chair of Sanskrit, Oxford observed: "Endowed with an intelligence of rare serenity and informed with the wide philosophical culture of the eighteenth century". The genius of Sir William Jones, "the most enlightened of the sons of men," as Dr. Johnson said, "was ideally fitted to conceive the grand role which Asia had enacted in human history and its wealth of materials for the study of the arts and sciences".

Tartaj says, "A man who was acclaimed by one of his contemporaries on the continent as early as 1774 in the words of the classical Arabic as 'the incomparable one of his age and the most profound one of his time.'

33

The Long Journey from Portsmouth

"There is a tide in the affairs of men which taken at the flood leads to fortune" – *Julius Caesar*, Shakespeare

That tide in the life of Sir William Jones was when he sailed from Portsmouth on the 14th of April 1783 on the frigate 'Crocodile' for his long journey to India.

William Jones was a most unusual passenger. It was not the knighthood nor the judgeship that he obtained at the early age of thirty-five which set William Jones apart from the usual crowd of East India Company soldiers, clerks and merchants on board the ship. Jones did not have to travel to the East in search of fame. He was already acknowledged to be the foremost linguist in Europe and the leading Oriental scholar in England. He was a member of the newly formed Royal Society. Samuel Johnson to whose select Literary Club he belonged had called Jones "the most enlightened of the sons of men." A man such as this was a very rare passenger on an 'Indiaman'– a ship bound for India.

The year 1783 was an unusually eventful year in his life. It was the year in which he was knighted, a very young knight at the age of thirty-five. It was also the year in which he had been appointed to the long awaited judgeship of the Supreme Court Judicature of Bengal. It was the year in which he had married his beloved Anna Maria, the daughter of his old friend, the Bishop of St. Asaph. All these events had followed in swift succession; his feelings must have been tinged with regret as he looked back on the receding shores of England. He had sought a political career and high office in his own country but in an England where patronage and influence prevailed, the prizes he sought had been denied to him. His judgeship and his knighthood had come to him after six arduous and frustrating years of waiting. The road to Portsmouth for him had indeed been a long one.

Despite his prodigious intellect, his genius for languages, William Jones had never been a cloistered scholar. He had political ambitions but lacked political experience and was therefore disappointed in the naïve pursuit of power and position. He turned then to the profession of law where he excelled but once again without appropriate connections did not make the name or fortune he sought. He wanted to make a fortune and like many young Britons of the day considered India the best place to make an easy one. It is rather sad to read his correspondence where this brilliant young man puts up a brave front about his not-so-successful legal practice, and sadder still when the future greatest Indologist declares his intention to earn thirty thousand pounds in India and return home to procure a seat in Parliament.

And now here he was with his wife on the deck of the *Crocodile* seeing the receding shores of England. Great Orientalist that he was and critic of British society though he had become, he was a child, though an exotic one, of the England of his time as he had written in his *Ode to Liberty*. He could not have known as he looked back on the receding shores of England that he was looking at the loved shores of Albion for the last time.

The motives which drove the general run of passengers on board the ship to India were personal gain and commercial profit. Young Englishmen spurred on by the precedents of Governor Pitt and Robert Clive and by the visions of the vast fortunes which could be made by "shaking the pagoda tree" were willing to brave the long ocean journey, the rigours of the Indian climate and the ever present spectre of an early death. Edmund Burke painted a vivid picture of them when he said, "animated with the avarice of age and the impetuosity of youth, they roll in one after another, wave after wave; and there is nothing before the eyes of the native but an endless hopeless prospect of new birds of prey and passage with appetites continually renewing for a food that is continually wasting."

Though the scholarly Jones certainly did not belong to the rapacious breed described by his friend Burke, it must be confessed that the journey of William Jones to the East was inspired not by his interest in Oriental studies or by a desire to establish proper judicial institutions in India. Like the other young men on the *Crocodile*, William Jones went to India in search of a fortune. In a letter written in 1778 to his friend, George John Shore who was to be Governor-General of India at the turn of the eighteenth century, he said frankly "and it shall be my good fortune to return to England at the age of seven or eight and thirty years with thirty thousand pounds in my chest. I shall then be able to concur with you and other friends of liberty and virtue in defending our Constitution, amending our laws and encouraging letters."

These letters seem to reflect a premature cynicism in one so young. They also seem to be inconsistent with the idealism that inspires all William Jones' writing on politics and constitutional reform. We have to evaluate these remarks against the context of the milieu in which they were written and we have also to look at the experience of William Jones that gave rise to these remarks.

Jones combined a touching blend of naivete and worldliness. As tutor to Lord Althorp, son of the Earl of Spencer, and sister of the dazzling Georgiana, Duchess of Devonshire, he had been able to study the intricate structure of patronage and political corruption on which the edifice of Parliament rested and he had early come to the conclusion that to a young man like himself with no family connections, the doors of Parliament were closed without a personal fortune. And it was in quest of this fortune that Jones like other young men of his time left the verdant shores of England for the marshy plains of Bengal.

Notwithstanding what Schopenhauer said of the supremacy of the human will, shaping of destiny is never entirely in our hands. It is destiny that had prepared a very different script for William Jones and it was in consonance with this journey to immortality that he was on his way to India.

34

The England of William Jones

> People bought land who were peculiarly susceptible to considerations of social prestige and political power. Among them were a few large merchants namely Chairmen of the East India Company, who went in for politics; but most of the newcomers were either in some way connected with government or were judges who desired to have that significance in society which only possession of land could give. They bought up blocks of land in different parts of the country, bought out some of the surrounding gentry, sought admissions and in many cases the manorial rights of Parliamentary boroughs. They were not so much investing their money in land as buying up the perquisites of a social class, the undisturbed control of the life of a neighborhood. When they looked over the fields they wanted to see their own land and nothing but their own land. The hatred of the small squires for the great lords, whether old or new, who were buying them out is the theme of many a contemporary play (G.M. Trevelyan, *Social History of England*).

Trevelyan's description of eighteenth century England in *History Review* is vivid:

> Country-house grandees filled their rural palaces with pictures from Italy, furniture from France and editions of Italian, French or Latin authors which they not only collected but read. There were philosopher lords like the third Earl of Shaftesbury, scholar statesmen like Montagu, and the greatest of all antiquarian collectors, Robert Harley.
>
> Thanks to the East India Company's great ships not only tea but coffee was now a usual drink among the wealthier people. Every respectable landowner had his favourite coffee house. The coffee house occupied the position now occupied by the Club but in a more cheap and informal manner and with a great admission of strangers. In days when men stood much on their rank, it had a leveling influence.

> London was governed by her own freely elected magistrates; policed in so far as she was policed at all by her own constables; guarded by her own militia and rendered formidable to the neighbouring seat of government by the largest and least manageable mob in the island.
>
> In the England of Dr. Johnson during the years 1740-80 we find a generation of men wholly characteristic of the eighteenth century ethos, a society with a mental outlook of its own, self favoured, self judged and self approved and freed from the disturbing passions of the past and not yet troubled by the anxieties about a very different future which was soon to be brought upon the scene by the Industrial and the French Revolutions. It was an age of aristocracy and liberty, of the rule of law and the absence of reform; of individual initiative and institutional decay; of Latitudinarianism above and Wesleyianism below and the growth of humanitarian and philanthropic feeling and endeavour, of creative vigour in all their trades and arts that serve and adorn the life of man. It is a classical age, that is to say, an age of unchallenged assumptions when the philosophers of the streets such as Dr. Johnson had ample leisure to moralize on the human scene in the happy belief that the state of society and the modes of thought to which they are accustomed are not mere passing aspects of an ever shifting kaleidoscope, but permanent habitation, the final outcome of reason and experience. Such an age does not aspire to progress though it may in fact be progressing, it regards itself not as selling out but having arrived. And therefore the men of this classical age look back with a sense of kinship to the far off Ancient World. The upper class regarded the Greeks and Romans as honorary Englishmen, their precursors in liberty and culture.
>
> To the typical men of the period of Blackstone, Gibbon, and Burke, England appeared to be the best country possible in an imperfect world requiring only to be left alone where providence and the Revolution of 1688 had placed her. However Hogarth, Fielding and Smollet and the Philanthropists saw the defects of the society of their time; they exposed the evils as unsparingly as Dickens.

William Jones also saw the defects of his time very clearly. He looked forward to Calcutta but also to his return when he could play the part of reformer.

What strikes one as bizarre is that while the English legal system itself needed reform and rationalization, it was imposed on India, a society that had its own ancient laws. Blackstone held an uncritical view of English laws which he passed on to William Jones. Jeremy Bentham offered his 'first blast' to Blackstone in 1776 in "Fragment on Government".

William Jones showed his concern for insolvent debtors who had to drag on their wretched existence in prison. He wrote: "I have visited the prison in disguise and though it is much neater and more comfortable than I expected to find it, yet I deplore the fate of the poor wretches who must pass their hot months in it." He suggested law reforms similar to England's laws.

Two Englishmen produced two classics of the modern age; Gibbon published his epic *The Decline and Fall of the Roman Empire* and Adam Smith inaugurated the discipline of Economics with *The Wealth of Nations.* It is amusing that the celebrated historian lamented in his Autobiography that he had not "embraced the lucrative pursuits of the law or of trade, the chances of civil office or India, (sic) adventure or even the fat slumbers of the Church."

It was a society which with all its faults was brilliant above and stable below. Though separated by eighteen centuries, the flavour of eighteenth-century England reminds one of the Ujjain of Kalidasa's time. Perhaps it is this familiar flavour which drew William Jones to the poet of that bygone age.

35

The Making of William Jones

For a fuller understanding of the man William Jones was when he set out for India in 1783 and the reasons which sent him there, we need to know more of his early life. We owe most of the biographical details we have to the *Life of Sir William Jones* written in 1799 by John Shore, first Baron of Teignmouth, who by then had served as Governor-General of India between 1793-1798.

Lord Teignmouth tells us that the parent of Jones' father – also named William Jones – came from a family of yeomen or 'little farmers' from the island of Anglesey in Wales. This William Jones' father published a treatise on navigation, and was acquainted with such luminaries as Sir Isaac Newton, Halley the famed astronomer, Dr. Mead and Dr. Samuel Johnson. His learning brought him to the notice of Lord Chief Justice Hardwicke who made him Secretary for the Peace. We are also told that the origin of the family of Jones on the maternal side had been traced to the ancient princes and chieftains of Wales. Teignmouth adds with somewhat heavy handed humour that

> with whatever delight however the Cambrian genealogist might pursue the line of his ancestry, a barren catalogue of uncouth names would furnish no entertainment to the reader. I shall only transcribe from the list a single and remarkable name in one of the collateral branches, that of William Dreiganaian, who died in one thousand five hundred and eighty one at the age of one hundred and five years with a note annexed to it, that by three wives he had thirty six children, seven more by two concubines and that eighty of his issue during his life, were living in the parish of Tregaian in Anglesey.

Jones' maternal grandfather was notable in a somewhat less spectacular fashion. This was his grandfather George Nix, the cabinet-maker in London, the rival of Chippendale, and who from "the honest and pleasant frankness of his conversation, was admitted to the tables of the great."

It is in this family that William Jones was born on 28th September 1747, on the feast of St. Michael. Jones' father died when the boy was only three. His capable mother Mary took up his education and training. She is described by her husband as "virtuous without blemish, generous without extravagance, frugal but not niggard, cheerful but not giddy, close but not sullen, ingenious but not conceited, of spirit but not passionate, of her company cautious and in friendship trusty." The boy was fortunate in that his mother knew algebra and trigonometry and was a born teacher. At the age of four, the boy William could read English fluently and could recite Shakespeare. In 1753 he entered Harrow. He was bullied by the older boys but shamed them into silence when he shone as a scholar, mastering Latin and Greek, French and Italian, Hebrew and a little Arabic. At the age of twelve he had translated into English verse several of the epistles of Ovid, all the pastorals of Virgil and had composed drama on the story of Miliager. His master in the subject at Harrow declared that Jones knew more Greek than himself and was better acquainted with the idiom in that language. While still at Harrow, young William acquired knowledge of French and Italian.

Jones had that sine qua non for proficiency in linguistics – a remarkably retentive memory. This is illustrated by an anecdote recounted by his biographer Lord Teignmouth, of how, in his twelfth year of his choice he and his school friends decided to stage Shakespeare's *Tempest* and how on not being able to readily procure a copy of the play, Jones wrote it for them correctly from memory. It is also mentioned that Jones assumed the part of Prospero. Time would show that Prospero the scholar 'rapt in secret studies', the archetypal teacher of language, was an appropriate role for the young Jones to play. A warning against the insensitivities of colonialism is one of the themes of the *Tempest* and this makes the choice of the play prophetic because Jones in his career in India battled ceaselessly against the cultural obtuseness of eighteenth century Europeans in the Oriental context. The choice of the play is interesting because it is the only one of Shakespeare's plays which shows a game of chess played on stage. Jones was a passionate chess player himself and in his seventeenth year wrote a 360 stanza poem to his invented muse of chess, *Caissa.*

At seventeen Jones had to choose between the Inns of Court and University; he was a prodigious scholar and linguist and the portals of Oxford seemed like a natural destination. At the age of eighteen he was preparing for publication of Greek and Latin compositions including a comedy on the language and measures of Aristophanes.

It was natural that he should gravitate towards University College of Oxford University which was famous for Oriental scholarship. The trend was set by Edward Pococke, who was appointed the first professor of Arabic in 1636. William Jones learned Arabic from a Syrian named Mirza whom he had met in London and whom he brought back to Oxford. In 1768 Jones had mastered both Persian and Arabic and had become well known as an Orientalist. He was deeply impressed by Saadi's *Gulistan.* He graduated that year with a degree in Bachelor of Arts. Jones rejected the suggestion of a legal career on the ground that law books were written in poor Latin! He was only of twenty-one years. In between he studied Milton who was Jones' hero whom he called "the most perfect scholar ... sublimest poet that our country has produced." During his brilliant academic career in Oxford he established the foundations of his reputation as the greatest Orientalist of his time and a linguist whose span covered twenty-eight languages. Eminently suited to the academic life, Jones would probably have pursued an academic career at Oxford had not the judgeship of Bengal come to him.

By 1765 Mary Jones was finding it difficult to defray the educational expenses of her son. This forced Jones to support himself by taking up the position of tutor to Lord George John Althorp, who later became First Lord of the Admiralty. Jones took pleasure in teaching his young charge Cicero, Blackstone, Locke and Euclid, while he made full use of the excellent library at the Spencer estate at Althorp. His taste for classical literature led him to love what he called 'ancient wisdom' which he believed found expression in contemporary Whig philosophy and the English Constitution. While on a three week visit to a Spa along with the Spencer family he learnt German while at the same time "finding leisure to participate" all the amusements of his place. Along with his pupil he learnt dancing. It was during these holidays in Europe that he began studying Arabic, Persian, Spanish, Portuguese, and even Chinese. When in 1768 Jones published his translation of

Rousseau's *History of Nadir Shah,* and a *Grammar of Persian Language* in 1771, his reputation as an Orientalist was firmly established. He was drawn to subjects beyond the Western literary horizon. While translating Petrarch's *Canzoni,* he wrote *Commentaries on Asian Poetry* and began a tragic drama on Sultan Suleiman the Magnificent and his son Mustapha who was blinded by a vicious concubine. He picked up the keys to Chinese and was able to read Confucius in translation at the royal library in Paris.

Jones expected that serving in the propinquity of such an influential Whig family as the Spencers would be an advantage in his search for office. He gradually became more and more disillusioned with the aristocratic milieu in which he moved. He was also frustrated by his somewhat menial role in the Spencer household. Back in Oxford he concentrated on Asiatic studies; he translated the second *Ode on Hafiz,* and dreamt of an appointment at the British Embassy in Constantinople so that he could absorb more of Asian literature. Though nothing materialized in the way of an appointment, the Ode made his name. The literary critic Irwin describes William Jones significantly in one of his poems as the "British Hafeez". William Jones was described as having "the imaginative glory of Milton, the picturesque phraseology of Collins and foreshadows Shelley." Jones' translation of Asian poetry marks a landmark in that it revealed to the West the Eastern outlook of life. The idea of *kismet,* the recurrent motif in *Seven Poems* set up epochs in later English poetry. In Jones' translation of *A Persian Song of Hafeez,* he says:

Speak not of fate: ah! change the theme
And of odious talk of wine
Talk of the flowers that round us bloom
Tis all a cloud tis all a dream
To love and joy thy thought sublime
Nor hope to pierce the sacred bloom

A Persian Song of Hafiz first appeared in his *Grammar* and was later published in his *Poems,* gave him a place among the minor eighteenth century poets. But it would be a mistake to portrait Jones as a Romantic poet. In the same volume that he published *'Persian Song',* he also published his *Ode to Petrarch – Laura, Elegy to Petrarch* and *Arcadia* which demonstrates the eighteenth century neo-classical spirit. (Edward Fitzgerald, the celebrated translator of the *Rubayyat of Omar Khayyam,* was initially inspired by William Jones. Indeed echoes of Jones' work may be found in Fitzgerald.)

Jones continued to compose verses on Asian themes. He wrote a poem *Solima* about an Arab princess, and *The Palace of Fortune* based on an Indian fable and *The Seven Fountains*, a Syrian tale. While translating Petrarch, Jones discovered the similarity of styles between Arab poetic forms and Petrarch's sonnets and realized that these literary styles had come to Italy through the Moors of Spain. Inspired by this knowledge and smitten by Arab letters, he began at the age of twenty-one his *Commentaries on Asian Poetry*. Here he says: "It is probable that poetry was originally no more than a strong and animated expression of the human passions of joy and grief, love and hate, admiration and anger, sometimes pure and mixed, sometimes variously modified and combined."

Though William Jones took little interest in Indian affairs until his actual appointment as a judge came, he had read widely on India's cultural heritage from Herbelot's *Bibliotheque Orientale*, Dow's *History of Hindostan*, Robert Orme's *Wars in India*, Persian works of India – *Babur Nama, Akbar Nama* and Hyder Ali's work on Kashmir that contained pre-Muslim history of Kashmir largely taken from Kalhana's *Rajataragini*. Pre-Muslim India was at that time admittedly a "dark period for him". He expresses the view that though India has produced the fables of Bidpar and invented the game of chess she had no poetry. Mughals carried Persian poetry to India and the Indian poets in his day composed their verses in imitation of them. At this stage Jones was looking at India through Persian eyes. His considerable erudition in Sanskrit literature was still very much in the future. (*On the Poetry of Eastern Nations*)

At Oxford, William Jones wished to make Asia more acceptable to Europe. In his presentation of Nadir Shah and his introduction of the Persian poet he wrote – "The poets of Asia have as much genius as ourselves. They have a Homer in Firdaus, a Virgil in Hafiz and some of the Persian songs have a striking resemblance to the Sonnets of Petrarch."

According to historian S.N. Mukherjee, "William Jones had all the qualities of subjectivity, emotion, reference to uncommon names and far away places which appealed to poets like Southey and Byron."

Jones, like his German literary contemporary Herder, was fascinated by world literature. Coming across Confucian philosophy at the Royal Library in Paris, he set to work on the theory of education as perceived by Eastern philosophers.

While studying at Oxford William Jones was branded as a Radical because of his two works, *Ode to Liberty* and *Ad Libertatem Carmen*, and his opposition to the suppression of the Gordon riots. He felt monarchy should be limited in powers and slavery should be abolished. In 1780, when the parliamentary seat for Oxford University fell vacant he applied as a candidate. However he did not get the support of the Radicals. Sensing the mood of the electorate he withdrew his candidature a day before the election. The only encouragement came from Mrs. Elizabeth Montague, a lady from fashionable society, who felt that the voters ought to elect him.

This was undoubtedly a period of great personal bitterness – his long working for the judgeship in Bengal for four years and his failure in the Oxford election. Reaction set in when he felt that "England had no freedom." This feeling of bitterness found vent in a letter to Benjamin Franklin on 17th September 1781. "All virtue and public spirit are dead in this country. We have the shadow of a free constitution but live in truth under the substance of despotism." He also wrote to Georgiana, Duchess of Devonshire, in October 1782 – "In the great orchestra of politics I find so many musicians out of humour and instruments out of time that I am more tormented by such dissonance than the man in Hogarth's print and I am more desirous than ever of being transported to a distance of five thousand leagues from all this fatal discord." Jones was not a votary of the pleasure-seeking life led by persons in aristocratic circles and liked to think of himself as "a philosopher among courtiers." Nor was he aware that his exodus was imminent. In 1781 Jones wrote to Edward Gibbon: "Any system is purely speculative and has no relation to my seat on the bench in India where I should hardly think of instructing Gentoos with the maxims of the Athenians."

Thanks to the Spencers, young Jones had acquired a distinguished circle of intellectual friends, of whom one was the Hungarian diplomat and Orientalist, Count Reviczi. It was the beginning of a long friendship based on an abiding interest in Asian civilizations. The Count's interest in India and the Orient was taken up in the next centuries by fellow Hungarians such as Sandor Csoma de Koros, Armenius Vamberry, and later Aurel Stein.

Amidst his scholarship one pastime remained with him throughout his life – the game of chess. His lasting attachment to the game found expression in two forms, both of which bore the distinctive hallmark of his unique personality. One was the poem *Caissa* which he wrote when he was still a schoolboy at Harrow. The other was his essay on *The Indian Game of Chess*, which he wrote towards the end of his life in Calcutta for *Asiatic Researches*. While the first reveals the awesome precocity of young Jones, the second is an example of the depth and range of his later years.

Jones' idol was Cicero. And like Cicero he wished to be a leader of opinion and a guide in the affairs of men. In the Whig milieu of his time one needed to cut a figure in society. And for this William Jones realized very early that one needed the advantages of either family or wealth. He had neither. He was not like Burke and Sheridan whose golden tongues opened all doors including those of Parliament. Samuel Johnson 'the great champion of literature' of his time had called Jones the 'most enlightened of the sons of men.' But enlightenment was not passport enough to Parliament. A fortune was needed. Financial considerations made him turn to law once more.

Finding that his connection with the Devonshire and Spencer families was not leading to any advantage, he parted company with them. The ostensible cause for difference was over the education of the young Lord Althorp. He pleaded with the boy's mother to send Lord Althorp back to public school but the mother felt her son was not strong enough. Nor did they agree upon Jones' plan for the young aristocrat's education. Jones resigned from the tutor's post and left the world of sinecure and patronage but remained on cordial terms with both Lord Althorp and his sister Duchess Georgiana. In fact during his eleven years in India, not a single month went by without a letter from Jones to Georgiana.

In the meantime the literati of London had discovered William Jones, the versatile scholar, linguist, poet and commentator. He was invited to join as a Fellow of the Royal Society by the celebrated Dr. Samuel Johnson who was the moving spirit of the Society. He also joined the Turk's Head club in Gerard Street in Soho that had been founded by Burke, Johnson and Joshua Reynolds. He was respected for his scholarship, his modesty and linguistic genius. He met Samuel Johnson at these gatherings who later presented Warren Hastings with a grammar of the Persian language. Jones persuaded both the Bishop of Asaph and Lord Althorp to join the Club on the grounds that: "There is no branch of knowledge concerning which we could not give the world good information." Here were Oriental scholars such as William Chambers, Francis Gladwin, Charles Hamilton. But most important of all was the presence of Charles Wilkins, the Sanskrit scholar, the future translator of the great *Bhagavad Gita*. Jones decided to learn Sanskrit and began to dream his Indian dreams.

Between 1770 and 1783 William Jones wrote a number of books – at least nine – connected with Orientalism. His fame as an Orientalist enabled him to become a member of Johnson's exclusive literary club in 1773 and a fellow of the Royal Society of London.

In 1773 Jones was a lawyer at Middle Temple. In 1774, William Jones was called to the Bar and in the following year he was appointed Commissioner of Bankrupts – a dismal office with Dickensian overtones. He wrote about this in later years. The work was dreary and uninspiring and in a moment of despair he felt like renouncing his literary and linguistic pursuits. It is a matter of interest that Macaulay almost fifty years later was to occupy the same, though somewhat travanoguled, office. Macaulay was also incidentally responsible for winding up this office on grounds of redundancy.

When Jones' attempt to enter Parliament ended in failure he applied for a Judgeship in Calcutta that came after a long period of waiting. He had knocked long at the doors of patrons. Speaking on a point of delicate serupulosity of moral conduct Jones said to one Mr. Langton, "Men of harder minds than ours will do many things from which you and I would shrink; yet Sir they will perhaps do more good in life than we. But let us try to help one another. If there be a wrong twist it may be set right. It is not probable that two persons can be wrong in the same way." (This could apply to Warren Hastings who was undoubtedly a man of harder mind.)

Jones' brilliance and fame made him a sought after guest at parties and receptions given by aristocratic hostesses like the Duchess of Devonshire, Lady Lucan, Lady Henrietta Bessborough, and his admirer Mrs. Elizabeth Montague. Men of letters and politicians such as Dr. Johnson, Horace Walpole, and the actress Fanny Burney were proud to have his acquaintance. A contemporary, Thomas Maurice, said of him, "To know Jones was to know the whole literary world, so exalted was his character, so anxiously sought after was his company." Young ladies swarmed around the handsome and eligible bachelor. He enjoyed the social life of London – the dancing, riding, fencing with the broadsword that were the transient pastimes of a young man with an eye on 'cutting a figure' in Georgian London.

His heart however was already engaged – to the refined, accomplished Anna Maria Shipley whom he had met in 1766 while he was immersed in scholarly pursuits at Oxford. She was the daughter of the Bishop of Asaph, and a relation of Duchess Georgiana of Devonshire. The Bishop was an intellectual and a covert radical; his son William was known for his firebrand views. Through him young Jones came to meet other radicals and supporters of the French Philosophers who were the catalysts of the French revolution. He also met the American revolutionary Benjamin Franklin who ironically had been well received in the court of King Louis XVI. Franklin was warm in his praise of Anna Maria but William Jones was given to understand that the erudite Anna Maria was affianced to someone else. This had saddened him but he refused to consider a marriage of convenience that was customary among the upper classes in Europe. Anna Maria belonged to an affluent family whereas his fortune had yet to be made. He wrote to his former pupil Lord Althorp in 1781: "I have ever abhorred it and solemnly declare that I would not marry a woman whom I did not love with the truest affection if she had all the mines of Peru and the diamonds of Golconda for her portion."

Jones' last years in England were not successful; he did not do well as a lawyer and suffered financial problems. Though he was not a cloistered scholar and enjoyed the company of kindred souls, his political aspirations were not supported by experience. His fervent hope that the Spencer and Devonshire families would launch him in society and politics did not materialize despite his scholarship, reputation as a notable Orientalist and a formidable authority on English law.

The idea of going to India germinated in his mind as early as 1778 when he wrote to the historian Edward Gibbon of his desire for financial security and plans for using the funds for pursuing a political career. There was an unquestioned assumption that without a personal fortune, no position in politics or society was possible. The situation had changed in the time of Macaulay who was already a member of parliament when he left for India.

Jones turned his sights once more to India; in a letter to George John Spencer he mentioned: "A noble offer that has been made to me by the noblest of men among whom I may not only plead causes but make laws and write them on the bank of my own river and under my own oak." He received the appointment for judgeship in 1783. It is once again a matter of interest that it was for the precise sum of L30,00 that the young Macaulay also set sail for India.

It may be asked how he reconciled his political views with the Indian situation. In England maintenance of laws is the aggregate will of the people and the state is made of the whole people and rulers are but the servants of the people. Dean Tucker posed this question in his sequel to *Dialogues*. "I wish to know whether he himself allows the consequence of his own doctrine? Doth he or doth he not permit the poor enslaved Gentoos and the plundered Indians to dispute his authority and disobey his commands by telling him to his face that they never chose him to be judge of their country?"

One may ask here how much did the young Jones owe for his theory of the General Will to Rousseau? Was he reconciling this anomaly which a man of his sincerity must undoubtedly have recognized by becoming more Indian than most Indians and a greatest scholar than most? There were no such misgivings in Macaulay's mind.

The search for a fortune in India was the usual motivation but to picture William Jones in the role of potential *Nabob* would be patently wrong portraiture. His friend Johnson was fond of quoting a Spanish proverb: "He that desires the wealth of the Indies must take the wealth of the Indies with him." There was no other passenger on the *Crocodile* except William Jones of whom this was true. For even before he set sail for India, the cultural riches of the Orient were very much part of his intellectual treasury.

36

The Literary and Political Scene in London

William Jones was influenced by the life and works of Cicero and imitated his style of correspondence and modelled his life on the Roman man of letters. In his historical writing Jones tried to follow the rules of the perfect historian that he learned from Cicero in his book, *On Oration.* Cicero believed that the historian should not only be free from bias but should also be a shrewd judge of all public personalities and should write elegantly and copiously. Jones realized that this was just an ideal to which all the works human genius are constantly tending, though like the logarithmic spiral they never reached the point which they are infinitely approaching.

William Jones believed that the essence of history was truth – which most historians do not possess nor the qualities mentioned by Cicero. Some of them are great and judicious, some bold and impartial, others polished and elegant but none of them seemed to have possessed all those qualities in a perfect combination of which is required in the character of an accomplished historian. Even about the accounts of Herodotus William Jones had his doubts. As for Thucydides the facts might be authentic but the language was poor. William Jones thought that Tacitus's style was defective. Voltaire pleased him most – "His style is lively and spirited, his descriptions animated and striking, his remarks always ingenious, often deep but he is inclined to un-necessary brevity and his wit is often ill-placed. He cannot give an abstract of Newtonion philosophy without interspersing it with strokes of humour." Jones was more interested in the essence of history than in facts.

William Jones read voraciously and acquainted himself with the writings of Diderot and the Encyclopaedists. Many modern scholars have considered Jones as a precursor of the Romantic movement. One senses the attraction of the sophisticated being for the simple life, a yearning for the primitive and a search for the noble savage in his early writings on the Arabs. He admired the Arabs because they had been able to retain the simplicity of their ancestors for three thousand years. Moreover they had never been subdued by another nation. Arabia he claimed was the only country left in the world that was simple, free and happy especially since the Mughal conquest of Kashmir. The Abbasid Arab poets with their nomadic life, violent loves and thrilling adventures and their 'dramatic pastoral poems' charmed him. The passion for the simple tribal life is understandable in November 1780 when Jones had lost all chances to win a seat in Parliament. "In these rambles in the wilds of Asia I soften the anguish which I feel whenever I reflect on the melancholy times in which we live." (Jones' letter to E. Cartwright).

Jones' attraction for the free and happy Arabs could only have been an intellectual fancy. As an eighteenth century Western man he could not love the irrational. Nor did he advocate emulation of the Arabs by Europeans. Though Jones had read Rousseau's works and found them "wonderfully absurd", he did not find the life of the *bon savage* attractive. Following William Jones four decades later, Pushkin, the greatest Russian poet, became captive to the enchantment of the East. The simple and unspoiled people of the Caucusus who had recently come under Russian rule formed the theme of his many poems and plays.

William Jones had great respect for Dr. Samuel Johnson and for his great achievement in compiling the English Dictionary. Jones observed that "as great men of antiquity such as Scipio Africanus had an epithet added to their names, in consequence of some celebrated action so my illustrious friend was called Dictionary Johnson from that wonderful achievement of genius and labour his dictionary of the English which I contemplate with more and more admiration." There were other names and epithets such as Hermes Harris, Pliny Melworth, Persian Jones, Demosthenes Taylor, Abbysinian Bruce, Leonidas Oliver, Hesiod Cooke and Corsica Boswell.

Dr. Johnson survives in history as 'the emperor of good company.' It was said that Dr. Johnson never had a friend whom he did not at times assault or snub in an outrageous fashion. His literary circle comprised of an extraordinary variety of persons. His erudition and wit made him 'an idol of the Club and the tavern as well as the elegant drawing rooms of the nobility. He was at once the perfect companion of the profligate, the toper, the scholar and the fashionable lady.' His enduring achievement however lay elsewhere.

Samuel Johnson was a celebrated lexicographer and literary critic. It is he who proclaimed Shakespeare as England's greatest writer. Johnson was the son of a bookseller; his home was not a happy one but he had "great powers of enjoyment". He was a sickly child, studied at Lichfield Grammar School where he excelled in Latin. He acquired his doctorate early. Johnson was an ugly man who suffered from scrofula and watery eyes. His ill-fitting clothes were not always clean and he delighted in crumpled bed linen.

Johnson's greatest contribution was the compilation of the English dictionary. He also excelled in 'engaging descriptions'. He was known for his quickness, irony and humour. He was a Conservative in politics who accepted class distinctions but he hated the slave trade with equal fervour. He was against imperialism and overseas empires and felt that order at home was more important. Though a conventional Christian, he called the Old Testament a form "of threats and promises." He loved London and declared in a memorable phrase "when a man is tired of London he is tired of life."

Despite his posturing and apparent arrogance, Johnson's great biographer Boswell observed that Johnson "never hesitates to appear in a humiliating light."

Soon after his return to London in February 1764 Dr. Johnson founded the Club which had existed but without a name. The title bestowed was Literary Club. Sometimes they met at the Turks's Head tavern in Gerard Street in Soho once every week and continued their conversation till very late hours. After about ten years of its existence the members decided to meet together and dine once a fortnight during the meeting of Parliament. The original tavern having been converted into a private house, the members moved to various places and finally settled down at Parsloes in St. James's street. A brilliant cluster of men were its members; Sir Joshua Reynolds, Dr. Johnson, Edmund Burke, Oliver Goldsmith, Sir John Hawkins, Adam Smith, Richard Garrick, Bishop Shipley of St. Asaph, James Fox, Richard Sheridan, Edward Gibbon, William Jones, Dr. Burney, Lord Spencer, Lord Ivean, Lord Palmerston, the Bishop of Peterborough, the Duke of Leeds, the Bishop of Salisbury, and of course James Boswell the chronicler of the times.

Hannah More describes how Boswell became drunk at Bishop Shipley's: "I was heartily disgusted with Mr. Boswell who came upstairs after dinner disordered with wine and addressed me in a manner which drew from me a sharp rebuke, for which I fancy he will not easily forgive me". This episode has a distinctly Wodehousian flavour; the Bishop's house, the gilded youth, the prim spinster.

Burke, Fox and Sheridan who were the Literary Club members were also the severest critics of Hastings and who later mounted the campaign for his impeachment. Johnson himself harboured anti-Whig sentiments. But William Jones nursed no prejudices against Warren Hastings on this account. They later became neighbours in Alipore and took a momentous initiative in the promotion of Indology.

Another luminary of the Literary Club was Richard Garrick. He was originally destined for law but became a wine merchant. He received a legacy of L 1000 from an uncle with which he set himself up in trade. However, not being a merchant by bent of mind, he lost much of his legacy in trade. The stage offered him an alternative career. He was aged twenty-four when he captured London with his performance of Richard III at Goodman's Field where before long he had a dozen dukes to see him. The poet Alexander Pope was among the most enthusiastic of his auditors, declaring that he was the greatest actor the world had ever seen.

Richard Brindsley Sheridan, an eminent eighteenth century Englishman, was author of the plays *The Rivals* (1775) and *School for Scandal* (1777) and was also a member of the Club. He was Under Secretary for Foreign Affairs and Secretary to the Treasury.

Oliver Goldsmith was as, if not more, famous than Sheridan. He wrote *She Stoops to Conquer*. By 1773 this play had already found a place in English drama. In 1776, the year of the Declaration of American Independence, Edward Gibbon began writing *The Decline and Fall of the Roman Empire* and would complete it in 1788, a year before the outbreak of the French Revolution.

During this period William Jones was in close correspondence with Burke, the fiery orator from whom Jones would later turn away. But in the late 1770s they were friends. Burke supported William Jones in his attempts to secure a judicial appointment in Bengal. Though they were friends, Jones did not give wholehearted support to Burke on India, as if intuitively anticipating the conflict that waited in the future between Burke and Hastings.

The Bishop of St. Aphas joined the literary persons now and then. "He was like other Chaplains looking for a vacancy. But that is not peculiar to the clergy. I remember that when I was into the army after the battle of Lateldt the officers grumbled that no general was killed."

On the question of whether Judges who went to India should be permitted to engage in trade Johnson maintained that they might "for why should not judges get riches as well as those who deserve them less?" Johnson's biographer Boswell said they should have sufficient salaries and have nothing to take off their attention from the affairs of the public. Boswell showed more sagacity than his master. There is no record of whether William Jones was present during the discussions.

After Jones was made Commissioner of Bankrupts in 1776 and was offered a Judgeship in India by Lord Bathhurst in 1778, he listened carefully to the debates on India in Parliament and read up about India. Burke invited him to discuss the Bengal Bill and said "the natives of the East to whose literature you have done so much justice are particularly under your protection for their rights." Like many Englishmen of his age Jones had little sympathy with the East India Company and shared the general suspicion that British rule in India might corrupt "freedom loving Britons". This led Horace Walpole to remark about William Jones that he was "a staunch Whig but very wrong headed".

On Sunday 10th October 1979 the conversation having turned to the prevailing practice of going to the East Indies in quest of wealth, Johnson said, "A man had better have ten thousand pounds at the end of ten years passed in England than twenty thousand at the end of ten years passed in India because you must compute what you give for money: and a man who has lived ten years in India has given up ten years of social comfort and all those advantages which arise from living in England."

William Jones obviously did not think so but Johnson proved to be more than true in the case of William Jones who gave up not only social comfort but life itself.

37
A Brush with Rebels

A group of extremists comprising of John Wilkes, Richard Price, John Cartwright, John Jebb, Charles Lennox, the third Duke of Richmond, who advocated both Universal Suffrage and annual Parliament, sought to begin a new movement. They appealed for the restoration of their natural rights and to share in the legislature. They identified the British struggle against tyranny with the American efforts for independence. Most of the extremists belonged to the Society for Constitutional Transformation which was founded by John Cartwright in April 1780 to propagate the cause of Parliamentary reform. They considered themselves the "real or honest" Whigs carrying on the tradition of fighting against tyranny and for toleration, individual freedom and natural rights. The ideas were shaped according to the basic tenets set out by the seventeenth century political thinkers and by the political experience of the civil war and the 'Glorious Revolution' of 1688.

The school boy Jones who was once brutally punished by a sadistic master grew up to fear uncontrolled power in one person. William Jones wrote to John Shore that "distrust in power is the very nerve of wisdom". But one may ask how did Jones reconcile these ideals with the new despotism of British rule in India and dual rule in Bengal. "Despotism compounded with despotism," as Burke commented.

William Jones came to know the radicals at Bishop Shipley's house who were friends of parliamentary reform and the American cause. Jones was not a formal member of any reform organization until 1782 when he was elected honorary member of Society for Constitutional Transformation. He was in close touch with Cartwright and Burke. He was a friend of Benjamin Franklin whom he used to meet in Paris when he travelled with the Spencer family. With Price and Priestley, Jones shared political and religious views. William Jones earned a place in the history of Reform Movement and history of ideas with his "popular pamphlet" *The Principles of Government*. In this pamphlet Jones advocated active participation of citizens in State affairs, and the sanctity of people's choice in formation of legislative branch of government. Ten thousand copies of this pamphlet were printed and is one of the most influential books on Constitutional reforms.

Another member of the enlightened circle, Reverend William Shipley, Dean of St. Asaph, was friend of William Jones and later became his brother-in-law. William Shipley was prosecuted by the Sheriff of Wiltshire but was acquitted of charges of publishing a libelous pamphlet. Thus inspired, William Jones published *Dialogue* which is in the form of a Socratic dialogue between a scholar and a peasant about Parliamentary reforms.

Jones declared that the State consists of a whole people and the law is the aggregate of the will of people and not the wish of a sovereign. "I differ from Blackstone – he defines law as a rule prescribed by a superior. I define it as the work of the whole community as far it can be collected with convenience."

Jones criticized Blackstone not on utilitarian grounds as did Gibbon and Bentham but on the final nature of authority in a society. He disagreed with Blackstone when he said character of civil law could only be guaranteed by a self-perpetuating sovereign to which all men had agreed. Men in civil society cannot live without a supreme power as has been shown by Hobbes. Jones agreed with Locke and the theory of social contract which stated that the State is governed by laws that have been handed through the ages as a heritage from forefathers whose wisdom and reason have approved such a set of rules. It is interesting to ask how William Jones, as a Judge of the Supreme Court at Calcutta, reconciled this view with British administration of their justice in India, replacing Indian system of law?

William Jones was not a revolutionary who wanted abolition of the monarchy and the nobility. He wanted to retain both because for him the "true spirit of the constitution was in the English common laws – the collective wisdom of many centuries having been used and approved by several generations." To him as to most Whigs the English Constitution was the summum bonum of human wisdom and aspiration for political liberty since the days of Athens and Rome.

The Gordon Riots conditioned Jones' thinking on democratic principles; his idea of democracy was not one based on universal adult franchise but that "all Englishmen having property are entitled to vote in choosing Parliamentary delegates". However, Jones held that the franchise should not be given to persons who cannot support themselves by their own labour. The works of Jones encouraged honest propertied citizens to arm themselves to defend their property against the rabble. The Gordon Riots frightened him enough to write a plan to suppress such occurrences in future in his tract, *An Inquiry Into the Legal Mode of Suppressing Riots.* In this he criticized the Riot Act and felt that the use of military power to suppress riots was un-necessary since the English constitution permits civil power in the shape of a citizen's militia to "repel such a rabble". In order to prove this point he ransacked English law books and showed that law allows citizens to take up arms against internal revolts.

When Sir Roger Newdigate, the Parliamentary candidate from Oxford decided to resign in April 1780, William Jones expressed his desire to stand as a candidate because membership of Parliament would have been an important landmark in his career. He issued an Address to Electors who were the young radical lawyers and the ladies of the salons like Mrs. Elizabeth Montagu who was among his most enthusiastic supporters. Mrs. Montagu wrote to William Pepys urging him to support William Jones "if the Muses were the electors he would carry the election from every candidate that could offer". But the Muses were not electors in Oxford. William Jones came late to the contest; the author of an *Ode to Liberty* was a suspicious character; his plan for suppressing riots was aimed at curtailing executive power and pulling down the masses. William Jones failed to get support from the old Whig families. Nor was there any solid support from any of the colleges. Further as a latecomer to the contest he had no clear idea of the political game.

Jones' political views were probably responsible for his political failures in late eighteenth century England. His opposition to England's war against the American colonies by Lord North's government, ensured that North's ministry would not offer him any post.

In 1772 William Jones wrote to Burke about his abortive scheme of migrating to America: "I wish now more than ever to be in India that I may be less afflicted at a distance by than I am on the scene of action by the dissension of my benefactors and friends, which I never cease to deprecate and shall never cease to deplore." Jones was ready to migrate to America and wrote to the Chancellor about "a noble offer which has been made to him by the noblest of men among whom I may not only plead causes but make law and write them on the bank of my own river and under my own oak". He invariably advised young people to go to America. However, the Shipley family prevailed upon him not to sail for America. He was destined for another long voyage.

Like Burke, Jones was sympathetic to the cause of the American Revolution. Sensing the turmoil in Paris, Jones had visited the French capital in 1782 with one Mr. Paradise; they were suspected of having been there on some covert mission of conciliation with the French government sponsored by Lord Shelburne. (*Life and Times of Benjamin Franklin* by James Part)

In 1782 the constitutional agitation for parliamentary reforms began. Inspired, Jones composed an Ode in the style of the Roman poet Callistratus which became an instant success. The Ode ended with an uncharacteristic jingoistic touch:

Rise Britannia, dauntless rise!
Cheered with triple Harmony
Monarch good and Nobles wise,
People valiant, firm and free.

The poet and rebel, scholar and free thinker wanted to appear a part of the Establishment.

As late as 1782 Jones wrote to Burke: "You see how the little skiff of my hopes and fortunes is destined to be tossed by the waves and winds of political changes! Yet I bear my destiny without repining and if my friends and country sustain no injury will submit with cheerfulness to my ruin. I dreamt that I was just sailing into the mouth of the Ganges when a sudden gust of wind drove me off so violently that, although still at sea I am as far from Bengal as ever." Jones obviously expected to be deprived of appointment as a Puisne Judge of the Supreme Court in Calcutta after the fall of Lord Shelburne's government.

He spent a month at the home of the Shipley family at Chilbolton, mainly to be with Anna Maria and ascertain her affections. He had been drawn to her for her "amiable qualities, sweet disposition, excellent understanding and virtues of every kind". She confirmed that she was not engaged and his hopes soared. In fact he said it was the first time he knew happiness since the death of his mother. However, he refused to propose marriage until he had a proper position. But he informed the Duchess of Devonshire, Lord Althorp and Benjamin Franklin of his intentions.

Jones' efforts were met with success. Lord North's government, hostile to Jones, was replaced by the Coalition government of the Duke of Portland. A member of the ministry, Lord Ashburton, was able to secure for Jones the post of a judge in Bengal. The King also intervened and expedited his appointment which was announced on 4th March 1783. Jones was knighted Sir William on 19th March. Congratulations poured in from all quarters followed by numerous farewell receptions. William Jones now formally sought the hand of the woman whom he had courted for sixteen years, the only woman he had loved. Bishop Shipley gladly gave his consent as Anna Maria joyously hastened to prepare for the momentous journey. Sir William Jones and Miss Anna Maria Shipley were married by a special license on 8th April and sailed for India on 12th April.

All London rejoiced at his success but were sad to lose such a scholar and friend. As they set sail the London Magazine observed "... and from the ideas which we have formed of his character, and from the opportunities which we have had of contemplating with admiration his exquisite taste, his extensive and diversified erudition, we may venture, without incurring the censure of rashness, to presage that his conduct, in the character of a judge will render him even a great ornament to his country".

William Jones now embarked on a momentous journey not only for himself but also in the dialogue of civilization.

38

The Advent of William Jones

His dreams seemed to be coming true. He looked forward to exploring the art and literature of Asia on the continent itself. As a Judge in Calcutta he would be earning L 6000 a year. He intended to stay six years; save L 30,000 to retire in England with the independence he so much desired. However, fate had prepared a more dramatic story.

Sir William's program for the six-month voyage was "my daily studies will be what they will be for six years to come. Persian and Law and whatever relates to India, my recreation will be chess, my exercise walking on deck an hour before dinner; but my great delight is the sweet society and conversation of Anna Maria." By 12th July he had drawn up his plan of study during his stay in Calcutta. "The objects of my inquiry," wrote Sir William, "during my residence in Asia will be (1) the laws of Hindus and Mahometans (2) the history of the ancient world (3) books and illustrations of sculpture (4) traditions concerning the deluge (5) modern politics and geography of Hindustan (6) best mode of governing Bengal (7) arithmetic and geometry and mixed sciences of Asiatics and mathematicians such as Bhaskara (8) medicine, chemistry, surgery and anatomy of Asiatics (9) natural products of India (10) poetry, rhetoric and morality of Asia (11) music of the eastern nations (12) the She-King or three hundred Chinese odes (13) the best accounts of Tibet and Kashmir (14) trade manufacture, agriculture and commerce of India (15) Mughal constitution (16) Mahratta constitution."

It is not known to what extent William Jones was able to do justice to this daunting agenda in the eleven years he spent as against the six years he budgeted for. One wonders what drove children of the age of reason to delve into the great deluge. Like Hastings, Jones was aware of the Indian contribution to the sciences;

unlike Macaulay he had an ear for music. The six months period for Jones was a preparation for widening of horizons as it was for Macaulay a soaking in established prejudices.

The sea voyage was a long one; later in the century the passages around the Cape route became cheaper. But then a single passage cost about L120 or for a reserved cabin L 150. The cabins were not properly furnished and the passengers were informed that they would have to obtain sofas with mattress, pillows, hanging lamps, mirrors, and chest of drawers from the East India docks.

Sir William Jones was no *condottiero* coming out East. Nor was he leaving England's cool water-laden air and the glitter of London because he had been banished like the Portuguese poet Camoens, or because he had scandalized his peers like the future Duke of Wellington. He was in fact a product of the Enlightenment of the 18th century, particularly of London. He wanted to participate in political life and believed that by making a modest fortune through hard work in India he would gain entry to the Parliament.

The first part of the journey was pleasant as *The Crocodile* sailed the seas stopping at the Madeira and Cape Verde Islands and then at the Cape of Good Hope. Captain Williamson was honoured to have such distinguished passengers on board and answered their queries about the places they passed. It was when the ship's sails unfurled over the Arabian Sea that William Jones began to think of a greater mission than that of making enough money to retire comfortably in England. All that he had studied in his youth of Persians, Arabs and Indians rose to the surface as *The Crocodile* ploughed through eastern seas. He began to think of a systematic research on the Orient.

He felt that a group of Europeans could study and do research on the various fields of Indian and Oriental civilization as well as their commerce, agriculture and manufactures. Jones had a true scholar's perennial thirst for knowledge but it was now tempered by a deeper concern – the need to promote greater understanding between the Orient and the Occident, which would in turn foster better relations between the two. Sir William hoped that the Royal Society in England would sponsor such studies.

This was perhaps the first time that this concept – a conscious cultural dialogue between nations – was envisaged.

There was yet another motive for William Jones' desire to encourage intellectual work in India. It was to improve the quality of Company officials whose reputation stank across ten thousand miles of sea.

As he set sail for India in 1783, the young, principled, independent minded Jones must have been distressed by "the parlous and tattered condition" of the reputation of his new employer, the East India Company. The British public had shared in the triumphs of Clive at Arcot and Plassey and Eyre Coote at Assaye. But now London was being increasingly treated to the spectacle of the returning *Nabob*, as the parvenu from the East was called.

On his way to India, while he played chess on board *The Crocodile* with wife Anna Maria, Jones must have mused that he was on his way to the land where chess was born. For it was in north-west India in the sixth century that the game of chess began to be played, desired some said, by pious monks as a surrogate to wean the mind of kings away from war.

The ship stopped at Madras where the Governor Lord George Macartney entertained the young couple and exchanged news. Sir William got his first impressions of India. Lady Jones walked around the stockaded grounds of Fort St. George facing the Bay of Bengal. After a few days' repose *The Crocodile* resumed its journey along the Coromandel coast towards Calcutta.

39

A River of Ruined Capitals

For the scholar or the historian interested in how cities grew from their parent-earth, the most suitable approach to Calcutta is by the sea. For it is here that one realizes that it was a city reclaimed from the swamp and silt of the Hooghly delta. It was this that inspired Kipling to write his much quoted lines:

As the fungus sprouts chaotic from its bed,
So it spread –
Chance directed, chance erected,
Laid and built
On the silt,
Palace, byre, hovel, poverty and pride
Side by side.
And above the packed and
Pestilential town
Death looked down
On the city of dreadful night.
(*Tale of Two Cities – Departmental Duties*)

In these lines Kipling was perhaps carried away by the clichè that the British Empire was built in a fit of absent mind. This is one of those half truths poured into the mould of a catchy phrase which has got caught the imagination of successive generations. It was to an extent true of the gentlemen of Leadenhall Street but it would be a grave injustice to attribute such absence of mind to Job Charnock and Clive or Warren Hastings and Wellesley. These were a breed of men who knew their own minds and who were determined to play a role in the shaping of the British presence in India.

In the second week of December 1783, the frigate *Crocodile* bobbed uneasily on the roadstead of the island of Saugar at the mouth of the Hughly. Only the melancholy sound of sea birds broke the silence of the drowned wastes of the swamps on the shoreline. The atmosphere was made sinister by the stories which sailors told of man-eating crocodiles as large as fishing boats, of sharks to which unwanted girl babies were thrown ritually on full moon nights, of predatory tigers swimming out into the estuary and menacing the fishermen. The Hoogly is very broad – almost sixteen miles across – at Saugar. On the other shore stood the English settlement which bore the quaintly Anglicised name of Kedgeree but which had nothing homely about it and was in fact the haunt of plague and pestilence. Bishop Heber who was to travel by the same route twenty years later was to write that the seamen and officers spoke of this shore with horror as the grave of those unfortunate to remain there.

The passage down the river however brought a change of landscape. The tidal marshes with their eerie detritus gave way to dense dark jungles with the bison and rhino wallowing in mud that in turn was succeeded by the green trees and palms, and birds of colourful plumage of the Sunderban or Beautiful Forests in Bengali. Then the woods receded and the green paddy fields, the clumps of coconut trees, the villages of thatched huts with mud walls, the immemorially dreamy landscape of rural Bengal appeared. And next the unmistakably British landing stage at Culpee, renamed Diamond Harbour where the 'budgerow,' (Anglicization of the Bengali baujra) or barge-ship, awaited, flying the Union Jack.

As Jane Jacobs says in *The Economy of Cities*, "Cities cannot be explained by their locations or other given sources. Their existence as cities and the sources of their growth lie within themselves in the processes and growth systems that go within them. Cities are not ordained; they are wholly existential."

And though the introduction to Bengal at Saugar was dismal, the six-day journey up the Hooghly, to the observant eye and ear of William Jones, must have been truly rewarding. As an object lesson in how cities evolve from their parent silt as an exercise in autochthony, no better route could be found for approaching a great city like Calcutta.

For the Hooghly was the great high road of trade from Bengal to the sea. The name itself is a degenerate Portuguese form of Ogli or warehouse. The Hooghly has been called the 'river of ruined capitals' by the perceptive traveller Sir William Hunter. On its banks Buddhist kings, Hindu rulers, Moghul Viceroys, Portuguese, Dutch, Danish, French, German and English traders had set up their trading posts, their emporia and their fortresses. The once flourishing port of Tamluk had seen Buddhist missionaries embark for Sri Lanka, Burma, Thailand, Cambodia and beyond to China and Japan.

To the keen eye of William Jones, the Hooghly must have told its story of capital after capital, port after river port, silted, abandoned and forgotten by the capricious river. The old Buddhist monastery of Tamluk silted up, its successor, the capital of the kings of the warrior caste, also swamped. One more coat of slime and the next capital of the aboriginal kings of the fishermen caste was also the river of the foreign settlements. Palta, once a busy Dutch river port, was where the British Governor and his Council sought refuge from Siraj-ud-doula in 1756. Above Calcutta was the old Danish town of Serampore. Further up the French settlement of Chandernagore which in time became landlocked by Hooghly silt. Above it was the Dutch port of Chinsura and a mile further the once flourishing Portuguese emporia of Hooghly. At Bandel upstream of Calcutta still stands the old Portuguese church of Our Lady of Happy Voyage built in 1559 and rebuilt in 1661, where the Virgin in her robe of cerulean blue with the Infant Jesus in her arms is flanked by two perpetually burning lamps to guide the great galleasses which can now never come up the river. Still further up stood the once proud German port of Bankipur which despite Carlyle's vapourings to the contrary was an indubitable Teutonic presence in this river, till it was sacrificed by the Pragmatic Sanction in 1733 to the Moghuls. One by one, the capitals, the emporia, the warehouses, the fortresses all fell victims to the mercilessly wayward river. All of them with one resounding exception, the city to which the budgerow was now carrying Sir William and Lady Jones – the city of Calcutta.

The journey to Calcutta by river reveals as nothing else can that the foundations of this metropolis are laid on silt.

The foundations of silt are undisputable especially when one has travelled up the river. While Kipling gave credit for Calcutta's pedigree of silt, he did less than justice to one of the most far-sighted pioneers that British colonial history has seen – the colourful Job Charnock, the founder of Calcutta. And it is strange that Kipling who in other cases was only too willing to praise the achievements of men with a streak of rascality in them should have withheld his just dues from Job Charnock who was the leader of that tribe.

On 25th September 1783 the long sea voyage of *The Crocodile* ended as the frigate reached Calcutta. The growing capital of British India was in the words of William Jones "large", "well peopled", with "houses generally well built and some often equal to Palaces". He went on to observe, "I will only say that disliking the politics and parties of Britain I am very glad to be out of their way and to amuse myself for a few years in this wonderful country."

As they left *The Crocodile* and rode up river in his 'budgerow', Jones must have recalled with wry amusement his words to Edmund Burke seven months earlier when he feared that at the last moment he was about to be deprived of his judgeship by Shelburne. "I was just sailing into the mouth of the Ganges when a sudden gust of wind drove me off so violently, that although still at sea, I am as far from Bengal as ever."

The Crocodile which was part of the scene in Plymouth and which had brought them so confidently across the sea now stood bobbing uneasily on the waters of the Hooghly at Chandpal Ghat. And walking down the gangway to meet the officers of the Court who were waiting at the quay, William Jones must have felt some uneasiness about the decision he had taken of embarking on a career in this strange country, the fringes of which were bewildering and in a way, depressing.

For Calcutta then had no grand vistas to uplift the spirit. It is a city set on a plane where the cool breezes of the sea do not reach and where the fetid air of the surrounding marshes settles heavily on the spirit. On the journey across the town to his lodgings, Jones must have been struck by the wide expanses of flat undotted landscape. He must have passed through Chowringhee with its half a dozen houses, set out in spacious grounds, seen the most visible architectural embodiment of the British presence at Fort William. Here again he must have been reminded of the gross lack of reputation from which the servants of the Company suffered. The builder of Fort William had retired to England with an immense fortune. Jones must have been prepared for the unfamiliar appearance of the natives and their manner of dressing, bare except for loin cloth in the case of coolies, the *dhotis* and loose fitting *kurtas* and turbans of those of higher rank. He must have accepted these national features and his reaction must have been quite unlike that of Cornwallis who upon landing at Chandpal Ghat and seeing the bare legs of the natives resolved that with as much speed as possible the Indians should be provided with shoes and stockings! And quite so much as the absence of houses, he must have been struck by the absence of white faces. And everywhere his observant eye, ear and mind were noting and registering the sounds of Bengali, the architectural evidences of the British presence, the nascent contact between East and West, which in cultural terms, in course of time, he was to bring to such magnificent fruition.

Burke and England must have seemed very far away among the purlieus of Justice Impey's Deer Park, the tigers and dacoits of Chowringhee, and the engrossing wonder and strangeness of this infinitely varied land, of which the Englishman in the closed circuit of his colony and the restricted ambit of his business circle saw so little.

When William Jones landed in Bengal in 1783, the Mughal Empire had already passed its apogee. The Battle of Panipat in 1761 had left it as a hollow shell. After a last gleam of prosperity under Mirza Najat Khan like the dying flicker of a guttering candle the imperial power was finally extinguished by the excesses of Gulam Kader Khan in 1788. However, the Englishman who dominated Calcutta in 1783 was a totally different kind of person with his own conception of the British destiny in India. If the story of Clive is a schoolboy yarn with an appendix by Sigmund Freud, justice can be done to the complex personality of Warren Hastings and the life punctuated by great and lasting achievements and punctuated by equally great and lasting disappointments, through the arts of drama. For Hastings was indubitably a man of contradictions. The brooding figure in the Hounslow painting peering out of the chiaroscuoro portrait gives indication of the mystery of this undoubtedly great man.

The achievements of William Jones in India, the zest with which he and his colleagues could take up the study of Indian civilization, in making Indian civilization known to the West, was possible because Warren Hastings, the Governor-General, who consolidated British rule in India was also fascinated by India's past heritage.

It is in this setting that Sir William Jones and Lady Anna Maria Jones arrived in Calcutta. Their new home was in a spacious bungalow in Garden Reach almost opposite the Bishop's College. Within a short time Sir William was immersed in his Oriental studies.

There began a new chapter in Indian history.

40

Calcutta in the Time of William Jones

St. Petersburg was established by Peter the Great at the same time as Calcutta was founded by Job Charnock. Eight years before Job Charnock founded Calcutta it had been the site of flourishing cities. Both cities were erected in swamps amidst an unhealthy climate. Both became capitals of great empires. How little could the founders have anticipated that by 1860 both the British-Indian and Russian empires would meet in Asia separated by a mere few hundred miles.

Old Fort was called Fort William. It was built in 1692 in the reign of William III, the Dutch Prince of Orange who became King of England through his marriage to Mary Stuart, Queen of England. The fort was built in the same year in which the French at Chandernagore and the Dutch at Chinsura built their forts. As in feudal times, the old fort served as the nucleus of the town.

Calcutta remained a small town in the seventeenth century. In 1702 the Company surgeon Hamilton wrote: "Governor had a handsome house in the Fort, the Company has a pretty good garden which furnishes the Governor with herbage and fruits at table and some fish ponds to serve his kitchen with good carps, callots and mullet."

The population of Calcutta was a reflection of its commercial past and present: 'the Jew that excels the Bengali in cheating, the Armenian with his semi Asiatic habits, the rich Mughal merchant, the dark Portuguese, the muddy looking East Indian. There were also Persians and Chinese here.' Calcutta was not a city only of black and white. It was a medley of Englishmen, Portuguese, Armenians and Parsis and the occasional Dane. Before the advent of Europeans Chinese traders had come to Bengal. China Bazaar was the result of the commerce between the two people. The Armenians were among the oldest foreign inhabitants. The

Armenians had settled in this quarter in the days of Job Charnock. Their locality with its quaint houses contrasted with the conspicuous Western-style buildings of Calcutta. The Armenians like the Jews were noted for their mercantile zeal and in the early days were much employed by the English as *Gumastas* or clerks. They adopted local habits and wore Moghul court dress. Though the Armenians did not have social intercourse with the English, they were considered valuable as trading agents.

The Portuguese had come in the mid-sixteenth century to explore the possibilities of conquest but the Moghul Viceroy had snuffed out these reconnoiters. So they concentrated on trading of clothes, especially the famed Dhaka muslin. They were called 'harmaad' after the armadas in which they sailed up the Hooghly. Thereafter the word 'harmaad' in Bengali came to denote men with rough manners as indeed the Portuguese displayed in their transactions with Indians. Up to the middle of the eighteenth century the Portuguese often acted as liaison agents between various nationalities. For almost two centuries they had carried on a flourishing trade including that of slaves. In the eighteenth century many Europeans employed slaves to wait at their table. In 1781 the following advertisement appeared in a Calcutta newspaper "to be sold by private sale – two Kaffri boys who play remarkably well on the French horn; about eighteen years of age, belonging to a Portuguese padre lately deceased. For particulars enquire of the Vicar of the Portuguese church".

Hamilton writes in 1708, "Portuguese is the language most Europeans learn for general converse with one and other as well as with the different inhabitants of India." The epithet "Rice Christians" that was applied to native Christians was handed down from the Portuguese who called such persons Christian de Amoz. The name Portuguese in those days was a term of reproach, while the term Portuguese Ayah was synonymous with *femme de plaisir*. The men who boasted of being countrymen of Albuquerque became petty clerks or cooks.

The cosmopolitan character of eighteenth century Calcutta was due partly to the conditions of service and the connections of many of the Company's servants with political circles in England; they neither expected nor desired to serve long in India; their interests therefore remained those of the richer classes in London. But when fortunes could not be picked up in five years and a return to Europe was the final reward of long service, narrowness of outlook and a philistine suspicion of culture became the rule. Toynbee has found extraordinary the progress of Anglo-Indian character from a placid Jos Sedley of *Vanity Fair* to the ruthless John Nicholson of the Mutiny.

An epitaph to William Jones reads: "If we are to believe those marvels, the inhabitants of ancient Calcutta were a race of virtuous industrious and honourable men, of pious and beautiful women enlivened society in general and afforded every domestic and social comfort to husbands far distant from the home of early consanguinity and the joys of England."

Busteed's *Chronicle of Calcutta,* written in early nineteenth century, refers to old inhabitants of Calcutta who remembered Sir William Jones and Warren Hastings. These persons claimed that they have heard a tiger roar adjacent to the spot where the St. Paul's Cathedral and Episcopal residence stands. In the early nineteenth century there were people who remembered the period when Chowringhee was outside the limits of town, when shots were fired in the evening to frighten away the dacoits and when servants attending their masters at dinner parties left their good clothes behind them lest they be plundered in crossing the Maidan – the Hownslow Heath of those days.

Calcutta was regarded as the place of exile and death. The scholar Gladwin gives the following view which was entertained by even the Mussalmans of Bengal that Calcutta was considered "a gloomy prison, the land of specters and the mansion of death. But they had chiefly to blame themselves with tables groaning under the weight of heavy joints of meat, washed down with arrack punch".

The Calcutta of 1783 was divided distinctly into the English quarter and the native quarter. It was not yet the "city of palaces" it was to become when Macaulay came to it fifty years later. It was a city in which the road that was to become in time the main thoroughfare was bedeviled by tigers and dacoits where the main *maidan* or field was in the area where that sugar-cake monument of British rule – Victoria Memorial – now stands, was an extensive paddy field. Men like Hastings in Alipur and Impey with his palatial house and his deer park had made themselves elegantly comfortable. Most English people lived in windowless houses set hotchpotch. They seemed to save all their architectural inspiration for their return to England.

The centre of attraction in the Calcutta of 1784 was the large Palladian style, porticoed mansion called Belvedere, now the National Library, where Governor-General Warren Hastings lived with his wife Maria. Its spacious lawns were full of flowers and ornamental trees and shrubs that were often tended to by Hastings himself, wearing a shirt and breeches and a straw hat. At first Warren Hastings occupied a small town house on the site of present Government House but Mrs. Hastings preferred what is now 1 Hastings Street which was occupied a century later by a British commercial firm 'Burn and Company'. Stavorinus mentions visiting Belvedere in 1768 where the Governor of Bengal resided.

A Calcutta resident, Mrs. Fay, describes Belvedere in 1780: "The house is a perfect bijou; most superbly fitted with all that unbounded affluence on display, but still deficient in the simple elegance which the wealthy so seldom attain from circumstance of not being obliged to search for effect without much cause, which those but moderately rich find to be indispensable. The grounds are said to be tastefully laid out."

Nearly opposite Alipur bridge stood two trees called the trees of destruction. The place was notorious for the duels fought under their shade. Hastings and Francis had exchanged shots there. Had Hastings fallen in the duel the stability of British power in India might have been shaken with such a playboy as Francis guarding the Chariot of State. In the days when European women were few, jealousy often gave rise to these affairs of honour. Thus, this early account cast an unsuspected light on the famous duel. Was there an unsuspected romantic aspect to this episode? Was Maria Imhoff Hastings involved? These may be one of the great 'ifs' of history.

The old district of Govindpur which had been the residence of Seths and Bayanks – the oldest Hindu families of Calcutta – later was named Tollyganj when it was named after Colonel Tolly who improved the place at his own expense and was given the right to collect tolls from it in 1775. This gave him an income of Rupees 4,300/- per month – a handsome fortune in those days.

Calcutta had in former days an ill name as "the graveyard to Europeans". However, physicians were also at fault as Doctor Goodere states in his "On the Progress of European Medicine in the East": "Patients were ordered in these cases pillaos, curries, gulled fowls and prepared chicken broth and libitum into a glass or two of medicines, a little brandy and water, and a dessert of ripe fruit. Native doctors had their hot and cold remedies with their mantras." Mrs. Kindersley says,

> "The Portuguese doctors prescribed as the grand cure 'the changing of all European blood in their patients bodies into natives'. This they endeavored to accomplish by repeated venesections till they conceived that the whole mass of their circulating fluid had been abstracted. And then by a diet consisting exclusively of the country they hoped to substitute a liquid entirely Indian which would render their patients proof against maladies under which they had previously laboured.

A unique form of transplant to be sure!

Recreation in the 1780s comprised of rides in chaises or palanquins in the fields or to the gardens, and walking and fishing. Racing at the Old Race Course is mentioned in 1780. But later, during his administration, Lord Wellesley set his face decidedly against horse racing and every other species of gambling. The assembly rooms were used for holding balls, parties and meetings. In the middle of the eighteenth century the Tank Square was the scene of many midnight escapades of young people while elderly ones amused themselves on the banks of the fishpond in the park "inhaling the evening breezes and thinking of friends they had heard of nine months before." Esplanade was the meeting point of five streets, and was the favourite promenade of "elegant walking parties" on moonlit evenings.

The chief strangers who came to Calcutta in those days were the Captains of the Indiamen, great personages in their day, the Lords of those splendid ships, the old Indiamen and whose position often pointed to a position in the Court of Directors. One of the charters provided that six members of the Court of Directors should always have been commanders of their ships but the Company rented accommodation for these magnates by hiring houses during their stay at rupees five hundred per month.

Fort William College or Writers Building was appropriated for the residence of writers or young civilians. Mention is made of it in 1780 as a monument of commercial prosperity. The buildings were rented by the government from the Barwell family. Mr. George Barwell returned to England with a fortune of eighty lakh rupees.

In this boisterous age English etiquettes were discarded when found tiresome and decorum was not observed even in church.

There was considerable argument about seating. Mrs. Fay sniffs disapprovingly, "ladies are approached by all gentlemen indiscriminately, known or unknown, with offers of their hand to conduct them to their seat, those gentlemen wishing to change their conditions repair to this holy home and tender their services to the fair strangers in hope of matrimony". There were very few English women in Calcutta in the eighteenth century and as their numbers were small they were in great demand for courtship, matrimony or escapades by the men who vastly outnumbered them. European ladies were afraid to face India. Lord Teignmouth's lady refused to go to India with her husband.

Here mention must be made of what is probably the earliest European novel about India, written from first-hand experience – *Hartley House, Calcutta*. The work of an anonymous author, apparently a lady, was published in London in 1789. Evidently the writer had first hand experience of the Calcutta of Hastings. Her work combines the characteristics of a novel and a travel book. Like many of the novels of the period it is in the form of a letter written by the heroine, Sophia Goldborne, to a close lady friend in England. It is of small literary merit but it gives an interesting picture of the luxurious lives of the Calcutta *Nabobs*. Its most significant feature from the historian's point of view is its very sympathetic attitude to Hinduism. The novel is also a striking comment on the effects of self-confident imperialism and the rise of the evangelical movement on the attitudes of the British in India.

The construction of Government House commenced in 1799 under the orders of the Marquis of Wellesley who was called 'the Augustus of Calcutta,' an Occidental greatly addicted to Oriental pomp. Wellesley believed that "India should be governed from a Palace, not from a counting house, with the ideas of a Prince, not a retailer dealing in muslins and indigo."

The Supreme Court was the scene of many dramatic events. In the eighteenth century it was here that the sentence on Nanda Kumar was pronounced, here Impey maintained the independence of the power of justice against the East India Company, and where William Jones dispensed justice. Here enormous fortunes were made by lawyers in the early days when the attorneys were limited to only twelve in number. Many lawyers came from England after the establishment of the Supreme Court in Calcutta resulting in the loss of work and employment of native lawyers. Philip Stanhope, an English visitor to India in 1774, wrote, "The numerous dependants which have arrived in the train of the Judges and of the new commander-in-chief of the forces will of course be reappointed to all the posts of any importance; and I must do this gentlemen the justice to observe that both in number and rapacity they exactly resemble an army of locusts sent to devour the fruits of the earth."

North of the Hastings building lies Kuli Bazaar where there is a platform where Nanda Kumar, once Dewan to the Nawab of Murshidabad, was executed on 5th August 1775, the first Brahmin to be executed by the English in India. His death exerted as great a revulsion among the natives as the execution of Louis XVI among the French royalists. The foremost among the Mahapatak, enemies of the highest degree or mortal sins, is killing a Brahmin. Hindus went to the river to wash the offence committed in serving the executioners. For three days they ate nothing. Menaces were held out to the judges that if they proceeded to Court their lives would be sacrificed as victims of popular fury but regardless of menaces they marched in procession to the Supreme Court attended by the parapharnelia of justice. On that day the Hindus went to the other side of the river to eat considering that Calcutta had been polluted by the execution of a Brahmin.

Halsi Bagan, the headquarters of Nawab Siraj-ud-dulla, had been a military fort with cannons mounted on the ramparts in 1757. Later Amirchand, the accomplice of Clive in chicanery, took over the mansion. He was the Rothschild of his day and made a fortune by usurious practices with the troops. For forty years he was the chief contractor for providing the Company's investments and made about a crore of rupees. He had enough influence to shape policies in Murshidabad. On the decline of Murshidabad the aristocratic families went to the north-west frontier. Those who stayed back were haughty and remembered their days of glory.

A French traveller observed, "Few of the streets bear any marks of antiquity and the English like the Americans had the bad taste to give them European names instead of euphonious expressions drawn from native associations."

'Adventurer' was the term applied to every man who came out to India not in the service of the Company. 'Kings' Troops' were all noted for their young officers without any knowledge of local conditions which nearly caused the loss of India – ignorance and interference with local customs.

The most important landmark in the life of William Jones in India is the building of the Asiatic Society which stands on the corner of Park Street built on a piece of ground granted by the government. This great Society was founded on 15th January 1784. That same year gave Calcutta its first church erected by the public. It was the first time after the Battle of Plassey that religion and literature went together.

41
Social Life in Calcutta

Denis Kincaid describes Calcutta of the late eighteenth century in *Social Life In India – 1608-1937*:

> After many months on sea, English travelers reached Calcutta, considered 'the greatest and gayest of the Anglo-Indian cities'. It was the city that Clive described as 'one of the most wicked Places in the universe'. Corruption, licentiousness and a want of Principle seem to have possessed the Minds of the Civil servants, by frequent bad examples they have grown callous, Rapacious and luxurious beyond Conception and the Incapacity and Iniquity of some and the Youth of others ... Fortunes were made and lost in a night at cards. Francis at a single sitting won L 20,000 and on another occasion Barwell lost L 40,000. Hastings once made up his mind to end his squabbles with his opponents in the Council by buying them up for L 100,000 a piece.

It was here that Mrs Sherwood found the material for her descriptions of

> the splendid sloth and languid debauchery of European society in those days – Englishmen overwhelmed into the consequences of extravagance, hampered by Hindoo women and by crowds of olive coloured children, without the will or the power to leave the shores of India ... Great men rode about in state coaches with a dozen servants running before and behind them to bawl out their titles; and little men lounged in palanquins or drove a chariot for which they never intended to pay, drawn by horses which they had bullied or cajoled out of the stables of wealthy Baboos.

The sudden change in funds, lifestyles, and power made the *Nabobs* indolent upstarts. They had an army of servants to attend to every conceivable task, never bothered about their accounts which was left in the hands of *sircars* or *munshis*, while they smoked their *hookahs*, took long siestas, went riding in the *maidan*, attended interminable parties, danced, gambled, intrigued, flirted, and plotted how to plunder and get richer still. These gaieties would suddenly be terminated by a deadly fever or a duel. But life would continue at its frenetic pace.

The *sircar* or *munshi* hired the servants and arranged for the daily expenses of the house and a favourite subject for contemporary satirists was that of the 'lordly European lolling in a long chair, the mouthpiece of a hookah in his hand, a glass of Madeira at his elbow while standing with bent head before him the *sircar* read from an enormous role of parchment, the expenses incurred by him on behalf of his employer'. Most unmarried men in Calcutta had Indian mistresses. Those of the higher officials were usually pretty and accomplished. One Norman Douglas congratulated Hickey's contemporaries on their freedom from colour prejudice.

Reading the contemporary chronicles of the English in Calcutta one sees not a spectacle of imperial decadence that characterized the last days of Rome but the clamour and frenzy that came with the Black Death in 14th century Europe, of people enjoying themselves with a gloomy fatalism because they knew the end could be a breath away.

The Calcutta of the 1780s was dominated by the East India Company officers who had become *Nabobs*. They lived in a world of their own, avidly pursuing profitable trade and hoping to return to England to buy up estates and fashionable homes. In the meantime they enjoyed themselves with a kind of unnatural frenzy indulging in illicit liaisons "which flourished and died with the sudden blossoming and the equally abrupt wilting of a tropical bloom". As the climate of Bengal produced maladies for which the Englishmen knew no cure, a sort of fatalism enveloped them that encouraged hedonistic spirit with the motto "eat, drink and be merry for tomorrow we die". Indeed knowledge of the tropical diseases and their cure was so primitive that life was a permanent hazard and the cemetery full of those who could not realize their ambition of an early retirement with a comfortable fortune. The general impression of eighteenth and early nineteenth century Calcutta is an atmosphere of extravagance and frivolity.

Social life in Calcutta must have been in odd contrast to the refined and erudite literary and intellectual circles in which William

Jones had been initiated first by the aristocratic Spencers and then Samuel Johnson and his circle.

It must be remembered that there were different types of societies within the English community. While Hickey and Francis presided over the ones described, Hastings and his friends amused themselves by composing Latin verses and translating Latin poets. Hastings was considered to be an arbiter of literary taste and these verses would be sent to him for his approval. He himself made translations from the Indian epics. They were rough and ready versions without poetic fire; he would compose them in his palanquin as he jolted over the plains of Bihar or the steaming paddy fields of Bengal. He sent them to his wife with a modest little preface: "If you read this with a Composed Mind and admire it only as a production of mere poetical Merit (for so much I am sure from the Partiality of your Judgment) burn it; for it is good for nothing." But if these solemn poems had little value there is no doubt that Hastings could turn a skilful epigram when he chose as his lines on Burke prove.

Oft have I wondered that on Irish Ground
No poisonous reptiles ever yet were found
Revealed the secret strands of natures work
She saved her venom to create a Burke.

When weary of versifying he would take up a book of extracts from the *Mahabharata* and the lean disdainful face of the Governor-General would soften with emotion as he read of the old chivalrous heroes of the Hindus, the divine charioteer Krishna, of Arjun, the noble warrior and his brother Yudhishtira who would not enter heaven until his faithful dog accompanied him. Hastings' intellectual pursuits were interminable – his entourage was surprised at the Governor General's interest in Hindu philosophy and his 'undignified pundit hunting'. Hastings studied Persian which he considered should be promoted to a status of a serious subject in English universities as a companion classical language to Latin. A Persian lady Panna Begum, wife of Colonel Pearse (Hastings' second in the duel with Francis), used to write him long letters in Persian.

It was not long before the Governor-General realized the valuable role that the newly appointed Judge William Jones could play in his plans to promote Hindu traditions and learning for their own administrative purposes.

Calcutta was a far cry from the London that Sir William Jones had left behind. But instead of repining and yearning for England's pleasant clime and green glory he brought to the growing boisterous capital a new dimension. The serious intellectual pursuits of scholars and statesmen helped to make Calcutta the second city of the British Empire.

42

The British Justinian

Jones' reputation for scholarship and integrity had preceded him. Britons and Indians alike looked forward eagerly to his arrival. Calcutta was a whirlpool of intrigues; Governor-General Warren Hastings was engaged in constant attrition with members of his Council led by Philip Francis. His ally Sir Elijah Impey was the Chief Justice of the Supreme Court who was polite, cynical and quite amoral when it came to furthering his own interests. The other judge was John Hyde, an elderly, easy-going man. Sir Robert Chambers was of a scholarly bent and was the only other jurist of the Supreme Court. Sir Robert offered his home to the young couple until they found one of their own and Sir Elijah lent money to William Jones to get clothes made that were suited to the Bengal climate. Then there was the irascible William Hickey, the first press person in Calcutta who enjoyed exposing scandals of the Company officials. After the first round of parties, William Jones took his first step as the new Justinian.

The native administration of law appeared to be arbitrary and the severity or levity of punishments appeared to be subject to the whims of the individuals who served as judges. There were no codes but there appeared to be different systems of law for Hindus and Muslims. There did not appear to be any fixed principles for determination of the quantum of the land revenue. To add to this state of institutional chaos, the mechanism of dual role had introduced an element of uncertainty as the judges and tax gatherers did not know whether to serve the Nawab or the British. Further, vitiating the situation were the hordes of Englishmen who came to India, in Burke's phrase, like 'birds of prey', with no motive in their minds except personal gain. In Bengal, in 1783, there were the 'firmans' of the emperor, the shadow Nawab at Murshidabad and the very real presence of the East India Company which at the outset had no intention of playing a significant role in the politics of the country but which was being inexorably drawn into it, by the vacuum created by the collapse of the Moghul empire and by the territorial imperatives of trade.

The compilation of Indian law from the traditional sources both Hindu and Islamic was one of the tasks that Hastings had addressed himself to but was not able to complete as he was recalled to England. In 1790 William Jones was entrusted with this mission. All his interests as a linguist, historian and lawyer were aroused. As far as Hindu law was concerned he found that the sources were numerous. For identifying the sources and for obtaining accurate translations Jones took as his assistants the eminent Sanskrit scholars Jagannath Tarakapanchanan and Radhakanta Sharman. One of the documents which they led him to was the *Bhavisya Purana* where he also found much of the material for his essay on chess.

Jones' legal background was to prove valuable. In 1781, while still in England, he had written an essay on Law of Bailment. This became a standard authority on the subject.

The legal system and the procedures convinced Jones that a wholesale reform of legislation was of urgent necessity. With a wisdom ahead of his times, Jones saw that the Indians had to be protected from the arbitrary attitude and actions of the British. He insisted that not only should Indians be heard but that the British judges should record evidence. "A system like this, consisting of reciprocal checks and balances of power would bring security and satisfaction to the natives, the government, and the English subjects in India." But the man who could have helped him push through such reforms – Burke – had turned hostile and could not be counted upon to cooperate.

Jones was concerned about the state of the jails where prisoners were kept in inhuman conditions. Murderers, debtors, common felons – all shared the same cells. Jones urged for separate prisons for different types of offenders. He showed his concern for insolvent debtors "who have to drag on their wretched existence in prison." He wrote: "I have visited the prison in disguise and though it is much neater and more comfortable than I expected to find it, yet I deplore the fate of the poor wretches who must pass their hot months in it."

In his correspondence with Prime Minister Pitt, Jones described the frightening conditions in the prisons that endangered the lives of the hapless prisoners. Aware of the rigidity of the caste system among the Hindus, Jones suggested that separate cells should be maintained for different castes. He strongly suggested to the Prime Minister to take up law reforms similar to England's laws.

Another concern of William Jones was the plight of the Indians who suffered miscarriage of justice. They could not afford to come to court in view of the high fees of lawyers, especially in the Supreme Court. If the Indian had suffered wrong at the hands of a Briton, it became doubly difficult for him to secure redressal of the wrong. Jones therefore suggested that the judges could hear the complaints in their chambers and cut short the procedure of argument conducted by avaricious and procrastinating lawyers.

It was William Jones' wish to be the Justinian of modern India. Seeing the legal system he felt it imperative to codify all existing laws as the Byzantine Emperor Justinian had done in the fifth century. In a letter to Lord Cornwallis in March 1788, Jones pointed out the urgent need to prepare a Digest of Hindu and Mohommedan laws. The Governor-General agreed to the proposal. Jones began the daunting work himself and recruited a large group of Hindu and Muslim scholars to assist him. Jones composed *The Mohommedan Law of Inheritance* in 1792 and the Institute of Hindu Law or the *Ordinances of Manu* in 1794. He did not live to complete the digest of Hindu and Muslim laws; the work was completed by the Sanskrit scholar Colebrooke.

As William Jones set about preparing a digest of native laws, he discovered that there were Hindu laws of a very old date including the celebrated Code of Manu or *Manusamhita,* the greatest of Hindu law books. In 1789 he translated into English the famous version of the *Code of Manu*. The Sanskrit text appeared only in 1813. It became the basis of civil law, which was to be applied to the Hindus. In Indian mythology the legendary author of *Manu Smrithi*, the Sanskrit Code of Law, was also known as the first king from whom most Indian medieval rulers traced their ancestry either through his son (the solar line) or through his daughter (lunar line). The *Satapatha Brahmana* recounts story of the great flood. Manu combines the characteristics of both Noah and Adam.

At first William Jones depended on the translations of Wilkins from Sanskrit texts. Wilkins was acknowledged as the expert, especially after his superb translation of the *Bhagavad Gita* but Jones realized that the only manner in which he could have mastery over old law texts was to learn the language himself.

Sir William Jones went to the old university at Nadia, the seat of Sanskrit learning, and sought a good instructor in Sanskrit. No Brahmin agreed to his request; they refused to teach a non-Hindu and a non-Brahmin the sacred language. After several refusals Jones was able to obtain the services of a non-Brahmin teacher who laid down certain conditions to which Jones readily agreed. In 1785 William Jones began his study of Sanskrit with diligence and determination. He wanted to have direct access without the intrusion of Persian translators to the crucial text *Manava Dharma Sastra* for preparing a digest of Hindu laws. With his genius for languages it was not long before William Jones acquired proficiency in Sanskrit.

At court the new judge declared his impartiality before the law. He had been appointed a judge to ensure that British laws applied to Britons in India while Indians were to be judged by their own laws and customs. However, to pave the way for better understanding between Indians and Britons, the former would be informed about the British legal system. Where the laws of Britain and India conflicted he would attempt to reconcile them by affecting changes in the law. While instructing the jurors he made it clear that he would not be a party to policies of exploitation or injustice to the Indians.

In the meantime instructions recalling Impey had come from London on the charge that he at the instance of Warren Hastings had connived at the judicial murder of Nanda Kumar. Though William Jones had established cordial relations with Impey and Anna Maria had become friends with Lady Impey, he refused to be drawn into any political controversies. Sir Elijah and his family soon sailed for England to answer charges of corruption and murder.

William Jones' relation with the Governor-General was more complex. He recognized at once that Warren Hastings was a man of exceptional abilities, both as an administrator and scholar. When they met at the gubernatorial residence at Belvedere, Jones was impressed by Hastings' knowledge of Indian culture. Jones realized that Hastings was no *Nabob* who had come out East to make a fortune; Hastings was a visionary who had plans of reviving the grandeur of Indian civilization that had been forgotten. It was to be expected that the two men of formidable intellect and insatiable craving for knowledge should become friends. They discussed Indian civilization as well as how to improve the administration of British India. In Calcutta, a city so far removed from all that was familiar, William Jones must have found in the elegant ambience of Belvedere something of the atmosphere he had liked and enjoyed in the Devonshire, Montagu and Spencer houses. He was drawn to the Governor-General who believed that revival and preservation of Indian traditions was necessary both for India and Britain. When Hastings waived his prerogative to be President of Asiatic Society and proposed Jones in his place, the latter felt kindly towards him. Besides, William Jones realized the immense responsibilities borne by Hastings and respected his addressing them with sagacity and firmness. In contrast Francis and his confederates in the Council seemed like hollow men thirsty for power.

William Jones therefore refused to join the intrigues against Hastings. He hoped that Burke would understand that Hastings was acting in the best interest of Britain without allowing the rapacious conduct that had received tacit support from Clive. Jones also hoped that Burke would realize that he and Burke held common views on governance of India. This guarded neutrality angered Edmund Burke who was sharpening his knives against the powerful and enigmatic Governor-General. Burke even hinted to Sir William's father-in-law, the Bishop of Asaph that if he heard that Jones was siding with Hastings, Burke would ensure Jones' recall from India. Jones wrote to Burke expressing his dismay. In retaliation Burke refused to consider or recommend to Parliament Jones' suggestions for reform of the judicature in India. The opportunity to reform the legal system in India was lost. Burke revealed what was to become obvious in the ensuing decade – that for all his posturing about oppressed Indians, he only pursued his immediate personal agenda.

In the meantime Jones was encountering problems with Chambers who was now acting Chief Justice. His indolence, tardiness, refusal to attend court in time was making it difficult for Jones to keep to the schedule of hearing cases. Hearings and trials were delayed because of Chamber's indiscipline. Both Jones and Hyde recorded their protests.

While the political turmoil gathered momentum, Sir William and Lady Anna Maria enjoyed their private idyll. Unlike some Britons who dressed and ate as if they were in England's cold climate, the young couple gracefully adjusted to the local food and wore clothes suited to the humid warmth of Bengal. Sir William wore Indian clothes at home. They maintained a house in the centre of the town and another in the suburb of Garden Reach and their daily schedule was governed by discipline. They rose at dawn and after a bath Sir William sat down to study Sanskrit or his legal papers, while Anna Maria tended to her garden, making sketches of the exotic blooms that grew in profusion in the fertile clayey soil. She sought details about them in *Systema Naturae,* a book written by Swedish botanist Carl von Linnaeus.

As the work increased and demands on his time grew, William Jones felt he needed more time and tranquility to pursue his studies. They found a pretty thatch-roofed cottage in Krishnanagar, some fifty miles north of Calcutta in the district of Nadia, the home of the mystic-saint Chaitanya and the seat of Vaishnav culture and learning. Nearby was the famed town of Nabodwip, the Benaras of Bengal.

Preparation of the *Digest of Indian Laws* took up his leisure hours but he was enthused by the prospect of doing this for Indians whose gratitude he said was more precious to him than the thanks of the King of England. Usually modest, he said that to be the legislator of the Indians was his greatest desire and he felt that this would be his legacy to India. It is strange indeed that he thought his legal contribution was greater than this cultural one.

William Jones upheld the independence of the judiciary by saying, "I always thought before I left England that a regard for the public good requires the most cordial union between the executive and judicial powers in this country; and I lamented the mischief occasioned by former divisions. Since I have no view of happiness on this side of the grave, but in a faithful discharge of my duty, I shall spare no pains to preserve that cordiality which subsists, I trust and will subsist between the Government and the Judges." (Letter to George John Spencer – 1793)

William Jones was a judge of unswerving integrity and refused to participate in political intrigues. His scholarship and his integrity made him a rara avis in the judicial circles of British Bengal. He was however drawn into matters concerning governance of Bengal such as the power and authority of the Supreme Court, the relationship between the Supreme Court and Supreme Council, the relationship between Indian Courts and the British Supreme Court and the administration of criminal justice.

However, William Jones could not escape the inherent contradiction of his position. The political theories which he had imbibed in England about the sovereign will of the people and the authority vested in officers by the community sounded hollow in a situation where the will of the people – the Indians – did not exist and the authority of a foreign government was imposed upon the people. He was well aware of the contradiction and tried like all members of an imperial government to find an acceptable compromise. He did this by paying handsome tribute to Indian civilization but concluded that since India had not known democracy and the rule of law it was the duty of British Government to introduce it in India. However, he contradicted himself on another occasion by saying that Indian civilization could not have developed if Indian rulers had been cruel and despotic. He therefore relied on the traditional legal system of India as a reflection of the collective will of the people to be applied to them. Agreeing with Burke, Jones believed in allowing Indians to live under their "immemorial usages".

The Indian legal system was not new to William Jones. He had been consulted by Lord North's government in 1773 prior to the enactment of the Regulation Act whereby the Supreme Court had been established in Calcutta and the Act of Parliament of 1781. William Jones had made an extensive study on prevailing laws on inheritance, property, succession, the law of contracts, etc. After coming to India he decided to acquaint himself with Hindu and Muslim laws from their original source and it was for this reason that he took up the study of Sanskrit and Arabic. As he acquired knowledge of the two systems of law, he saw the necessity of codifying them. This would not only facilitate the administration of justice but would make it easier for British administrators to become acquainted with the laws of the country. Perhaps he saw himself as a British Justinian.

43

Poet, Historian and Philologist

Indology started with Sir William Jones who declared in his presidential address to the Asiatic Society in 1786, that Sanskrit, Greek, Latin and probably the Celtic and Teutonic languages sprang from a common source no longer existing. This theory led to the foundation of the science of comparative philology by Frank Bopp in 1816. Jones began Sanskrit Philology. He also drew up a transcription of the Sanskrit alphabet in Latin letters.

In Calcutta William Jones met a group of young officers who were as keenly interested as himself in Asian and Oriental studies. Nathaniel Halhed had already published *A Bengali Grammar* and the *Code of Gentoo Laws*. In 1785, Charles Wilkins published a translation of the *Bhagavad Gita*, the first rendering of a Sanskrit work in English. Other scholars such as John Shore, Francis Baldwin, John Carnac, Jonathan Duncan, and William Chambers were eager to promote Oriental learning. All of them later became founding fathers of the Asiatic Society and made regular contributions to Asian studies. The work of the Asiatic Society and the epochal contribution made by it in the dissemination of knowledge and understanding of India is dealt with in a later chapter.

In 1789, a Brahman pundit told Jones of the existence of Sanskrit drama and in that year he astonished the Western world by a translation of Kalidasa's famous masterpiece *Shakuntala*. Scholars now began a systematic and eager search for Sanskrit. At first scholars had been confined to classical Sanskrit though Jones and Colebrooke had both read some of the Vedic texts.

The search for linguistic affinities had begun in medieval Europe by Latin scholars. The great medieval poet Dante's attempts to understand the classification of languages was taken up by the German scholar Schaliger. Earlier, Stevens, an English missionary and Sassetti, an Italian trader, had observed the affinity between

Sanskrit and European languages. Attempts were made to look for affinities between German and Greek, German and Persian. Debates ensued as to whether various languages developed simultaneously or consecutively. A seventeenth-century Dutch scholar, Marcus Boxhorn mooted the theory of a common Indo-European language in view of the fact that words of common origin were found in several European languages. Further studies were developed in Hungary and Russia on the affinities of certain languages. Though it was evident that many languages were related and connected, there was no attempt to explain the similarities. Scholars like Boxhorn and Scaliger subscribed to the theory of simultaneous and independent evolution of languages while others felt that migrations and invasions could have affected linguistic patterns. European linguists such as Lidoff, Heras, Gyernathi, Pallas, Freret offered various theories. A French Jesuit Pere Coeurdoux suggested that various factors could be responsible for the affinity of languages such as proximity, common creed, trade, invasions and large scale migrations. However, being Europe-centric the Western scholars were inclined to believe that Persian and Sanskrit were derived from Greek and Latin rather than the other way round.

William Jones believed that languages developed similarities through physical proximity and close interactions. The more he studied Sanskrit, the more he saw its close structural connection with Greek and Latin. This is when he made his famous statement on Sanskrit before the Asiatic Society – "... is of wonderful structure; more perfect than Greek, more copious than Latin and more exquisitely refined than either, yet bearing to both of them a strong affinity both in the roots of verbs and in the forms of grammar; so strong indeed that no philologer could examine them all three without believing them to have sprung from some common source which no longer exists."

The theory of a far away and ancient land of origin appealed to the votaries of the unfolding Romantic movement in Europe led by German men of letters.

As a genius at languages, Jones obviously believed that acquiring knowledge of a new language was acquiring a new soul. The languages known to Sir William Jones were English, Latin, French, Italian, Greek, Arabic, Persian, Sanskrit (less perfect but all intelligible with a dictionary), Spanish, Portuguese, German,

Runick, Hebrew, Bengali, Hindi, some Turkish, a sketchy knowledge of Tibetan, Pali, Pahlavi, Deri, Russian, Syriac, Ethiopic, Coptic, Welsh, Swedish, Dutch and Chinese. This itself was a phenomenon virtually unknown in his or other times!

William Jones toured North India in the winter of 1784-85 and stopped at Banares to see the holy city of the Hindus and Bodh Gaya the centre of Buddhism. It was a momentous trip. He met many famous pundits with whom he discoursed with the help of an interpreter. He obtained a manuscript of *Dharma Shastra;* the work interested him both for its literary value as well as for its legal contents. The codification of Hindu law and its application to Hindus was of great concern to him. The pundits introduced him to the *Bhagavata Purana,* and *Yogavashishta,* and the epics of which the *Mahabharata,* impressed him so much that he composed *The Enchanted Fruit or Hindu Wife,* which deals with the story of Draupadi, the wife of the five Pandava brothers. Jones the poet tells the story in couplets.

Jones was deeply impressed by the saga of the *Ramayana* and the *Mahabharata.* As early as August 1784 he wrote to his friend Richard Johnson in England: "I am charmed with Crishen (Krishna), an enthusiastic admirer of Raama, a devout adorer of Brihma, Bishen, Mahaser not to mention that Judishteir, Arjen, Corno and other warriors of the Mahabharat appear greater in my eyes than Agamemnon, Ajax, and Achilles appeared when I first read the *Iliad.*"

He also wrote an essay titled *On the Gods of Greece, Italy and India* where he pointed out, "A resemblance too strong to have been accidental, between the popular worship of the old Greeks and Italians and that of the Hindus and between their strange religions and those of Egypt, China, Persia, Phrygia, Phoenicia and Syria and even remoter regions."

William Jones was brought up as a Christian but the spirit of tolerance and enquiry of eighteenth century Europe made men's mind receptive to other systems of thoughts and beliefs. He was drawn to the variety, the mystical quality as well as the intellectual aspects of Hinduism. Instead of denigrating the gods and goddesses Jones wrote hymns to them.

In the first two volumes of *Asiatick Miscellany,* Jones' contributed nine *Hymns* addressed to Indra, Surya, Lakshmi, Narayan, Saraswati, Kamdev, Durga, Bhavani and Ganga. These were published along with twenty tales and fables of Nizami. To each hymn he gave an explanatory note for the benefit of the Western reader. This not only contained a comparative study of Hindu mythology but also showed Jones as the first Anglo-Indian poet.

The *Hymn to Narayana* is regarded as the greatest of all as it touches on the Hindu doctrine of *Maya* or illusion. Before leaving Europe Jones had read the letter of the French Jesuit, Pere Pons, written from Thanjavur on 23rd November 1740 adressed to a fellow Jesuit, Pere du Halde, which was called *An Essay On Certain Aspects of Indian Literature.* It is from this composition that Jones first became acquainted with the Hindu doctrine of *Maya*. The example taken is of the rope being mistaken for a snake. He also learnt of the concept of deliverance of the soul from *Maya* that can be attained by repeating the mantra *aham param Brahma* or 'I am supreme'.

The following hymn was written in 1785 while Jones was in the court room. In this poem he describes the divine attributes of the almighty; the creator, the preserver and the destroyer. Jones describes the moment of creation –

First and all – potent all – pervading sound
Bade flow the waters – and the waters flowed
Exulting in their measureless abode
Diffusive, multitudinous, profound
Above beneath around ...
Brightest of beings, greatest of the great
Who not as mortals steep their eyes in dewy sleep
But heavenly – pensive on the lotus lay
That blossomed at his touch and shed a golden ray.

His *Hymn to Saraswati,* the goddess of learning, reflects his knowledge of Indian music. He composed *Hymn to Ganga* in 1784 while he was sailing up the river Ganga in his 'budgerow' or barge. Jones describes Ganga's birth in the Himalayas and her joining with the river Brahmaputra (son of Brahma) in a celestial marriage. The hymn to Indra whom he calls the King of Immortals is seen as mounted "on the Sun's bright beam". His hymn to Surya has echoes of the Vedic salutation to Surya who rides on a chariot drawn by seven horses. In this poem William Jones used all the fifty names of the Sun god. The hymn to Lakshmi depicts her as the mother goddess who is the consort of Narayan who preserves the world and nature. Quite different in mood is *A Hymn to Camdeo* describing the god of love's attempt to rouse in Lord Shiva amorous feelings for Uma. The austere god turns Kamadev into ashes for his impudence.

Lest he be considered a pagan by his orthodox Christian countrymen, Jones stated that: "In learning the pagan theology of old Greece and Rome we must consider that the allegories contained in the Hymn to Lacshmi constitute at this moment the prevailing religion of a most extensive and celebrated empire and are devoutly believed by many millions whose industry adds to the revenue of Britain and whose manners which are interwoven with their religious opinions nearly affect all Europeans who reside among them."

One gets the impression that William Jones, swept away by poetic ardour about Hindu gods, wanted to give a practical reason for being enchanted by them and enjoined others to be equally enchanted. Jones' hymn to *Prakriti* or nature is ornamental in style. The *Hymn to Durga* is inspired by Kalidasa's *Kumara Sambhava.* Jones had just begun to read Kalidasa and was captivated by the great Indian poet's dramatic imagination. He describes Durga's passionate love for Lord Shiva and then her mystical union with him.

These poems were immensely popular in England and Europe. Jones was able to convey what was essentially Hindu in content in the form of European poetic idiom. The Western reader was fascinated by the rich imagery of Hindu mythology, the novel sentiments and values that William Jones portrayed with such empathy. So popular were they that many of them, especially *The Enchanted Fruit* and the *Hymn to Kamadeva* were sold in London in pirated versions!

Sir William Jones delivered eleven lectures as the President of the Bengalatic Society. He identified Sone as the Erannoboas of Megasthenes, the river that stands at the confluence of the Ganges near the ancient city of Pataliputra or Palibothra as the Greeks called it. His readings of ancient Sanskrit classics revealed that Hiranyabahu was another name for Sone. His study also led to the discovery that the King Sandrocottas mentioned by the Greeks in 315 BC, who defeated the Greek general Seleucus, was the famous Indian monarch Chandragupta Maurya who ruled his empire from the capital at Pataliputra.

Jones had several gigantic literary projects in mind concerning India, Arabia, China, Persia and Tartary that he named *Desiderata*. Unfortunately he did not live to complete this monumental work. Jones was the first European to edit a Sanskrit text, Kalidasa's *Ritusanhara* or *Pageant of the Seasons*. This was translated into English followed by the *Gita Govinda* of Jayadeva, the *Hitopadesha* – a collection of fables containing stories in which the philosopher Vishnu Sharman tries to teach morality to his sons. As in *Aesop's Fables* the stories are told through animals and a moral is attached to each story. He also translated large parts of the *Vedas*. Through these intellectual activities Jones in collaboration with Wilkins and Colebrooke began a serious study of Oriental subjects that was called "the new scholarly movement".

These Englishmen were the heralds of the Indian Renaissance.

It was William Jones who by his search for a common linguistic origin commenced the science of Comparative Philology. He was the very first European who realized the importance of Sanskrit in the family of Indo-Germanic languages. The exploration of a common religious heritage between India, Rome and Greece led him to evolve the discipline of Comparative Mythology. His search took him to Benaras and other centres of learning where he collected manuscripts.

Affinity of language, Jones believed, must have led to common traditions in religion, myths and legends. The search for common language ancestry led to speculation about the history of these people. Jones felt that the Egyptians, Ethiopians, Persians, Indians, Romans, Greeks, and Goths belong to a common group while the Semetic races formed another group and that the Chinese and Japanese originally came from India and that they developed a different group of language.

William Jones is now considered the father of Comparative Philology. His interest and knowledge of Sanskrit led to his study of languages and their inter-relationship while his vast linguistic background and proficiency in various groups of languages gave him the facility to look into the origins and cultural evolutions of languages. The main impetus for comparative philology came towards the end of eighteenth century when it was discovered that Sanskrit bore a number of startling resemblances to Greek and Latin. William Jones brought them to the attention of the scholarly world and put forward the hypothesis in 1786 that all three languages must have "sprung from some common source which perhaps no longer exists". By this time a number of texts and glossaries of the older Germanic languages (Gothic, Old High German, Old Norse) had been published and Jones realized that Germanic and Old Persian and perhaps Celtic had evolved from the same common source. Sanskrit may have been the common source.

Sanskrit – Sanskrita means 'prepared, cultivated, refined' – is the classical language of India and is considered a branch of the old Indo-European tongue from which Prakrit and modern Indo-European languages have evolved. Vedic Sanskrit based on a dialect of north-west India was used from Circa 1500 BC to about 200 BC. Classical Sanskrit overlapped Rig Vedic period dating from Circa 500 BC to AD 1000. This began with standardization of grammar in the important grammar of Panini (fifth century BC). It was the vehicle of a rich literature prior to fifteenth century. It is now written in Devanagari script and is widely used in India as scholarly second language with a status similar to Latin in medieval Europe. Sanskrit continues to be a learned and sacred language.

Juan Masecaro, the latest translator of the *Gita*, says of Sanskrit:

> Sanskrit literature is a great literature. We have the great songs of the Vedas, the splendour of the Upanishads, the glory of the Bhagvad Gita, the vastness of the Mahabharata, the tenderness and heroism of the Ramayana, the wisdom of the Fables, the stories of Jataka, the scientific philosophy of Sankhya, the psychological philosophy of the Yoga, the poetical philosophy of the Vedanta, the laws of Manu, the grammar of Panini, the scientific writings, the lyrical poetry and drama culminating in the great poetry and drama and Kalidasa.

Professor Arthur Besreldale Keith in the Preface to his *History of Sanskrit Literature* wrote:

> The great poets of India wrote for audiences of experts. They were masters of the learning of their day. Long trained in the use of language and the aim to please by subtlety not simplicity of effect. They had at their disposal a singularly beautiful speech, and they commanded elaborate and most effective meters ... It is in the great writers of Kavya alone headed by Kalidasa that we find depth of feeling for life and nature matched into perfection of expression and rhythm ... The Kavya literature includes some of the great poetry

> of the world. But it can never be expected to attain wide popularity in the West because it is essentially untranslatable ... we cannot possibly give the reader the same poem as the original.

William Jones was greatly interested in the Indian grammarian Panini who lived in the fifth or sixth century BC and was the author of *Ashtadhyay* or *Eight Chapters* which is regarded as the oldest known grammar of Sanskrit and perhaps the oldest extant grammar in the world. Grammar scholarship had an impact on Western studies of classical languages.

William Jones studied the *Grammar* of Panini whose contribution was the presentation of a clear systematized description of Sanskrit phonology and morphology and syntax. Panini's grammar appeared to Jones more systematic than Greek, Latin, Arabic or Persian. He stated that Panini gave him insight into "relationships between explicitly stated basic morphemes and the similar implicitly intuited basic morphemes which he already knew in the classical languages". (Holgar Pedersen, *Linguistic Signs in the Nineteenth Century*.) Jones also found in Panini phonetic and structural similarities between Sanskrit and Greek which suggested simultaneous development. He reluctantly discarded the theory that Sanskrit had travelled from India to Greece since such a journey in the third or second millennium BC would have been hazardous. He therefore reiterated his theory that Sanskrit was the autochthonous language of India. Panini's system provided in detail of grammar and syntax that he tried to apply to Greek and Latin. Jones compared the similarities and differences between the languages and presented his thesis before Asiatic Society in February 1786.

His next pre-occupation was the reconstruction of Indian history on the basis of religious texts such as the *Puranas* and the *Vedas*. He found that the story of the great flood of Noah and Moses had been referred to in the *Puranas* and that the Cush of Moses was the same as the Kusa of Valmiki, the author of the *Ramayana*.

However, dating Indian history from Hindu mythology was difficult. He tried to reconcile Hindu mythology with Biblical traditions as well as to Graeco-Roman myths. He said that Ganesa of the Hindus was the same as Janus of the Romans and the Greek Zeus-Pitr was the Hindu Brihaspati. This, he declared, indicated their common ancestry, their common gods, worshipped by different names. The zodiac, he observed, was known in India long before it is mentioned in Greece. He held the view that the method of instructing by apologues, the decimal notation, and the game of chess were all invented by the Hindus. The ancient Indians carried all this information with them at the time of their migrations to their new homesteads. The antiquity of Sanskrit proved that Indian civilization was older than any in Europe and even that of Persia.

This theory would be contradicted in the next century when Orientalists such as Max Muller, eager to find favour with the growing spirit of imperialism, explained away the greatness of ancient India by formulating a theory that 'Aryans' invaded India and produced the Vedic civilization. Never was the actual homeland of the 'Aryans' identified nor the reasons given for such a mass migration. The discovery of the Indus Valley civilization imparted a new dimension to the interpretation of Indian history and gave rise to new theories that are still being debated. William Jones' thesis – that Sanskrit and Vedic culture was autochthonous and not brought by invading or migrating Aryans – is now being accepted by Indian historians and archaeologists on the basis of linguistic evidence.

In building up the chronology of events Jones relied mainly on the *Bhagavat Purana.* His guide was Radhakant Sharman who interpreted the *Puranas* in terms of history and the reckoning of time. Joining them was Goverdhan Kaul a Kashmiri pundit who joined in the efforts to reconstruct ancient Indian history.

The real breakthrough in Indian historiography came with the identification of Sandrocottas as Chandragupta Maurya and Palibothra as Pataliputra. Since these names were referred to in Greek records it was possible to establish the chronology of the various dynasties of ancient India. There were no other historical or epigraphical evidences on which to proceed though epigraphical inscriptions written in the old Kutila script were available throughout the country. A decade earlier Wilkins had deciphered some inscriptions in the later Brahmi script of the Pala period in Bengal which enabled him to state that this dynasty ruled Bengal in the sixth and seventh centuries. He could not decipher Asokan inscriptions that were written in the early Brahmi script. This decoding would have to wait for another half a century when James Prinsep entered the scene. In the meantime Buddhists inscriptions and Chinese records and travelogues written by pilgrims were able to establish the dates of events in the early Christian era.

By demonstrating how to gather corroborative evidence from coins, ancient texts and inscriptions on ancient monuments, William Jones established the methodology for reconstructing ancient Indian history.

Despite his rational eighteenth century education William Jones seemed to have been touched by the spiritual ambience of India. Perhaps he presaged the mood that would gather momentum in Europe – of withdrawal from the entirely cerebral outlook of eighteenth century Europe. In Germany the first stirrings of this was visible in Schlegel and would be brought to a culmination in Wagner who turned to mystical medieval traditions for his inspiration in music. It was natural that a Europe wearied of rationalism sought in Hinduism a deeper significance, a harmony and serenity that eluded a Europe soon to be caught in the throes of bloody revolutions and wars of conquest.

It would not be surprising if the spectacle of Britons immersed in making fortunes by whatever means was possible, as well as the frenzy of pursuing pleasure, made Jones the scholar and poet distance himself from his compatriots. Was it the sight of the brevity of life among the Europeans in India, the maladies and sudden deaths which terminated frantic money-making and equally frantic hedonism that made Jones pause and wonder about the purpose of existence? How else can one explain the man of law, the classical scholar, a true product of the Enlightenment turn to Hindu deities for poetry, to the tender *Gita Govinda* of Jayadeva and finally the romantic pastoral idyll of Shakuntala? Had India opened a new inner world to him?

His interest in Hinduism deepened. Before he had mastered Sanskrit he relied on Persian translations of Hindu texts such as Prince Dara Shikho's *Upanishads* and *Dharma Shastras*. The classical scholar found the influence of the *Vedanta* in Greek philosophy, especially that of Pythogoras and Plato. He was attracted to the monotheism of Sankaracharya's *Advaitavad* and the theory of the transmigration of souls. He felt that the *Vedanta* was based on lofty principles that may not be comprehended by everyone but a religion that propounds a selfless surrender to God is great.

It is not known whether his enthusiasm for Hinduism attracted the disapproval of his orthodox Christian compatriots; he made his position clear without fear when he wrote in 1787, "I am no Hindu but I hold the doctrine of the Hindus concerning a future state to be incomparably more rational, more pious and more likely to deter men from vice than the horrid opinions inculcated by the Christians on punishment without end."

Perhaps his ardour for Indian thoughts was generating resentment both in official circles in Calcutta and in London. So he also declared that the greatest achievement of the intellect was to be found in the British constitution. This sounds like a recant – after extolling the achievements of Indian metaphysics, and going so far as to say in his article, *On the Philosophy of the Asiaticks*, in *Asiatick Researches* that Newtonian science had elements of the Vedas that refer to "a force universally attractive".

Sir William and Lady Anna Maria sought their own pastoral idyll far from the clamour of Calcutta and even Garden Reach. The couple went to the Governor General's formal receptions since these were *de rigeur* but otherwise held themselves aloof from the lavish parties thrown by British officers and merchants. However, Sir William always went to the weekly meeting of the Asiatic Society and people with serious interests were welcome to the Jones home. An English traveller, Thomas Twining records in his book *Travelling In India a Hundred Years Ago* of how he went to dine with Sir William and Lady Jones at their home in Garden Reach. The scholar was dressed in white kurta pyjama and at the dining table called for Othello, his pet turtle whom he fed.

They retreated to the tranquillity of Krishnagar on the river, not far from the famed seat of learning in Nabodwip. There they lived in a two-story thatched cottage surrounded by deer, sheep, an occasional tiger and the singing of nightingales. Brahmin pundits came to discuss Sanskrit texts with Sir William while Lady Anna Maria read Italian poets. The pundits listened with interest when Jones told them about Europe and its culture and traditions.

Anxious to see more of Bengal, William Jones and Anna Maria journeyed to Chittagong on the ship *Phoenix*. They were charmed by the hilly forests and the mighty estuary of the Ganga flowing into the Bay of Bengal. It was an idyllic period for them; while Jones worked on legal matters, philology and poetry, Anna Maria sketched and painted Indian plants. Sometimes they went hunting for rare plants in the lush forests. In the evenings by the light of candles they played chess together. It was during the sojourn at

Chittagong that William Jones with the help of a Persian teacher read Firdausi's epic *Shah-Namah*. Jones was deeply impressed by the Sohrab-Rustam story. He planned to write a tragic poem on the theme in English but in the Greek style. He was not able to take up the work; a century later Mathew Arnold wrote the poem that Jones had envisaged. His original attraction for Persian returned briefly when he decided to publish his manuscript of *Laila Majnun* for Indian readers.

When the Supreme Court closed in June they usually went to Krishnanagar to escape the humid heat of the monsoon in Calcutta. There William Jones could study without disturbances. From dawn until mid-morning he worked on Sanskrit and then sat with his wife to read Italian poets or teach her Algebra. Sometimes they made experiments in chemistry. On Sundays they read books on theology as there was no church in Krishnanagar. Now that Brahmins and scholars had come to know of the extraordinary English judge's pursuit of Sanskrit studies, pundits from Nadia came to assist Sir William. His vocabulary expanded swiftly. He was not only interested in ancient legal codes of India but in her ancient and magnificent literature and metaphysics. Where better to learn about that than the home of Shri Chaitanya who had transformed Bengal in the middle ages with his message of the brotherhood of man.

Their happiness was clouded by Anna Maria's declining health. Doctors advised her to leave India's harsh climate for Europe as her frail constitution may not be able to withstand the rigours of Indian summers. William Jones had been planning to leave for England in 1790 but now he asked her if she would like to leave India before him. Anna Maria refused to leave him and he, cherishing her support and company, did not insist. Immersed in his study of Sanskrit and research on philology, he left his wife to deal with his correspondence with friends and relatives in England. They planned to save up enough money in order to retire comfortably and leave India in 1795.

44

William Jones and the Indian Game of Chess

"Chess is the art of human reason" – Gustav Selerius, Duke of Brunswick, 1616.

"There are two classes of men; those who are content to yield to circumstances and play whist, those who aim to control circumstances and who play chess" – *Attic Salt* by Mortimer Collins (1827-1876).

"The game of chess is the touchstone of the intellect" – J.W. von Goethe.

William Jones was a passionate votary of the game of chess. While still in school at the age of sixteen, he wrote a poem of 425 stanzas on Caissa, the goddess of chess, and the consort of Mars. The mythological figure Caissa, who was a product of his school boy mind has now been enshrined in chess lore – though the poem itself is long and out of print, perhaps deservedly so, as the ponderous pentameters amply demonstrate. The interesting story is told with the typical euphemistic elaboration of poetic expression of that age. The poem is not written by a chess player but by a scholar who is familiar with the chess moves of the game and the value of the pieces.

The pattern of movement of individual chess pieces is shown for instance by the description of the movement of the thoughts on the chess-board. A good memory is an indispensable asset in the armoury of a chess player and this William Jones had in abundant measure. His interest in chess did not vanish with his youth; it was not merely an adolescent interest because one hears of him playing chess up to the end of his days in Calcutta and Krishnanagar. And his interest must undoubtedly have been rekindled in the land where chess was invented by a philosopher in the sixth century who wanted to devise a game that would depict a battle between two armies which he called Chaturanga or army game. In India chess became the game of kings.

It was in India that chess literally became the royal game with the Emperor Akbar (1542-1605). This great Moghul liked playing the game on a mammoth open air chess board at Fatehpur Sikri, near Agra, using real horses, elephants and camels as chess-pieces. His grandson, Emperor Shah Jahan built a chess palace at Jehanpore where he indulged in his predilection for both chess and feminine pulchritude by using the ladies of his harem as pieces. Early Indian chessmen were miniature reproductions of the animals or persons whose names they bore. Many were of ordinary shape, cheap to produce, for use by the common player. Other tastes were reflected in models elaborately carved, mostly in ivory.

The poem *Caissa* tells the story of the wooing of the wood-nymph Caissa by Mars, the god of war. When his overtures were repulsed, Mars seeks the assistance of Euphron, the god of sport, for devising a recreation to beguile the damsel. Euphron obliges and invents the game of chess which he names after Caissa. The poem is 425 stanzas long, and is a rococo effort. Among the trills and runs of Augustan poetry, Jones included several graphic passages on the pattern of the moves of chess pieces on the board. As poetry *Caissa* has dated but it is notable even today because unwittingly the school boy Jones had created for chess a Muse who remains enshrined as the patron-goddess of the game more than two hundred years later. Tongue in cheek, the school boy also fabricated an etymology for the word chess in the last lines of his poem:

He taught the rules that guide the pensive game,
And called it Caissa from the Dryad's name,
When Albion's son who most its praise confess
Approved the play and named it thoughtful chess.

And though all four hundred and twenty-five stanzas of the poem are a virtuoso exercise in liberally ornamental Augustan prosody may not be memorable, there are several which deserve quotation. For instance, the lines on the movements of the knights and the final tongue-in-cheek lines with which the schoolboy Jones contributed a resoundingly false piece of etynmology to the theology of chess 'Caissa-Chess'. In the essay on chess, interest in chess, etymology, law, all converged in a very interesting amalgam. It was an essay that only Jones and no one else could have written.

The poem *Caissa* has an interesting artistic and linguistic pedigree. It was obviously inspired by the poem *Scacchia Ludus* – the game of chess written by the 15th century Bishop of Alba, the Italian Marcus Hieronymus Vida. Like Jones, Vida was both a lover of chess and poetry and who in his day was known as the 'Christian Virgil'. Jones, already a Latin scholar at seventeen, had read Vida's poem in the original and with youthful virtuosity fashioned a variation on the theme of chess as a game of divine origin.

It is also likely that it was Jones who in the circle of Dr. Johnson introduced the poem to another habitué of the Literary Club – Oliver Goldsmith. The chain of chess and poetry continues with Oliver Goldsmith. Jones had known Goldsmith since 1769 and in 1772 when his *Collected Poems* was published, they were both members of Johnson's Literary Club.

During his years in India, William Jones pursued his researches into the origins of chess. In his essay on *The Indian Game of Chess*, which he contributed to *Asiatic Researches* in 1790, he wrote, "If evidence be required that chess was invented by the Hindus, we may be satisfied with the testimony of the Persians who, though as much inclined as other nations to appropriate the ingenious inventions of a foreign people, unanimously agree that the game was imported from the west of India together with the charming fables of Vishnuvarman in the sixth century of our era." He also established that the name was derived from the Sanskrit word Chaturanga – "that is four angas or members of an army which are said to be in the Amaracosha to be hastya-swaratha-padatam or elephants, horses, chariots and foot-soldiers. Now by a natural corruption of the pure Sanskrit word, it was changed by the old Persians into Shatarang when the game was introduced to Persia in the 6th century AD". He also traced how "it has been transformed by successive changes into axedraz, searchu, ecichs, chess and by a whimsical concurrence of circumstances given birth to the English word check and even a name to the Exchequer of Britain." He also propounded the theory that "the beautiful simplicity of the game as it is commonly played in Europe and Asia convinces me that it was invented by one effort of some great genius, not completed by gradual improvements but formed to use the words of the Italian critics by the first intention."

H.J.R. Murray in his authoritative *History of Chess* concluded that it was the descendant of an Indian game that was transmitted to the West in the shape it had assumed sometime in the 7th century. The game was most likely passed on by the Moors to the Spaniards and to the Italians by the Byzantines and thus made its way further into Europe. Chess became a favourite pastime of the aristocracy; the young lovers in Shakespeare's *Tempest* are shown playing chess. However, the clergy frowned on it as a wasteful and compulsive distraction from spiritual commitment.

The genius of the Essay, *On the Indian Game of Chess*, is of special interest as it illustrates Jones' special propensity for dovetailing different lines of enquiry and, in a sense combining work with play. At the time when this essay was written, Jones was engaged with the task of compiling the *Digest of Hindu and Islamic Law*. He had enlisted the assistance of his noted Sanskrit scholar Radhakanta Sharman and his preceptor Jaganath Tarakapanchanan of Tribeni for identifying the sources of the Hindu law and for giving firm authoritative translations. It was a coincidence that both these pundits were chess players and in the words of Jones "both of them, especially the venerable sage of Tribeni understood the game". Quoting the *Bhavisya Purana* Jones points out, "One circumstance from the Puranas seems very surprising; all games of hazard are forbidden by Manu yet the game of Chaturanga in which dice are used is taught by the great Vyasa himself, whose law tract appears with that of Gotama among the eighteen books which form the *Dharmashastras."*

One pleasing aspect is the way that the three scholars, an Englishman and two Indians, bound by the bonds of erudition, mutual respect and common love of the 'exquisitely contrived' game of kings, unravelled the chess lore of India by their forays into the scriptures and ancient writings. They must have often sat, of an evening, in the gardens of Alipore or in Jones' country villa in Krishnagar, Jones and Jaganath locked in the combat, playing on an old board of onyx and crystal with ornamental chessmen of silver and ivory with king and queen on elephants, ministers in place of bishops and the pawns as sepoys. Their friend Radhakant would have looked on. All the three were linked by the strong bonds of the magic masonry of the chess game whose lore, scholarship and etymological derivations they shared.

45
Jones Discovers Kalidasa

It was inevitable that while studying Sanskrit William Jones would discover the great poet of India – Kalidasa. It was inevitable too that the poet in William Jones would be irresistibly drawn to this epochal figure of classical Sanskrit literature. He extolled the great works of Kalidasa - *Meghaduta, Ritu Samhita, Raghuvamsa* etc.

Kalidasa was an outstanding master of Sanskrit poetry and is considered the greatest writer of any Indian epoch excluding the ancient seers Valmiki and Vyas who composed the *Ramayana* and the *Mahabharata*.

There is little historical or biographical data about Kalidasa. The date of Kalidasa's birth is not certain. If he was a poet in the court of Samrat Vikramaditya, he would have been born in the first century before Christ. However some scholars place his reign in the fifth century of the Christian era. His poems suggest Brahmin origin and judging by his name, Kalidasa or servant of Kali, he probably belonged to the Shaivite sect. He is regarded as one of the nine gems or *Navaratna* in the court of Vikramaditya.

Kalidasa reflected the cultural values of a prosperous and peaceful era, where a secure and sophisticated aristocracy gave patronage to poets, artists and scholars. His *Sakuntala* is generally regarded as the best Indian literary effort of any period. *Vikramivasi, Malavika Aghumitra, Raghuvamsa, Kumara Sambhava and Meghaduta* are his important works. In his book on Kalidasa Purasu Balakrishna says "beauty of nature is depicted with a precise elegance of metaphor difficult to match in any of the worlds literatures...The society depicted in Kalidasa is of a courtly aristocracy...Kalidasa has done more than any other writer to wed the older Brahmanical religious traditions in its natural concern with Sanskrit to the seeds of a new and brilliant secularism. With the collapse of the Gupta empire Kalidasa became a memory of the perfection that neither Sanskrit nor the Indian aristocracy would know again."

Kalidasa's epic poems were the earliest Indian works to be translated into a Western language by William Jones. The translations awakened the interest of Goethe who did a German translation and influenced other German men of letters and inspired English and French men of letters. A poem of William Blake (1808) shows the influence of Kalidasa.

Bring me my bow of burning gold
Bring me my arrows of desire
Bring me my spear, o clouds enfold,
Bring me my chariot of fire.
Kalidas exulted in similes –
a silver car air borne
whose silent wheels
fresh wet from clouds of morn
son of a dazzling dew.
One wonders if Keats in the *Endymion* was inspired by this.
The ocean forming
against my bridges which
divides it as far as
the Malaya mountain like
the milky way dividing
the autumnal sky.

William Jones' translation in 1789 of *Sakuntala* by Kalidasa and *Gita Govinda* and *Manusamhita* in 1794 brought the greatness of Sanskrit literature to the notice of the world for the first time.

In his *Glimpses of Kalidasa*, Purasu Balakrishnan states:

> It is sometimes regarded that in greatness Kalidasa comes next to Valmiki and Vyasa and only after them comes Kamban and Tulsidas. Kalidasa created a new genre of *Duta Kavya* – messenger poems or message poems. These are lyrical love poems or love letters where love is recollected and anticipated in separation half in tranquility and half in flame. Jayadeva the great poet of twelfth century of India called Kalidasa *Kavikula Guru* or the poet's poet. The German poet and dramatist Schiller used the motif of *Meghaduta* or Messenger of the Clouds in his play *Maria Stuart* where the captive Mary, Queen of Scots, sends a message to her native land through a cloud. Goethe modeled the *Prologue to Faust* on the prologue to *Sakuntala.*

"Kalidasa is not only a poet's poet but a painter's poet and a sculptor's poet." C. Shivarama Murthy wrote of sculptures inspired by Kalidasa.

> He was also a patriot's poet who knew and loved India and dwelt lovingly on her charms of body and soul. India lay before him with her mighty mountains and humble hills, her great mother river and her little streams and her rolling fields spreading from the Himalayas to seas, her birds and beasts, her trees and every little flower, her populous cities and her luxurious palaces, her tranquil and friendly and godly hermit groves, her gentle and gracious men, her lovely and steadfast women, her sages of great learning. He gathered them all in one sweeping embrace of love and he gave us the quintessence of them all in visions of beauty that shined and shined forever. To him it was given poetically and spiritually to see these visions as one unity.
>
> In *Meghaduta* Kalidasa's hero exhorts a cloud to visit Ujjain where his beloved lives. In *Raghuvamsa* Kalidasa did for India what Virgil did for Rome in his *Aeniad.* Kalidasa was also the people's poet in which he shows a whole spectrum of society, tenderness of feeling, brilliance of imagination, opulence of imagery, subtle suggestions, sublime grandeur of description, mastery of rhythm and melody that is a spell, a perfect marriage of sound and sense. Kalidasa had a profundity of elucidation and a magnificent versatility. All these gave Kalidasa a unique place among the loftiest poets of the world.

William Jones said that Kalidasa was the Shakespeare of India in aesthetic beauty and sensuous delights. Kalidasa, he said, "had the large imagination of an ancient, a Hindu who was brought up in the universal philosophy of the Upanishads and his love of nature is an ideal, as true as the philosophy of the Upanishads".

Because literature consists of conventional symbols there exists in literature the problem of translation which does not exist in any of the other arts when we want to extend the audience to non-native speakers of the language a great deal of the works of the original character is lost.

In his treatise *Transformation,* William Jones observed that

> those who watch India most impartially see a vast transformation going on there but sometimes it produces a painful impression on them and they see much that is destructive and goods things together. Sometimes they doubt whether they see many good things called

> into existence. But they did not see any enormous improvement under which we may fairly hope that all other improvements are potentially included. They see anarchy and plunder brought to an end and something like the immense *Majestas Romanae Pacis* established among two hundred and fifty millions of human beings. (Sir John Robert Seeley, 1909, *The Expansion of England* – Lecture 8)

William Jones opened up a new world of ideas and heritage before the Western world. Another Indologist, Robertson, was influenced by Jones. He observed, "Indian Metaphysics is as acute as Greek and Indian Astronomy as accurate." Deriving his knowledge from William Jones he thought that 'Indian drama was refined in taste and content.' By eighteenth century standards he found some defects in the *Bhagvad Gita* and thought that it was ill constructed and could not understand why philosophy was introduced into the epic at a moment when two armies were about to clash. Robertson failed to appreciate the immense drama of the great poem. It was this very halt in the midst of preparations for a mortal combat as the two armies are about to annihilate each other that Lord Krishna presents to the baffled Arjuna a vision of the universe and its immutable moral laws.

Jones urged the British as the paramount power to undertake the preservation of this literary heritage especially at Benaras, the Athens of India.

Not all Englishmen shared his enthusiasm for Hinduism. Robertson, a contemporary of Jones, observed, "As for Indian religion the elaborate ceremonial and the superstitious practices as corrupting elements that inflamed the passions instead of leading men to virtue." He was surprised that "such mild people as the Hindus should have such fierce gods". He was disturbed by the sensual character of the religion, by the inordinate love of pleasure, the indecent temple dances and visual representations of Indian religion in sculpture and painting. The saving quality of Indian religion he believed was the theism of the Brahmins. If only, Robertson commented, the Brahmins had spread their belief in a single deity to other castes! But as a Conservative he believed that the problem of reforming Indian religion must be left to the Indians. He did not urge the spread of Christianity. At most he suggested circulation of ideas for the benefit of society so that the whole of society might benefit from new ideas and new scientific knowledge.

Fundamentally conservative, both William Jones and Robertson insisted that all the civilized achievements of India had to be preserved, not only because they were notable contributions but also because they were prerequisites to the future development of India. They emphasized that the political order, social improvement and cultural achievement of India could not be developed unless the development was founded on the traditions and laws of the country. With deep foresight and understanding of cultural evolution they realized that progress must come from an inner revival of the nation's spirit.

46

Establishment of Asiatic Society

It is one of the great ironies of history that the Indian Renaissance began under the auspices of East India Company scholars within the portals of the Asiatic Society.

The establishment of the Asiatic Society in Calcutta in 1784 was a landmark in the cultural history of India. This led to the development of Indology and Indian archaeology as serious academic disciplines. The guiding spirit for the foundation of the Asiatic Society was Governor-General Warren Hastings who saw the need to establish an organization that would collect, impart and disseminate knowledge of India's material and intellectual civilization to the rest of the world. Supporting him in this endeavour was Sir William Jones, then Supreme Court Associate Justice, and the scholar-officials of the East India Company. He has been called the father of Indology. William Jones had expressed the desire "to know India better than any other European ever knew it". While doing this he also searched around for other Englishmen who would be interested in starting an organization to study "the history and antiquities, arts, sciences and literature of Asia".

Ironically, while Hastings was consolidating British political power in India he also saw the need for British officials to know about India's vast and ancient heritage. While making India known to the world the Asiatic Society succeeded in awakening the awareness of Indians to their own traditions and heritage at a time when belief in themselves was being undermined by foreign conquest and the impact of the West.

As early as 1778 William Jones was regarded as an authority on India. Inviting him to discuss the Bengal Bill over breakfast Edmund Burke told William Jones, "The natives of the East to whose literature you have done so much justice are particularly under your protection for their rights."

Soon after arriving in Bengal Jones realized that his plan to promote Asian studies and researches would not be realized unless scholars worked in collaboration since the subjects for study were vast and varied. In January 1784 William Jones wrote a letter in which he mooted the plan to establish a society for Oriental studies in Calcutta.

In his Inaugural Address at the founding of the Asiatic Society of Bengal William Jones said,

> When I was at sea last August on my voyage to this country which I had long and ardently desired to visit, I found one evening on inspecting the observations of the day that India lay before us and Persia whilst a breeze from Arabia blew nearly on our stern .... It gave me inexpressible pleasure to find myself in the midst of so noble an amphitheatre, almost encircled by the vast regions of Asia which has ever been esteemed the muse of Sciences, the inventress of delightful and useful studies, sets the scene of glorious action fertile in the production of human genius, abounding in natural wonders and infinitely diversified in the forms of religion and government, in the laws, names, customs and languages as well as in the features and complexion of men .... How important and extensive the field was still unexplored ... in this fluctuating, imperfect and limited conditions of life such inquiries and improvements could only be made through the united efforts of many.

The first meeting of the Asiatic Society was held on 15th January 1784 in the Grand Jury room of the Supreme Court under the presidency of Chief Justice Robert Chambers. Others present were Mr. Justice Hyde, John Carnac, John Shore, Charles Wilkins, Francis Gladwin and Jonathan Duncan. All of them shared William Jones' interest in Oriental studies and had resolved to form a society to further studies on Asia.

The Governor-General, Warren Hastings, who had been the guiding spirit was requested to become the first President of the Society but he declined the offer. William Jones was elected President. G.H. Barlow was selected as the Secretary.

The word 'Asiatic' substituted 'Oriental' since the Society would concern itself with Asian civilizations rather than those of Egypt and Abyssinia who were also considered under the loose generic term of 'Oriental'.

The inspiration for the Society was not entirely original. Six years earlier in Indonesia (or Batavia as it was then called by her

Dutch rulers) an organization, Koninklijk Bataviaasch Genootschap, to study Indonesian culture, had been founded by the Dutch administrators. However, the Batavian Society did not acquire the eminence or celebrity of the Asiatic Society which was the parent of all other Asiatic Societies including the Royal Asiatic Society of Great Britain and Ireland that was formed in 1823. In other countries, the Asiatic Society inspired the establishment of Oriental Institutes like the Institutes of Oriental Studies in Constantinople and Damascus, in Germany and Russia. All Orientalists agreed that "this oldest learned society of Bengal has accelerated the growth of the larger part of subsequent scientific activity in India, itself being well known for its own solid work, in literature, history, archaeology and philology." It may be regarded as a mother of the Indian Science Congress Association which held its first meeting in 1914 and the National Institute of Sciences of India established in 1935 which is the nearest equivalent in India to the Royal Society of London, as well as the Indian Historical Congress of later years.

The circumstances were favourable in Bengal because there was a group of young officers who shared William Jones's fascination for Asian studies. They did not form a homogeneous group; they were divided by political differences. However, Halhed and Wilkins had become friends and had worked in collaboration to produce the first Bengal typeface in 1778 and produced works of their own which will be described in another part of the book. Gladwin had written *Institutes of Emperor Akbar* which was a brief version of Abu Fazl's *Aini-I-Akbari.* Creditable as their individual efforts were, there was no organised attempt to promote Oriental studies.

At the inaugural meeting William Jones outlined his plans for the Society as well as the purpose of Oriental studies which would help Europeans to understand the laws, religions, forms of government and the natural wonders of India. Not only would this extend the horizons of knowledge but would also help Britain to rule India better. He subscribed to the views of Francis Bacon who had said that memory, reason, and imagination were the three aspects of the human mind and it would follow that history, science and art would be the product of these three faculties.

In his usual democratic manner Sir William emphasized that there would be no formalities or regulations imposed on the members of the Society. He suggested holding of weekly meetings in the Grand Jury room where original papers would be read and discussed. No translations except of those papers written by Indian authors would be permitted. It is strange however that he did not recommend the admission of Indian scholars to the Society established for the benefit of promoting Indian studies!

Sir William Jones laboured assiduously to strengthen the Asiatic Society. He advocated a balanced and pragmatic approach to facilitate work. The enrollment of members was sparse and the attendance at meetings was thin. The main interest of Britons in Calcutta after trade was social entertainment and discussing political events. That the Society survived is due mainly to official sponsorship that had been bestowed from the beginning by Warren Hastings and later by his successors. Moreover, Sir William Jones discouraged any attempt to turn this academic institution into a place of social gathering or political discussions.

The success of the Society depended on actual studies to be discussed at meetings. Old manuscripts were collected from Indian scholars from various centres of learning such as Benaras, Gaur, Nabodwip and Gaya. Dissemination of knowledge was necessary if the work of the Society and the scholars was to be known. Jones personally attended to correspondence with his Orientalist friends in England and Europe. Various universities in Europe, including Oxford and Cambridge, suggested that Oriental institutes should be established in these universities. A steady and regular source of information on the work of the Asiatic Society was sought to be made known by establishing a magazine – *Asiatick Miscellany* – in 1785 which contained translations, poems, extracts from old texts as well as research papers. Production of the journal became a labour of love; when there were not sufficient contributions to the journal from scholars Sir William Jones himself wrote articles and research papers. Wherever he went – Banares, Malda, Nadia, Patna, Gaya, Gaur – Jones collected information, manuscripts and books. He discussed diverse subjects with Muslim and Hindu scholars. His friends were the historian Ghulam Hussain, the Sanskrit scholars Pandit Ramlochan, Radhakanta Sharman and Jagannath Tarakapanchanan who would help him to prepare the *Digest of Hindu and Muslim Laws*.

At the second anniversary of the founding of Asiatic Society, Jones delivered a lecture on the purpose of establishing the Society.

It was as much for the benefit of Indians as for Europeans. In order to foster amicable relations between the rulers and the ruled it was imperative for British officials to be acquainted with Indian history and culture, her laws and customs. Astute lawyer that he was, Jones said what would appeal to his compatriots – that a better understanding of the flora and fauna of India would enable the British to have a better diet, and that knowledge of Indian crafts would pave the way for improving manufacture and industry.

Asiatick Miscellany was published by the East India Company Press. The journal was priced at twenty rupees. As the President of the Society, William Jones attended to all the details of publication including proof reading and correction. This tedious and time-consuming work was in addition to his official duties at the Supreme Court and writing judgments. Under his guidance the journal became very popular; scholars and those interested in the Orient awaited the arrival of the journal to England where politicians and the literati discussed its scholarly and sometimes exotic contents in Parliament, aristocratic homes and in coffee houses. Pirated editions were sold in London while the journal was translated in various European languages as well as in the young United States.

The Bengali renaissance that spread to other parts of India and encouraged a flowering of works in Indian languages, was a direct product of the efforts of these great scholars.

The founders were true cosmopolitans, a rare phenomenon in the age of aggressive colonialism, and they took upon themselves the difficult task of starting the dialogue of civilizations that would foster affinity between the East and West.

Seldom has the establishment of an organization had such far-reaching consequences on the exchange of ideas and cultural heritage as did the Asiatic Society in the eighteenth and nineteenth centuries. This is described in later pages.

Thus began a dialogue between civilizations that is still continuing, enriching all the participants. This was the legacy of Sir William Jones.

47
Farewell to Arcadia

By 1788, the Indian scene was improving. William Jones exerted a benign influence on the Governor-General and John Shore. To improve administration of justice, Jones had recommended preparation of a *Digest of Hindu and Muslim Laws*. Cornwallis conveyed his approval and offered funds for the assignment and gave Jones full freedom in the selection of *pundits* and *moulvis* to assist him. For the first time there was cooperation between the judiciary and the executive in Calcutta. Cornwallis now agreed with Jones that Hindus and Muslims should be governed by their own laws and not the ones imposed upon from Britain. Hastings had held this view two decades earlier. The work progressed expeditiously; the Governor-General conveyed these developments to the Court of Directors with a sense of satisfaction. William Jones felt that at last he was able to accomplish the tasks dear to his heart, both in the field of law as well as in academic matters. He realized perhaps that India had provided him an arena for the realization of his gifts which London could not have done where he might have been a mere Member of Parliament or a Minister at best. Here he was in a position to transform a country both in its administration as well as in its outlook, and to transform the manner in which the world looked at India.

The French Revolution erupted the following year and unleashed a chain of events that were epochal in character and which changed the face of Europe. Gone were the oppressive *ancien regimes* of feudal monarchies, gone too was the medieval idea of the monarch's divinity. It was a cruel yet cleansing time. The seeds of freedom and fraternity sowed by the French revolutionary armies would blossom and be mowed down and would blossom again throughout the nineteenth century. The ideas of national self-determination and representative government would spread from its European frontiers to Asia and Africa, eventually spelling the end of empires.

One wonders what would be the attitude of the great scholar and the great humanist if he had been in his own country instead of the self-imposed exile in India. Would he have tried to justify the Jacobin blood letting, the execution of the French monarchs and their aristocratic friends? Would he, a poet, like Byron and Shelley, have seen the events in France as a liberating movement? Or would he have joined the chorus of fighting 'the Corsican ogre'? At any rate his comment to his friend the Earl of Spencer on Burke's *Reflection on the Revolution in France* was "the wickedest, the silliest and the worst written book in our language".

1790, the year of their planned departure, came and went. Neither William Jones nor Anna Maria were in a hurry to leave India. Her health seemed to be improving while he, after bouts of fever, felt much stronger. While European governments were mobilizing soldiers to unleash twenty years of bloodshed, William Jones was preoccupied with thoughts of how to improve the law and order situation in Calcutta, the reduction of crime, preparation of law digests and his all consuming interest in Sanskrit studies. His interest in philology led him to evolve an International Phonetic Alphabet in four languages.

Accolades came in from different parts of the world. Delivering a lecture on William Jones, T. Walker, an American scholar said, "I have never heard of a linguist to compare with him. He could address gifted scholars of every civilized nation in his own dialect." The *European Magazine* observed, "The man of whom all this and much more may be said is now only in the bloom of manhood; possessed of integrity unimpeached, and of manner the most attractive; in his judicial capacity the glory of the British name in India; and as a scholar still indefatigable in his pursuits which render him at once the patron and example of the poet, the philosopher and the critic."

With seven hundred copies of *Asiatick Researches* going to England and Europe every month, Jones was a celebrity. His work and his thoughts were appreciated by politicians, scholars, traders and even the off-and-on mad King George III. Jones was more famous living in India than when he was in the heart of London.

The early 1790s were very fruitful years for William Jones; he had said that they were the happiest years of his life except for his constant concern for the health of Anna Maria. In 1792 he had published three books and was translating Kalidasa's *Ritusamhara* which he called *The Seasons – A Descriptive Poem*. When this was published in Calcutta he was the first European to have printed the original Sanskrit text of any work. During this period he also published *On The Musical Modes of The Hindus* in which he compared Hindu and Western music and the Hindu system of music based on Sanskrit text. The year 1791 saw the publication of *The Lunar Year of the Hindus* that was a translation of a Sanskrit tract by Raghunandana which contained accounts of the rites and ceremonies in the Hindu Lunar year. This was followed by another publication, *On the Musical Poetry of the Persians and Hindus*, which also contained the first English translation of a part of *Mathnaii* by the great Persian Sufi poet Jalal-ud-din Rumi.

By 1793 William Jones' reputation as a great Sanskrit scholar was firmly established. The publication of *Sacontala* took Europe by storm. The *Gentleman's Magazine* pronounced him "one of the most extra-ordinary characters which England has furnished". Through all his international acclaim, Sir William Jones remained as modest and amiable as in his youth.

Unknown to Anna Maria and William Jones, dark clouds were gathering around them. The constant reading of old manuscripts, writing of judgements and his own articles and discourses was taking a toll on Sir William's eyes. His doctor advised him not to read by candlelight – a pastime both he and Anna Maria enjoyed after the day's work. She had just recovered from a spell of illness when news of her father's death reached Calcutta. Out of concern for the frail wife Sir William concealed the news from her and saw that no letter mentioning the Bishop's death reached her. But one letter did slip through and Anna Maria fell ill again.

Another misfortune befell Sir William. In spite of his absolute superiority of character, intellect, and achievement he was overlooked for the post of Chief Justice of the Supreme Court. Prime Minister Pitt, a Tory, could not forget that William Jones had as a youth held radical views. So notwithstanding Jones' Herculean work, Pitt decided to promote Chambers to the high office – Chambers who did not come to court in time, who knew little of law, and who was openly accused of corruption. Chambers displayed his dishonesty in his judgements while Sir William had an impeccable reputation for fair play no matter how powerful the litigants. But William Jones had no patron in England. So he accepted the setback without a comment and continued with his work. Added to the deplorable state of affairs was Cornwallis's disastrous administrative measures in the field of commerce, land revenue, police, civil and criminal justice which both William Jones and John Shore had opposed.

His friend and one time collaborator for promotion of Oriental studies – Warren Hastings – was now standing trial in England for all the caboodle of falsehood and misrepresentations that Burke, Fox and Sheridan had gathered to indict the man who had consolidated the British Empire in India and who had tried to bring a measure of decency to the Company rule whose immoralities had been inaugurated by Clive, and who had been honoured by a baronetcy for his misdeeds. Hearing of the proceedings of impeachment of Warren Hastings, Jones felt sad but was powerless to help him. Perhaps if he had been in England he would have stood by his side as Charles Wilkins had done.

In 1791 several doctors had advised William Jones to send Anna Maria away to England in order to safeguard her health. She had postponed the departure as she did not want to leave her husband. By 1793 it was becoming obvious that she would not be able to withstand another harsh Indian summer. So William Jones toyed with the idea of accompanying her back to England but he was in the midst of the work both legal and literary and did not want to leave India without accomplishing his self imposed tasks.

On the tenth anniversary of the founding of Asiatic Society Sir William Jones gave a discourse in which he declared the advantages that would come from the Society's research on Asia's natural history as well as geography and astronomy. He believed that many scientific texts in Sanskrit should be translated as they contained unusual information on the subject. But his mind was not entirely on his work as it became clear that Anna Maria's departure could not be postponed further without endangering her life. Her condition became serious enough for them to cancel their annual holiday in Krishnanagar as there were no English doctors there. Instead they rented a house in Bandel, a former Dutch colony. Both of them went walking by the river and explored the nearby countryside to find rare plants and flowers. It was he who fell ill in Bandel and they hastily returned to Calcutta.

In November 1793 Anna Maria Jones embarked on the ship *Princess Amelia* which was to take her to England. Despite his longing to accompany her Sir William decided to remain behind and complete his work which was vital for improving the judicial system in British India. Sir William Jones watched her sail away, assuring Lady Anna Maria that he would join her within two years.

News came from Europe of the Reign of Terror in France and declaration of war on that country by England. Sir William Jones suffered deep anxiety as Anna Maria was now on the high seas and there was no knowing when French warships would intercept *Princess Amelia.* Lonely and dispirited he went on working on the *Ordinances of Manu*. He had been working on this book for seven years; it was now nearing completion.

In the Preface he wrote:

> The work now presented to the European world contains abundance of curious matter extremely interesting both to speculative lawyers and antiquaries with many beauties which need not be pointed out and with many blemishes which cannot be justified or palliated. It is a system of despotism and priest craft, both indeed limited by law but artfully conspiring to give mutual support though with mutual checks; it is filled with strange conceits in metaphysics and natural philosophy, with idle superstitions, and with a scheme of theology most obscurely figurative, and consequently liable to dangerous misconception. It abounds with minute and childish formalities, with ceremonies generally absurd and often ridiculous; the punishments are partial and fanciful, for some crimes dreadfully cruel, for others reprehensibly slight; and the very morals, though rigid enough on the whole are in one or two instances (as in the case of light oaths and of pious perjury) unaccountably relaxed. Nevertheless a spirit of sublime devotion, of benevolence to mankind, and of amiable tenderness to all sentient creatures, pervades the whole work. The style of it has a certain austere majesty, that sounds like the language of legislation and extorts a respectful awe; the sentiments of independence on all things but God, and the harsh admonitions even to Kings are truly noble. It must be remembered that those laws are actually revered as the word of the Most High, by nations of great importance to the political and commercial interests of Europe and particularly by many millions of Hindu subjects.

As William Jones worked a tumour on his right side became extremely painful but he did not pause as he worked with a frantic energy to complete his work and join Anna Maria. In a mood of deep sadness he wrote *A Hymn to the Night.* With superhuman effort he was nearing completion of this work and like a Yogi was almost able to overcome the acute physical pain that was now his constant companion. For some reason he did not even consult a doctor about the tumour and nursed a childish belief that the tumour would dissolve on its own. The fervent hope of joining Anna Maria in England and living comfortably in retirement drove him on.

He fell ill on the night of 20th April 1794. At first it looked like a fever. But the doctor diagnosed the tumour as an inflammation of the liver. On 26th April Sir William Jones' condition improved. Two ships that were soon to depart for Europe were anchored in the harbour at Calcutta. His physicians urged him to immediately embark on the ship and sail for England. On the morning of 27th April 1794 Sir William Jones passed away, his head resting on his right hand. The breeze of the Ganga, to whom he had offered a hymn, blew around him as if in benediction.

48
The Legacy of Sir William Jones

William Jones was a pivotal figure in development of both Oriental studies and British policies of the eighteenth century. By establishing the Asiatic Society of Bengal, a systematic attempt was made for the first time to study the history, society and culture of India. His works on Indian civilization caught the interest and imagination of the post-Napoleonic European mind and stimulated further research on the subject. In England he had been an ardent supporter of America independence and of the movement for Parliamentary reforms. In India he evolved a definite theory of law and government for the British Raj in Bengal. William Jones maintained contact through correspondence with men in power who often consulted him on policy matters. His *Digest of Indian Laws* was considered as important in jurisprudence as Cornwallis' Permanent Settlement was in revenue administration. Eric Stokes says, "In fact Jones occupies a larger place in the history of British attitudes to India than has hitherto been recognized."

His career is important because it shows more clearly than anything else that dichotomy of the attitudes of some of the British officers in India. Many were radicals at home and they were attracted by India, her 'glorious past' and her 'simple people', yet they had to uphold an authoritarian rule. Jones epitomized this dichotomy in his life and works.

Even after two centuries William Jones remains one of the most fascinating figures in the history of British India; not only because he was an erudite scholar who knew twenty-eight languages and made numerous great discoveries in Indian languages nor because he was a pious man who treated Indians kindly. His treatment of Indians was not as exceptional as is made out in the eighteenth century. British officers had close contact with Indians although Indians were never treated as equals, not even by Jones. Some of his discoveries were known to other scholars while others like that on Orthography were of small importance. However, some of his discoveries were of great significance. His translation of Kalidasa's *Sakuntala* had a profound effect on India. He retrieved Kalidasa from the domain of Sanskrit scholars and medieval commentators and made the great classic accessible to English readers. It was the awakening of India to her own heritage.

In the last years of the eighteenth century there was a transformation in the attitude of human outlook due to the ideas that stemmed from the Enlightenment. When Warren Hastings and William Jones founded the Asiatic Society of Bengal, they began an intellectual movement that was to have far-reaching consequences not only in the field of academics but in reviving a dormant nationalist spirit through the development of Indology and Comparative Philology. Jones inaugurated *Asiatick Researches*, the journal of the Asiatic Society that became a landmark in the study of Indian language, literature and philosophy. His writings and translations of a number of Asian classics "opened up for civilized Europe a new chapter in the Science of Man and that was Orientalism".

Indology as a subject commenced with the awareness of Indian heritage by colonial administrators and savants which led to a revaluation of Indian culture. However, the study of Indian civilization goes back to earlier times. Greek interest in India led to an exquisite cross-pollination of culture. Chinese pilgrims came to India during Maurya and Gupta eras to study Buddhist texts in Sanskrit and Prakrit that led to their translation in Chinese. Arab travellers and scholars delved into Indian medical and mathematical texts while Western scholars and travellers kindled intense curiosity in the East. A decisive role was played by German scholars on the sacred language of the Brahmins, the teachings of Buddha, the works of Zoroaster and Confucius. This marked a new epoch and a new Orientation towards the study of Asia.

The modern age of Indological studies may be said to have started in a regular manner with the three noteworthy acts of William Jones: the founding of the Asiatic Society in 1784, his definite assertion of the affinity of Sanskrit with Greek and Latin in 1786, and his translation of *Sakoontala* in 1789. The ground had been prepared by the efforts of the Governor-General Warren Hastings to have a compilation of Hindu Law made by Sanskrit pundits (1776) and the English translation of the *Bhagvad Gita* by Charles Wilkins in 1785 who as the 'Indian Claxton' played a notable part in the starting and growth of printing in Indian languages in India. Henry Thomas Colebrooke who came to Calcutta in 1782 built on the foundations laid by these and translated and edited Sanskrit texts of lexicography, grammar, poetry and fable and gave accounts of Vedas, systems of philosophy and Indian astronomy and mathematics. A collection of Sanskrit manuscripts was made by Colebrooke which formed the nucleus of the India Office collection – a catalogue of Sanskrit works was the publication of the *Suchipustaka* of the works in Fort William, Asiatic Society and Sanskrit colleges at Calcutta and Benaras.

The extension of European interest from the purely material to the intellectual concerning the East was due largely to William Jones who took a leading part in this movement. Of course there were his contemporaries also: the Arabists of Europe, the Jesuits in China who mastered Chinese, sometimes men of vast erudition but generally of a singularly orthodox or narrow outlook, and there were the scholarly pioneers like Esterao in Konkan, Beschi in Tamil, Anquetil du Perron (so much misunderstood by even Sir William Jones) in Avestan, Manoel de Assumpsao, Nathaniel Brassey Halhed in Bengali and Charles Wilkins in Sanskrit.

Professor Eric Stokes has observed,

> Ever since the famous Nanerite revolution in historical scholarship it has become fashionable among a group of scholars to neglect the role of ideas in history. It has been suggested that the ideas have no validity of their own. They are merely a rationalization of human activities, which are motivated by a thirst for power. According to Sir Lewis Nanes men in the eighteenth century went to Parliament 'to make a figure' and they no more dreamt of a seat in the House in order to benefit humanity than a child dreams of a birthday cake that 'others may eat it'. It is not for me to say whether all politicians in the eighteenth century went to the House of Commons only to 'make a figure' but it is certainly true that ideas played a significant part in the history of modern India. Men went to India for a variety of reasons; to make money, for adventure, and as a help up the social ladder in Britain. But the majority of men also had definite missionary zeal to help the future of the country.

Sir William Jones did not belong to either categories whatever may have been his previous intentions.

Sir William Jones was the embodiment of the intellectual curiosity of the highly cultivated and humanistic eighteenth century Europe; he was also something more. Like all leaders in the domain of thought he had the soul of a poet. Inspired by the *Rig Veda* and the *Puranas*, William Jones composed poems to Hindu gods and goddesses. His poem on Narayana has been compared to Shelley's *Ode to Intellectual Beauty.*

When he took up Eastern classics for translation he selected two masterpieces of Arabic and Sanskrit – *Muallaquat Al Saldh* or the *Seven Suspended Poems* of pre-Islamic Arabic literature where we find the spirit of desert Arabs in his earliest and most characteristic form and the drama *Shakuntala* of Kalidasa is one of the most exquisite creations of literature which has become a classic for all humanity. He thought that "reason and taste were the grand prerogatives of the European minds while the Asiatics have soared to greater heights in the sphere of imagination".

William Jones was rooted in the conventional and generally accepted dogmas of Christianity. Otherwise he would not have obtained the approval of his biographer Sir John Shore who became Lord Teigenmouth. An ardent Christian, Shore became a fervent patron of the British Bible Society. William Jones sought to use this rational knowledge that he believed to be part of his European heritage to the languages, culture and civilization of Asia. But he shunned any form of dogmatism, either political or religious. This scholar from the world of an English public school and an English university could with the "mystic intuition of the first explorer draw out some of the noblest and most abiding things in eastern civilization".

Foundation of the Asiatic Society stimulated the development of Indology as a serious academic discipline. The impact of Asiatic Society was evident from the very beginning. Drawing on the material available in Asiatic Society, European scholars began work on Indian studies. Faculties for study of Indian and Asian history and art were established in European universities during the nineteenth century. William Jones laid down the scope of the investigation to be taken up by the Society – it was to be man and nature: whatever is to be performed by the one or produced by the other.

Scholars in the United States also took a keen interest in the work of the Asiatic Society. Since India was *terra incognita* for

Americans they were eager to learn about this land and its culture. From the earliest days of its inception in 1796 the Secretary of the American Academy of Arts and Sciences in Cambridge, Massachusetts, sent a set of its Memoirs to the Asiatic Society and requested Sir William Jones for information on Indian literature. In 1835 an American, Professor Ashley of Philadelphia, was elected an Honorary Member of the Asiatic Society. Benjamin Franklin, a close friend of Sir William Jones, drew inspiration from Asiatic Society and founded the American Philosophical Society. In the next century American scholars such as Henry Princeton, Whitney and Lanmann were included as honorary members of the Asiatic Society. The Asiatic Society had interaction with Harvard University, the American Oriental Society, the Smithsonian Institution, the Library of Congress and other organizations interested in preservation of archives and manuscripts. One of the famous honorary members was a professor of Princeton – Dr. Albert Einstein.

Taking the lead from Britain, Russia established the Asiatic Academy at St. Petersburg in 1810. The Societe Asiatique of France was established in Paris in 1822.

The Asiatic Society vigorously sponsored pioneering work and studies in archaeology, epigraphy and historiography. Decades later scholars and epigraphists were able to decipher the Indian Pali and the Aryan Pali alphabets. This enabled them to read the ancient inscriptions and rock edicts that gave information on ancient Indian history. This in turn enabled scholars to reconstruct Indian history on the basis of epigraphical evidence. This is dealt with in some detail in Part V of the book.

Through their researches the scholars of the Asiatic Society proved that no country except Greece and Rome had made such substantial contribution to the science of Philology. Scholars of the Asiatic Society not only studied Sanskrit and its vernaculars but went on to do philological research on China, Armenia, Turkestan and other Central Asian communities.

These translations and other scholarly publications over many decades encompassing every branch of ancient studies, particularly on Indian civilization, had a significant effect in shaping the attitude of the Western world towards the Orient and her heritage.

In 1805 the Indian government granted the Asiatic Society a plot of land between Park Street and Chowringhee Road where

Captain Lock of the Bengal Engineers built a edifice to house the society. Construction was begun by the builder Jacques Pinchon in the same year. The building was completed in 1808 at a cost of thirty thousand rupees. The building was typical of eighteenth century colonial architecture; a combination of the neo-classical styles in vogue in England but modified to suit tropical climate such as verandahs and lattices to keep out the monsoon rain and summer heat.

In 1806 the Asiatic Society started its famous publication, *Bibliotheca India*, where translations of treatise, drama, prose and poetic works in Sanskrit and other Asian languages were published. Extracts of these works were also printed. The first volume was published in 1847. Hundreds of texts in Sanskrit, Arabic, Persian, Bengali, Tibetan and other languages have been published, some in the original and some in translation. Books on Hindu astronomy and medicine have also been included in the *Bibliotheca.*

In 1814 the Asiatic Society established a Museum "for the reception of all articles that might be sent to illustrate Oriental manners and history or to elucidate the peculiarities of Art and Nature in the East".

Established in 1814 the Indian Museum was the first museum in the Pacific-Asia region. As a result of archaeological excavations many valuable antiquities and objects were found and placed in the Indian Museum. Most notable was the Bharhut Rock Edict of Emperor Asoka of third century BC. Innumerable edicts and copper-plates inscribed in Pali, Brahmi Kharoshti, Nagari and Bengali scripts are housed in the Indian Museum. There are also valuable manuscripts, artefacts, and archival material dating from fifth century AD onwards. Added to this are contemporary paintings by British artists. Manuscripts in every language of India, illuminated and illustrated manuscripts of various schools and periods, are preserved in this Museum along with books in numerous European languages. The earliest palm leaf manuscript is *Kubjikamatam*, a Tantric text on the worship of goddess Kubjika dated to the seventh century AD. The *Nilamata-Purana* is inscribed in Sharada script on Kashmiri paper while the *Ganapalka* is in Bengali script. There are scripts written on birch bark and on gold lacquered leaves in Burmese script and the *Miracle of Jesus* in Armenian script in parchment. These manuscripts with their unique calligraphy, composition, colour and style are unique. A valuable collection was of ancient coins. Over the years the collection expanded, the contributions coming in from both private donors and from finds retrieved from excavations. A major acquisition was acquired in 1859 when the Society purchased "the magnificent and representative collection of Colonel Stacy". The valuable coins were deposited in the Indian Museum. The numismatic collection offered valuable information on historical events and conditions.

Indians were admitted as members of the Asiatic Society in January 1829. The first Indian members were Prasanna Kumar Tagore, Dwarkanath Tagore, Russamay Dutt, Ram Camul Sen and Raja Radhakanta Dev. A few years later Ram Camul Sen was appointed as the first 'native secretary' of the Society. It is significant that in 1885 the year in which the Indian National Congress was founded the first Indian President was elected in the person of Rajendra Lala Mitra. Despite the preponderance of European members much of the research and deciphering work was done by Indian pundits such as Ramlachan Pundit, Radhakanta Sarman and Goverdhan Kaul.

The literary renaissance in India which began paradoxically after the battle of Plassey was due both to stability of the government – albeit a foreign one – and the external stimulus which came with English scholars. The English rulers realized that a sympathetic knowledge and understanding of the languages of the Indian people was an essential ingredient for political stability. Warren Hastings and Sir William Jones had realized this a century earlier.

John Gilchrist encouraged the study of Urdu prose and translated *Bagh-e-Bahar* into English. Mirza Ghalib of Delhi continued the Urdu prose tradition. The Protestant missionaries in Serampore led by William Carey set up a Bengali press there and translated the New Testament into Bengali. This encouraged the writing of Bengali prose. Carey wrote the life of Pratapaditya, a celebrated Bengali ruler. When Persian was replaced by English as the official language, Indians began to study English in earnest.

Carey's printing press at Serampore and publication of his Bengali grammar led to the promotion of Bengali literature. It is an interesting irony that the towering figure of Bankim Chandra Chatterjee regarded as the greatest of Bengali novelist, who wrote novels on fiercely patriotic themes such as *Anandamath* (for which Bankim Chandra composed the national hymn of India – *Bande Mataram)* was greatly influenced by the works of Sir Walter Scott.

While Bankim Chandra was the herald of literary nationalism, there grew another school that derived its inspiration from western values. These were Henry Derozio, Kashiprasad Ghose (who delivered a stinging critique to Mill's *History of British India*) and Shoshee Chander Dutt who wrote under the pseudonym of J.A.G. Barton. Ram Mohan Roy had been an ardent advocate of Western education and believed that India could be modernized only through this.

A westernized Bengali family – the Duttas of Rambagan – produced several novelists, dramatists, and civil servants. The most famous of these 'westernized' litterateurs was Michael Madhusudan Dutta. Rejecting Hinduism he converted to Christianity, married an English woman, and then repudiating his alienation he returned to his cultural roots and wrote in Bengali. His poetic epic, *Meghnath-badh-kavya* (Ballad of Slaying of Meghnath), was a revolutionary work and is considered a major work of Bengali literature. Here Ravana and his son Meghnath are portrayed as heroes instead of the god-king Rama and his brother Lakshmana. Bengalis, always smitten by novelty, were delighted by this unconventional and dramatic approach. Another member of the family, Romesh Chandra Dutta, was a member of the Indian Civil Service who resigned in order to write a powerful denunciation of British economic policies in India. Then he composed the English transliteration of the *Ramayana* and the *Mahabharata* in mellifluous verse. The family literary tradition was continued by two women – Aru Dutta and Toru Dutta – who learnt French and English and composed *Ancient Ballads* and *Legends of Hindustan*. Following in their wake was the poet Sarojini Naidu who produced several volumes of poetry on Western and Indian themes.

Progress in Bengali literature in turn stimulated prose and poetry in Urdu, Marathi, Hindi, Gujarati, Tamil and other South Indian languages. This nurturing of vernacular languages and literature was what Jones and Hastings had envisaged.

Ram Mohan Roy, one of the heralds of the Indian Renaissance founded the Brahma Samaj, a reformist group that emphasized and propagated the monotheism of the *Upanishads*. He published a treatise called the *Precepts of Jesus – A Guide to Peace and Happiness*. With this he stole the thunder from Christian missionaries by calling upon Hindus to follow the teachings of Christ who he said was a great man, an avatar, and whose teachings he felt were in consonance with Vedantic Hinduism.

The Tagore family played a vital role in the Bengali renaissance in literature, painting and music. They reached a brilliant climax in the effulgent and versatile genius of Rabindranath Tagore whose *Gitanjali* earned him the Nobel Prize in 1913 and brought modern Indian literature to the notice of the West. His educational innovation – Vishwa Bharati at Shantiniketan – drew scholars and artists from the world over where dialogues between civilizations were mandatory.

In his article, "Indological Studies in India", from *Rabindranath Tagore – A Centenary Volume* published by Sahitya Academy, New Delhi, Venkatarama Raghavan observes:

> In the regeneration which he (Tagore) envisaged for this country and for which he worked, the recovery of the cultural heritage was according to him to play a vital role. He said 'we must not imagine that we are one of those disinherited peoples of the world. The time has come for us to break open the treasure lore of our ancestors and use it for our commerce of life. Let us with its help make our future our own and not continue our existence as the eternal rag-pickers in other peoples dustbins.'
>
> In the letters Tagore exchanged with Professor Gilbert Murray he wrote, 'Meanwhile the system of education in India remained and still remains absurdly un-Indian, making no provision for our own culture. We have here not even the facility which the German student has for the study of the lore of Hindu and Muslim. And if we have become conscious of this vital deficiency in our education that is because of the spirit of the times'.
>
> Consequently when the great poet established Vishwa-Bharati at the end of 1921 which was not only an educational center which recaptured the ancient Indian ashram ideal but it also provided for the study of Art which was so completely neglected in Government Schools and Colleges. But it also had as an integral part a Vidya Bhavan where higher studies could be pursued in ancient Indian culture and its trans-Indian scripts.
>
> Indology had grown long before this time but Tagore's efforts at Vishwa-Bharati resulted (a) in a collaboration between Indian and foreign scholars (b) fresh enthusiasm for study of cultures of neighbouring countries with which India in the past had close cultural ties – promoted by visiting Professors – Sylvan Levy,

Formichi, Tucci, Sten, Korod, Winternitz, and Lessing as well as indigenous Sanskritists such as Vidhushekara Bhattacharya and Kshitimohan Sen.

John Galsworth, Fellow, Royal Society of Literature, London, gave this tribute to Sir William Jones in his poem, *In the Shade of Sir William Jones at the Royal Asiatic Society:*

How far lies Harrow Hill from Hindustan,
Viewing the Hooghly I reflect a thought
I sense you shared. Bengal was not our clan;
Yet it provides still solaces unsought.
... Your times were gracious, the insidious clerk
The unlettered bourgeoisie had not closed the doors
Upon the lamp of knowledge is craved dark,
Had not dowsed with, to silhouette the boors,
I pace, Sir William, your cool avenue
Of sanctuary, grateful for its share
In such a scoundrel hour returned, you
Would be the first to press
Home Rome's clean shade
Yet shall your Bengal beacon light
Flicker on and sublime their Eblis plan.

One of the greatest legacies of Sir William Jones and the Asiatic Society was the establishment of the Archaeological Survey of India in 1861. The Asiatic Society had declared its intention of enquiring among other things 'into the History, Antiquities, Arts, Sciences and Literatures of Asia'.

Archaeology is the study of the material remains of a civilization, and is the handmaiden of scientific historiography. The ruins of monuments and sites enables the archaeologist to build up the sequence of cultures and events, assisted by the patient efforts of epigraphists who can provide corroborative evidence to archaeological discoveries. It is a means of gleaning information of pre- and protohistory, as well as recorded history. By doing this a nation or society is able to unravel the mysteries of the past, learn of its heritage and acquire an enlarged identity.

There had been no dearth of interest in India's past; scholars and savants, travellers and dilettantes had dabbled into the myths and legends of Indian civilization in a sporadic and amateurish manner.

While Indian civilization has produced lofty metaphysics, speculative philosophies, great literature, science, astronomy, mathematics, medicine, it did not evince any interest in either history or geography. Unlike the Babylonians who recorded important events in steatite seals and in tombs, Egyptians on papyrus scrolls and in the pyramids, ancient Crete and Greece in documents, Indians wrote no chronicles of events. Time past was seen as Time future. Western scholars feel that the phenomenal world did not interest her sages and savants; they were immersed in discovering the mysteries of the mind and spirit and the nature of Time. India had no Nabonidus who enquired into the Babylonian past, no Thucydides, Tacitus, Herodotus, Pliny or Periplus to chronicle events.

Composed some three millennia before Christ, the *Rig Veda* gives an idea of the migration of people from the north, their encounter with a darker race. But the accounts are coloured by prejudice and fear and cannot be relied upon as historical chronicles. The *Ramayana* and *Mahabharata*, like the *Iliad* and the *Odyssey* and the *Aeneid*, indicate some epic events but they are so woven with myths and legends that it is difficult to fix time and place of the events described. While the age of classical Sanskrit literature gives vivid descriptions of contemporaneous society, its beliefs, rituals and organizations, they do not provide data on chronology of events.

In the eleventh century the poet Kalhana reconstructed the history of Kashmir in his epic poem *Rajatarangini.* A certain amount of glorification of the rulers, such as Lalitaditya and Avantivarman, reduces its objectivity but not its magnificence. Kalhana's work gives a vivid description of the political and cultural scenario of Kashmir's golden age. Islamic travellers and historians recorded events through their own values though Al-Biruni's and Ibn-Batuta's chronicles are as near to modern travelogues as can be expected of medieval travellers. Italian travellers such as Marco Polo, Nicolo Conti, Nicolao Manucci, the Russian Afnasy Nikitin, the Frenchmen Tavenier and Bernier, the Portuguese Barbosa, Nuniz and Paes, have all left records of their travels and described the cities and kingdoms they visited as well as their customs and conditions. The eighteenth-century historian Duguigne went further and suggested study of the civilization of India and Central Asia, and their influence on each other.

In 1774, Samuel Johnson had written to Governor-General Warren Hastings even before Jones' arrival in India of the need to "examine nicely the traditions and histories of the East that he will survey the remains of its ancient edifices and trace vestiges of its ruined cities; and that at his return we shall know the arts and opinions of a race of men from whom very little has hitherto been derived". However, it was only with the advent of William Jones that the movement for a systematic study of India's past began in earnest. He recognized the need to organize investigations in a scientific manner.

Founding of the journal *Asiatick Researches* in 1788 encouraged scholars and amateurs alike to publish their finds and theories on the antiquity of India. These were men who delved into India's past through her literary and religious texts rather than exploring the material remains of the past. Through these brilliant scholars – interpreters as well as translators – the world came to know of India's intellectual and spiritual heritage. Henry Thomas Colebrooke observed that "in the scarcity of authentic materials for the ancient and even modern history of the Hindu race" all that the monuments could do was to provide some information to supplement that found in Indian literature. Nevertheless the search for India's antiquity had begun, fuelled sporadically by finds of coins or ancient ruins.

It has been narrated earlier of William Jones' identification of the figure Sandakottas found in Greek records with Chandragupta Maurya, the city of Polibathra with Pataliputra that could fix the chronology of events of ancient India. Jones' conclusion that Sanskrit was the oldest member of the family of Indo-European languages was the commencement of comparative philology. It also led to theories of migration of ancient peoples to centers of civilization. Jones' Sanskrit pundit Radhakanta Sharman assisted him in editing Sanskrit texts that provided information on various periods.

The great Sanskrit scholar Charles Wilkins who translated the *Bhagavad Gita* into English had in the course of studying Sanskrit found the key to the Gupta and the Kutila script and laid the basis for epigraphical studies. Colebrooke and Wilson continued these works. The latter went on to do research on ancient Afghanistan; his work *Ariana Antiqua* was the result of his labours.

Others also were at work; Polier described the pillar at Firoz Shah's fort; James Hoare made a copy of the Asokan inscription of the pillar. Both were army officers. Duncan reported his findings on urns found in a *stupa* at Sarnath and in the nineteenth century Elphinstone discovered a *stupa* at Manikiyala that would provide information on the Scythian period. Another army officer, Fell, discovered the *stupa* at Sanchi which would lead to further investigations into Buddhist remains. Warre Malet studied the script found at the caves in Ellora that were similar to Asokan inscriptions found in pillars.

While these activities were being conducted in North India, scholars were at work in the south. In 1772 William Chambers wrote about the ruins of the shore temples at Mahabalipuram for the *Asiatick Researches.* Colin Macenzie, Surveyor General of India, devoted himself to the task of inspecting ancient monuments and sites, made drawings to scale, collected coins, images and inscriptions which provided the material for further studies and research into South Indian history and social organization. This dedicated army officer met the expenses of these investigations from his own resources. Other individuals contributed to furthering information on Indian antiquity such as Francis Buchanan who surveyed the newly annexed kingdom of Mysore, monuments in Bihar, inscriptions at Bodh Gaya.

However, these explorations and investigations remained individual efforts, without methodology and without the support or the resources of an organization. Nor was there any awareness of the significance of monuments, or of the stories they told. Since the importance of monuments was not realized there was also no understanding of the need to preserve monuments. Throughout this period the Asiatic Society vigorously sponsored pioneering work and studies in archaeology, epigraphy and historiography.

Epigraphists worked on the Kharoshti script, which according to Levi, had come from Kashgar in Central Asia, while Franke believed it originated further south. Some have found similarities with old Aramaic while others have found similarities with the ancient Phoenician script. Like Arabic it is written from right to left. Pryzluski and Das Gupta declare that the original name of the script Kharaposta, meaning hide of a donkey, indicates the material on which it was first written. Whatever the origins of the script, Kharoshti was used on Asokan rock edicts. Greek, Scythian,

Parthian and Kushana records were written in Kharoshti. The script was in wide use from the 3rd century BC to 4th century AD spanning an area from the Hindu Kush, Turkestan, Baluchistan, and Ladakh to Patna.

Origins of the Brahmi script have been the subject of many theories. The name 'Brahmi' was given by the Indologist Buhler. William Jones believed it had Semetic origins. Nineteenth-century scholars fix the evolution of Brahmi script around the 8th century BC. But in the early twentieth century the discovery of writing in the Indus Valley sites indicates the antiquity of the Indus Valley script to the third millennium BC. The relationship between these two scripts is not clear. Edward Thomas feels the Brahmi script is of Dravidian origin while Cunningham, Ojha and Dowson feel the script evolved in 'Aryan' or Vedic times. Some have ascribed either Greek or Semetic origins to the Brahmi script though this seems unlikely in view of the fact that an autocthonous script was in use in the third millennium BC.

In 1837 there was a landmark development through the path-breaking discoveries of James Prinsep. He was Assay Master at the Government Mint in Calcutta and became Secretary of the Asiatic Society. Through his deep knowledge of numismatics and epigraphy Prinsep guided archaeological research and investigations with a thoroughness and diligence that resulted in great discoveries. He realized the importance of excavation in the Indus-Jhelum region where the material remains indicated the presence of the Kushanas, a hitherto unknown race from Central Asia. He interpreted the findings of the ancient *stupas* in Afghanistan where there had been settlements of Greeks, Bactrian and Scythian dynasties as well as the Asokan rock edicts at Dhauli.

Prinsep began working on the Brahmi script between 1834 and 1837. Coins from Bactria and Gandhara were engraved on one side with the portrait of the ruler; on the reverse side the coin legends were inscribed in Brahmi and Kharoshti script. By working on a bilingual and biscriptal code, Prinsep was able to decipher the Brahmi script on Asokan inscriptions. Until then the inscriptions on pillars, *stupas* and coins could not be interpreted since the Brahmi script had fallen into disuse and forgotten. By deciphering the Brahmi script Prinsep enabled the reading of all Brahmi and Kharoshti inscriptions; this opened the door to information of events and individuals who had shaped that age. The reading of

James Prinsep

Asoka's edicts and the discovery of his contemporary meeting with some kings outside India furnished firm landmarks to work out Indian chronology and corroborative history. It was now possible to obtain historical information of that era and fix a chronology of events and obtain information on ancient India, its language, its art and commerce, and the rulers of that period. Scholars could now reconstruct Indian history on the basis of epigraphical evidence. In 1838 Prinsep identified three Graeco-Bactrian kings – Antiochus II, Ptolemy Philadelphos, and Magas of Cyrene in the Asokan inscription found on the Girnar rock. This identification led to the establishment of the contemporaneity of the author of these inscriptions with those rulers and helped to place Indian archaeology for the first time on a secure chronological basis.

It was a great step forward in Indian historiography. Prinsep's untimely death in 1840 was a setback to the progress of epigraphy and archaeology. The momentum that had been generated under his erudite and brilliant leadership was lost and archaeology went again into the shallows. Then again in the closing years of the decade a group of scholars resumed the work begun by Prinsep; Alexander Cunningham, Markham Kittoe, Edward Thomas, Walter Elliot, J. Stevenson, and Bhau Daji prepared surveys and undertook excavations. Cunningham took up the investigation on the Indo-Greek and Indo-Scythian dynasties to continue the work of Prinsep. In collaboration with Maisey and Kittoe they prepared surveys of Buddhist monuments in Bihar along with large number of drawings of the sites and monuments. He undertook excavations at Sarnath, which indicated the presence of Buddhists monasteries. Impetus of the work was interrupted by the outbreak of the conflict of 1857. Edward Thomas continued Prinsep's work on numismatics and studied coins from third century BC to fifteenth century AD.

It was found that the Brahmi script was in wide use beyond the frontiers of India. Many of the scripts of Eastern Asia are derived from Brahmi. In India the Devanagari script evolved with local variations from the ancient Brahmi script.

In South India, the remarkable antiquarian Colonel Macenzie built up a prodigious collection between 1822 and 1828 comprising eight thousand inscriptions, drawing of about ten volumes and local arrivals and accounts. Elliott continued the work began by Mackenzie and from various archaeological evidence, mainly coins, was able to reconstruct the history of the Chalukyas and other

Alexander Cunningham

dynasties of South India. Epigraphy made headway with Stevenson and Bhau Daji who were able to decipher records of King Rudradaman and Skandagupta from the Ajanta epigraphs. Between 1829 and 1847 Fergusson made a survey of Indian architecture.

James Fergusson and Meadows Taylor made extensive surveys of ancient buildings and evolved a system of classification of buildings. Taylor was the first to understand the importance of excavation as a means of reconstructing history. This was about the same time that Leonard Woolley was making landmark discoveries on Minoan civilization.

These individual attempts awakened the Court of Directors at London to the need to preserve the remains of an ancient civilization that was beginning to emerge from oblivion. There was a growing awareness both in India and in England of the value of Indian monuments and other archaeological remains and the need to explore, understand and interpret them. These efforts culminated in the formation of the Archaeological Society of Delhi that was the first voluntary organization to engage itself in archaeological work such as investigation of sites, drawings, historical researches in the area around Delhi.

The foundation for systematic archaeological work was laid by Alexander Cunningham, a military engineer, who wanted a nation-wide survey of sites and monuments. He was able to persuade Governor-General Lord Canning of the need for preserving monuments and the inscriptions thereon "in the total absence of any written history form the only reliable sources of information as to the early condition of the country". Cunningham voiced his fears that the monuments "would soon disappear altogether unless preserved by the accurate and faithful descriptions of the archaeologists". He warned the Governor-General that "it will not be to our credit as an enlightened ruling power if we continue to allow such fields of investigation, as the remains of the old Buddhist in Behar, the vast ruins of Kanouj, the plains of Delhi, studded with ruins more thickly than even the Campagna of Rome and many others to remain without more examination than they have hitherto received ... There are European Governments if they had held our rule in India would not have allowed this to be said".

The Archaeological Survey of India was established in November 1861 and Cunningham was appointed Archaeological

Surveyor. He spent the next few years travelling across North India, studying monuments, Asokan rock inscriptions, identifying cities and peoples described in Greek accounts of the expedition of Alexander of Macedon. Cunningham's zeal and enthusiasm convinced both the Governor-General as well as the British Government of the need for preserving monuments in India. Local governments were instructed to make a list of historic buildings accompanied by photographs along with descriptions of the monuments. Eminent archaeologists Sykes, Burgess, Cole, R.L. Mitra worked on this project and surveyed a large number of monuments. Bayley who was Secretary to the Home Department supported their activities and stated that not only should monuments be protected but that extensive excavation projects undertaken in sites where explorations had not yet been made.

Around this time (1870) Eduard Schliemann decided to explore and excavate the site of ancient Troy. Taking the poet Homer as his sole guide, accompanied by his Greek wife and numerous assistants Schliemann embarked on his celebrated excavations in the Turkish village of Hissarlik. The discovery of tombs, jewellery, masks, coins indicated that this site of an ancient civilization could be the Troy of Homer's *Iliad*.

Enthused by these developments, Indian archaeology also progressed; the massive *stupa* at Bharhut was discovered followed by the Greek sites at Taxila, and inscriptions from the Pala period in Bengal. Going by the travel records of Chinese pilgrims Buddhist monuments were identified at Shravasti, Kausambi and Sankisa. More Asokan pillars were discovered enabling epigraphists to interpret the information contained in them. A branch of the Archaeological Survey was devoted entirely to epigraphy including Persian and Arabic epigraphy. In 1878 the government passed the Treasure Trove Act which protected monuments and new finds from going into hands of private people by placing them under government possession.

After Cunningham's pioneering work his successors continued his work on a more systematic basis. South India came under close scrutiny thanks to the efforts of archaeologists such as Robert Sewell, Alexander Rea and James Burgess. Action was taken to train epigraphists who knew Sanskrit, Pali and Dravidian languages to translate the inscriptions that would facilitate expansion of knowledge about the events and conditions of the period they described. Hultzsch, a great linguist and epigraphist, undertook this work. Burgess established the quarterly publication *Epigraphia Indica* in 1888; it contained information on valuable inscriptions contributed by renowned epigraphists such as Fleet, Hiltech, Buhler, Kielhorn, Eggeling, Sten Konow, Vogel, and later Indian experts like Venkatayya, Krishnaiah Shastri, Hirananda Shastri and N.P. Chakravarty. These scholars and their officers brought over 30,000 inscriptions in diverse scripts such as Brahmi and Kharoshti.

The information contained in the epigraphs and inscriptions contributed greatly to the expansion of knowledge on various periods and eras. In 1848 there were more editions of Sanskrit and other texts such as the *Biblioteca Indica*. The Asiatic Societies of Bombay and Madras started their journals as well in 1838 that went on until 1841. James Burgess started the *India Antiquarian* in 1872 that went on until 1938 during which period sixty-two volumes issued. These volumes contained varied material on history, epigraphy, religion, literature and folklore.

Further impetus was given to archaeology by Lord Curzon who was Viceroy of India between 1899 and 1905. It is indeed a strange phenomenon that this die-hard imperialist was also a fierce protagonist for preservation of Indian heritage. Among his numerous tasks he chose to personally scrutinize the organization of the Archaeological Survey of India, its functions, its funding and its achievements. He felt that no scientific principle was being adopted for conservation and restoration of monuments and that the attempts made for excavation of art objects was unsatisfactory. He proposed that much larger financial assistance should be given for the conservation of monuments and antiquities. To head the Archaeological Survey of India he invited John Marshall who had earlier distinguished himself in excavation and restoration work in Greece, Crete and Turkey. The powers and functions of the new Director General were defined. Lord Curzon also took keen interest in epigraphy, which was an essential adjunct to historical research.

He succinctly summed up the work of the Archaeological Survey when he said, "It is in my judgment equally our duty to dig and discover, to classify, reproduce and describe, to copy and decipher and to cherish and conserve." Curzon's outstanding contribution to Indian archaeology was the enactment of the Ancient Monuments Preservation Act of 1904 that gave the Archaeological Survey wide powers to maintain monuments and antiquities. For the first

John Marshall

time legal power was given to the Survey to implement its aims. In the five years that Curzon was Viceroy he completely transformed the organization and function of the Archaeological Survey of India.

Curzon's vision was shared by John Marshall who ushered in a new age to archaeology. He had already gained wide experience in excavation of ancient cities in Greece and Mycenae and planned to restore edifices of ancient India in all their material grandeur. He was fortunate to obtain the co-operation and assistance of brilliant archaeologists such as Henry Cousins, Alexander Rea, T. Bloch, Vogel, D.R. Bhandarkar, D.R. Sahani, K.N. Dixit, M.S. Wats, A.N. Longhurst, and D.B. Spooner. Added to this list was the great Indologist and explorer Sir Aurel Stein whose path-breaking work in Kashmir and Central Asia was a unique contribution to Indian historiography.

It was during Marshall's leadership that the great discovery was made of Mohenjodaro and Harappa by Rakhal Das Banerjee in 1922. Earlier, Cunningham had seen the mounds but had not seen its potential or significance. Bannerjee's preliminary investigation led to whole-scale excavation of these two major cities of the hitherto unknown Indus Valley civilization that gave a new dimension to Indian history.

Indology received strong support through the establishment of Indian universities. The Benaras Hindu University was established in 1866 when it also began its publication *Pundit* which continued until 1920. Texts, studies, and translations relating to different branches of Sanskrit literature were taken up in right earnest. The establishment of the Indian Historical Records Commission in 1899 gave a encouragement to the documentation necessary for historiography. Nirnaya Sagar Press in Bombay and Chowkante Press, Benaras were established in 1886 and 1880 from which the growth of modern Sanskrit studies cannot be separated. The Oriental Research Institute at Poona was established by Bhandarkar in 1917, the Kuppuswamy Research Institute at Madras and the Adyar Library, also at Madras to further studies on ancient India.

The Universities of Calcutta, Madras and Bombay were founded almost a hundred and fifty years ago. It is well known that when the Company thought of taking the responsibility for education, there was keen controversy as to the kind of education they should provide, whether it should be the indigenous one or the modern one from the West. The Minute of Macaulay is notorious. Naturally in the scheme of education introduced it took a long time for the universities to take in Indian humanities and still longer time to develop higher studies in ancient history and culture and Indian languages and literature. The spirit of the time promoted study of the above disciplines. There was the zeal of scholars like Ashutosh Mukherjee (Vice-Chancellor, Calcutta University, 1914) for linguistics, ancient history and culture, art, Sanskrit, Pali and Prakrit. In time these subjects were included in the curriculum for post-graduate subjects and eventually incorporated in degree courses in more and more universities.

After independence and the establishment of the University Grants Commission, further development has taken place with the founding of Chairs in Indian history and archaeology, Sanskrit and Indian philosophy, Indian linguistics and the opening of Indology department where these were not available.

The Sanskrit Commission was appointed and on its recommendation a Sanskrit board was appointed. In 1919 the All India Oriental Conference was founded. It functioned as a premier forum of Indian Indology. In 1925 the Indian Philosophy Congress was founded followed by the Linguistic Society of India established in 1928 and the Indian History Congress founded in 1935.

To begin with, the institutions for research were in the hands of foreign scholars and Christian missionaries. In addition to the leading names, others such as Muir, Ballantyre, Thibant, Vems, and Griffith were all associated with the Sanskrit College at Banaras. Wilson Cowell, Pargiter who worked from Calcutta, Gough, Hall, Hodgson, Hocsule, Growse, Koer, Foulkes, Schaader, Loofues and others carried forward these researches.

Greerson's Linguistic Survey of India (1903-27) was the basis for all further linguistic studies in India. In South India, the pioneers of linguistic studies were Kittel, Rice, Browse, Caldwell, Kingsbury, Pope and Gundaest. Works of Vincent Smith became text books in history. Foreign scholars like Havell did pioneering work in the study of Indian art.

It is well known that all the leading foreign Orientalists had pundits at their elbows who were privately associated with all that the former produced. But gradually Indian scholars like

R.G. Bhandarkar led Indology studies and a later generation produced Suniti Kumar Chatterjee "the most outstanding linguist and versatile scholar of our times".

In the renaissance which transformed India there have been scholars, men of thought, leaders of cultural and spiritual movements, whose contributions have been decisive. Among national leaders there were Bal Gangadhar Tilak and Bhagwandas who were Sanskritists and research scholars as well as the Vivekanandas and Aurobindos and Ananda Coomaraswamys whose interpretative and provocative explorations have made Indian thought and culture live again. Their ideas have helped modern Indians brought up on alien modes of education to recapture the enduring values of Indian life and spirit. In the brilliant galaxy of great Indians stands the luminous personality of the poet Rabindranath Tagore who described Shantiniketan as his 'tangible poem' – 'the boat that carried the best cargo of his life'.

Part V

European Indology

European Indology

Indology blossomed within the boundaries of the British Empire, nurtured in the early years by men of vision such as Warren Hastings and Sir William Jones and then sponsored by the British Government once they realized the value of Indian studies. Scholarship and governance went hand in hand. There were however European nations where Indology burst into splendour through other forces.

Though Germany had no imperial ambitions in India, it was in this country where Indology flourished in the 19th century. A brilliant cluster of scholars, linguists, philologists read, analysed and interpreted a vast number of Sanskrit texts. A noted Sanskritist of India has observed that it is doubtful if even Indian universities had such facilities for the study of Sanskrit and Indian history as German universities. In fact Bonn was called the Benaras of Europe. German scholars brought to their studies a fresh intensity, fuelled perhaps by the Romanticism of the times, inspired in the early years by myths and legends about India, and a belief that India and Germany had cultural links before recorded history. Aquiring knowledge about India was a sort of intellectual Holy Grail. Their studies were never touched by the imperatives of imperialism because Germany had no empire in Asia. Goethe's words on Kalidasa's *Shakuntala* demonstrate this effusive enthusiasm.

Russian Indology developed through very different forces. Russia has always straddled two worlds – the Asian and the European. The forces that moulded Russian culture have been as much determined by history and geography. The Greek historian Herodotus stated that the meeting of Asia and Europe was on the banks of the River Don. The Orient was no stranger to Russia; she was half Oriental. Many of the races that lived on her borders were Oriental. They influenced her music, letters, costumes and customs.

Old Slavonic ballads and legends indicate that pre-Kievan Russia was nearer to Iran and India than Europe. The names of Russian gods are akin to those of Vedic and Avestan deities. It was only in the eleventh century when Grand Prince Vladimir accepted Byzantine Christianity that Russia moved closer to Europe. The rule of the Tartar Golden Horde cut her off from Europe until the time of Ivan III who through his marriage to Princess Zoe Palealogue of Byzantium renewed Russian ties with Europe. Afanasy Nikitin's travelogue quickened Russian interst in India. Paradoxically it was the establishment of British rule in India that expedited Russian interest in Indian culture. Here again the perceptions were different. Russian scholars did not look upon India as part of the imperial dream. They felt sympathy for a people who were under foreign domination and Russian intellectuals and scholars spoke in defence of this subjugated race. Though the response of Russian government to these denunciations varied according to political expediencey the Tsarist government gave every encouragement to the establishment of institutes for the study of Indian and Oriental civilization. The nineteenth century saw the flowering of Indology in Russia and in the twentieth century Indology reached great heights. With official sponsorship by the Soviet Government scholars delved into munerous aspects of Indian studies – in language, history, political science, sociology.

Italy had the oldest connections with India. Travellers and envoys of imperial Rome have left behind interesting chronicles of these encounters while archaeology has yielded details. Others followed in medieval times. But Indology as a subject began in the early twentieth century with the establishment of the Institute for Studies in Near and Middle East which was later extended to India and Tibet through the efforts of the brilliant GiuseppeTucci.

Another nation that produced great Indologists was Hungary. It began with William Jones' meeting with Count Reviczi in the 1770s. Count Reviczi was a diplomat by profession and was interested in Asian civilizations. During his travels the Count collected material to further Oriental studies. This forged a deep friendship between Count Reviczi and William Jones. Following in Count Reviczi's footsteps were there other Hungarian Orientalists – Armenius Vamberry, Sandor Csoma De Koros and Aurel Stein. The two scholars – Csoma and Stein – were diametrically opposed in their attitudes, their perceptions and in their occupations. But both carried with them their nations' subconscious memories as they traversed mountains and deserts to find answers to questions about their nation's origins and ties with India. Aurel Stein was however part of the British Government and worked with them.

This brief Part V attempts to describe the work of Indologists of Russia, Germany, Italy and Hungary.

49

Germany and Indology

The legacy of William Jones, the father of Indology, influenced India and the West. His work, especially his translation of Kalidasa's *Shakuntala*, made a deep impact in Germany where Indology became a subject of serious interest in academic circles. William Jones' *Sacontala* fired the imagination of German scholars and men of letters. The Germans refer to this as the 'Shakuntala Experience.' There were great Indologists in Germany who took their inspiration and guidance from William Jones and gave Indology a new depth and dimension. Perhaps William Jones unleashed an unconscious fascination that harked back to early times.

Calling India 'the dreamland of medieval pilgrims and poets,' the German scholar Walter Leifer says that there were invisible ties between India and Germanic Europe. The name 'India' stirred German imagination from early times. The eighth-century scribe Alcuin mentions India in his chronicle on Charlemagne. He believed that India, like Africa and Europe, was a separate continent. Another medieval historian-geographer Theodulph spoke of India as if it was the continent of Asia. The twelfth-century Anno-Lied observes – "They say that in that region there are still people who speak German – very far towards India."

Futile attempts have been made to locate the homeland of the Indo-Germanic people. The location has ranged from Uzbekistan to Siberia, from the Iranian highlands to the Alps. In his book *Cultural History of the German People* Henne am Rhyn says,

> According to the common legends and vocabulary of the Aryan peoples and languages we are able to assume with approximate reliability the following about the unknown cradle of these languages: it was a rather cold and bleak land in which ice, snow, clouds, fog and rain were familiar and winds frequent. The country was mountainous ... It is doubtful whether the land bordered on

> the sea. Birch and fir trees grew there as well as various cereals; tropical plants were as unknown as the Asiatic animals – lion, tiger, donkey, camel, elephant. Whereas wolf and bear haunted the region ... the inhabitants lived by agriculture, baked bread, drank mead made from honey ... the horse was also known but neither bred nor used for riding ... The inhabitants made paths and fords over the rivers; they propelled ships or boats (modern German Nachen: Sanskrit nau, Latin nava: old German nauen) ... They had fortified places (Sanskrit puri or pura: Greek polis). But there were no towns. They worshipped gods, resembling humans all of which they originally named after forces of nature; they revered their ancestors under the term of man and their heroes (Sanskrit vira – Latin Vir) and believed in the immortality of the soul.

Throughout the middle ages the belief persisted that there were people who spoke German in India and Iran. Impressions of India were based on Greek and Roman texts. One such early text was *De Moribus Brachmanorum* (The Customs of the Brahmins) written in Greek by St. Ambrose of Milan. This work gave details of the religious practices of the Brahmins as well as their asceticism. St. Ambrose took the view that the German people had migrated to India. The German emperor Charlemagne sent emissaries to Baghdad where various nations of the East gathered to pay homage to the Caliph. The Arabs, especially the Moors of Spain, brought to Europe fairy-tales and folklore from India contained in the Sanskrit *Katha-Sarita-Sagara*. These stories spread to European countries with local variations. The early German Indologist Benfey held the view that India was the source of all fables and stories. The German Indologist Ludwig Alsdorf states that the wise and cynical stories in *Panchatantra* were adapted in various countries. Walter Leifer feels that Indian spiritualism may have influenced the literature about the search for the Holy Grail. In the middle ages the Hohenstaufen princes such as Manfred and Sigismund were concerned about the relics of St. Thomas in India.

Portuguese activities in India aroused the interest of Germans in the sixteenth century and though attempts were made to join the scramble for colonies in the eighteenth century a fragmented Germany remained far behind. Under the Pragmatic Sanction the Austrian emperor had ceded Bankipura to the British. On her accession to the throne Empress Maria Teresa wanted to regain the Austrian colony. India was a perpetual lure.

South India became a favourite destination for German missionaries in the eighteenth century such as Ziegenbalg who studied Tamil and Malayalam to further his missionary activities. He translated the Bible into Tamil and began to preach. He was followed by Rottler who came to the Danish colony of Tarangavadi or Tranquebar in 1776. A versatile scholar and linguist, his main object was the conversion of Hindus to the Protestant faith. Bernhard Schmidt was also a missionary and a philologist who set up his home in the Nilgiris where he translated numerous Tamil works into German and German texts into Tamil.

Christian Friedrich Schwartz came to Tranquebar and set up the Society for Promoting Christian Knowledge. He later established a missionary school and a church in 1765. He built an orphanage in Thanjavur and sometimes acted as a liason officer for the British in Madras as well as advising the Raja of Thanjavur. Karl Graul made a significant contribution by preparing the *Bibliotheca Tamulica* in which he describes for the first time to European audience the richness of Tamil literature. It is through him that Europeans came to know of the *Kural* of Thiruvalluvar that is a collection of some thirteen hundred adages. Albert Schweitzer praised the *Kural* and placed it higher than the *Dharmasastra* of Manu or even the *Bhagavad Gita* on the grounds that these adages celebrate life and human love and does not stress as the Sanskrit texts do the life of renunciation and asceticism. Great Tamil works of the classical age such as *Silappathikaram* and *Manimeghalai* were translated.

However, it is with the publication of William Jones' *Sacontala* that German Indology took a great leap forward. The man who translated Jones into German was Georg Forster. He was an unconventional young man who loved traveling and espousing revolutionary causes and was not afraid to flaunt his views at a time when liberal ideas were dangerous possessions.

Forster first became acquainted with Indian culture in England. He had asked a friend for a letter of introduction to Warren Hastings who was then Governor-General in India. Though he did not go to India as planned he came across William Jones's *Sacontala* in London. He translated Kalidasa's drama from English to German and sent it to Johann Peter Fischer, a bookseller who lived in Mainz. The German translation was accepted at once. Kalidasa's drama was printed in May 1795. Forster sent copies to the great German poet Goethe, the philosopher Herder, and Heyne, professor of philosophy at Gottingen University.

Forster opened a door to the unknown; German Indology blossomed like a spring flower. He brought the land of the Indus-Ganges to the German intellectual world. With a message far ahead of his time Forster made a plea that great literature should unite humanity and that division of people should not be on the basis of colour and creed but between good and evil.

Tributes came flowing in beginning with Heyne and followed by the great dramatist Schiller who published a scene from *Shakuntala* in his journal *Thalia.* Humboldt declared, "In the whole Greek antique literature there was no poetic portrayal of beautiful womanhood and beautiful love comparable to *Shakuntala.*" The philosopher Herder was even more enthusiastic about Kalidasa's poem and said about the heroine "a true flower of the Orient; and the first, the fairest of her kind". In the introduction to his article on *Shakuntala,* Herder commands his readers, with a deeper understanding of Indian thought and philosophy. When the pioneer Forster passed away, Herder published the second edition of the poem in 1802.

Indeed Kalidasa's *Shakuntala* became a subject of discussions and debates in Germany and especially in Weimar. Goethe was rapturous about Kalidasa's poem and felt that the acclaim it had received in England and Germany encouraged one to believe in the concept of world literature as a common heritage of mankind. Edition after edition of the great Sanskrit poem began to come out. The four well known lines of Goethe, so often quoted in relation to the Indian drama may here be repeated:

> 'Willst du die Bluthe des fruhe, die Fruchte despateren Jahres
> Willst du was reizt und etzuckt, willst du sattigt und nahrt
> Willst du den Himmel, die Erde, mit einen Namen begreifen
> Nenn' ich Sakontala, dich, und so ist Alles gesagt!

> Wouldst thou the young ears blossoms and the fruit of its decline
> And all by which the soul's is charmed, enraptured, feasted, fed?
> Wouldst thou the earth and heaven itself in one sole name combine?
> I name thee O Sakoontala! and all at once is said!

Not content with the German translation of William Jones' English version, Bernhard Hirzel learned Sanskrit and translated *Shakuntala* into German. Numerous Indologists began translating *Shakuntala* in different versions – Boethlingk, Meiner, Lobedanz, Fritze, Kellner and Schroder to name a few.

The success of *Shakuntala* prompted German writers and scholars to translate other works of Kalidasa into German; *Urvasi* by Robert Lenz, *Vikramorvasi* and *Malavikagnimitra* by Bollensch and Weber. Hillebrandt became a renowned Kalidasa scholar who wrote extensively on the great Indian poet.

German Indology, as a serious discipline, was established by Friedrich Wilhelm von Schlegel. He had met an English prisoner of war in Paris in 1803 from whom he learnt Sanskrit. India – her literature, philosophy and art – became the focus of his interest. In 1808 the University of Heidelberg published Schlegel's *Uber die Sprache und Weisheit der Inder – On the Language and Wisdom of the Indians*. The book stimulated a systematic study of Indian civilization. Friedrich's brother August Wilhelm joined the movement. He corresponded with the great men of letters of Germany – Goethe, Schiller, Schelling, Humboldt – on Indology. He commissioned works on Indian culture and his book dealt with Indian philology. August Wilhelm von Schelling was drawn to the *Rig Veda* and Hindu mythology. He also studied Indian Buddhism and tried to answer his own questions about the difference between Buddhism and Brahmanism.

Augustus Wilhelm von Schlegel in his first lecture on Dramatic Literature says, "Among the Indians the people from whom perhaps all the cultivation of the human race has been derived plays were known long before they could have experienced any foreign influence. It has lately been made known in Europe that they have a rich dramatic literature which ascends back for more than two thousand years. The only specimen of their plays (*natakas*) hitherto known to us is delightful *Sakoontala* which notwithstanding the colouring of a foreign clime, bears in its general structure a striking resemblance to our romantic drama".

Alexander von Humboldt in treating of Indian poetry observes: "Kalidasa the celebrated author of the *Sakoontala* is a masterly describer of the influence which nature exercises upon the minds of lovers. This great poet flourished at the splendid court of Vikramaditya and was therefore contemporary with Virgil and Horace. Tenderness in the expression of feeling, and richness of creative fancy have assigned to him his lofty place among all the poets of all nations".

It is interesting to note what Heinrich Heine, the political philosopher, wrote to A.W. Schlegel –

August Wilhelm Schlegel

Wilhelm Humboldt

> As to the study of Sanskrit itself, time alone will tell how useful it will be. Year after year Portuguese, Dutchmen and Englishmen have been dragging home the treasures of India in their big ships; we Germans have been onlookers. Yet the spiritual treasures of India shall not escape us. Schlegel, Bopp, Humboldt, Frank etc are our East India travelers. Bonn and Munich will make good trading stations.

Germany, not yet a colonial power, could view India with admiration and romanticism, without overtones of patronization or condescension.

Franz Bopp was of the first generation of German Indologists. Inspired by Sanskrit works, his studies gave rise to a new branch of Indology – comparative linguistics. The philological researches of Franz Bopp demonstrated that the laws of sound, structure and basic vocabulary of the original Indo-Germanic language shows several groups: The eastern group comprising of Iranian, Phrygian, Armenian, Thracian, Albanian, Baltic, Slavonic and Indo-Aryan languages, and the western group comprising of Greek, Illyrian, Celtic, Italic and Germanic.

In the wake of interest in Indian metaphysics the German philosopher Schopenhauer studied the *Upanishads* and hoped that this ancient discourse on life and death and the soul would flourish on Western soil. Of *Nirvana* or liberation he writes, "The highest reward awaiting the loftiest deeds and utter renunciation goes to the woman who voluntarily died on her husband's funeral pyre in seven consecutive lives, to that person whose pure lips have never told a single lie. This reward can only be expressed in a negative way by the myth in the language of that world, without the so frequent promise of never more being reincarnated."

Whether it was due to the belief that ancient Indians were part of the Indo-Germanic family or whether it was the predilection for metaphysics or because Germans found in the gods of the *Rig Vedas* echoes of the deeds of Germanic gods and mythology, German Indologists had a particular fascination for the *Rig Veda.* There were numerous translations of the *Rig Veda* by German scholars beginning with Hermann Oldenberg (*The Religion of the Veda*), P.T. Hoffmann (*The Wisdom of the Veda*), Hillebrandt (*Vedic Mythology*), Hermann Grassmann (who did complete translations of the *Vedas*), Heinrich Zimmer (*Ancient Indian Life and the Culture of the Vedic Aryans*).

Long before the *Vedantas* were known outside India, Paul Deussen translated the *Upanishads* and wrote *The System of the Vedanta and The Philosophy of the Upanishads*. He wrote: "The Upanishads have intrinsic value as early testimonies of the human spirit which reaches for the highest goals." The *Puranas* were translated by Zimmer and Schack. The *Puranas* are the personal experiences of pious men. However, side by side with them exists literature that radiates authority and is recognized by all Indians.

Moriz Winternitz was drawn to Rabindranath Tagore's world-university where he studied and taught. His *Indian Literary History* describes and analyses the magnificence of Sanskrit literature from the *Rig Veda* onwards.

If the *Rig Veda* with its undercurrent of Aryan-Indo-Germanic origins fascinated Germans, the grandeur of the *Mahabharata* and the *Ramayana* impressed them equally. Numerous are the German Indologists who have translated the two epics and the various stories contained therein.

Finally the *Bhagavad Gita* made a deep impression on German scholars.

> All that is to be learnt in Europe of the metaphysics the views and ideas of Indian philosophers is here reflected in language which is as beautiful as it is simple and convincing. This part of the *Mahabharata* describes the inner struggle of a man exposed to the strife of his time with psychological profoundity of a kind one would scarcely have expected from writers of millenniums ago ... Here the sacred texts speak to us in a language reminiscent of Kant's ethics of duty; in the idiom of the Ganges plains we hear words echoed much later by the categoric imperative (Walter Leifer).

Willhelm von Humboldt called the *Bhagavad Gita* "the finest, nay, perhaps the only true philosophical poem produced by any literature known to us".

German translations of the *Bhagavad Gita* are legion; it has come to be regarded as the principal Indian work.

Numerous universities in Germany became centres of Indological studies. These were at Tubingen, Gottingen, Munich, Bonn, Nurnberg, Marburg, Heidelberg and Leipzig. The enormous interest in Indology would be realized when one hears of the galaxy of German scholars who studied and taught Indology at these universities. As V. Raghavan, a renowned Sanskrit scholar has observed:

> Though the credit of discovering Sanskrit for the West goes to England and though it was at the feet of French pioneers that the first German Sanskritists like Bopp and Schlegel sat, Germany had taken to Sanskrit studies with such enthusiasm and disinterested love, that outside India, one can say without exaggeration, that it has been a second home for Sanskrit. Before the war there were fourteen full chairs for Sanskrit at German universities which is something that could not be said of even India .... Bonn had played the role of something like a Benaras to entire Europe. To give an account of German contribution to Sanskrit would be to write the history of Sanskrit studies in modern times.

William Jones had ignited the flame of Orientalism not only amongst his countrymen but on the continent of Europe as well. The most famous of his followers was the German scholar Max Muller who was born in the duchy of Dussau in 1823. Max Muller studied Sanskrit in the University of Leipzig. He was not the first German to be fascinated by Oriental studies; there was Professor Brochaus at Leipzig, Franz Bopp and Schelling at Berlin. He came into contact with British Orientalists and settled down in Oxford in 1848. Queen Victoria's German husband Prince Albert took a keen interest in Max Muller who was shortly appointed Professor of Modern European languages at Oxford. He translated the *Rig Veda* that was sponsored by the East India Company. Though his interest was in the development and science of languages, he advanced the cause of Sanskrit. In 1872 Muller established an endowment of Sanskrit lectureship at the University of Strasbourg. The science of language gave him insight into the development of human civilization. He wrote, "If history is to teach us anything, it must teach us that there is a continuity which binds together the present and the past, the East and the West. And no branch of history teaches that lesson more powerfully than the history of language and the history of religion."

It took some courage for a Christian in nineteenth century to write of Hinduism in the following eulogistic manner. "Even the highest heights and the deepest depths which can be reached by the human mind are lighted up by the omnipresence of Brahman, the Indian name and concept of what we mean by the omnipresent Father, or if you like, of that ineffable Godhead of which even the Father is one person only." And again he says, "I deeply sympathize with your *shraddha* ceremony; I wish we had something like it in our own religion. To keep alive the memory of our parents, to feel their presence during the great trials of our life, to be influenced by what we know they would have wished us to do and to try to honour their name by showing ourselves not unworthy bearers."

Max Muller was not averse to underline the difference between the East and West when he said, "Some of the most beautiful poetry of ancient and modern India was inspired by that sentiment of unworldliness – the very opposite of that passionate love and attachment which forms the constant theme of European poetry."

Max Muller's history of ancient Sanskrit literature is a work of great scholarship along with his other book *The Six Systems of Indian Philosophy*. His book, *The Sacred Books of the East*, brought Oriental studies to the attention of the world.

Max Muller's tribute to India comes in a moving passage:

> If I were to look over the whole world to find out the country most richly endowed with all the wealth, power and beauty that nature can bestow – a very paradise on earth – I should point to India. If I were to be asked under what sky the human mind has most fully developed some of the choicest gifts, has most deeply pondered on the greatest problems of life – I should point to India. And if I were to ask myself from what literature, we, here in Europe would have been nurtured almost exclusively on the thoughts of Greeks and Romans, may draw that our inner life more perfect, more comprehensive, more universal, in fact more truly human, a life not for this life only, but a transfigured and eternal life – again I should point to India.

Georg Buhler was a great German Indologist and was probably the scholar who first contributed to the study of Indology in Europe. He was born in 1837 in the old kingdom of Hanover where he received his early education. Thereafter he went to study at the university at Gottingen where he studied under a famous linguist Theodore Benfey. It is under Benfey's guidance that Buhler learnt Sanskrit in order to read the *Vedas.* It is not generally known that Benfey's work promoted the study of Sanskrit literature and philology in Europe and particularly in Germany.

After completing his studies in Gottingen Buhler went to Paris, Oxford and London in order to study Orientalism in the libraries there. He copied Sanskrit manuscripts containing the *Vedas*. In London he met Max Muller and became librarian at the Royal Library at Windsor. After a few years Buhler felt that unless he studied Sanskrit with the pundits in India he would not be able to expand his scholarship. In India he was made Professor of Oriental Languages at Elphinstone College, Bombay in 1863. He remained in the educational service of Bombay Presidency and served in various capacities. While studying Sanskrit and collecting manuscripts Buhler made contributions to the educational system in the Bombay Presidency. He traveled widely in Central India, the Rajput States, in Punjab and Kashmir. He collected texts on philology and archaeology.

Buhler returned to Europe in 1880 and was offered the chair of Sanskrit and Indology at the University of Vienna. Buhler wanted to make Vienna, then the capital of the Austro-Hungarian Empire, a centre of Oriental studies. He received official encouragement and sponsorship which enabled him to establish the Oriental Institute of Vienna University. He commenced publication of the *Vienna Oriental Journal* soon after. Many scholars contributed articles and research material on Indian history and epigraphy. In recognition of his pioneering work in Indology in Europe he was made a member of the Imperial Academy of Sciences at Vienna. He prevailed upon academics as well as the Austrian government to fund Oriental studies particularly research on Sanskrit. Buhler completed the *Encyclopedia of Indo-Aryan Research* which was a major enterprise in the field of Oriental scholarship. As his fame spread he was invited to be a member of the German Oriental Society, the American Oriental Society, the Berlin Academy of Sciences, the Imperial Academy of Sciences in Vienna, St. Petersburg, and at the Institute of France in Paris. He was made a member of the Asiatic Society of Bengal in recognition of his work.

Dr. Buhler's literary and scholarly production was prodigious. Like William Jones he had a special fondness for Sanskrit pundits and he liked spending his time with them. He described them as "the representatives of the traditional knowledge of Sanskrit". He tried to combine the discipline of classical European education with the traditional methods of teaching of Sanskrit scholars. His work in western India inspired illustrious Oriental scholars such as R.G. Bhandarkar, Kashinath Telang, Shankar Pandit and Apte. Like Colebrooke he prepared a *Digest of Hindu Laws of Inheritance, Partition and Adoption*. He produced two volumes on the legal *Sutras of Apstamba, Gautama, Vasistha* and *Baudhayana*. He translated the *Manu Samhita* or *Laws of Manu* and wrote a treatise on Indian inscriptions and *Kavya* (epic) literature. With the help of Sanskrit literature he was able to contribute to the chronology of events of ancient India. Like William Jones Buhler maintained that India had a far older and more developed civilization than Greece or Babylon. His numerous articles in *Indian Antiquary* contain his interpretation of Indian history. He took a keen interest in archaeology as well.

By that time Buhler left India he had collected 2330 Sanskrit manuscripts which he placed in Government Archives. He rescued many ancient and Sanskrit texts from oblivion. These texts and manuscripts paved the way for future research on various subjects on Indian history and Sanskrit literature. Dr. Buhler left behind a host of German Indologists such as Hultzsch, Fuhrer and Winternitz who carried Indology forward. Much of the work thereafter in this field was accomplished by German-speaking scholars, who found much affinity between the construction and grandeur of German and Sanskrit. Nineteenth-century German philosophers such as Herder, Nietzsche and Schopenhauer, were influenced by the *Vedas* and *Upanishads*.

Professor Buhler of Vienna aided by thirty scholars of different nationalities prepared a comprehensive encyclopedia of Vedic and Sanskrit literature. His work was completed by Professor Kielhorn of Gottingen. Other German scholars, most notably Max Mueller, added to the science of comparative philology.

By the beginning of the twentieth century the entire range of Vedic and Sanskrit literature which in quantity exceeds that of Greek and Latin put together have been studied and commented upon; texts were edited and translated by Europeans scholars such as Macdonell, Hopkins, Horowitz, Winternitz, Pargiter, Oldenburg, Peterson, Hertel, Edgerton, Ridgeway, and Keith.

The fascination that scholarly Europeans have for the *Upanishads* is explained by H.W. Schomerus when he says,

> The European mind has searched no less earnestly than the Indian for a transcendental quality as something real, nay, as the coronation of reality. But inspite of all occasional higher evaluation of the transcendental, the European mind has never succumbed to putting it down as being the essential quality as though it were opposed to the world in principle in all its parts... This is a kind of philosophy which contrary to pantheism proceeds not from the realities of the world around us but from something standing outside the world and in essence quite distinct from it.

German enthusiasm for Hindu metaphysics may be because there was no imperial purpose in their studies. They felt no need to 'reform' the Hindu character from 'the abyss of ignorance and superstition' through the propagation of missionary activities. Since philosophy flourished in nineteenth century Germany, Indian philosophy had a natural attraction for educated Germans. Nietzsche and Schopenhauer borrowed certain tenets of the *Upanishads* in the formulation of their philosophical ideas. In the twentieth century German men of letters, notably Herman Hesse, was inspired by Indian philosophical themes and based his two famous works – *Sidhhartha* and the *Glass Bead Game* – on them.

50

Russia and Indology

The renowned Indologist, G. Bongard-Levin states that India has fascinated Russians from times immemorial and that there are many references to India – her traditions, customs, and beliefs – in ancient Russian literature. The image of India was that of a land of both wisdom and wealth, a place of wonders. This was not very different from the picture of India in France or Germany but in the case of Russia there were references to India in ancient Russian literary texts, especially in the realm of folklore. While these do not reflect direct contacts between the two peoples, they indicate a handing-down of a written literary tradition going back to the distant past. It is obvious from this that Russia as well as the multinational former Soviet republics had similar ancient cultural traditions as India.

Explorations around the northern shores of the Black Sea have found evidence of Indo-Iranian tribes who were ancestors of the Vedic people. Knowledge of India was transmitted through Alexandrine-Greek texts to Byzantine scholars and then to the Bulgarians who in turn passed them on to old Rus. The Romance of Barlaam and Joaseph is said to be a transposition of the legend of Lord Buddha. Mention of this legend is found in the 7th century *Anushirvan* of Shah Khusrau in the Pehlevi language. The Indian game of chess or Chaturang was transmitted around this time to Iran where it came to be called Shatrang. And from there it went to Russia. The Georgian Rafail Daribegashvli made several trips to India and brought stories from the *Panchatantra* that came to Russia. Armenia had trading posts in India. A Hindu temple was built in Baku in Azerbaijan where pilgrims came from India. There was brisk trading between India and Trans-Caucasia. One of the nationalities of the region – the Ossetians – is regarded as the same race that created the Vedas. Indian traders came to the Volga region and settled in Ashtrakhan. Merchants and craftsmen from India came to Ashtrakhan and settled there bringing with them skills in weaving and pottery. Indians and the 'Brahmin language' are mentioned in the *Laurentian Chronicle* in 1377.

The *Golubinaya Kniga* or the Dove Book with its cosmogenic theme is reminiscent of the *Purushashukta* of the Vedas. India is mentioned in old Slavonic texts such as the *Visit of Zosima to the Rahmans* (Brahmins), and *The Narrative of the Rahmans and their Amazing Life*. It is astonishing that in early medieval Christian Russia there was interest in Brahmin rites and Hinduism. India is mentioned in ancient Slavonic ballads such as the *Bylina* of Volkh Vyacheslavich and the tale of Sadko of Novgorod. The Tartar rule brought Southern Russia, Central Asia and India closer to trade.

One of the most fascinating medieval travelogues on India was written by Afnasy Nikitin, a merchant of Tver who has left a vivid description of India in the late fifteenth century. There was no religious intolerance in his observations. Though frequently homesick Nikitin adopted the customs of his hosts such as fasting during Ramzan. He describes Hindu rituals and says "they pray like Russians and bow in Monkish fashion". In his description of the wealth of India there is no sign of envy or greed. His work was incorporated in *Sofiiskaya Chronicle*.

The interest of the Russian government in India began when Tsar Peter the Great ordered all documents pertaining to India to be collected and annotated.

As William Jones was founder of Indology in Western Europe, in Russia Indology commenced as a serious study with Gerasim S. Lebedev who was born two years after William Jones in 1749. Unlike the scholarly Jones Lebedev was a gifted musician who was imbued with a passion to see the world. He came to Madras in 1789 (Sir William Jones came to Calcutta in 1784) and then went to Calcutta in 1791. Lebedev earned his living by giving music recitals and teaching music. It is most likely that he met Sir William Jones who was then a prominent scholar and judge because he was inspired to study Sanskrit, Bengali and Hindi. While Sir William Jones cultivated the acquaintance of pundits and scholars Lebedev made friends with Bengali intellectuals and was a prominent member of cultural life of Calcutta. He is remembered as the person to establish the first European style drama theatre in Calcutta where plays were staged. The Calcutta theatre developed under his inspiration and guidance.

Gerasim Lebedev, like William Jones, had admiration for the civilisation of India. He praised the poetic genius of Kalidasa and the wisdom of the Vedas. He also found in late eighteenth century India much to be admired such as high standards of morality, a vibrant culture, a well ordered social life and the respect given to learning. He observed that public and private schools both in cities and villages imparted education. Unlike his British contemparories who spoke of Indians as destitute of honesty and sunk in vice, Lebedev had respect for his Indian friends who "although tyrannized and tempted in many ways remained staunch in piety". He found that the scriptures as well as common sense governed the conduct of the people. This fundamental difference in outlook between Lebedev and his British contemporaries (with the exception of Warren Hastings and William Jones) naturally influenced Lebedev to regard that British rule was a tragedy and not a blessing which had fallen on great people. He states that "far from being savages these words might describe those who had come to rule them". Lebedev's observations aroused the sympathy of Russians for Indians who were suffering under Colonial rule.

Many Russian journals in the eighteenth and nineteenth century described the appalling features of British rule in India. This same view was expressed by the radical writer A.N. Radischev, a contemporary of Lebedev. Nowhere will we find so severe an European indictment of British rule in India as in Radischev's words in which he laments the fate of the heirs of a great civilization at the hands of cruel colonizers. Nikolai Novikov, a votary of 18th century Enlightenment, wrote denunciating British tyranny in India. In fact this attitude prevailed over much of Russia in the late 18th and early 19th centuries. The Slavophil thinkers and writers (who were opposed to Westernization) advocated ties with India and the study of Indian and Sanskrit culture. The poet Alexander Khomayakov observed that Sanskrit and Old Slavonic were different dialects of a common language. The works of Russian Indologists were read not only by the intellectual elite of Russia but it percolated to ordinary people as well. As a result the average Russian had more knowledge of India than his British counterpart. Interest in India drew a galaxy of Russian scholars to study India's cultural heritage as well as her present conditions. Further they approached their study and research without pre-conceived notions or condescension. In this way the Russian Indologists were closer to William Jones than his own compatriots.

This sympathy and interest may be ascribed to the rivalry between Russia and Britain for dominance in Asia, especially as the 19th century progressed and 'The Great Game' became bitter and hostile. This however is refuted by a renowned modern Russian Indologist, Dr. Evgeniya Vanina who points out in her article *Russian Indology: Past and Present* that while Russian scolars and the general public may have been sympathetic to India's plight, the Tsarist government adopted a different policy. While Britain supported Japan against Russia in 1905, she reversed her policy towards Russia as German military power increased and concluded a treaty with Russia in 1908. When the Russian Consul in Bombay, V. Klemm, expressed sympathy with Indian revolutionaries such as Tilak, he was immediately recalled to Moscow. But the Russian people continued to lend moral and sometimes tangible support to India; they organised funds during famines and epidemics. Dr. Vanina feels that this empathy for Indians sprang from Russia's own past – of invasions from Sweden, Poland, and France as well as the fact that Russia stood on the crossroads between Europe and Asia, with a civilization that was half Western and half Oriental. "Both India and Russia had therefore to struggle for the preservation of their traditional values and culture and world outlook against the outside forces which strove to suppress and subvert their civilizational identity. The Russian Indologists and their readers never represented the institutions and ideas of the Indians as 'manifestations of an alien mentality'."

Perhaps Russian Indology began even before the arrival of Lebedev to India. In 1762 fables from the *Panchatantra* and *Hitopadesa* were translated and published in Russian. Charles Wilkins' translation of *Bhagavad Gita* in 1784 and Governor-General Warren Hastings' ardent sponsorship of it made news in Europe. A German translation followed and then came the Russian translation in 1788.

Russia came to know of Kalidasa's *Shakuntala* through her poet Nikolai Karamzin who was living in Europe in 1790 when George Forster's translation appeared. Karamzin wrote about *The German Shakuntala* in the *Moskovskoy Zhurnal* and gave excerpts of Forster's translation. To him Kalidasa was as great as Homer. Years later *Shakuntala* was produced at the Moscow Playhouse. To the Russians who had lived on the borders of Europe and Asia the Orient was no stranger. But this was the first time that the intellectual treasure of Asia was opened to them. Karamzin's introduction on *Shakuntala* unleashed a new source of inspiration. Thus, the foundations were laid for the further development of Indian studies in both the Tsarist and the Bolshevik era. Russia's vast Asian territories in the reign of both Tsars and Commissars prompted her to widen her knowledge and understanding of Asian people.

These translations were not published in academic documents such as William Jones' *Asiatick Researches* but in popular journals and were widely read both by the Russian intelligentsia and the general public.

As early as 1820 a Czech composer J.W. Tomaschek composed an opera – *Shakuntala.* This was followed by another Opera on the same story by Leopold Schefer Perfalls and *Shakuntala Ballet* by S. Bachrich. Sir William Jones had made *Shakuntala* an international phenomenon.

Around the same time Russia's greatest poet Alexander Pushkin burst upon the literary scene. He was the bard of the people as was Kalidasa, Dante, Shakespeare and Goethe. While in exile in the Caucasus he discovered the heritage of the Asian people who lived on the periphery of the Tsar's empire. Pushkin was influenced by his school friend Kuchelbecker who had knowledge of the East and Oriental literature. Pushkin spoke of his "ecstatic raptures over the splendour of the East." The great Russian novelist Tolstoy said of Pushkin: "He was bent on getting into the soul of a man of foreign culture and depicting his inner world the way it was against the backdrop of natural settings, customs, mores and the very life that had begotten his inner world." Pushkin's famous works, *Fountains of Bakchiserai, Prisoner of the Caucasus, Tale of Tsar Saltan, The Gypsies,* explore the lives and customs of these people. After Pushkin his disciple Mikhail Lermontov set his famous work *A Hero of Our Times* against the background of Oriental peoples. Russian composers such as Glinka, Borodin, Rimsky-Korsakov, would turn to Oriental legends for their musical compositions.

Affected by the efflorescence of Oriental and Indological studies, the Russian government established the Institute of Oriental Studies in Moscow in 1818 and the Institute of Oriental Studies of the Russian Academy of Sciences in St. Petersburg in 1823. Ninety years earlier the Asiatic Museum had been established to house Indian manuscripts. The collection burgeoned as diplomats, scholars and travellers brought back Sanskrit and Tamil manuscripts on numerous subjects ranging from Vedic hymns, dramas, poems, medicine, astronomy and mathematics. This had served as the nucleus of Indological studies. By the time of the Bolshevik Revolution, the Oriental Institute at Petersburg was well established as a renowned academic institution. In mid-nineteenth century Russia there was an unprecedented flowering of Indological studies. Archaeological discoveries in Central Asia (such as the 'New Troy') in Turfan Oasis, in Eastern Turkmenistan evoked keen interest amongst Russians for Indology. In fact so deep was this interest that classical Sanskrit language was made a compulsory subject in the faculties of History, Philology, and Slavonic studies in all Russian universities in 1890. Other centres of Indological studies were founded in Samara, Ryazan, Kazan and Tashkent; these received special attention during the Soviet era. In fact the Bolshevik Revolution ushered in a new relationship with India. St. Petersburg and Moscow continue to be the main centres of Indological study and research on Indian history, linguistics and literature as well as contemporary social studies and economics.

A brilliant cluster of scholars made major contribution to the development of Indology. The Vedas, *Upanishads* and Buddhist texts were read and analysed and interpreted.

P.Y. Petrov (1814-1875) was born in 1814 and learned Sanskrit at St. Petersburg University. In 1842 Petrov was appointed Professor and Head of the newly founded Sanskrit chair in Kazan University. Hindustani, Marathi and Bengali were taught there along with the the art, history, and literature of India. In 1855 P.Y. Petrov became Professor of Moscow University, where the Department of Oriental Languages was established. The important achievements of Professor Petrov were:

Translation into Russian of some chapters from Kalhana's *Rajatarangini* which was published in the journal of Moscow University in 1872. He also translated into Russian the 'Matsyopakhyanam' and 'Savitryupakhyanam' episodes from *Mahabharata*. These were published in different literary journals.

He analysed and translated some of the cantos of *Gitagovinda* of the Bhakti poet Jayadeva. These were published in the *Moskovsky Zhurnal* in 1841. His other works include *On the Spiritual Literature of the Hindus* and *On the Qualities and Composition of Sanskrit*. These were published in the Ministry of Education Journal in 1845 and 1842. *The Sanskrit Anthology* that included aphorisms, fragments from epic poems, tales, fables, descriptive fragments and lyrics, was published by the Oriental Institute at Kazan in 1846. *The Sanskrit Grammar* was published in Moscow in 1865.

In the mid-19th century Petrov was regarded as one of the foremost Sanskritologists in Europe. F. Bopp, the leading German Sanskritologist, said about Petrov: "He has nothing to learn from me!"

Professor Petrov's close friend was the famous literary critic and revolutionary V.G. Belinsky. Petrov contributed to the journals edited by Belinsky. These journals carried articles that were very sympathetic to the Indian people's struggle against colonial rule.

O.O. Bothlingk (1815-1904) was born in 1815, graduated from St. Petersburg University and then became a member of Russian Academy of Sciences. Of German descent he contributed to the school of Russian Indology and brought the German Indologists into contact with the scholars of Russia. Most of his research articles were written in German. His main contribution was the Petersburg Sanskrit – German dictionaries (Bothlingk O und Roth R., Sanskrit – Worterbuch. Vols. 1-7, St. Petersburg, 1855-75). He has also published the Sanskrit text of the *Abhidhanacintamani*, a lexicon by Hemacandra in 1847.

K.K. Kossovich (1815-1883) was born in 1815, and studied at St. Petersburg University. He held the post of Professor of Sanskrit in the Department of Oriental Languages and headed the team of scholars which prepared the first Sanskrit-Russian dictionary. This was published in 1854. Until then most Russian Indologists, like their European counterparts, concentrated their researches and study on classical works. Kossovich was the first Russian Sanskritologist to study medieval Sanskrit literature. He felt that, "We should not consider the Sanskrit poetry of the later periods as devoid of any originality. On the contrary, through the exquisite guise of its fancy wordings the heart beating of a genuine feeling is conspicuous and sometimes the pearls and diamonds of its human adornment disappear, struck down by the lightning of such a divine thought, that could not be borrowed even from the ancient sages."

His major works include the Russian translation of the 'Sunda' and 'Upasunda' episode from *Mahabharata* published in 1844, the Russian translation of *Prabodhacandrodaya* by Krishna Misra published in 1847, the Russian translation of Jimutavahana episode from Somadeva's *Kathasaritsagara* also published in 1847, the Russian translation of *Nalopakhyanam* published in 1851-52, the Russian translation of the scenes from Sudraka's *Mrcchakatika* published in 1849, and the Russian translation of some Vedic hymns in 1854. He published articles on his researches on Sanskrit literature.

P. Minayev was born in 1840 to a middle-class family. He graduated from the Faculty of Oriental Languages at St. Petersburg University. At first he studied Chinese, but when his interest was aroused in Buddhism, he decided to study Sanskrit, Pali and Prakrit. In St. Petersburg he studied with Russia's famous Sanskrit scholar K. Kossovich, then in Europe with the celebrated German Indologists, Benfey and Bopp. From 1873 until his premature death in 1890 Minayev was a Professor of St. Petersburg University. He was a friend of R.G. Bhandarkar, met Surendranath Banerji, Bal Gangadhar Tilak (then a young teacher), Bankim Chandra Chatterji and corresponded with them. During his travels in India Professor Minayev collected a rich library of Sanskrit and Pali manuscripts which, according to Minayev's will, became the property of St. Petersburg University.

His works include: *A Review of the Phonetics and Morphology of the Pali language*, which was translated into many European languages, *Paradigms of the Sanskrit Grammar*, publications of many Buddhist texts in Sanskrit and Pali, including the *Jatakas* and most important Buddhist *sutras*, *A Review of the Most Important Works of Sanskrit Literature*, *Indian Fairy Tales and Legends* (collected in Kumaon in 1875) and *Buddhism: Studies and Materials.*

Pyotr Minayev, the leading Russian scholar of Buddhism and Jainism, kept a diary of his travels in India during the period from 1874 to 1886. He wrote: when I find myself in an under-developed country, devoid of nearly all comforts of civilized life,with not enough sleeping, unhealthy food and limbs crushed by horrible roads I feel it would be wonderful if this country be possessed by a Western master. But wonderful for whom? For a Western man accustomed to living according to the standards produced by European culture. But should it be a must for those who have never lived according to these standards and had no idea of them? And in case these standards be established who is to benefit? And would not these standards be established at the expense who had never and would never use them?

From the lecture delivered in St. Petersburg University in 1884 he said: "For a Russian scholar the Orient can be neither lifeless, nor an object of an exclusively bookish interest ... We in Russia have to study not only the India of yore, but the India of today. The research into old India should not diminish the scientific and practical importance of studies of modern India."

S.F. Oldenburg (1863-1934) was Professor at St. Petersburg University, and became Member Secretary of the Soviet Academy of Sciences in 1916. He was from 1930 Director of the Asian Museum which was later re-organised as the Institute of Oriental Studies. Professor Oldenburg was founder of the renowned *Bibliotheca Buddhica*. He is known as the best translator of Indian folktales into Russian. These were first published in 1921. He wrote tracts on Indian literature and religion such as *Buddhism and Popular Cults, Four Periods in the History of Indian Art*, and *The Indian Theatre.* He gave lectures on *The Foundation of Indian Culture, Oriental Influences Upon Narrative Literature of Medieval Europe, and Introduction into the History of Indian Art.* These were later on published as research works. Many eminent Russian Indolgoists were pupils of S.F. Oldenburg.

The following quote is taken from Professor Oldenburg's lecture *Introduction into the History of Indian Art:*

> The many-handed and ugly statue of a Hindu deity may look monstrously rude and even disgusting if placed on a shelf in a European museum. But in the half-darkness of an Indian temple, on the altar, illuminated by the twinkling lamps and glow worm-like incence-burners, wrapped in the scented smoke, decorated by flowers, the same idol may appear to us as an immortal monument of art, temple's living soul, a source of the highest inspiration. The very features which looked so ugly in a museum, will now possess a great charm. India has understood it centuries ago – the mystery of the enchanting beauty of its art and literature lay in their blood connection with Life and Nature.

F.I. Scherbatsky (1866-1942) was one of Russia's most famous Indologist whose special field of interest was in the religions, philosophy and literature of India. He was Professor at St. Petersburg University, a member of the Russian (Soviet) Academy of Sciences, honorary member of Royal Asiatic Society of Great Britain and Ireland, Die Deutsche Morgenlandische Gesellshaft, Societe Asiatique de Paris, etc.

He was a student of Minayev and a friend of Indian scholars such as R.G. Bhandarkar. F.I. Scherbatsky studied manuscripts from the Hemachandra library and met Sanskrit pandits who helped him in his work. He was a regular contributor to the famous *Bibliotheca Buddhica*.

His works include: Publication of the Sanskrit text of the *Nyayabindu*, the treatise on the Buddhist logic; *Philosophical Teachings of Buddhism* (Petrograd, 1922); *The Central Conception of Buddhism and the Meaning of the Word "Dharma" (London, 1923; Calcutta, 1956)*, the Russian translation of Dandin's *Dasakumaracharita, The Conception of Buddhist Nirvana (Leningrad, 1927; Tokyo, 1957)*, Publication of the Buddhist treatises by Dharmakirti, Vasubandhu, etc. *Towards the History of Materialism in India (Leningrad, 1927).*

A.P. Barannikov (1890-1952) was a leading Soviet scholar whose specialization was in modern Indian languages and literatures. He studied under both S.F. Oldenburg and F.I. Scherbatsky. He did research in the field of Sanskrit and Buddhist literature and translated the *Jatakamal* by Aryasura. Later on he turned to medieval Indian literature and vernacular languages. He was a Professor at Leningrad University, and the Director of the Institute of Oriental Studies. His translation of Tulsidas' *Ramacharitamanasa* into Russian and the introduction to this work marked the commencement of Soviet studies into the Bhakti movement. A.P. Barannikov taught many Soviet Indologists, including his son who became a specialist in Hindi linguist and daughter who translated Telegu works into Russian.

His works include: Hindi and Marathi textbooks, translation of Tulsidas' *Ramacharitamanasa* into Russian in verse (1948), the translation of Lalluji Lal's *Premsagar* into Russian, *A Brief Review of Urdu Literature* (1930), *The Hindi Press* (1935), *The Indian Philology* (1959), which was jointly written with his son, P.A. Barannikov.

P.L. Smirnov (1891-1967) was trained to be a doctor and practiced medicine for many years in Turkmenia. His career as an

Indologist began with a strange encounter. He was still young when he found a Sanskrit textbook at a railway station. As he glanced through it, he became interested in the culture of ancient India and began to learn Sanskrit and gained fluency in the language. He was recognized for his scholarship as well as his skill as a doctor. He became a distinguished member of the Academy of Medical Science.

From medicine to metaphysics is a long journey but Smirnov made the journey and in 1956 he published the first translation of *Bhagavad Gita* from Sanskrit into Russian. Thereafter in 1960 he published an enlarged and annotated version of the *Gita* titled *The Philosophical Texts from the Mahabharata.* He then translated episodes from the *Mahabharata* – the 'Nalopakhyanam' and 'Savitryupakhyanam' under the title *The Lady of Nala* and *The Spousal Fidelity*. These were published after his death.

Y.N. Roerich (1902-1960) was the son of the renowned Russian painter N.K. Roerich.

When the family emigrated to Britain after the Bolshevik revolution, Roerich studied Sanskrit and Pali under famous Indologists such as Sylvan Levy, Paul Pelliot, and Demison Ross at the School of Oriental Languages of London University. He went on to study Sanskrit at Harvard University, Indian Philology at Sorbonne University as well as comparitive grammar, the influence of South-West Asia on the art of South Russia. He also studied Tibetan, Mongolian and Chinese.

In 1923 Yury Roerich arrived in India with his father and joined the expedition to Sikkim where the team visited Buddhist monasteries, studied local folklore, Tibetan art, and religious beliefs. Along with his artist father, Yury studied Tibetan tankhas or scrolls and was struck by the similarity with Russian icons. In fact they were convinced that the inspiration came from a common source. They saw similarities in the manner in which the Russian icon as well the figure of the Buddha were seated in isolation.

As in the case of many Indologists, such as Csoma de Koros and Aurel Stein, Roerich's attention turned to Central Asia, to study Buddhism art and philosophy. In the case of Russian Orientalists there was also a strong impulse to find the origin of an Indo-Iranian-Russian language, the migration of races to and from Russia, and the search for the original homeland of the 'Aryan' people. Accompanying his father on the Central Asian expedition, Yury Roerich collected manuscripts, scrolls, paintings, sculptures which became the foundation for the Urusvati or Himalayan Research Institute. This institute collaborated with other institutes specializing in Oriental and Indological studies. Roerich's keen interest in Tibetan studies led to the commencement of the journal *Tibetica*. He headed the Institute of Himalayan Studies in Kulu and Indo-Tibetan Seminarium in Kalimpong.

After many years in India, Professor Roerich returned to Russia to revive the Russian School of Oriental Studies in Moscow where he became the head of the faculty of Indology. His researches paved the way for deeper understanding of Tibetan traditions and philosophy and created a new generation of scholars in this field.

Indology made great strides in the Soviet Union, covering not only classical studies but also research on contemporary India.

Yury Roerich drew many Russian scholars into the study of Sanskrit. He was Honorary Member of Royal Asiatic Society of Great Britain, Asiatic Society of Calcutta, and wrote countless works on Buddhism and Tibetology. Some of his works include: *Biography of Dharmaswamin: A Tibetan monk Pilgrim (Patna, 1959, 2 vols.), Tibeto-Russo-English Dictionary with Sanskrit Parallel (Moscow, 1983-86, 11 parts), Towards the Study of Kalacakra (Kharkov, 1990).*

V.I. Kalyanov was born in 1908, and graduated from the Institute of History and Philology in 1932. He carried on research in the Institute of Oriental Studies (Leningrad Branch) from 1937. He obtained his Ph.D. in 1941 and soon after joined the Soviet Army to fight in the Second World War. After the war he taught in Leningrad University where he was head of Indian Chair until 1968. Dr. Kalyanov was awarded the Jawaharlal Nehru Prize in 1982. He is the author of more than 100 works of which the most notable are:

Russian translation of *Mahabharata: Adiparva* (1950), *Sabhaparva* (1962), *Viratparva* (1967), *Udyogaparva* (1976). All these are published in Leningrad.

Russian translation of *Arthasastra* (1959). This was published in Moscow.

Kalidasa: An Outline of His Works which was jointly written with V.G. Erman (1958) and published in Moscow.

The Image of Indian Women in the Mahabharata: This was published by the Bhandarkar Oriental Research Institute in their Golden Jubilee Volume, 1977-78.

N.R. Guseva was born to a peasant family in an Ukrainian village in 1914. She studied at the Institute of Literature and Philology and graduated in 1940 and obtained a Ph.D. in 1951 and D.Litt. in 1978. She did research at the Institute of Ethnology. Madame Guseva taught at the Institute of Foreign Languages from 1952. She was awarded the Jawaharlal Nehru Prize and is the author of some 100 works. The most notable of them are:

Modern Applied Arts of India (Moscow, 1958).
Jainism (Moscow, 1968). This book has been translated in English and has been published in Bombay by Sindhi Publications in 1971.
Hinduism: History and Cult (Moscow, 1978).
India: Millenniums and Modern Times (Moscow, 1971).
The Multi-Faced India (Moscow, 1971).
The Arts and Crafts of India (Moscow, 1982).
Rajasthani People and Their Problems (Moscow, 1989).

I.D. Serebryakov is recognized as a renowned scholar of Sanskrit and Punjabi literature. He also did research on the civilization of medieval India. He was born into a working class family in the year of the Bolshevik revolution in 1917 and graduated from Leningrad University where he studied under the great Indologist F.I. Scherbatsky. He perfected his Sanskrit and Bengali under the guidance of the famous Indian scholars and freedom fighters – Rahula Sanskrityayana and Virendranath Chattopadhyaya. As a student of Bengali he wrote a letter of homage to Rabindranath Tagore who sent a reply of encouragement. He studied Hindustani at the Institute at Tashkent for military officers.

Serebryakov fought in the second world war and then joined as a newspaper correspondent in "Pravda". He was posted to India of which he wrote:

> The inhabitants of India whom I have met impressed me most favourably. Endowed in many regions with the richest soil and other treasures of nature, densely populated, in possession of a glorious historical past and of a few most ancient cultures, the cradle of education and intellectuality, this country has a full right for a better future and the cherished desire of its best sons to see their motherland free from foreign ravagers.

From 1960 and until the end of his life in 1998, he was a staff member of the Institute of Oriental Studies in Moscow. He received many honours in India – the Jawaharlal Nehru Prize and Bhai Vir Singh Award. He participated in numerous international seminars and world Sanskrit conferences. His notable contributions in the field of Indology are:

Russian translation of the full text of Somadeva's *Kathasaritsagara.*
The Russian translation of Bhartrihari's *Satakatraya and Vakyapadiya.*
A Comprehensive work on *Bhartrihari's Poetry and Ideas* (Moscow, 1983).
The Russian translation of Haribhadra's *Dhurtakhyana.*
The Russian translation of the dramas by Bhavabhuti – *Malatimadhava* and *Murari.*
The Russian translation of some chapters of Bana's *Harsacarita,* publication of text and annotated translation of Bakhtavar's *Sunesar,* an early XIXth century philosophical poem in Hindi.
Literary Process in India, VII-XIIth Centuries (Moscow, 1979).
Somadeva's "Ocean of Tales" as the Monument of Medieval Indian Culture (Moscow, 1989).
Sanskrit Literary Works from Kashmir (Moscow, 1982).
Punjabi-Russian Dictionary.
The Punjabi Literature, An Outline (Moscow, 1968), also in English and Punjabi.

E.P. Chelyshev was born in 1921 in Moscow and graduated from the Oriental Faculty of the Military Institute of Foreign Languages. Thereafter he joined the Red Army and fought in the second world war. After the war he returned to academic life. He obtained a D.Litt. Chelyshev has been a professor since 1965. From 1961 to 1987 he did research at the Institute of Oriental Studies, Moscow. He headed the Department of Literatures from 1966 to 1987 and became a full member of the Russian Academy of Sciences in 1987. He received the Jawaharlal Nehru Prize in 1967 and participated in international and UNESCO conferences of Orientalists and Sanskritists. Professor Chelyshev was Co-chairman of Indo-Russian Joint Commission on Co-operation in Social Sciences and was appointed Chairman of the Russian Society of Friendship with India.

E.P. Chelyshev observed, "Indian cultural legacy has until now been the basement for the multi-storey edifice of Indian literature with all its superstructures and decorations. It also fertilizes the literature of many South-East Asian cultures who have referred to their ancient Indian cultural legacy." He believes that Indian classical legacy is a complex synthesis of different cultural, spiritual and material values accumulated by the people of India. He regards Rabindranath Tagore as the founder of contemporary Indian culture. While rejecting colonialism he tried to form a synthesis between Indian and Western civilization. "No one did more than Tagore to enrich Indian culture with the finest achievements of other world cultures." Chelyshev hails Tagore's visit to Russia in 1930 and his statement that the Revolution of 1917 was a turning point in world history. Even today, says Chelyshev, Tagore is the best known and most popular Indian writer in Russia today. The epistolary friendship between Mohandas Gandhi and Leo Tolstoy, says Chelyshev, was a "remarkable milestone" in Russo-Indian relations.

Professor Chelyshev has written and published more than 350 works of which the most notable are:

Modern Hindi Poetry (Tradition and Innovation in the Poetry of Sumitranandan Pant and Suryakant Tripathi Nirala) (Moscow, 1965).

Hindi Literature: An Outline History (Moscow, 1968).

Sumitrananandan Pant (in Hindi, Delhi, Rajkamal Prakashan, 1970). This book has been published in Russian in 1978).

Indian Literature – Yesterday and Today (Moscow, 1989).

G.M. Bongard-Levin was born in 1933 in Moscow and graduated from Moscow University. Thereafter he was engaged in research at the Institute of Oriental Studies up to 1956 and obtained a D.Litt. in 1970. He vecame a full member of the Academy of Sciences in 1990. He was Editor in chief of the "Ancient History Bulletin" journal. Dr. Bongard-Levin won the USSR State Award, Jawaharlal Nehru Prize, and the Golden Medal of the Asiatic Society of Bengal. He was Honorary member of the Archeological Society of India, of Indira Gandhi International Sanskritological Society, and the Italian Institute of Near and Middle East, Royal Asiatic Society of Great Britain and Ireland. He is Vice President of the World Sanskritology Association. He has also contributed for international seminars. He is the author of more than 200 works and the following are most important:

Mauryan India (Moscow, 1973). This book in English was published by Sterling Publishers in 1985.
History of India. An Outline. (Moscow, 1973). The book is jointly written with K.A. Antonova and G.G. Kotovsky and has been published in English, Hindi, Punjabi, Tamil, Malayalam, Bengali, Czech and other languages.
From Scythia to India. The Enigmas of the Ancient Aryan History (Moscow, 1974). This book has been written jointly with E.A. Grantovsky and has been translated and published in English and French.
Sages and Philosophers of Ancient India (Moscow, 1975). This book has been written jointly with A.V. Gerasimov.
Ancient Indian Civilization, Philosophy, Science and Religion (Moscow, 1980). This book was published in English by Arnold Heinemann Publishers in 1985 and is also available in Bulgarian and Serb languages.
A Complex Study of Ancient India: A Multi-Disciplinary Approach. The book has been published in English by Ajanta Books International, Delhi, 1986.
Ancient India (Moscow, 1985). This book was published in English several times.

While the above-mentioned scholars have contributed towards Russian understanding of India and Indian civilization, other Russian Indologists have brough fresh insight into the subject of Indology, both modern and ancient.

N.A. Vishnevskaya, Indologist and literary critic, feels that the renaissance of Indian culture occurred in the middle ages with Bhakti poetry which was contemporaneous with Petrarch, Ariosto and Tasso and saw resemblance between Bhakti and Sufi poetry. S.D. Skazkin sees the Hindu renaissance as a result of resistance to Islam whereas A.M. Dykov sees the Bhakti poetry as a protest literature against the caste sytem and attending rituals. A.V. Martynov studied and wrote about Hinduism and the theory of the transmigration of souls in *The Inscrutable Path: Philosophical Etudes*.

What German Indology was in the late 18th and 19th century, Russian Indology has been in the 20th century. The older bonds of empathy and interest between the two peoples has been strengthened by political friendship as well. Perhaps no other country has produced so many Indologists in the 20th century as has Russia.

51

Italian Indology

Italian interest in India commenced in the ancient Roman world. In the centuries before and after Christ, when the Kushanas were taking over Bactria and parts of the Hellenic-India kingdoms, Rome was acquiring remnants of the Alexandrine Empire in Syria and Egypt. When Rome became the legatee of Greece's Asian territories, she acquired a keen interest in the customs of these countries, not for intellectual interests but for trade. Alexander's Asian campaigns had been spurred by a desire for territorial expansion rather than trade. Rome's territorial expansion was motivated by both glory and wealth. As Pax Romana under the stern hand of Augustus Caesar brought order, peace and prosperity, the desire for luxury, expecially Oriental luxuries, grew. Frankincense from Arabia, silk from China, spices from Malacca and beyond, fine muslin, pearls and beryls from India were in great demand. The presence of gold coins in South Indian ports is a testimony to the commerce between the two nations. The volume of the trade increased under the emperors who succeeded Augustus, reaching a peak in the time of Nero. Beset by inflation and the loss of bullion, Vespasian and the Antonines tried to curb the extravagance of the Roman patricians.

It is this trade that focused attention on India. The earliest writer was Strabo, an Asian-Greek who travelled to the mouth of the Nile and saw ships embark for India. The Roman sailors appeared to have reached the estuary of the Gaṇga but their descriptions were vague. So Strabo turned to earlier writers for information such as Eratosthenes from the city of Alexandria who in turn derived information from Megasthenes, Arisobulus, Onesikritus, and Nearchus – all of whom had participated in Alexander's campaigns. Then there was Arrian who wrote *Indika* in 150 BC. Pliny the Elder describes India in his treatise *Natural*

History. Another important work was the *Periplus Maris Erythraei* written by an unknown Alexandrian sailor who had seen the coasts of the Red and Arabian Seas and the western coast of India. In the early Christian era many envoys and emissaries came from India to Rome – Kushanas, Pandyans, and Yavanas. These envoys offered information on contemporaneous commerce and politics. Apart from muslin, silk and spice the Roman world now imported wood from India – blackwood, teak, ebony and the much prized sandalwood from the populous port of Barygaza in western India.

Ptolemy's *Geography* describes the prevailing situation in the first centuries AD. As the Roman polity began to disintegrate, the soldiers who had served in the proud Roman legions now sought employment with foreign rulers as mercenaries – as the Vikings were to do a few centuries later. They are referred to as 'dumb Mlechhas' or powerful Yavanas in Tamil literature. To facilitate trade, Roman colonies were established along the Coromandel coast. The last of the Roman travelogues was written by a monk, Kosmos Indikopleustes. It is from his writings and others like him that we derive our information of India in the early Christian era, of Indian expansion eastwards, her trade, commerce, religion, art and philosophy.

Then as the Germanic tribes descended upon Rome, India faded from Roman concerns and remained a gilded memory of halcyon days. Many centuries were to pass before Italians ventured beyond the Mediterranean lands.

Of them the most famous was the Venetian trio, Nicolo, Matteo and Marco Polo. *The Travels of Marco Polo* or *Il Millioni* as the original text was called (composed by Marco Polo in prison and dictated to a fellow prisoner Rustacelli) provides an abundance of information on China and India. The authors believe that this book had far-reaching consequences. Venice, a powerful commercial republic, awoke to the possibility of trade with India and China once more. Merchants from Spain and Portugal were fired with curiosity to see and trade with these lands.

The next notable traveller was Sassetti, a trader-scholar of the 16th century who came to India as a pepper merchant. Among his many letters is the one that made him famous in which he speaks of link between Sanskrit and Italian, thus becoming progenitor of the linguistic theory that was to result in the concept of Indo-European languages. "All their sciences are written in a language that they call Sanskrit which means 'well articulated' and which they do not remember as a spoken language ... It takes six or seven years to learn and their present language has much in common with it. There is also much in common between our language and this one, especially the words for certain numbers such as six, seven, eight, nine and words for god, snake and such like."

The first European who made a serious attempt to understand Indian thoughts and customs was ironically enough, an Italian Jesuit, Roberto de Nobile, who arrived in India in 1606 a few years after the visit of Sir Thomas Roe to the court of Emperor Jahangir. De Nobile came to India to win souls for Christ. He realized that Christianity as a product of Western culture would not appeal to Indians. Christianity had, per forza, to be Indianized. He and his followers shed their Jesuit robes, adopted the saffron garments of the sanyasi, shaved their heads, wore the sacred thread, ate vegetarian food, learnt Sanskrit and Tamil and then began preaching the word of Christ. He won many converts from various castes including Brahmins. He allowed their converts to retain the caste system and caste rituals. He even segregated them in Church according to their caste. His disciple Father Beschi became a literary figure in Tamil literature. Establishment of Jesuit schools and colleges in South India began under De Nobili's inspired guidance.

Less pious and perhaps more interesting was Niccolau Manucci, the Italian traveller, scholar, and soldier of fortune who came to the court of Shah Jahan and described the Moghul Empire and court at its dazzling height in his book *Storia de Moghor* or History of the Moghuls which gives a fascinating account of two emperors, a star-crossed crown prince, fratricidal murders, wealth, power and glory and impending tragedy.

With the decline of the Moghul Empire, Portuguese, Dutch, French and British merchants and envoys came to fish in troubled waters. Italy – fragmented and chaotic, with the French, Spaniards and Austrians spoiling for loot on Italian soil – could only remember imperial Roman glory. It was after the *Risorgimento* or unification of Italy that she could turn for inspiration to the past to plan future glory.

It was North Africa rather than Asia which interested her now. Libya was hers and Ethiopia waited for Italian conquest. India was far away. It was one man who established Italian Indology on a sure and scholarly footing.

Giuseppe Tucci started as a student of history. The Orient fascinated him; he went to India in the late 1920s to study Sanskrit. In Calcutta, then the intellectual and commercial capital of India, he met a group of scholars such as Benoy Ranjan Sarkar and linguists such as Suniti Kumar Chatterjee. He went to Shantiniketan and met Rabindranath Tagore. Then, following the footsteps of Csomo de Koros and Aurel Stein Giuseppe Tucci, explored Central Asia and the Buddhist Silk Road. Fascination for Buddhism and Tantrism took him to Tibet. He already knew Sanskrit and Pali; now he learnt Tibetan under the guidance of the Lamas. He had stepped into a strange and fascinating world, a world into which very few Europeans had gained admission. Professor Tucci read scrolls, manuscripts and ancient texts, analysed them, and took some with him back to Rome.

Politics and Indology sometimes go together. The Italian leader Benito Mussolini encouraged Oriental studies. He thought it incongruous that Italy which along with Greece had relations with India and the Orient from ancient times did not have an Institute for Oriental Studies while Germany and France – latecomers to the Orient – should have such institutes. He gave all assistance and patronage to establish the Institute for Middle and Far East or ISMEO as it was generally called. GiuseppeTucci drew a group of scholars to study the Orient while Indian scholars from the Asiatic Society of Calcutta came to study and teach at ISMEO. He had renowned colleagues – Formichi and Levy – who specialized in Sanskrit, Pali and Bengali. ISMEO published the journal *Trans-Himalaya* with articles on Indology and Tibetology. (One of the co-author's father, Moni Moulik, was a student of Tucci and taught Bengali at ISMEO).

As the age of empire ended with the liberation of Asian countries following the second world war, ISMEO continued to sponsor Oriental studies as a means of gaining knowledge of civilizations that now formed the comity of nations.

* * * * *

The legacy of William Jones stretches beyond India, Britain, Germany, France, Russia and Italy. There are some sixtry institutes that have been established for Indology and Oriental studies also in Poland, Norway, Sweden, Denmark, The Netherlands, Japan, Australia, Switzerland, Canada and USA.

52

Sandor Csoma De Koros – The Pilgrim-Scholar of Hungary

Sandor Csoma de Koros was the most intriguing of Oriental scholars. He was born in a remote Transylvanian village in Hungary on 4th April 1784 – a momentous year for Indology – when the Asiatic Society was established in far-away Calcutta by a group of Englishmen. His life would be inextricably bound with the work of the Asiatic Society. That was however in the years to come.

The family belonged to a class of military nobility called Szekely who claimed their ancestry from the Huns and who had guarded the frontiers from Turkish intrusion. Their fortunes had dwindled; they compensated for this by educating themselves. Csomo went to high school and then to the University of Gottingen. He studied Greek, Latin and English. His professor Eichhorn introduced him to Arabic. The straitened circumstances of his family impeded his studies and it was sometime before he could obtain his degree.

As a subject nation living under Austrian rule his youthful concern was the search for national identity. He decided to journey to Asia and do research on the original homeland of the Magyar or Hungarian race.

Csomo de Koros had the cosmopolitanism that is the hallmark of great scholars and like many of them he began with a love for his own country. Hungary stands in the heart of Europe, a landlocked nation surrounded on three sides by powerful neighbours. They had once been a part of the Roman world but that heritage was soon forgotten in the welter of events that overtook the rich fertile country on the banks of the Danube. The Hungarians liked to remember the distant past when their ancestors – the Huns – had overrun Europe. When the Huns disappeared

Alexander Csoma de Koros

into the Steppes as abruptly as they had appeared, a Turkic race, the Magyars, conquered the land and became the ruling class. Their original language, said to be a branch of the Romance group was lost in the Magyar-Turkic tongue. Added to this confusion was the belief that the Gypsies or Romany people of Hungary were of Indian origin.

While much of Eastern Europe became Christian and part of the Byzantine empire, Hungary struggled to maintain her freedom from both Europe and Asia. The only other European nation which did not belong to the Byzantine or Roman Commonwealth was Russia. In the eleventh century pagan Hungary, like Russia, was converted to Christianity. While Russia chose the Greek Orthodox Church, Hungary's King Estevan (or Steven) embraced the Roman Church. But like Russia, Hungary straddled two worlds.

At the time of Csomo's birth Hungary was a part of the sprawling Austrian-Hapsburg Empire, ruled by a son of the great Maria Teresa. The French Revolution would touch her with a grim hand in a decade when a daughter of Maria Teresa, Queen Marie Antoinette of France, would be executed before a blood-thirsty Jacobin multitude in Paris. Hungarians had little interest in these matters; they were poor and the only use the Austrians had for them was the young men who filled the imperial army. It is in such circumstances that a nation searches for its identity. Csomo felt a magnetic pull towards Asia. At the age of thirty-five he set out in search the Hungarian homeland in Central Asia.

Csoma's biographer Professor Geza Bethlenfalvy of Budapest wrote,

> The beginning of the nineteenth century was a time of quest for a new national identity of Hungarians, an oppressed community, a time of search for truth, more than myth, for a truth which would meet the requirements and new norms of science and learning. Csoma decided to unravel the mystery of the mythic early history of his nation, to devote his life to this problem and to prepare himself for this enormous task. He learned to sleep on the floor without bed or blankets, he learned to suffer hunger ... he walked to Gottingen and learned what scholars knew about Central Asia, about philology, history and geography ... There were many theories about the origins of Hungarians ... as descendents of Attila's Huns. Other hypothesis showed they could be traced to Hebrews, Turks, Tanguts ... only one fact was certain – they came from the east.

Csoma set out for the East in November 1819. He travelled across Rumania, to Alexandria, Aleppo, Damascus, Tehran, Samarkand, arriving in Bukhara in 1821. Hearing of the approach of the Russian army he turned south towards Kabul and then finally Lahore. From there he planned to travel to Ladakh and then to Yarkand and Turkestan. On 16th July 1822 in the village of Drass in Kashmir, he met another scholar-explorer, George Moorcroft. Together they travelled to the kingdom of Ladakh. In June 1822 they arrived at the capital, Leh. Moorecroft's enthusiasm for Tibetan studies deeply interested Csoma; he was persuaded to prepare a dictionary and grammar of Tibetan language. Moorcroft gave him three hundred rupees and letters of introduction to influential persons in Ladakh. Moorcroft gave Csoma a rare book, *Alphabetum Tibetanum*, and said the Tibetan language would be valuable for him in this region. Persuaded by his British friend, and with letters of introduction, Csomo trekked through mountains roads to the monastery of Zangla in the Zanskar taluk of Ladakh. There the Rimpoche, Sangs-rgyas Phun-tshogs, received him warmly and arranged Tibetan language lessons for Csoma.

At this stage a question arises – why did the Hungarian scholar in search of the Magyar homeland suddenly decide to study Tibetan in remote snow-bound Zanskar? Moorcroft was a British officer in the employ of the East India Company, ostensibly a veterinary surgeon in charge of buying stud horses. It is more likely that he was also an agent of the British Government involved in the 'Great Game' in which Russia, China, Afghanistan and Britain were involved. Was Csoma persuaded to gather information for the British? Did Moorcroft remind him that an English endowment at Gottingen University had funded his education? Did Csoma wish to repay the kindness? There are scholars such as C.L. Dutta, G. Bethlenfalvy and Theodore Dukas who strongly deny this and say that Moorcroft was acting on his own initiative. The answers will never be known.

Nevertheless one is intrigued by Moorcroft's instruction about the documents to be prepared by his Hungarian friend. "These in the event of my decease or of his departure from Ladakh before my return will be deposited with Anwar Baba the Imam of Leh, with Khoga Tanzeen of Nobhra or Mohin Ulee the British Factor at Leh and on the occurrence of the event first mentioned (death of Moorcroft) these (documents prepared by Csoma) will become property of the Honourable Company ..." Moorcroft ends the letter by a request to his book agents in London to send several volumes on Greek and Latin for facilitating Csoma's studies. The postscript of the letter is written in Latin. These are not the normal preoccupations of a horse trader-procurer!

The Lama Bande (Pundit) Phun Tshogs, a man of deep and wide learning, began to teach Csomo Tibetan and Buddhism. The monastery had some three hundred printed volumes on Tibetan Buddhism, literature and folklore. No outsider, least of all a foreigner, had had access to such material before. Csoma patiently copied all the texts in the order in which they stood. He had been admitted to sacred texts that had been open only to *Lamas* and their students. Rajendra Lal Mitra, the renowned Indian archaeologist commented: "No European had studied Tibetan language and philosophy with greater dedication."

Dedication it certainly was. When daylight dwindled Csoma returned to his tiny stone cell and lay down on sheepskin rugs, trying to keep warm in the intense cold. Food was austere. Sometimes he would wake in the morning to find the door of his cell blocked by snow. As he later observed, "At twenty thousand feet Zangla Monastery was a picture of desolation and grandeur." Assured of Csoma's sincerity and his readiness to undergo all privation in order to learn, the *Lama* eventually invited the scholar to live at his house. Sandor Csoma de Koros stayed in Zangla from June 1823 to October 1824 where he copied manuscripts and books, and learned whatever the *Lama* would teach him. Then he moved to the villages of Ste-sta and Phug-thal in Zanskar for another year. Then gathering his precious manuscripts the Hungarian pilgrim-scholar began the descent to the plains and came to the river Sutlej and crossed into Punjab to meet Moorcroft. But the British officer had passed away. Why should Moorcroft, a vigorous young man anticipate his death unless he was involved in a dangerous game?

Once more we are puzzled; Csoma was kept in civil detention at Sabathur, 'half a guest and half a prisoner.' Why? Did the scholar refuse to participate in the Russo-British games over Tibet and act as a cat's paw? His plea to return to Ladakh was turned down. Csoma felt friendless and alone. He took up residence in the village of Kanam in the Kinawar Himalayas for four years between 1827 and 1831 where he worked on his Tibetan research material. Csoma decided to go to Calcutta and continue his studies. In 1831 the Hungarian Tibetologist set off for Calcutta on foot.

H.H. Wilson was then the head of the Asiatic Society and received the austere scholar warmly and offered facilities for continuing his Tibetan researches. Csoma gratefully accepted the offer but was curt in declining financial assistance. He refused to be under obligation to the British Government. Did they once again ask him to be an agent or an informant?

Csoma de Koros now began to work at his corner in the Asiatic Society building in Calcutta. He could now tell the world about Tibet and India's ancient ties with that kingdom in the clouds. He described how in the eighth century a Buddhist monk Shanta Rakshita was invited by the King of Tibet to teach Buddhism, the evolution of Tibetan philology and mythology, to teach Buddhism and the doctrine of ten virtues. After this, the great teacher Padma Sambhava came to Tibet and made significant contribution to Tibetan mysticism.

Csoma set to work on preparing a Tibetan Grammar and Dictionary as an improvement on the book Moorcroft had given him. These were compiled entirely from authentic sources and from the material given to him by the *Lama* of Zanskar. Modestly Csoma spoke of "the elementary works herewith published as a key to unlock the immense volumes, faithful translations of the Sanskrit texts which are still to be found in Tibet on the manners, customs, opinions, knowledge, ignorance, superstitions, hopes and fears of a great part of Asia especially Indian in former ages."

While the great scholar may have called them elementary works they were in fact of great significance because until then knowledge of Tibet was shrouded in mystery. His grammar of Tibetan language in English was a great achievement as well as his Sanskrit-Tibetan-English Vocabulary. Csoma indicates in his writing that the literature of Tibet was mostly derived from the Indian originals that were again translated from Tibetan into Mongol, Manchu and Chinese. As a result, he discovered, the Tibetan language like Latin in medieval Europe became the language of the scholar and the vehicle for transmission of northern Buddhism. Csoma wrote on lexicography, grammatical literature, description and analyses of Tanjur and Kanjur and other non-canonical works, historical literature, chronology, the different systems of Buddhism such as

Madhyamika and Kalachakra, medical literature of Tibet, translations of wise sayings, on amulets, scarves and banners.

It was said of him, "Csoma de Koros did more than the armies of Ochterlony and no less than the diplomacy of Hodgson to pierce the mysteries of Tibet." Long before any scholar traversed the formidable Himalayas, Csoma de Koros had gone to Ladakh and addressed himself to a formidable task – a survey of classical Tibetan literature. Painstakingly and with unswerving dedication he culled out details of Tibetan history from the manuscripts and religious treaties including tracts on Tantra.

After arriving in India Csoma de Koros taught himself Bengali, Hindustani, Marathi and Mythili. He already knew Hebrew, Arabic, Greek, Latin, Slavonic, German, English, French, Russian, Tibetan, Persian and Pushtu. During the years 1834 to 1837 Csoma lived and worked at the Asiatic Society in Calcutta, where he translated Tibetan works into Sanskrit and English. Much of the information about Tibetan history and religion known today is due to this extraordinary man. Other great scholars like James Prinsep befriended him. They listened to accounts of his travel with awe and growing interest.

It is sad that this towering scholar was given the rank of a sub-librarian in the Asiatic Society. But he did not mind because this gave him a tiny place that was his room and where he worked for many years. Csoma was a man of ascetic temperament who could live in the most trying circumstances in the most difficult of climate and terrain. During his travels he sometimes lived in a hut and subsisted on boiled rice and tea. He was totally unpractical and never sought financial assistance for the pioneering work that he was doing.

In 1842, when he was fifty-eight years old, Csomo de Koros had a great urge to visit the Himalayas and undertake a tour of Central Asia. The youthful dream of finding the Hungarian homeland had not entirely left him. He wrote a farewell letter to the Asiatic Society and from Calcutta set off to travel northwards along the course of the Ganga. But the dream remained unfulfilled. By the time he reached Darjeeling he was ill with malaria and it is there in the sight of his beloved Himalayas that the pilgrim scholar breathed his last.

It is an indisputable fact that Csoma de Koros was a great pioneer in Indo-Tibetan studies at a time when no one else dared to enter the field and who by his silent example influenced a host of scholars in this.

Csoma de Koros inspired several generations of scholars, archaeologists and explorers of Tibet. His Hungarian compatriot Aurel Stein was inspired by him and set out on his travels of exploration in Central Asia and through his excavations drew attention to the network of civilizations that flourished in Central Asia. Sven Hedin, the Swedish scholar-explorer, followed in the footsteps of Csoma de Koros in the early twentieth century and has left behind a detailed account of his travels in Tibet, of Tibetan Buddhism, and Lamaism in three volumes of *Trans-Himalaya*. In the 1930s came the flamboyant scholar Giuseppe Tucci, founder of the Oriental Institute of Italy or Istituto Media e Estremo Orientale (ISMEO), who followed Csomo de Koros to Ladakh and Tibet and deepened the knowledge of the world on that remote mountain nation.

Long before the inter-connections of civilizations were recognized, especially in the variegated cultural patterns in Asia and in the inaccessible areas such as Tibet and Ladakh, Mongolia and Manchuria, Csomo de Koros brought to light the close ties between Indian and Tibetan culture and was able to demonstrate the influence of Sanskrit on Tibetan thought, its outward flow from Tibet to even remoter places such as Manchuria. He endorsed William Jones' theory of the antiquity of Sanskrit.

The Hungarian inscription on his tombstone in Darjeeling reads – 'Alexander Csoma de Koros, a poor lonely Hungarian, without money or acclaim but inspired by determination and staunch patriotism who sought to find the cradle of Hungarians finally succumbed to the fatigues of his journey. He sleeps his everlasting dream far from his homeland, but lives in the heart of every good Hungarian.'

In recognition of his dedication and his pioneering researches and writings on Buddhism, its outward trajectory from India to Ladakh to Tibet and beyond, the University of Taisho in Japan canonized Sandro Csoma de Koros as a Bodhisattva. Sandor Csomo de Koros, the pupil of a Buddhist Rimpoche, would not have asked for a greater honour.

Part VI

Oriental Scholars and Dialogues in Civilization

"This (mutual understanding between Britain and India) will survive when the British dominion in India shall have long ceased to exist and the sources which it once yielded of wealth and power are lost to remembrance."

— Warren Hastings, Governor-General of India, 1776-1785

"If history is to teach us anything, it must teach us that there is a continuity which binds together the present and the past, the East and the West. And no branch of history teaches that lesson more powerfully than the history of language and the history of religion."

— Max Muller, German scholar and Indologist

53

Warren Hastings – Imperialist and Orientalist

Now when the British Empire is a phantom of the past, and its Governors-General and Viceroys relegated to the detritus of history, Hastings is being remembered for the contribution he made not to the clash of civilizations but to their dialogue and reconciliation.

More than fifty years ago Dr. Jowett said, "Englishmen cannot govern a people without understanding it and the understanding of it must be gained through a knowledge of its languages, its literature, its institutions, its customs, its poetry and mythology, its land and agriculture." Warren Hastings realized this a century and half before Dr. Jowett.

Sometimes it takes one man to change the tone and temper of an epoch. It is sometimes the vision and the action of one man that sets into motion a chain of events that transforms an age and its outlook. Such a man was Warren Hastings. Initially it might be felt that there is an incongruity in the choice of Hastings in the galaxy of extraordinary scholars who opened the grandeur of Indian civilization to the West, but the more you look at Indology under the East India Company's rule, the more you see the influence that Hastings exerted in the choice of scholars for different assignments, in setting the parameters for their work, in making the administrative and financial arrangements which made their work possible. Hastings' role can be seen in Halhed's *Gentoo Laws* and the *Bengal Grammar*, in Wilkins' translation of the *Bhagvad Gita* for which he wrote both the Introduction, and the Recommendation to the Directors of the East India Company, in the sponsorship and encouragement of the scholar Colebrooke, and in the formation of the Asiatic Society for which the scholars wanted him to be the first President. The scholars respected Hastings because he was himself a scholar who knew Persian and some Sanskrit and who had a knowledge and empathy for India that was superior to their own. Warren Hastings was the patron of the Company scholars and this book therefore pays tribute to him.

The scholars were all articulate men and it is refreshing to hear their authentic voices across the span of centuries. The approach of the authors is not one of *de mortuis nil nisi bonum*, that is, speak not ill of the dead. While their virtues, their talents and their achievements are worthy of commemoration, the fact that they were human beings living in an age in which scholarship and low life could coexist quite compatibly is always kept in mind.

Hastings not only presided over a momentous period on two spheres, he actually shaped the era. In the world of politics he was eminently successful; it was his astute diplomacy, his occasional chicanery, his cautious cogitations coupled with a remarkable audacity that extended the boundaries of the British Empire in India. It was in the region of nurturing a cross fertilization of cultures that lay his enduring achievement. By delving into the forgotten heritage of India, by getting gifted scholars to learn and write about it, Hastings began the movement that came to be called the Indian Renaissance.

Hastings the scholar knew that empires are built on shifting sands. He had spoken of the day when British rule would end in India and the need to leave behind something worthwhile that will survive when British rule ends.

It is something of a dialectical phenomenon that while he brought more and more Indian territories under the Company's rule, he also laid the foundations for the nationalism that would one day dismantle his empire. It is possible that while building the British Indian empire, Hastings had grown to love the people and customs, the languages and philosophies of that land. And so he wanted to let his compatriots in England and the world know more about the vast country that had been conquered. Nowhere is this empathy and esteem for India more clearly reflected than in the letter he wrote to the Chairman of the East India Company recommending the publication of Charles Wilkins' translation of the *Bhagavad Geeta* which is presented in a later chapter.

This part of the book attempts to describe the contribution of the handful of brilliant and dedicated British scholars who assisted

Hastings in his task. We have tried to show their backgrounds, their academic and social reputations before they landed in India, their motivations, their proficiency in Sanskrit and other Oriental languages, the support and patronage they received especially from Hastings and other Governor Generals, their personalities, their access to pundits, their attitude to religion, their attitude to Indian customs, traditions, religion – to *sati*, female infanticide, child marriage, etc., the depth and sincerity of their scholarship, the changes in the men who went to India and the men who returned, the durability of their contribution, whether their work has lasted, their subsequent careers in England. One wonders whether they would have been able to achieve so much if they had remained in England. Perhaps it was India that gave them an arena for realizing their gifts just as it was India, the jewel in the crown, that gave grandeur to the British Empire.

If extolling the contribution of Hastings and his scholars seems politically incorrect at a time when colonial empires are discredited, one has to cast a glance backward to see what might have happened if India had been ruled by Portugal.

Sir William Jones wrote of the first summer in India:

> I should not therefore have written now merely to say that it is hot in April or that mango fruit are in season but a passage from a letter from the Bishop of St Asaph which I have just received makes me desirous of expostulating a little with you ... You have declared I find that 'if you hear of my siding with Hastings you will do everything in your power to get me recalled.' ... Ought you not to know after your long experience of my principles that whilst I am a Judge I would rather perish than side with any man. The character of justice (and I am sorry for it) indeed makes me multilateral; it gives me an equity side, a law side, and a ecclesiastical side, a crown side, a admiralty side and the worst of all in the case of ordinances and regulations, a legislative side but I neither have nor will have nor should any power or allurement on earth give me a political side. As to Hastings I am pleased with his conversation as a man of taste and a friend to letters but whether his publick conduct to be wise or foolish I shall not in my present station examine; and if I should live to mention it after examination in the House of Commons, I should speak of it as it deserves without extenuation, if it be reprehensible and without fear of any man if I think it laudable.

Hastings encouraged a large group of scholars who worked under the auspices of the East India Company and the Bengal government. They are sometimes called the Company Scholars. The Indologists whom Hastings encouraged were Nathaniel Brassey Halhed, Charles Wilkins, William Jones, Henry Thomas Colebrooke, John Shore, Francis Gladwin, John Carnac and Jonathan Duncan.

Nathaniel Brassey Halhed, Charles Wilkins, Henry Thomas Colebrooke, William Jones and Warren Hastings, the patron for Indian studies in India, are often and rightly quoted together by contemporary sources and later as a chapter in the history of Sanskrit scholarship. Yet they form a group in terms of personal contact and influence only. From the point of view of scholarship, Halhed's name, as Raymond Schwab well expressed it, comes last in the list of pre-Indology.

Many of them joined together to form the Asiatic Society with Warren Hastings as their patron. He tried heroically – and against the growing arrogance of the British – to *reconcile British rule with Indian institutions*. That is why he placed so much importance on the study of Indian religion, culture and the Indian way of life.

Hastings was more than a pragmatic ruler. It is not difficult to discern his personal touches; he quoted the *Bhagvad Gita* in his letters to his wife. In retirement we find him discussing Indian classics with Halhed. Hastings admired the simple Indian way of life. In his introductory letter to Nathaniel Suks, Hastings wrote that the British prejudice against the Indians "was not yet wholly eradicated though surely abated". He felt any work which brought the real character of India home for observation was of intrinsic value. He was therefore always in favour of publication of Indian scriptures in English. In fact he made the prophetic statement that, "This will survive when the British dominion in India shall have long ceased to exist and the sources which it once yielded of wealth and power are lost to remembrance."

54
Procuring Pundits

The first problem facing Western scholars for commencing Indology and the study of ancient India was language. English scholars were confronted with a language that was more ancient than Greek and Latin, the disciplines in which they had been initiated during their studies at Oxford or Cambridge. Greek and Latin had been the monopoly of the priests in the Christian monasteries and a few scholars during the dark ages in Europe when invasions by Gothic and Vandal tribes had disrupted civic life. Paradoxically it was in the court of Andalucian Emirs where Moorish scholars such as Averroes and Avicenna kept alive the Hellenic-Roman traditions. The Byzantine or the Eastern Roman Empire was also the repository of the same heritage until 1453 when Constantinople fell to the Ottoman Turks. The flight of Cardinal Bessarion from Constantinople to Rome together with his fabulous library opened the floodgates of classical learning from the essentially Greek Byzantine empire to Italy. Old classical works were read, discussed and analysed among the Italian scholars of the fifteenth century. The Renaissance flowered in this ferment of intellectual and artistic ideas. By the late sixteenth century Latin and Greek were no longer the monopoly of churchmen; they became the possession of educated people.

In India per contra Sanskrit over the centuries had become the preserve of the Hindu priesthood who were the interpreters of religious texts and learning to the masses as well as the performers of sacred rites. Sanskrit remained a closely guarded intellectual property of the Brahmins.

To obtain teachers was difficult at first. The Brahmins shunned contact with the foreigners who were considered as *mlecchas* or impure. However, as English power grew and looked as if it was there to stay, the rigidity of Sanskrit pundits decreased. Halhed observes in his *Preface to the Code of Gentoo Laws*, quoted from a Minute in December 1783 in which Warren Hastings recommends that Charles Wilkins should be permitted to continue his studies in Benaras and in which he proudly attributed the pundits' new cooperation to the enlightened policies that were initiated with the compilation of the Code.

A team of pundits was engaged for this task. Halhed comments on the difficulties of getting their cooperation. Halhed noted in the *Preface to the Code*: "The pundits who compiled the *Code* were to a man resolute in rejecting all his solicitations for instruction in this dialect, and that the persuasion and influence of the Governor-General were in vain exerted to the same purpose". Yet soon after he was 'happy enough to become acquainted with a Brahmin of more liberal sentiments, and of a more communicative disposition.' He promised, 'profiting by the help of so able a master ... to exert his intelligence upon so curious and uncommon a subject.' Little is known of Halhed's pundit. His name is not recorded. Halhed testifies both in the *Preface to the Grammar* and in his letter to Costard that the cooperative pundit was reproved by his fellow pundits. We also know that "while he readily displayed the principles of his grammar, he has invariably refused to develop a single article of his religion."

There were allegations that Warren Hastings had coerced the pundits into cooperating. He took pains to refute the allegation which emanated from London that he had used press gang methods to get the services of the pundits!

There is no doubt that the pundits were then reluctant to instruct foreigners. Yet the situation soon changed. Within a decade, Jones had 'more Brahmanical teachers than (he) could find time to hear' and another ten years allowed Colebrooke to exclaim, "I cannot conceive how it came to be ever asserted that the Brahmins were ever averse to instruct strangers; several gentlemen who have studied the language find, as I do, the greatest readiness in them to give us access to all their sciences." In 1783, Hastings rejoiced to witness this changed attitude. Halhed, the translator of the Code, was the first beneficiary of this punditic instruction, even though it came too late in his stay to allow the prolonged and advanced study that was to make of his *Princeps Litteraturae Sanscritae*. (Text on inscription of medal awarded to Wilkins by the Royal Society of Literature in 1825.)

Halhed elaborated on the point:

> It has been a generally received opinion that the professors of the Shanscrit learning were prohibited by some religious precept from communicating that language to strangers. This supposition has been of late years discovered to be ill-founded. The reserve which they have maintained distance which has given birth to it proceeded originally from the intolerant spirit of Mahometan bigotry and was merely a caution of policy not of prescribed obligation. The means which were used some years ago to conciliate the pundits who were employed to compile the *Code of Hindoo Laws* for the use of this government and the liberal and beneficent purposes for which the work has been since applied, have totally removed their former objections and I myself have found them not only willing but forward in gratifying every disposition manifested by the individuals of our nation to be instructed in their sacred language, in their sciences, and even in the mysteries of their religion.

(Quotation from a minute in 1783 in which Warren Hastings recommends that Wilkins should be permitted to continue his studies in Benares and in which he 'proudly attributed the pundit's new cooperation to the enlightened policies which were initiated with the compilation of the Code' [RR.79] (Minute to Board of Revenue, 9th December 1780.)

Warren Hastings recognized the need for understanding of Sanskrit grammar as well as the grammar of other Indian languages. It was he who was primarily responsible for "cultivation of a right understanding and a general medium of intercourse between the Natives of Europe who are to rule and the Inhabitants of India who are to obey". Halhed's Grammar as it was called marked the birth of the modernizing of printing and publishing industry in Bengal though the printing machine had come to India two centuries earlier in 1556 when Portuguese officials had brought the printing machine to their colony in Goa.

Inspired by Warren Hastings, Charles Wilkins, the printer of the book, "cut by the application of personal labour" a set of Bengali typefaces which are remarkable for their novelty and beauty.

55

Nathaniel Brassey Halhed and the Bengali Grammar

If there was a time when scholarship and sensuality rode so easily in double harness it was the Augustan Age in English letters and a practitioner of the art of living life so naturally on the sacred and profane levels was young Nathaniel Brassey Halhed.

Young Halhed was in the mould of an Elizabethan personality; a gifted scholar, a profligate with a romantic disposition, prone to tempestuous relationships, and writing effusive epistles to numerous young ladies. This trait showed itself in later life in Calcutta where he displayed a penchant for married women. Born to a rich and indulgent father, Halhed grew up in affluence unlike William Jones and Charles Wilkins. He grew to be unbusiness-like in early publishing ventures. Halhed suggested a second volume of his poems even when the first was not a commercial success in the hope that the success of the second would persuade readers to buy the first! In fact he was the most colourful character among the East India Company scholars with a literary bent.

Halhed invites comparison to the Portuguese poet Luis Camoens, author of *Os Lusiads* who was forced to leave Lisbon for India after a dangerous liaison with a court lady. Halhed the poet who was disappointed in love and who translated *The Love Epistles of Aristenetus,* from Greek into English meter, turned his attention to more practical matters after his arrival in India.

The magnificent promise shown in his youth burnt out quickly. In fact his greatest achievements were from the age of twenty-two to twenty-seven when he compiled the *Code of Hindu Laws* and the *Bengali Grammar.* Thereafter the years were in shallows, miseries and messianism. He was a part of the brilliant 'Bengal Brigade' in England and formed the talented group around Warren Hastings whom he warmly defended during the latter's persecution in England. After returning to England Halhed missed India intensely and lamented that the documents he needed for his scholarly work were not available in England. He ran into financial reverses; the combination of an active mind, penury and frustration led him to the eccentric millennial prophets such as the Richard Brothers and Joanna Southcott.

Rosane Rocher gives this summary in her book *The Chequered Life of Nathaniel Brassey Halhed*, 1751-1830:

> Nathaniel Brassey Halhed left his mark on many aspects of his times which are now of concern to diverse disciplines. To Orientalists he is not only the man who gave the West correct notions of Sanskrit, he is also the author of the first English grammar of Bengali, the man who first sought to purify it from foreign accretions and who by causing the creation of a vernacular printing press, set the Bengal Renaissance on its course. For historiographers of linguistics he is the precursor of William Jones, a pioneer in the comparison of Indo-European languages. For historians of British India he is one of the most faithful intimates of the Governor of Bengal, Warren Hastings, and a political pamphleteer on his behalf. To students of English literature, he is the youthful coadjutor of the famed playwright, Richard Brindsley Sheridan, in his first literary ventures. For exponents of millennial, messianic cults, he is the most celebrated supporter of the popular prophet, Richard Brothers.

The arrival of Halhed coincided with the assumption of *Diwani* by East India Company which thereafter ceased to be a mere trader but now had to assume administrative responsibilities including the administration of justice. "The Court of Judicature in Calcutta was a parody of an English court where judges in wigs and ermine perspiring in the Calcutta heat ... but even more ludicrous trying to apply incongruously English common law in an alien atmosphere" (Busteed). This Court tried miscellaneous cases – civil, criminal, maritime, and personal.

After assumption of *Diwani*, Warren Hastings was able to exert greater power. From the outset he wished to guard against the mindless imposition of English practices to Indian administration – a very real danger if Leadenhall Street had its way. The London officials of the East India Company had no conception of the needs of Indian administration. Only men who had endured the rigours of the Madras heat and the monsoons of Cossimbazaar, who had traded with the Indians, and who understood their customs and traditions arising from a complex history and culture of several millennia, were able to grasp the nuances of the situation. With the assumption of *Diwani* there came in its train administrative and judicial responsibilities well beyond the functions of a trading company. It was fortunate that there was at this critical juncture, a man at the helm of affairs who understood the magnitude and complexity of these responsibilities. That man was Warren Hastings.

It is one of the paradoxes of Indology that Halhed the poet was chosen for two works of purely practical utility – the compilation of the *Code of Gentoo Laws* and the *Bengali Grammar.* However fortuitous the choice, in the case of both he showed that the man was more than equal to the task.

Nathaniel Brassey Halhed was born on the 5th May 1751. Halhed's intellectual exploration of India began early; like William Jones he was a classical scholar with proficiency in Greek and Latin. His father was the Director of the Bank of England and sent him for schooling at Harrow and then to Christ Church College at Oxford University. Encouraged by William Jones he began learning Persian at Oxford. And like Jones he also studied Hebrew, Sanskrit and Bengali. He was a friend of Sheridan at school and William Jones at Oxford and collaborated writing *Epistles of Diatarebus.* This was not a notable commercial success.

Halhed the Oxford scholar, was aged twenty-one when he was forced to make 'a lover's leap' during a liaison with a renowned singer of her time. Halhed left for India in self-imposed exile because he was jilted by a colourful lady, Ann Elizabeth Linley, who became the wife of Sheridan and the reputed mistress (in exchange for a card debt) of the Prince of Wales. Halhed the linguist and grammarian was not a dry-as-dust scholar. Reading about these long and momentous voyages of the past, one cannot but help reflect on advantages of long ocean voyages as preparation for career in a new country when the traveller could read and think about the country of his destination. In contrast, modern air travel does not give enough time for even reading a guidebook thoroughly.

The scholar was a complete contrast to the calculating and avaricious soldiers of fortunes who came to India. Unlike the East India Company officials, Halhed did not go to India of his own volition. The decision was taken by his father who hoped that young Nathaniel would have a go at 'shaking the pagoda tree' though the young man had no inclination in that pursuit. Even his long journey to India was different from Clive's who almost drowned, losing hat, wig, shoes, buckles in the process. It is likely Halhed had shipboard romances in between cogitations, correspondence, formulating projects, and recording places seen.

Unlike other Englishmen who went to make their fortune in India, Halhed's genteel background had not prepared him for the rough existence of the East India Company life. Halhed compiled the *Code of Gentoo Laws* when he was twenty-two. He wrote the *Bengali Grammar*, which was to be his lasting achievement, when he was twenty-seven. He remained a true scholar and became famous for his two landmark works.

Halhed was a true product of the Enlightenment and a typical 18th century intellectual – eclectic, skeptical, tolerant and curious. A Europe wearied by religious strife and bigotry looked askance on dogmas and doctrines. Such a disposition was ideally suited to Halhed's destiny as an explorer of an alien civilization. His religious and political views were initially a help to his career of scholarship in India. Perhaps having brought his decadence with him to India he was not inclined to be censorious.

In November 1772 Halhed was appointed as a Writer in the Office of the Persian Translator in Calcutta. He lamented that the "wealthy, luxurious and lucrative India was so excessively ruined" that he could not "procure even a decent subsistence". Halhed held a succession of temporary jobs such as Interpreter to the Supreme Court and Commissary General. He could not obtain a higher position. A daughter of Colonel Clavering in Calcutta charmed him into a dalliance. By then he had become famous for his *A Code of Gentoo Laws*.

This Herculean task had been undertaken with a team of eleven *pundits* who translated twenty Sanskrit texts into Persian for Halhed. For this enormous effort the poor pundits were paid an honorarium of one rupee a day for two years – that is three hundred and sixty-five rupees per year. This financial arrangement provides a stark contrast to the emoluments of the Company officials who earned eighty thousand rupees annually. The Company documents do not record how Halhed was rewarded for his effort.

Halhed's immense scholarship and knowledge appears in his copious *Preface to Bengali Grammar* in which he discusses Sanskrit and its structure, rhythm and meter, along with a detailed account of Hindu chronology and customs. His contemporaries held his religious views as "wild" which probably meant that he was eclectic in his views and not circumscribed by Christian dogma. Halhed modestly admitted in his *Preface* that his knowledge of Sanskrit was deficient. However, this deficiency was redeemed by his awareness of the intrinsic features of the language. In 1778 Halhed was "astonished to find the similitude of Sanskrit words with those of Persian and Arabic and even of Latin and Greek". Sir William Jones, who is considered the "father of comparative philology," expounded his theory of Indo-Aryan group of languages much later than Halhed when he wrote "either Greek or Latin is derived from this language (Sanskrit)".

In 1787 Halhed translated the Moghul Prince Dara Shikoh's Persian version of *The Upanishads* into English. This indeed was a landmark in the history of translations as this opened to the West the immense depth of ancient Hindu philosophy and metaphysics. Halhed's other notable translations are – Radhakanta's *Puranavtha Prakasha (1788), Bhagavat Purana (1791), Swapurana* and a part of *Brahmavawartha Purana* and finally the massive epic, The *Mahabharata.*

Halhed belonged to the enterprising band of people who set the trend in the collection of Oriental manuscripts. He collected these at a time when Europe was indifferent to the study of Sanskrit language and literature and Bengali, along with other Indian languages, was considered by many as a 'Moor's language'.

Both Halhed and Wilkins were exceptionally brilliant men and remained lifelong friends. They were both in Calcutta at the time of the publication of *Bengali Grammar.* As in the case of *Gentoo Laws*, the main sponsor of the publication of *Bengali Grammar* was Warren Hastings. In fact Warren Hastings was the grand patron of all official publications on Indian civilization during his time.

By early 1778 Halhed's health deteriorated and he returned to England on 29th July 1778. He was no longer a forlorn lover; he took with him as his wife Helena Luisa, daughter of the Dutch Governor of Chinsura, Johannes Mathaeus Ross. Halhed returned to India in July 1784 and left Calcutta by January 1785 along with Warren Hastings to whom he was a loyal and devoted friend. They moved freely in the seemingly incompatible worlds of

England and British India, at the juncture of the eighteenth and nineteenth centuries.

After years of intense creativity he led 'an atrophied existence as a Nabob' when he returned to England. The later part of Halhed's long life was rocked by disasters. He managed to enter Parliament and plunged into politics. His performance in Parliament was not noteworthy. He lost money in political ventures and in speculation. By 1808 Halhed was a financially ruined man. He sold his house, the rare Indian manuscripts he had brought from India and most tragically his only remaining copy of *A Bengali Grammar.* Notwithstanding his reduced circumstances, Warren Hastings and Sir Elijah Impey continued to befriend him. With the assistance of influential friends, he was appointed Chief Assistant to Examiner of Correspondence in India House on a salary of L 600 per annum. Halhed passed away on 18th February 1813.

Halhed opens his *Preface to the Grammar* by carefully explaining the rationale for the work which is the need for cultivation of a right understanding and general medium of intercourse between government and its subjects. He points out that "the Romans, a people of little learning and less taste had no sooner conquered Greece than they applied themselves to the study of Greek. They adopted its laws even before they could read them and civilized themselves in subduing their enemies".

The implication that the English were dealing with a superior civilization in India could hardly have passed without comment even in the least jingoistic of times and the protests duly came.

A contemporary English reviewer, John Gillies, wrote that

> were England to follow the policy of Rome, she would be at the utmost pains to extend the knowledge of the English language over her dominions ... If any books were to be discovered in the Arabic, the Persian or the Sanscrit tongues which deserve notice on account of the regularity of invention, beauty of composition and force of reasoning, which distinguish the Greek and Roman classics, England would be particularly careful to translate such writings and adopt them as her own but she would never condescend to employ a foreign dialect as the medium of either commercial or political intercourse with the people she regarded as her subjects.

This view presages the stand taken by Macaulay in his *Minute on Education.* It was however the age of Hastings; Macaulay was still seventy-five years in the future. The sentiments expressed by

Halhed were in tune with Hastings' conscious policy of building bridges between the local administration and the native population that arose from his deep respect and understanding of Indian society, which Halhed came to share.

Halhed declares in his *Preface,*

> ... my principle aim has been to comprehend everything necessary to be known: not contenting myself with a superficial or partial view, nor confining my observations to the more obvious particularities. A short treatise, when preceded by more copious and diffusive compilations on the same subject may perhaps pass for a judicious abstract or an elegant compendium; but every omission of the writer who has chosen an unhandled topic will be imputed to ignorance or neglect by those whose subsequent discoveries may have furnished more complete information.

> The grand source of Indian literature, the parent of almost of every dialect from the Persian Gulph to the China Seas is the Shanscrit, a language of the most venerable and unfathomable antiquity, which although at present shut up in the libraries of Brahmins, and appropriated solely to the records of their Religion, appears to have been current over most of the Oriental World; and traces of its original extent may still be discovered in almost every district of Asia. I have been astonished to find the similitude of Shanscrit words with those of Persian and Arabic and even of Latin and Greek and these not in technical and metaphorical terms which the mutation of a refined arts and improved manners might have occasionally introduced but in the main ground work of language in monosyllables, in the names of numbers and the appellations of such things as would be first discriminated on the immediate dawn of civilization. The resemblance which may be observed in the characters upon the medals and signets of various districts of Asia, the light which they reciprocally reflect upon each other, and the general analogy which they all bear to the same grand Proto-type afford another ample feel for curiosity. The coins of Assam, Napaul, Cashmeere and many other Kingdoms are all stamped with Shanscrit letters, and mostly contain allusions to the old Shanscrit Mythology: the same conformity I have observed on the impressions of seals from Bootan and Tibet. A collateral inference may likewise be deduced from the peculiar arrangement of Shanscrit alphabet, so very different from that of any other quarter of the world. This extra-ordinary mode of combination still exists in the greatest part of the East, from the Indus to the Pegu, in dialects now apparently unconnected and in characters completely dissimilar; but is a forcible

argument that they are all derived from the same source. Another channel of speculation presents itself in the names of persons and places, of titles and dignities, which are open to general notice and in which, to the farthest limits of Asia, may be found manifest traces of the Shanscrit. The meager remnants of Coptic antiquities afford no scope for comparison between that idiom and this primitive tongue: but there still exists sufficient grounds for conjecture that Egypt has but a disputable claim to its long boasted originality in language, in policy and in religion.

In support of this opinion, I shall mention only one circumstance. The Rajah of Kishenagur, who is by much the most learned and able antiquary which Bengal has produced within this century, has very lately affirmed, that he has in his own possession Shanscrit books which give an account of a communication formally subsisting between India and Egypt; wherein the Egyptians are constantly described as disciples not as instructors, and are seeking that liberal education and those sciences in Hindoostan which none of their own countrymen had sufficient knowledge to impart. A few passages which are extant in the ancient Greek authors reflecting the Bracmans at the same time that they receive a fresh light from this relation, very strongly corroborate its authenticity.

But though these several proofs of the former prevalence of the Shanscrit are now thinly scattered over an immense continent and interspersed with an infinite variety of extraneous matter arising from every possible revolution in the manners and principles of the nations who have by chance cultivated or destroyed; that part of Asia between the Indus and the Ganges still preserves the whole language pure and inviolate; still offers a thousand books to the perusal of the curious many of which have been religiously handed down from the earliest periods of human existence.

The Jesuit Dupont has misled many subsequent writers, by his fabulous account of the wonderful structure of this dialect. According to him, it holds the most extensive and copious harvest of words to a very inadequate number of primitive roots, and these he chuses to call the *caput mortuum* of the language: as not being words of themselves but certain sounds bearing a relation to certain ideas. The element to which he alludes and of which he has misquoted and instance, fall far short of those comprehensive faculties which he has bestowed on them. They are firmly the Roots of Verbs, and are even so denominated in the very title of the book from whence he must have borrowed his inaccurate examples. Their number is about seven hundred; and it must be granted to them as to the verbs of most other languages, a very plentiful stock of verbal nouns owes its origin; but I by no means believe that they exceed those of the Greek either in quantity or variety.

The fundamental part of the Shanscrit language is divided into three classes: Dhaat or roots of verbs (Dupont's primitive elements) Shubd or original nouns and Evya or particles. These are ever indeclinable as in other idioms: but the words comprehended in the two former classes must be prepared by certain additions and inflexions to fit them for a place in composition. And here it is that the art of the grammarian has found room to expand itself and to employ all the powers of refinement. Not a syllable, not a letter can be added or altered but by regimen; not the most trifling variation of the sense in the minutest sub-division of declension or conjugation can be effected without the application of several rules: and all the different forms for every change of gender, number, taste, person, tense, mode or degree are methodically arranged for the assistance of the memory; resembling (though on a seal infinitely more extensive,) the compilations of proppria quae maribus and as in presenti.

It is obvious from Halhed's *Preface* that there was need to educate Englishmen about the languages in current use in Bengal. Halhed patiently explained the position and in the process implicitly gave the rationale for his *Bengali Grammar:*

Exclusive of the Shanscrit, there are three different dialects applied, (though not with equal currency) in the kingdom of Bengal: viz the Persian, the Hindostanic and the proper Bengalese: each of which has it own peculiar department in the business of the country, and consequently neither of them can be universally adopted to the exclusion of the others.

He then went on to elucidate: how each of these languages came to occupy its current position.

The Persian entered Bengal with the Moghul conquerors, and being the language of the court naturally gained a footing in the law and in the revenues; it had also for some centuries been the common medium of negotiation between the several states of Hindostan and from thence became an almost indispensable qualification for those who were to manage the extensive affairs of the East India Company ... This language is still used by all the Mogul officers of government, in their several departments of accounts and correspondence; as being the dialect of the former ruling power, of which the English

> has to some degree taken the place and whose system they have not yet laid aside. From hence arises one capital impediment to the uniformity of political arrangements in Bengal; for while the summary of all public business would be noted.

[Halhed, following the eighteenth century usage of the words 'dialect' and 'idiom' interchangeably as equivalents for 'language']. Halhed then proceeds to explain that 'Hindostanics' (Hindustani) is the language spoken for many ages throughout Hindustan and that it is indubitably derived from Shancrit 'with which it has the same connection as the modern dialects of France and Italy with pure Latin'. As for Bengali, Halhed explains to his eighteenth century reader who obviously stood in need of such enlightenment, 'what pure Hindostanic is to upper India, [Bengali] is to Bengal'.

Halhed took pains to explain that Bengal had a vernacular language distinct from "that idiom which under the name 'Moors' (Urdu) has been supposed to prevail all over India". He drew attention to the fact that the Board of Commerce at Calcutta and the Chiefs of the subordinate factories could not properly conduct the Company's correspondence without Bengali interpreters. He brought out the anomaly of a situation in which public business was transacted in Persian or Urdu while the people wrote letters and maintained their accounts in Bengali. He averred that 'it may even be doubted whether more than one third of all Gentoo zemindars, farmers and other lessees of the state can read a single word of their own accounts and representations, as delivered in their moonshee's Persian translation'. Apart from its importance in commercial use, Halhed pointed out that the adoption of Bengali would also be beneficial to the Revenue department "for although the contracts, leases and other obligations, executed between government and its immediate dependants and tenants, continue to be drawn out in the Persian dialect, yet under the leases and engagements which these in their turn grant to the peasants and cultivators of the ground, and all those copyhold tenures called pottahs are constantly written in Bengalese."

Having hammered home in various parts of the *Preface* the practical use of his *Grammar* to the Company's servants in Bengal, the scholar in Halhed could not resist a foray into philology. He traced the Sanskrit origins of Bengali but even more important was one of the first to sense the importance of Sanskrit as the fount of language – 'the grand source of Indian Literature, the parent of every dialect from the Persian Gulph to the China seas.' The description of 'Shanscrit as refined and 'copious' prefigures William Jones famous quotation on the superiority of Sanskrit over Greek and Latin.

Halhed had undoubtedly acquired considerable proficiency in the Bengali language by the time that Jones arrived. Sukumar Sen in his *History of Bengali Literature* was of the view that 'his knowledge of the Bengali language was astounding for the day'. He had in the interregnum since the *Gentoo Laws* also developed a love for the Bengali language even over Persian with which to begin with he was much more familiar. He wrote that Bengali was "much better calculated both for public and private affairs, by its plainness, its perfection, and regularity of constructions than the flowery sentences and the modulated periods of the Persians".

Halhed's *Bengali Grammar* was the first printed book in Bengali and he pays fulsome tribute to the efforts of Charles Wilkins of whom he writes that

> the advice and even the solicitation of the Governor-General prevailed upon Mr. Wilkins, a gentleman some years in the India Company's civil service in Bengal to undertake a set of Bengal types. He did and his success has exceeded every expectation. In a country so remote from all connection with European artists, he was obliged to assume himself with all the various occupations of the metallurgist, the engraver, the founder and the printer. To the merit of invention he was compelled to add the application of personal labour. With a rapidity unknown in Europe, he surmounted all the obstacles which necessarily clog the first rudiments of a difficult art, as well as the disadvantages of a solitary experiment.

In tone with the rest of the *Preface,* Halhed pointed out the specific advantages of the introduction of printing in checking "the various impositions and forgeries with which Bengal at present abounds in *pottahs* (or leases), in bonds and other written securities of property; in *rowanahs* and *dustucks,* in orders and notices of government issued in the country languages as well as in the transactions of commerce and also in the processes, warrants and decrees of the supreme and inferior courts of judicature, all of which afford ample scope for the exertion of Mr. Wilkin's ingenuity". But being Halhed he did not stop here but went on to foresee how the printing press would enable the spread of European literature in Asia.

The *Grammar* begins with an'Advertisement' on a very practical note, 'It is recommended not to bind this book till the setting in of the dry season as the greater part has been printed during the rains.' Those who have striven to protect their libraries against the ravages of the Bengal monsoon's humidity will appreciate the value of this helpful suggestion. One senses the practical hand of Wilkins.

The format of Halhed's *Grammar of the Bengal Language* owes much to William Jones' *Grammar of the Persian Language* to which Halhed pays homage – 'for that accurate and elegant grammar composed by Mr. Jones does equal honour to the cause of learning and service to his countrymen in Asia'. Halhed's *Grammar*, like that of Jones, is replete with quotations from the classics for illustrating points of grammar. Kasirama Dasa's *Mahabharata* is the main source. Other sources are Krittivasa's *Ramayana* and Bharatachandra Raya's *Vidyasundara*. All the sources were poetical works as there was no prose writing in Bengali literature at that time. Halhed went to the extent of speculating that the art of prose might never develop in Bengal. This was one instance where Halhed's usual prescience in literary matters failed him. The plethora of prose works which followed were printed in presses for which Charles Wilkins' Hooghly press was the forerunner.

In most of the landmarks of British Indology in the eighteenth century behind the British pioneer, there usually stands a shadowy Portuguese figure. In the case of the *Bengali Grammar*, it was Manoel da Assumpcam, the Jesuit priest who published his 600-page *Vocabulario Em Idioma Bengalla E Portuguez* in Lisbon in 1734 anticipated Halhed's work by almost half a century. Bengali commentators have said that Assumpcam's grammar teems with mistakes and it has generally been popular to denigrate his work. Though it was Halhed's *Grammar* that served as the model for subsequent Bengali grammars, most notably William Carey's, it would be grossly unfair to consign Assumpcam to oblivion. The single-minded resourcefulness of the Jesuit in obtaining the material for his work without the patronage of an established authority on the shores of Bengal is worthy of commemoration in the history of language. It was not love of the Bengali language that impelled Assumpcam in his labours. It was his belief that a Catholic priest owed a duty to learn the language of those whom he was proselytizing. Halhed's *Grammar* was on the other hand based on the thesis that a ruler had a duty to learn the language of his subjects. It was meant to facilitate the revenue and commercial administration of the East India Company. In the area of Bengal grammar production Mammon succeeded where God had failed. Halhed's work survived. In his famous *Grammar of the Bengalee Language* published in 1801, William Carey acknowledged his debt to Halhed. It is interesting that Carey published his *Grammar* as an aid to Christian missionary work. From Assumpcam to Carey, the wheel had turned full circle.

The circumstances of the Company's decision to sponsor Halhed's *Grammar* provide an interesting case study in the manner of functioning of the Bengal Council. When the book was still in the initial stages of its production in January 1778, Governor-General Warren Hastings placed a few stages of the printed material before the Council and recommended it for the Council's 'countenance and patronage'. The following February he read out a detailed *Minute* in which he gave his detailed proposal he explaining the practical value of the *Grammar* for Company administration. A practical politician that he was, he did not dwell unduly on his philosophic conception of what British administration in India should strive to achieve, as this was bound to raise controversy especially with contentious members like Francis. Steering clear of all abstract concepts, he presented the nuts and bolts of the project with his inimitable clarity, the gist of his proposal being the purchase of one thousand copies of the *Grammar* at thirty rupees a copy.

In June 1778 Warren Hastings placed a fragmentary specimen of a printed book before the Council – "specimen of a Bengali grammar" – written by Halhed. Hastings recommended financial assistance for purchase of a thousand copies at rupees thirty each for distribution to the Company's servants and those interested in learning Bengali. He suggested advance payment pending approval by Court of Directors. He offered to furnish his personal bond for the amount. Neither Francis nor Wheeler assumed their customary posture of antagonism. Hastings' personal bond was not insisted upon and Francis went to the extent of recording that he would bear his share of the loss if necessary. The only change made to Hastings' proposal was that the number of copies was reduced to five hundred. Pending the approval of the Company headquarters, an advance order was placed on the writer Halhed and the printer Wilkins. The author Halhed and the printer were paid for five hundred copies.

The *Grammar* was printed in the press at Hooghly, published in August 1778 and copies were delivered to the Superintendent of the Khalsa records in Calcutta. The transaction shows that even in the 1780s the Company was prepared to take a constructive long-term view of its responsibilities and to look if necessary beyond its immediate commercial interest. The members of the Council were willing to overlook their personal animosities while considering a project of this type. The price of thirty rupees was high but the Council did not deem it appropriate to resort to penny pinching. The Council took its decision and went ahead with execution pending the approval of Leadenhall Street. All in all, the proceedings show commendable speed of decision making and efficient dispatch of business.

There are clear lessons in this for current day Indian administration!

It is no exaggeration to say that the way shown by Halhed's *Grammar* and Wilkins' press led to the renaissance in Bengali literature in the eighteenth and nineteenth centuries with Ishwar Chandra Vidyasagar, Bankim Chandra Chattopadhyay, Michael Madhusudan Dutta, Sarat Chandra Chattopadhaya, and finally the effulgent genius of Rabindranath Tagore. *The Grammar* also served to introduce Englishmen to the glories of classical Bengali verse of Vidyapati and Chandidas.

Nathaniel Brassey Halhed, unlike Charles Wilkins and William Jones, could not read by himself from an original Sanskrit text. He lamented in respect to the *Mahabharata* that, "It grieves me that I never could master Shanscrit enough to read it in the original." But his contribution was that he broke ground for the founders of Sanskrit studies, Wilkins and Jones, and prepared the way for the first full-fledged Sanskrit scholar Colebrooke. The period during which Persian was a necessary channel for access to Hindu antiquities came to a close. "In antiquarian Oriented Europe, Sanskrit scholarship flourished, eclipsing continuing work in modern languages. Halhed's *Bengali Grammar* was soon forgotten while it remained famous in Bengal."

56

Codifying Hindu Laws

The Code of Gentoo Laws was a project inspired and financed by Hastings because he, unlike other colonial administrators of the time, was aware of the great antiquity of Hindu law and how much it was intertwined with Hindu religion and society. He wanted the English people to become aware of this. In the *Preface* to the *Code of Gentoo Laws* Halhed dwells on this aspect though he perhaps falls into a Halhed failing – an excess of scholarly enthusiasm when he antedates them to the Laws of Moses.

This Herculean task had been undertaken with a team of eleven pundits who translated twenty Sanskrit texts into Persian for Halhed. For this enormous effort the poor pundits were paid an honorarium of one rupee a day for two years – that is Rupees 365 per year. This financial arrangement provides a stark contrast to the emoluments of the Company officials who earned Rupees 80,000 annually. The Company documents do not record how Halhed was rewarded for his effort.

The decision-making process involved gives an idea of how the administration of East India Company worked. The manner of composition from Sanskrit to Persian to English is interesting. A college of pundits drawn from the educated Sanskrit-knowing Brahmins were involved in the work. It was not easy as Halhed has recorded. The work is all the more commendable that the East India Company who was then the agency for discharging political, administrative and judicial functions was the patron of this innovative scholarly work. This work was a commercial success and led to the establishment of Halhed's reputation as well as bringing in some financial gain though the earnings were not at all commensurate with the labour and talent employed.

The nature of the system of law that emerged from this document is interesting. The rationale of the work and its practical utility was to explore the foundations of the legal system in ancient India and assess how these could either be adapted or adjusted to the British system of law. There was no dearth of criticism from both Indians and the West about the acceptability of 'outmoded laws'. His efforts were in complete contrast to Macaulay's work fifty years later when he brought a modern Western legal system to India with the Indian Penal Code, that were followed later by the Criminal Procedure Code, the Indian Evidence Act and the Civil Procedure Code.

The title *Gentoo Laws* was not Nathaniel Brassey Halhed's idea but was given by Leadenhall Street. 'Gentoo' was a corruption of the word Hindu, a common and ludicrous mispronunciation of Indian words by Europeans which began with the Greeks who named the river *Beas* Hyaspes. The beautiful Tamil word *Taranganbadi* or 'haven of the waves' becomes the harsh Anglo-Saxon 'Tranquebar'. The name sits uneasily on an old port where the laterite ruins of the walls of the ancient Hindu temple and the 17th-century Danish fort merge into the waters of the Bay of Bengal.

Halhed's compilation of the *Gentoo Laws* was a complicated process. From the original Sanskrit, the Laws had been translated into Bengali and it was on this Bengali version that Halhed had to work. As Halhed at that time was not sufficiently proficient in Bengali, the Laws were translated into Persian and from Persian into English. In the process of this three-stage translation there were bound to be significant transmission losses in meaning. William Jones commented on this; he was of the view that the original Bengali/Persian version was suspect. The fact that William Jones declined to review it is significant.

John Gardi and Laurance Bunyon were eminent translators of Indian texts. The path of translation is fraught with dangers to the original. Review of *Dante Made Plain* underlines this.

> To translate a poem as long and complex as the *Comedy* you must find yourself abandoning the very things which moved you in translating it in the first place. The enjambucut, that rhythmic curve collocation, association, ambiguity, nuance. Most original of all you must abolish the original form of the poem to create an English equivalent. Much rubbish has been talked about translating a poem into 'identical meters'. There is no such thing for prosody is language specific.

These are the difficulties facing a translator. Halhed must have encountered similar dilemmas when he embarked on his translations of Sanskrit texts.

The financial arrangements for the production of *Gentoo Laws* give an indication of how even at the highest levels of the East India Company in India, personal and Company finances became intermixed. It also casts a sidelight on Warren Hastings' style of functioning. He claimed that he had funded the whole enterprise himself but shortly before he left for England for the last time he recouped the entire amount from the funds of the Company. Certain uncharitable comments have been made about this but they ignore the fact that Hastings advanced the funds from his own pocket in the first place. Secondly, considering that he was smarting under his virtual dismissal from the Governor Generalship by an ungrateful East India Company which had no conception of the great services he had rendered, getting himself reimbursed for payments undoubtedly made by him for work which was undoubtedly for public benefit and for the convenience of East India Company administration, cannot be held against him. Nevertheless it throws an interesting sidelight on the human side of Warren Hastings.

The Code of Gentoo Laws was a commercial success. It attracted the attention of scholars in Europe and opened a window to them on Hindu history, customs, traditions and law. The West became aware of the great antiquity of Indian civilization. Most important of all, Halhed's *Preface* contained certain tentative but very significant remarks on the Sanskrit language. It was a seminal work that led the way for later scholars like William Jones.

Halhed's *Code* is today only of antiquarian and historical interest. Even in its own time it was of limited practical value. It could not be used by judges and by litigants in the same way as the Indian Penal Code or the Indian Evidence Act or the Code of Criminal Procedure are used today. Its value was two-fold; it made British judges conscious of the fact that Indians had laws of their own that would be injudicious to ignore. Secondly, it made them conscious of the main principles behind Hindu law. However, Halhed's *Code* was not of any statutory value – it contained nothing compelling or binding. The application of law in one of the most sensational cases in Bengal – the trial of Nanda Kumar – showed that even fundamental tenets like the exemption of Brahmins from capital punishment could be ignored if realpolitik demanded it. And in Nanda Kumar's case it was ironic that it was Hastings, the inspirer of the *Gentoo Laws* who was the perpetrator of this blatant infraction. The reasons that led Hastings to take this course have their roots in the affairs of the Council, Hastings' continuously assailed position, his undoubted vindictiveness and his resort to ruthless and expeditious action. This is another instance of how the complex and infinitely intriguing psyche of Warren Hastings worked.

Was there any philosophy of law or jurisprudence behind the *Code*? There does not appear to have been any schema. A half century later, Macaulay appeared on the scene and turned his back on the whole caboodle. He turned Hastings' approach on its head. In an unaided virtuoso feat of genius, he produced a Code which was really a code of law which had very little to do with past practice. It was based on a patently low estimate of the Indian character. It is strange that a man who virtually had no empathy with India produced a Code of law which served the ends of justice perhaps in a much more effective way than envisaged by Warren Hastings and Nathaniel Brassey Halhed who had empathy for India and Indians.

Since the most articulate state in the National Movement was Bengal, it is no accident that the national anthem, *Jana Gana Mana* and the national song of India, *Bande Mataram* were composed by two Bengalis – Rabindranath Tagore and Bankim Chandra Chatterjee. It is however one of the numerous paradoxes in this most intellectual of all the States in the country that there is no hangover whatever of Anglophobia. The literary mandarins in the Bengali language, whose number is very large, tend to be finickily censorious of any departures from the set high standards of excellence in works of literature, pasts or present. When the bi-centenary of Halhed's *Grammar* came up in 1978, an excellent facsimile edition of Halhed's *Grammar* was published. Very appropriately, it was brought out by the press of the leading Bengali newspaper, the *Ananda Bazaar Patrika*. The Publisher's Note to this bi-centenary facsimile edition said – 'This is a landmark not only in the history of Bengali language and literature but also denotes the birth of the printing and publishing industry in Bengal and in the Bengali language.' The masterly Introduction to the book spoke of the memorable nature of the work, the fact that

Halhed was the first European to identify the Bengali language correctly, who advocated the learning of Bengali and who developed proficiency in the language. It also pointed out that a profound love of the Bengali language was the sterling quality of the book. The facsimile edition has been brought out with great artistry, the cover of the book caries Halhed's signature in letters of gold. The cover papers reproduce pages from the manuscript of the *Grammar.*

Bengal however got the printing press two hundred years after the Portuguese introduced it into the country. This event acted as the harbinger of the Renaissance in Bengali literature. James Hickey and the Bengal Gazette was also a step forward. Claims were made by Shepherd for reprinting of *Bengali Grammar*. The *Bengali Grammar* earned its printer the title 'Caxton of Bengal'.

57

Charles Wilkins and the Bhagavad Gita

"The first persevering adventurer in a service in which his example will have few followers ..." — Warren Hastings on Wilkins

From one portrait of Charles Wilkins one sees a man of elegant appearance – clear, level, light eyes, sturdy commonsense and very much of the man of business who set up the first successful commercial printing press in India. But in another portrait we see a face with a sensitive mouth, hint of humour in the eyes, and the scholar. He was both and achieved success to a large measure.

Charles Wilkins was born in Somersetshire in 1750 to Walter and Martha Wilkins. They were not well off and their son Charles grew up in that humble environment. He came as a Writer to India in 1770, that is two years before Halhed. Charles Wilkins was married twice and had three daughters. One of the daughters married William Marsden who was the author of the *History of Sumatra*.

Unlike Halhed, Wilkins had no academic background. He learnt Persian quickly and following Halhed commenced study of Sanskrit. He was one of the founders of the Royal Asiatic Society of Bengal. Wilkins, like many Company scholars was a protègè of Warren Hastings but seems to have been less affected by the vicissitudes of his mentor's fortunes than Halhed. He was not part of the repatriate Bengal squad and unlike Halhed he spent long years in India. Unlike Halhed, Wilkins enjoyed health, fame, affluence and a long life and seems to have completed all that he set out to do.

Wilkins returned to England in 1786 and settled in the mild climate of Bath and continued with his Indian studies. On return to England, Wilkins completed his career fittingly as the librarian of the East India Company Library. He was appointed Oriental Visitor at Haileybury in 1805 where he gave lectures on Sanskrit, Philosophy and Literature. He met Horace Hayman Wilson at Oxford who then occupied the Boden Chair of Sanskrit. Wilkins was made an Associate of Institute de France. His later years were happy ones; he was elected member of Royal Society in 1788 and was knighted in 1833 by King William IV and passed away three years later in May 1836.

Charles Wilkins is remembered as a pioneer in Oriental studies. He was the first person from the Western world to translate the *Bhagvad Gita* from Sanskrit into English in 1785. Wilkins's other translations were the *Hitopadesha* (1787) and finally *The Story of Sakuntala* in 1793. His translation of the *Bhagavad Gita* was translated into French, German and Russian.

Wilkins could be called the first epigraphist in India. Wilkins was also the first European to have deciphered Sanskrit-based inscriptions of any antiquity. He deciphered ancient inscriptions on copper-plates of King Vignapal that he found among the ruins at Monghyr in 1781. From the inscription Wilkins deduced that the Pala kings of Bengal were Buddhists. He ushered in a new era in Bengali literature by setting up in Hughly a printing press with type cast in Bengali alphabets.

If Halhed was the first grammarian of the Bengali language, Wilkins was one of the first European grammarians of the Sanskrit language. In 1806 he published a new edition of Richardson's *Persian, Arabic and English Dictionary*. Wilkins' famous *A Grammar of the Sanskrita Language* was published in 1808. In 1815 he published *Radicals of the Sanskrita Language.*

In the eighteenth century religious loyalties did not prevent English Christian scholars such as William Jones, Halhed and Wilkins, from translating Hindu scriptures in contrast to Englishmen such as Carey, Marshman and Ward who were interested in translating the Bible into Indian languages, but declined to translate Indian works into English.

Though unlike Halhed, Wilkins had no academic background or any connection with printing he became nevertheless father of Bengali printing. In this task he was assisted by a Bengali artisan Panchanan Karmarker and an English engraver Joseph Shepherd. In addition to setting up a Bengali printing press Charles Wilkins realized his cherished dream of making a Devanagari type for his *Sanskrit Grammar*. It was for these achievements that he has been called the "Caxton of Bengal."

Wilkins' greatest achievement and contribution to Indology was the full translation of the *Bhagavad Gita* from Sanskrit into English. His translation paved the way for the translation of the *Gita* into other European languages. The central themes of the symphony of the *Bhagavad Gita* are *Jnana*, *Bhakti* and *Karma*, light, love and life. "He who offers to me with devotion only a leaf or a flower or a fruit or even a little water, this I accept from my yearning soul because with a pure heart it was offered with love." – *Bhagavad Gita*.

The core philosophy of the *Bhagavad Gita* – that of performing one's duty without hope of reward as the road to salvation – is now a well known spiritual philosophy. For making this known throughout the world credit must go to Wilkins, the English scholar and his patron, the empire builder Hastings who venerated Hinduism.

As there are no references in *Bhagavad Gita* to Buddhism and there are few archaic words and references, scholars have considered the *Bhagavad Gita* to be pre-Buddhistic; the date varies from 2000 BC to 500 BC.

The frontispiece of Wilkins' translated work is thus described – "The Bhagvat-Geeta, or Dialogues of Kreeshna and Arjoon, in eighteen lecturers with notes – translated from the original, in the Sanskreet or ancient language of the Brahmans, by Charles Wilkins, Senior Merchant In The Service Of The Hon'ble East India Company And Their Bengal Establishment."

The next page called Advertisement is dated 30th May 1785 and says –

> The following Work is published under the authority of the Court of Directors of the East India Company, by the particular desire and recommendation of the Governor-General of India; whose letter to the Chairman of the Company will sufficiently explain the motives for its publication and furnish the best testimony of the fidelity, accuracy, and merit of the Translator.
>
> The antiquity of the original, and the veneration in which it hath been held for so many ages, by a very considerable portion of the human race must render it one of the greatest curiosities ever presented to the literary world –

On 19th November 1784 Charles Wilkins addressed a letter "To The Honorable Warren Hastings Esq. Governor-General etc." The letter reads:

> Honorable Sir,
>
> Unconscious of the liberal purpose for which you intended the Geeta, when, at your request, I had the honor to present you with a copy of the manuscript I was the less solicitous about its imperfections, because I knew that your extensive acquaintance with the customs and religious tenets of the Hindus would elucidate every passage that was obscure, and I had so often experienced approbation from your partiality, and correction from your pen. It was the theme of a pupil to his preceptor and patron. But since I received your commands to prepare it for the public view I feel all that anxiety which must be inseparable from one who for the first time, is about to appear before that awful tribunal; and I should dread the event were I not convinced that the liberal sentiments expressed in the letter you have done me the honor to write, in recommendation of the work to the Chairman of the Direction, if permitted to accompany it to the Press, would screen me, under its own intrinsic merit, from all censure.
>
> The world, Sir, is so well acquainted with your boundless patronage in general, and of the personal encouragement you have constantly given to my fellow servants in particular, to render themselves more capable of performing their duty in the various branches of commerce, revenue, and policy, by the study of the languages, with the laws and customs of the natives, that it must deem the first fruit of every genius you have raised a tribute justly due to the source from which it sprang. As that personal encouragement alone first excited emulation in my breast, and urged me to prosecute my particular studies even beyond the line of pecuniary reward, I humbly request you will permit me, in token of my gratitude to lay the translation of the Geeta publicly at your feet.
>
> I have the honor to subscribe myself with great respect, Honorable Sir, your most obedient and most humble servant, Charles Wilkins.

Warren Hastings forwarded the translation of the *Bhagavad Geeta* from Benaras on the 4th October 1784 to Nathaniel Smith, Chairman of the Board of Directors of the East India Company with the following letter.

> To You as a first member of the first commercial body, not only of the present age, but of all the known generations of mankind I

> presume to offer and recommend to you, for an offering to the public, a very curious specimen of the Literature, the Mythology and Morality of the ancient Hindoos. It is an episodical extract from the 'Mahabharat' almost a voluminous poem, affirmed to have been written upwards of four thousand years ago by Kreeshna Dwypayen Veias, a learned Brahmin; to whom is also attributed the compilation of 'the four Vedes or Bedes'. The only existing original scriptures of the religion of Brahma; and the composition of all the Poorans, which are to this day taught in the schools and venerated as poems of divine inspiration. Among these and of superior estimation to the West is ranked the Mahabharat. But if the several books here enumerated be really the production of their reputed author, which is greatly to be doubted many arrangements may be adduced to ascribe to the same source the invention of the religion itself, as well as its promulgation: and he must at all events claim the merit of having first reduced the gross and scattered tenets of their former faith into a scientific and allegorical system.

Hastings proceeds to give a brief and brilliant summary of the *Mahabharata* up to the point of battle of Kurukshetra. Thereupon he embarks on an eloquent summary of the *Geeta.*

> In this state the episode opens and is called 'The Geeta of Bhagbat' which is one of the names of Kreeshna. Arjoon is represented as the favourite and pupil of Kreeshna, here taken for God himself, in his last Obotar or descant to earth in a mortal form.
>
> The Preface of the Translator will render any further explanation of the Work unnecessary. Yet something it may be allowable for me to add respecting my own judgment of a Work which I have thus abnormally obtruded on your attention, as it is the only ground on which I can defend the liberty I have taken.
>
> Might I, an unlettered man venture to prescribe bounds to the attitude of criticism I should exclude, in estimating the merit of such a production, all rules drawn from the ancient or modern literature of Europe, all references to such sentiments or manners as are become the standards of propriety for opinion and action in our own modes of life and equally all appears to our revealed tenets a religion and moral duty. I should exclude them as by no means applicable to the language, sentiments, manners or morality appertaining to a system of society with which we have been for ages unconnected, and of antiquity preceding even the first efforts of civilization in our own quarter of the globe, which, in respect to the general diffusion and common participation of arts and sciences may be now considered as one community.

> Many passages will be found obscured, many will seem redundant; others will be cloathed with ornaments of fancy unsuited to our taste, and some elevated to attract of sublimity into which our habits of judgment will find it difficult to pursue them; but few which will shock either our religious faith or moral sentiment. Something too must be allowed to the subject itself which is highly metaphysical to the extreme difficulty of rendering abstract terms by others exactly corresponding with them in an other language to the arbitrary combination of ideas in words of expressing unsubstantial qualities, and more, to the errors of interpretation. The modesty of the Translator would induce him to defend the credit of his work by laying all its apparent defects to his own charge under the article loss enumerated; but neither does his accuracy merit, nor the work itself require that concession.
>
> It is also to be observed in illustration of what I have premised, that the Brahmans are enjoined to perform a kind of spiritual discipline, not, I believe, unknown to some of the religious orders of Christians Romish Church. This consists in devoting a certain period of time to the contemplation of the Deity, his attributes, and the moral duties of this life. It is required of those who practice this exercise not only that they divest their minds of all sensual desire, but that their attention be abstracted from every external object and absorbed with every sense in the prescribed subject of their meditation.

Hastings then goes on to describe a Sadhu at Banaris (Benaras) deep in meditation. He continues with the letter stating,

> The importance of this duty cannot be better illustrated nor stronger marked than by the last sentence with which Kreeshna closes his instruction to Arjoon and which is properly the conclusion of the Geeta: 'Hath what I have been speaking, Oh Arjoon, been heard with thy mind fixed to one point? Is the destruction of thought which arose from the ignorance removed?'
>
> To those who have never been accustomed to this separation of the mind from the notices of the senses it may not be easy to conceive by what means such a power is to be attained; since even the most studious men of our hemisphere will find it difficult so to restrain their attention that it will wander to some object of present sense or recollection; and even the buzzing of a fly will sometimes have the power to disturb it. But if we are told that there have been men who were successively, for ages past, in the daily habit of abstracted contemplation, began in the earliest period of youth and continued in many to the maturity of age each adding some portion of

> knowledge to the store accumulated by his predecessors; it is not assuming too much to conclude, that as the mind ever gathers strength, like the body, by exercise so in such an exercise it may in each have a quite the faculty to which they aspired that that their collective studies may have lead them to the discovery of new tracks and combinations sentiment totally different from the doctrines with which the learned of other nations are acquainted: doctrines, which however speculative and subtle, still, as they possess the advantage of being derived from a source so free from every adventious mixture may be equally founded in truth with the most simple of our own.

Hastings goes on to say,

> I hesitate not to pronounce the Geeta a performance of great originality; of a sublimity of conception, reasoning, and diction, almost unequalled, and a single exception, among all the known religions of mankind, of a theology accurately corresponding with that of the Christian dispensation, and most powerfully illustrating its fundamental doctrines.

Hastings then goes on to say that he places the *Mahabharata* on par with the *Iliad,* Odyssey and the sixth book of Milton.

The attention and understanding with which Hastings read the *Geeta* is clear from the above passages. He praises "the attempt to describe spiritual existences by terms and images which appertain to corporeal forms". No Western man before or after Warren Hastings has understood the essence of the *Bhagavad Gita* with such clarity, nor have many been able to present the work with such comprehension.

> It now remains to say something of the translator, Mr. Charles Wilkins. This gentlemen to whose ingenuity, unaided by models for imitation and by artists for his direction, your Government is indebted for its printing office and for many official purposes to which it has been properly applied, with an extent unknown in Europe, as united to an early and successful attainment of the Persian and Bengal languages, the study of the Sanskreet. To this he devoted himself with perseverance of which there are few examples, and with a success which encouraged him to undertake the translation of Mahabharat. This book is said to consist of more than 100,000 metrical stanzas of which he has at this time translated more than a third; and, if I may truly trust to the imperfect tests by which I myself have tried a very small portion of it through the medium of another language, he has rendered it with great accuracy

> and fidelity. Of its elegance, and the skill with which he has familiarized (if I may so express it) his own native language to so foreign and original, I may not speak, as from the specimen herewith presented, whoever reads it will judge for himself.
>
> Mr. Wilkins' health having suffered a decline from the fatigues of business, from which his gratuitous labours allowed him no relaxation, he was advised to try a change of air for his recovery. I myself recommended that Banaris, for the sake of additional advantage which he might derive from a residence in a place which is considered as the first seminary of Hindu learning; and I promoted his application to the Board, for their permission to repair thither, without forfeiting his official appointments during the term of his absence.

With the profundity of a true scholar Hastings goes on to reflect:

> Such studies, independently of their utility, tend especially when the pursuit of them is general, to diffuse a generosity of sentiment, and disdain of the meaner occupations of such minds as are left nearer to the state of uncultivated nature; and you, Sir, will believe me when I assure you that it is on the virtue, not the ability of their servants that the Company must rely for the permanency of their dominion.

Finally, Hastings reveals himself as a statesman of both foresight, wisdom and humanity who probably gave the British empire a new orientation by the following observations:

> Nor is the cultivation of language and science, for such are the studies to which I elude, useful only in forming a moral character and habits of the service. Every accumulation of knowledge, and especially such as is obtained by social communication with people over whom we exercise a dominion founded on the right of conquest, is useful to the State: it is the gain of humanity: in the specific instance which I have stated it attracts and conciliates distant affections; it lessens the weight of the chain by which the natives are held in subjection; and it imprints on the hearts of our own countrymen the sense and obligation of benevolence. Even in England this effect of it is greatly wanting. It is not very long since the inhabitants of India were considered by many as creatures spheres elevated from the degree of savage life; nor, I fear, is that prejudice yet wholly eradicated though surely abated. Every instance which brings the real character home to observation will impress

> with a more generous sense of feeling for their natural rights, and teach us to estimate them by the measure of our own. But such instances can only be obtained in their writings: and this will survive when the British dominion in India shall have long ceased to exist and when the sources which it once yielded of wealth and power are lost to remembrance.
>
> If you, Sir, on the perusal of Wilkins' performance shall judge it worthy of so honourable patronage may I take the further liberty to request that you will be pleased to present it to the Court of Directors for publication by their authority and to use your interest to obtain it? Its public reception will be the test of its real merit and determine Mr. Wilkins in the prosecution or cessation of his present laborious studies. It may in the first even clear the way to a wide and unexplored field of fruitful knowledge, and suggest to the generosity of his honourable employer, a desire to encourage the first persevering adventurer in a service in which his example will have few followers, and most probably none if it is to be performed with the gratuitous labour of years lost to the provision of future subsistence: for the study of the Sanskreet cannot, like the Persian language, be applied to official profit and improve with the official exercise of it which can only derive its award beyond the breath of fame in a fixed endowment. Such has been the fate of his predecessor Mr. Halhed, whose labours and incomparable genius into useful production have been crowned with every success that the public estimation would give them.

Hastings goes on to say that he has made "an attempt to introduce the knowledge of Hindoo literature into the European world, by forcing or corrupting the religious consciences of the Pundits or Professors of their sacred doctrines." This reflection was produced by the publication of Mr. Halhed's translation of the *Poottee* or *Code of Hindoo Laws.*

Hastings explains why the pundits were not willing in the beginning to share their knowledge of the Hindoo scriptures.

> Very natural causes may be ascribed for their reluctance to communicate the mysteries of their learning to strangers as those to whom they have been for some centuries in subjection, never enquired into them, but to turn their religion into derision, and deduce from them arguments to support the intolerant principles of their own. From our nation they have received a different treatment and are no less either to impart their knowledge than we are to receive it.

Hastings goes on to praise the Pundits who "contributed both cheerfully and gratuitously, by means of most respectable characters for sanctity and learning in Bengal, who refused to accept more than the moderate daily subsistence of one rupee each, during the term that they were employed on the compilation; nor will it much redound to my credit when I had that they have not yet received no other reward for the meritorious labour".

This letter reveals the extraordinary qualities of Hastings' mind. No other Governor-General or Viceroy of India came so close to an understanding of the spirit of India's intellectual heritage. No other representative of Britain saw the means by which a subjugated people could be reconciled to foreign rule through appreciation of her heritage. It is all the more extraordinary because Warren Hastings was an empire builder per excellence. The letter reflects the strange schizophrenia of this brilliant man – of the love for a country and a people whom he has conquered.

58

Henry Thomas Colebrooke – The Path Breaker

Colebrooke carried the mantle of Sir William Jones. He was not as versatile as the founder of the Asiatic Society but his scholarship was formidable. Through his translations of Sanskrit texts he made known to the West the world of Sanskrit – its language, literature, laws, astronomy, philosophy, mathematics. His translation of Visala Deva's inscription of the Delhi pillar was the starting point of Indian epigraphy.

A great scholar and the first man to employ scientific method in the study of Sanskrit language and literature, Colebrooke published texts and translation of some important works and also wrote essays dealing with different branches of Sanskrit literature which proved of great benefit to later Sanskrit scholars. Colebrooke's essay *On the Vedas* appeared in 1805 and gave a full account of ancient Hindu religion. This aroused great interest among European scholars, particularly German scholars, who devoted themselves to the study of Vedic texts. This was followed by numerous essays on Sanskrit and Prakrit, on Hindu metaphysics, on the mathematics of Bhaskara (who defined the concept of zero) and the algebra of Brahma Gupta.

Henry Thomas Colebrooke was born in London, on 15th June 1765. His father, Sir George Colebrooke was a rich banker and had considerable influence in the ruling elite of England. As a financier he was acquainted with the Directors of the East India Company. In 1769 Sir George became one of the Directors of the Company and later its Chairman. He had particular views on education and had his son Thomas educated at home. From an early age young Thomas displayed a great gift for languages and mastered Greek, Latin, German and French. He read widely on diverse subjects and had an aptitude for Mathematics. At the age of fifteen he acquired considerable knowledge through private study that was more than that of university scholars.

Due to his father's influence Thomas Colebrooke came to India as a Writer of the East India Company in 1783 – the same year as William Jones' arrival in Calcutta. It was said that when Colebrooke was on board the ship he had finished reading all the books that he was carrying along with him. As he had to read something fresh every time, he borrowed a few medical books from the ship's doctor and finished them in the absence of any other reading material.

He was first assigned to work in the Board of Accounts. Colebrooke was dismayed by what he saw of Company rule and did not enjoy being a part of a corrupt and exploitive system. He also found the life led by the young Writers and Cadets of the East India Company devoid of principles. It is surprising that he did not form close associations with the blossoming Indologists of those years, especially William Jones and Wilkins. In fact he could see no point in Wilkins' study of Sanskrit. In one of his letters to his father he described Wilkins, his fellow officer as 'Sanskrit Mad.' However the elder Colebrooke urged his son to learn Sanskrit and study Indian customs and culture. Knowing his son's insatiable thirst for knowledge, Sir George also sent him a large number of books.

In 1786, Colebrooke was posted as Assistant Collector of Tirhut (Muzaffarpur-Darbhanga region of the present day Bihar), which was then a part of the province of Bengal. In 1789, when Colebrooke was working as a Magistrate of Purnea District, the government entrusted him with the writing of a report suggesting how the government could earn more revenue in Bengal. Researching for the report Colebrooke collected a mass of materials concerning the state of agriculture, internal trade and industry in Bengal. In this report, Colebrooke presented a grim picture of the Company's unscrupulous exploitation of the people and showed how due to the trade policy of the Company, the small industries in the province were being ruined. It was one of the few voices of conscience in British Bengal of that era. Colebrooke's findings were received with great embarrassment by the Company administration. The authorities were furious with Colebrooke but they dared not take any punitive action against him as Sir George Colebrooke held a prominent position and had influence with the Court of Directors of the East India Company in London. It is not known what the father felt about the candour of his son's report.

Apart from being a great Sanskrit scholar, Colebrooke should be remembered for the immense honesty and courage with which he wrote a report on the economic situation in Bengal. Little did the East India Company officers realize what they had unleashed when they asked the young Collector of Purnea to look into the Permanent Settlement question in 1789. Colebrooke vehemently criticised the Company's commercial policy. He saw the immense damage done to the cottage industry of Bengal as a result of English competition. The export of cotton was harming the prosperity of Bengal. He pleaded eloquently in his report for saving those cotton weavers whose occupation and employment had been ruined by the monopolist policies of the Company.

In ringing tones Colebrooke denounced Company policy.

> To a Government enlightened ... it cannot be a trifling consideration to provide employment for the poorest classes. No public provision now exists in these provinces to relieve the wants of the poor and helpless. The only employment in which widows and female orphans incapacitated for field labour by sickness or by their rank can earn a subsistence is by spinning and it is the only employment to which females of a family can apply themselves to maintain the men if these be disqualified for labour by infirmity .... Their distresses are certainly great and among none greater than among the many great families which once enjoyed the comforts of life. These are numerous in India and whether they be entitled to particular consideration of Government or not they have certainly a claim on its humanity.

Colebrooke recommended that, "cotton yarn instead of cotton wool should be imported to England as that would provide employment for Indian labour."

While working in the solitude of Purnea, Colebrooke was seized by the desire to learn about India. He started learning Arabic, Persian and Sanskrit. Like Jones and Wilkins he fell in love with the beauty of the Sanskrit language. Delving into the Sanskrit language he realized both its grandeur and antiquity. The success of Sir William Jones and Charles Wilkins as Sanskrit scholars inspired him to proceed further. Colebrooke began to devote himself to the study of ancient *Smriti* literature (law of the Hindus). While he was working as a Collector of Natore in North Bengal (now in Bangladesh), the government entrusted him with the work of translating *Vivada-bhangarnava* (the ocean of settlement of disputes), a digest of Hindus Laws on contracts and inheritance compiled and written in Sanskrit. The compilation was done under the editorship of the most celebrated Bengali Sanskrit scholar of the day – Pundit Jagannath Taraka Panchanan who was a friend of William Jones.

The task of translating the Sanskrit works into English was first assigned to Sir William Jones. Due to his sudden and untimely death, the choice of the government fell on Colebrooke who had by that time become well known as a Sanskrit scholar. After about three years of intense work Colebrooke completed the translation. The work was published in four big tomes in 1797-98. Though Colebrooke's work is considered superior to Halhed's *A Code of Gentoo Laws*, which had been published earlier, he acknowledged Halhed's pioneering role. Colebrooke's *Digest* was re-published in London in three volumes.

Colebrooke's *Digest of Hindu Law* continued to be used in the law courts throughout the Company's jurisdiction in India for more than half a century. In 1874, the fourth edition of the book was published from Madras in two volumes. Sir John Shore, the then Governor-General of India, appreciated Colebrooke's translation of the *Vivada-bhangarnava* into English. He was paid Rupees 15,000 as honorarium for his work. The original *Vivada-bhangarnava* compiled by the great Pandit Jagannath Tarka Panchanan was never printed as the government was keen to have only the ancient Hindu laws on contracts and succession. Colebrooke's translation was considered sufficient for the purpose.

Colebrooke was a regular contributor to the journal *Asiatick Researches* of the Asiatic Society of Calcutta. He wrote on diverse topics such as status of Hindu widows, Indian weights and measures, enumeration of classes in ancient India, etc., which drew the attention of the Indologists all over the world. During this time he was posted at Mirzapur near Benaras where he was in charge of revenue matters. He utilized his stay here in learning Sanskrit from the traditional Sanskrit pundits of Benaras. After a few years' stay at Benaras, Colebrooke moved to Nagpur in Central India for sometime. In recognition of his great proficiency in Hindu Law Colebrooke was appointed Judge of the newly created 'Sadar Diwani Adalat' in Calcutta. In those days the power of this court was just below the Supreme Court of India, as there was no intermediary High Court. In this Court, cases were decided on the basis of Hindu or Muslim Laws according to the community of the parties concerned. Four years later, Colebrooke was promoted to the post of Chief Judge of the Court.

In 1800 Lord Wellesley Governor-General of India founded the Fort William College in Calcutta in order to train the Company's civil servants in Sanskrit and vernacular languages and literature. Lord Wellesley invited Justice Colebrooke of the Sadar Diwani Adalat to be Honorary Lecturer of Sanskrit and Hindu Law of Contracts and Succession in 1805. That same year Colebrooke published *Sanskrit Grammar* for the benefit of the students of the Fort William College.

Returning to Calcutta, Colebrooke resumed his study of Sanskrit and research on the language. In 1805, he published an article *On the Vedas and Sacred Writings of the Hindus* in the *Asiatick Researche.* In 1807, Colebrooke was made a member of the 'Supreme Council' of the Government of India. He occupied this post until 1812 in addition to his duties as the Chief Judge of the Sadar Dewani Adalat. From 1812 to 1814, Colebrooke served as a member of the Board of Revenue. In 1808, he published an English translation of the celebrated Sanskrit Lexicon popularly known as *Amar Kosa* along with the Sanskrit text. In 1810 he also published *Hindu Succession Law.* This was another of his contributions to Hindu legal literature. At the end of this period he resigned from the Council in order to pursue his Sanskrit studies and publish his research papers. Among his other interests was the antiquity of the Himalayan mountains.

Immersed in his studies and research Colebrooke did not consider matrimony until he was aged forty-five. Then he married Elizabeth, daughter of Johnson Wilkinson, in 1810. Three sons were born to the couple. Like many European women who could not withstand the rigours of the Indian climate and the strain of childbirth, Elizabeth passed away in 1814. She was buried at the South Park Cemetery in Calcutta. A year after Colebrooke left India for England along with three little sons. He had spent thirty-two years in India. After returning to England he first settled at Bath, and then moved to London where he spent his remaining years.

Colebrooke continued with his research and writings on India. In 1817, he published a book containing researches on Hindu

Arithmetic, Algebra and Mensuration. Some of Colebrooke's research papers on Hindu Mathematics and Indology were also published in the journals of the Geological Society and Astronomical Society of England. He also contributed some articles on scientific subjects in general in the *Quarterly Journal* of England.

In 1818, Colebrooke donated his vast collection of old Sanskrit manuscripts to the India Office library. He had spent about L 10,000 to acquire them. These formed the nucleus of the valuable India Office collection where scholars such as F. Rosen began to work on them. His edition of *Rig Veda* appeared in 1838. Rosen's work was followed by R. Roth who devoted himself to study of Vedic literature and published *On the Literature and History of the Veda* in 1846. In 1816 Franz Bopp published his work on the conjugational system of Sanskrit as compared with Greek, Latin, German and Persian, thereby taking comparative philology a few steps forward.

Colebrooke also made a catalogue of Sanskrit works and was responsible for the publication of the *Suchipastaka.* His other works were kept in Fort William, the Asiatic Society and the Sanskrit Colleges at Calcutta and Benaras.

When the Royal Asiatic Society of Great Britain and Ireland was formed in London in 1823 on the lines of the Asiatic Society in Calcutta, Colebrooke played a very important role. As he declined to accept its first Presidentship, he was made a Director. Many years later, his son Thomas Edward Colebrooke was appointed to the chair of the Society for three terms. Sir Thomas Edward Colebrooke, though not a celebrated Indologist like his father, had great attraction to Indian studies. Born in Calcutta, he felt a deep attachment for India. As a Member of Parliament, Sir Edward always fought for Indian interests. It was due to Sir Edward's efforts that all the articles by Colebrooke appearing in different periodicals from time to time were collected and printed in book form as *Miscellaneous Essays.*

From 1823 to 1828, Colebrooke delivered five long lectures on Hindu Philosophy – *Sankhya, Nyaya, Vaishesika, Vedanta, Buddhist, Jain, Charvak, Lokayata, Pasupata* and *Maheswara* systems at the Royal Asiatic Society, London. These were published in the Transaction of the Society. Later, they were included in his *Miscellaneous Essays*. In late life, Colebrooke published another book on Hindu laws.

Due to overstraining of eyes throughout life, Colebrooke lost his eyesight towards the end of his life. His later years were filled with sadness by the death of his two sons. Colebrooke passed away in London, on 10th March 1837, at the age of seventy-two.

Before the publication of the 'Centenary Review' (1783-1883), the Asiatic Society paid high tribute to Colebrooke as one of the main organizers of the Society in its first phase. A distinguished archaeologist Dr. Rajendra Lal Mitra described Colebrooke as

> a man of extra-ordinary industry, combined with rare clearness of intellect and sobriety of judgment, the first to handle Sanskrit language and literature on scientific principles, he published many texts, translations and essays dealing with every branch of Sanskrit learning thus laying the solid foundations on which the later scholars have built. As a great mathematician, zealous astronomer and profound Sanskrit scholar, he wrote nothing that did not at once command the highest attention from the public and notwithstanding the great advance that has been made in Oriental researches of late years, his papers are still looked upon as models of their kind...

Among the illustrious Westerners who worked to further Sanskrit learning and research, the name of Henry Thomas Colebrooke is ranked second after Sir William Jones. He was the first to reveal to the European world India's ancient culture long before Macaulay made his offensive and uninformed remarks. In fact Colebrooke has done a great service to India by his magnificent scholarship.

At a time when the conquered people of India hesitated to speak about their culture, Colebrooke astonished the European world by describing Indian religious thought and philosophy, philology, astronomy, law and mathematics. His essay on the *Vedas* published in 1805 acquainted Europeans with the oldest literature of the Hindus.

Colebrooke was the first European writer who inquired into the subject of Indian algebra, arithmetic and astronomy. His dissertation on the algebra of the ancient Indians categorically states that mathematical science was in a high state of development before the Greeks or the Arabs. The algebra and astronomy of Aryabhatta, the natural scientist Varahamihira and the arithmetic of Leelavati and Brahmagupta were translated by Colebrooke. He wrote:

> The Hindus had certainly made distinguished progress in the science so early as the century immediately following that in which the Grecians thought the rudiments of it. The Hindus had the benefit of a good arithmetical notation, the Greeks the disadvantage of a bad one. Nearly allied as algebra is to arithmetic the invention of algebraic calculus was more easy and natural where arithmetic was best handled .... They are sufficiently distinct to justify the presumption that both might be invented independently of each other. If however it will be insisted that a hint of suggestion that the seed of their knowledge may have reached the Hindu mathematicians immediately from the Greeks of Alexandria or to those of Bactria it must at the same time be confessed that a slender germ grew and fructified rapidly and soon attained an approved state of maturity in Indian soil.

Colebrooke founded the Royal Asiatic Society in England in 1823 when he declared,

> to those countries of Asia in which civilization may justly be considered to have had its origin or to have attained its earliest growth, the rest of the civilized world owes a large debt of gratitude ... and England is for that very cause the most beholden and by acquisition of dominion in the east is bound by a yet closer tie. As Englishmen they participate in the earnest wish that this duty may be fulfilled and that obligation required and we share in the anxious desire of promoting an interchange of benefits and returning in an improved state that which was received in a cruder form.

59

Horace Hayman Wilson

This eminent Oriental scholar began his career as a medical doctor. He took his medical degree at St. Thomas Hospital in London and joined the service of the East India Company as an Assistant Surgeon in 1808. He left England soon after on an East India Company ship. On the voyage he learnt Hindustani from a fellow passenger. Soon after arriving in Calcutta he changed his profession and left the post of Assistant Surgeon to work at the Calcutta Mint as Assistant Assay Master. He worked under the supervision of John Leyden who was also a distinguished poet and Oriental scholar and a close friend of Sir Walter Scott.

As a boy Wilson had seen the work of his uncle who was also employed in the Government Mint and had become acquainted with the process of chemical and metal analysis. Now the rudiments of that knowledge came in useful as he set about to learn his work in the Calcutta Mint. Dealing with coins provoked his interest in numismatics. He did extensive research on ancient coins of North India and became an expert on the subject. His later work, *Ariana Antiqua,* gave a detailed description of the coinage and history of Afghanistan. These studies naturally led inevitably to the study of Sanskrit. His pursuit of Sanskrit learning took him to Benares where he stayed for a year both to acquire proficiency in Sanskrit as well as to organize the Sanskrit College there. He became interested in Sanskrit drama and wrote a book on Hindu theatre.

Wilson was not a somber scholar. He took part in the social and cultural life of Calcutta and took delight participating in theatrical productions and concerts.

Wilson left India in 1832 to take up appointment as Boden Professor at Oxford. There he gave lectures on Sanskrit grammar, comparative philology, and the religious and philosophical system of the Hindus. In recognition of his intellectual attainments Wilson was elected a fellow of the Royal Society. In 1836 he was appointed to the post of Librarian at India House and gave lectures on Oriental studies at Haileybury College. He had by then acquired proficiency in a number of Indian languages such as Bengali, Hindustani, Hindi, Telugu, Tamil and Marathi along with Persian. He was a prolific writer on various subjects and compiled a Sanskrit-English dictionary. Following in the footsteps of his mentor Colebrooke Wilson wrote summaries of the *Puranas* and of the *Katha-Sarita-Sagara.* It was his translation of the *Rig Veda* that brought him scholastic fame. Wilson's translation of the *Rig Veda* was based on a excellent commentary of a Sanskrit pundit from South India. Unfortunately he could not complete the work which was taken over by Ballantyne who succeeded as Librarian of the India Office.

Wilson's early mentor John Leyden was appointed by the East India Company to its hospital in Madras in 1805. Once more the Scottish keeper of English conscience, Sir Walter Scott wrote –

> And thus set forth on his voyage, perhaps the first English traveler who ever sought India, moved neither by the love of wealth nor of power and who dispensing alike the luxuries commanded by the one and the pomp attached to the other was guided solely by the wish of extending our knowledge of Oriental literature and distinguishing himself as its most successful cultivator (*Miscellaneous Works*).

On his arrival at Madras in 1805 Leyden wrote to Ballantyre that he found the population came in two categories – "men whose natural occupation was to make money – the mercantile party." The other was those "who have discovered that they are not merely merchants in India but legislators and governors." Leyden wrote of India – "It has awakened in me energies which I scarcely imagined I possessed." He spent a substantial part of his salary on purchasing old manuscripts and Oriental works, determined to fathom the unplumbed depth of ancient India in the tradition of William Jones. Like Jones, Leyden knew several Indian languages. On this he wrote, "I may die in the attempt but if I die without surpassing Sir William Jones a hundredth let never a tear for me profane the eye of a borderer."

60
James Fergusson

One of the earliest scholars to discover archaeological remains was James Fergusson. Born in Scotland, young James joined a commercial company Fairlie and Fergusson where his elder brother was a partner in Calcutta. Unlike other British Indologists Fergusson did not have the benefit of a classical education. After his brother's business failed he became an Indigo merchant. In the midst of his commercial pursuits he became fascinated by ancient buildings and their history. He soon gave up his Indigo business and decided to devote himself to the research of ancient Indian buildings. He undertook extensive tours all over India between the years 1835 to 1842. He was admitted to the Royal Asiatic Society soon after. Fergusson presented various papers on the architectural heritage of India, particularly on the rock-cut temples of South India. It was after this paper that serious study began on Indian temple sculpture. His papers also brought to the notice of the directors of the East India Company of the wealth of Indian architectural heritage.

Fergusson returned to India in 1845 when he collected more material on the classical Indian monuments of the fifth and sixth centuries as well as on ancient Buddhist architecture in India. He was not a conventional archaeologist and encountered opposition to his theories. He wrote, "I have had the good fortune to spend the best years of my life in countries where art though old and decrepit still follows the same path that led it towards perfection in the days of its youth and vigour .... In the East men still use their reason in speaking of art and their common sense in carrying their views into effect. They do not as in modern Europe adopt strange hallucinations that can only lead to brilliant failures." In 1855 Fergusson published his major work, *Illustrated Handbook of Architecture*. His other book, *Indian and Eastern Architecture*, is a work of great scholarship in which he has described the development of various schools of architecture against their historical background.

His interest extended from India to West Asia especially Mesopotamian culture where he tried to establish common links between the Semitic and Aryan people. His work would be taken up a century and half later by Sir Mortimer Wheeler.

61

William Carey and the Serampore Mission

Along with Charles Wilkins, Nathaniel Brassey Halhed and Graves Channey Haughton, there were numerous European scholars in Bengali and other Oriental languages. Some of them belonged to the Serampore Mission. Of them the most remarkable was William Carey who started his life as a cobbler. It is an interesting point that the man who brought the Bible to Bengal was one of the catalysts of the Bengali Renaissance. The life of William Carey is the story of a different adventure and different ambitions. Power and glory, name and fame did not mean anything to him but a burning zeal to spread the Gospel to Indians all was he desired.

"Carey might be seen", wrote his fellow missionary, John Clark Marshman, "walking eight or ten miles to Northampton with his wallet full of shoes upon his shoulders and then returning home with a fresh supply of leather to fulfill his engagements with a government contractor." Carey came to India with a missionary zeal to redeem a people whom he felt were 'sunk in superstition, vice and idolatory.' He learnt Sanskrit, Bengali, Persian and Marathi 'not with a view to know the people or profit by the wisdom contained in Oriental books but with the object of bringing a large mass of humanity whom he sincerely believed to be groveling in darkness to light' (Dinesh Chandra Sen).

He was born in Northamptonshire where he began his career as a cobbler. Unlike other British scholars, Carey had no formal education; he studied only up to middle school. Despite this Carey managed to master four foreign languages including Greek and Hebrew. Later on he enrolled as a Baptist missionary in 1792 to work in India.

Since the British East India Company did not allow missionary activities within its territory with the apprehension that propagation of an alien faith might create political turmoil, Carey was denied permission to travel in an English ship and had to make the journey in a Danish vessel. He landed in Serampore which was Danish territory. Carey arrived in India on 11th November 1793 as a missionary of the Baptist Mission. He travelled secretly to the British territory of Calcutta in a fishing boat and then moved to Malda to work as an indigo planter. Initially Carey encountered rough time; his eldest son died and wife's growing insanity added to his worries. Conditions in the indigo plantation prompted him to leave it and join William Ward and Joshua Marshman who had been given security by the Danish at the settlement at Serampore near Calcutta. Here they founded a settlement that became a model and example of the humanist spirit. Here he worked till his death in 1834 making it one of the intellectual cradles of Bengal.

Carey, Marshman and Ward had come with the avowed purpose to spread the word of Christ. To do this they needed precision and sensitivity to language, idiom and cadence. The missionaries therefore had to learn the language and translate it themselves as Carey and others did. These missionaries established educational institutions partly for the upliftment of the native and also to pave the way for conversion.

First they set up a printing press and worked indefatigably at translating the Bible and other works into various Indian languages. Having gained proficiency in Bengali, Hindi, Marathi, Persian, Punjabi, Telugu and most important of all Sanskrit, Carey found the back of his task broken when these seven languages were learnt: secondary dialects could be quickly mastered. He translated the Bible into six languages including Sanskrit and Assamese: he also translated various parts of the Bible into twenty-eight other dialects. His friends Marshman and Ward were equally energetic and added Bibles in Chinese and Burmese. The group also encouraged their pundits to write original works in the vernacular and publish these. They thus laid the grounds for modern Bengali literature. Dictionaries and grammars were compiled. A four-volume survey of Hindu history, literature and religion was also published. The achievements of Carey, Marshman and Ward were great by any linguistic standards and so was their linguistic ability. Their motives sprang from their Christian fervour. The ordinary people, they knew, would not understand English; the translation of the Gospel in Bengali and other vernacular languages would give them access to Christian teachings. He became one of the greatest Western linguists of India.

Carey printed the first book in Bengali prose; Halhed and Wilkins had already paved the way to the art of printing with the Bengali typeface. Carey translated *The New Testament* into Bengali which was published in 1801 by his press in Serampore, a quaint Danish colony situated on the banks of the Hooghly river. Among his other achievements was the compilation a Bengali dictionary printed in 1815. A year after James Hickey brought out his *Bengal Gazette* in 1817, Carey started the first Bengali newspaper *Samachar Darpan* in 1818 and the famous *Friend of India*, another weekly in English which was later amalgamated with *The Statesman* of Calcutta in 1875. With the collaboration of two other missionaries, Joshua Marshman and William Ward, Carey founded the Serampore College in 1818. The Serampore Mission also provided education to the local people. By 1817 it was running forty-five schools for teaching two thousand boys in Bengali and in 1820 it began a school for Bengali girls.

It is now one of the educational institutions in the country imparting secular and religious education side by side. More than 2500 students are now enrolled in this college, known internationally for theological education and is one of the best Protestant institutes for theology in Asia. The College celebrated the bicentenary of Carey's arrival in India and the 175th year of its establishment.

After the translation of the *New Testament* into Bengali, he turned his attention to Bengali grammar and wrote textbooks of Bengali prose and grammar for his students at Fort William College, Calcutta, where he was appointed professor of Bengali and Sanskrit. In 1802 he undertook a daunting task – the translation of the *Mahabharata* and *Ramayana* into Bengali that ran into four and five volumes respectively. In 1812 Carey wrote a remarkable book in Bengali, the *Itihasamala*, an anthology of prose tales from East and West. His magnum opus was the compilation of the *Bengali Dictionary*, with the first edition of 616 pages printed in 1815, the second edition of two volumes in 1544 pages printed in 1818 covering 50,000 words. He wrote grammars for Marathi (1805); Sanskrit (1806) Punjabi (1812) and the language of Bhutan (1826).

It is a phenomenon not uncommon in colonial history to find members of the ruling race transformed 'into something rich and strange' by the encounter with the country they had come to civilize. In the case of William Carey the soil of Indian had converted the cobbler into a lexicographer.

Carey was also active on the social issues of his day and joined Raja Ram Mohan Roy who wanted the custom of *Sati* or widow burning to be abolished. Carey translated into Bengali the 1829 laws banning *Sati* and publicized them for the benefit of the people, especially women. He agitated against female infanticide and regularly rescued infant girls from the sea where they were abandoned.

Carey's object was to improve the lives of Bengalis by spreading education and by disseminating the truth of the Gospel. To him we permanently owe the rapid development of Bengali prose before Raja Ram Mohan Roy took up the work earnestly. The difficulties he faced were serious and numerous. His greatest ambition was to publish a translation of the Gospel in Bengali. When his translation of the *New Testament* was almost completed, the cost of printing 10,000 copies was Rupees 43,750, which he raised through donations and contributions from England. We may compare this to the business-like way in which Warren Hastings went about funding Halhed's *Grammar*.

There is a story that when Carey was lunching at Government House, one of the guests who did not know Carey by sight remarked that he had heard that Carey was a shoemaker by profession, whereupon Carey who had overheard this remarked that he 'was not a shoemaker – only a cobbler'. Carey was undoubtedly a man of genuine humility – a man who rose from humble beginnings unlike Jones and Halhed.

He and Marshman left nothing to bequeath when they died – not even money for their burial. Here again one contrasts them with Jones, Halhed and Wilkins who did well financially. Carey lived in Bengal from 1793 to 1834 when he passed away, a year after the death of Raja Ram Mohan Roy and was buried in the Danish cemetery in Serampore.

The contribution of Carey is very significant. The pioneering Bengali novelist Bankim Chandra Chatterjee appeared into the literary scene with a slender volume of poems, *Lalita-o-Manas* twenty-five years after the death of Carey. The eminent Bengali critic Susil Kumar De wrote, "To Carey belongs the credit for having raised the Bengali language from its debased condition of an unsettled dialect to the character of a regular and permanent form of speech, capable of becoming the refined comprehensive vehicle of a great literature in the future."

It is tempting to compare and contrast the attitude of William Jones who composed the *Hymn to Lakshmi* with the stern Christian attitude of Carey. One wonders whether it had anything to do with William Jones being a university man, a student of the liberal philosophy, a believer in Burke's teachings on the value of tradition. Despite their different backgrounds, the various scholars had proficiency in Oriental languages, though the degree varied.

One is tempted also to ask: who left the lasting contribution? The greater scholar Jones or the humbler Halhed or Carey? To ask this question one has to answer the larger question, did European culture benefit more by the opening of the doors of Sanskrit or did the Indians benefit by the introduction of printing and by the publication of the *Bengali Grammar*? Jones introduced into British as well as Indian minds the idea of systematic Indology and helped them to respect and preserve their great heritage. Carey and Halhed did something more practical and workmanlike – they taught the Indians to understand the structure of their own language and to propagate their own writings through the art of printing.

What Macaulay with the growing arrogance of imperialism preached was the antithesis of all that William Jones and the Company scholars stood for. His contempt for everything Indian, from the great epics to 'gods ten feet high' was a far cry from the curiosity and admiration of the eighteenth-century English scholars for Indian culture. But Hastings and the Company scholars were vindicated when Curzon promulgated the 'Ancient Monuments Act' to strengthen the functions of the Archaeological Survey of India.

62

Sir Monier Williams and Development of Sanskrit Studies

Historians have rightly pointed out that wars ironically commence dialogues between civilizations. When the old order of Europe ended with the French revolution it brought Europe into contact with Eastern civilizations. Napoleon's Egyptian campaign and the development of Egyptology coincided with the conquest of India and the discovery of Indian heritage by British scholars and the development of Indology.

Sir Monier Williams was a great Sanskrit scholar who popularized Sanskrit as a serious subject of study in the West. Monier Williams was an intellectual heir of Sir William Jones. Seventy years after William Jones "astonished the learned world by the discovery of Sanskrit dramatic literature Sir Monier Williams brought the study of Sanskrit literature to its fruition". He relates how Sir William Jones was initiated into acquaintance with Sanskrit literature by a learned Brahmin pundit who was "conversant with European manners, removed all his doubts and gave him no less delight than surprise by telling him that the English nation had compositions of the same sort which were publicly represented at Calcutta in the cold season and bore the name of Plays."

He was born in Bombay in 1790, educated in England and was selected as a Writer in the East India Company's civil service. However, he chose to stay in England and studied Sanskrit at Oxford University and a few years later became a Boden scholar and thereafter Boden Professor of Sanskrit, Persian and Hindustani at Haileybury. The chair was founded by Colonel Boden who stated in his Will of 15th August 1811 that the special object of his "munificent bequest was to promote the translation of the

Scriptures into Sanskrit so as to enable his countrymen to proceed with the conversion of the natives of India to the Christian religion".

Far from spreading knowledge of Christian scriptures Sir Monier became immersed in Sanskrit literature which brought him into contact with the ancient philosophy of the *Vedantas* and *Upanishads* as well as the secular works of the great poets and dramatists of the classical age of Sanskrit. It was not only an academic pursuit; like William Jones, Monier Williams believed that educated Englishmen should be aware of the culture of the vast and ancient land that was under British rule. He wrote,

> The need felt by the British public for some such translation as I have here offered can scarcely be questioned. A great people who through their empire in India command the destinies of the Eastern world, ought surely to the conversant with the most popular Indian dramas, in which the customs of the Hindus, their opinions, prejudices, fables, their religious rites, daily occupations and amusements are reflected as in a mirror.

His enduring contribution to Indology was through the *Sanskrit-English Dictionary*, a monumental work reflecting his expertise in Sanskrit. Thereafter he compiled *English-Sanskrit Dictionary* as a sequel.

In the Preface to the new edition of the Sanskrit-English dictionary Sir Monier Williams observed,

> Speaking for myself I may say that blended with thankfulness for the longevity that has enabled me to see a protracted undertaking brought to a completion is a deep consciousness that I am not young enough to consider myself infallible. Indeed it is at once the joy and sorrow of every true scholar that the older he grows the more he has to confess himself a learner rather than a teacher and the more morbidly conscious he becomes of his own liability to a learner's mistakes.

Sir Monier was a great admirer of ancient India. His knowledge of Sanskrit literature led him to observe "in some subjects too especially in poetical descriptions of nature and domestic affection Indian works do not suffer by comparison with the best specimens of Greece and Rome while in wisdom depth and shrewdness of their moral apothegms they are unrivalled. More than this learned Hindus had probably made great advances in astronomy, algebra, arithmetic, botany and medicine not to mention their admitted superiority in grammar long before any of these sciences were cultivated by the most ancient nations of Europe." His tribute to the Hindu epics is glowing.

> In exhibiting pictures of domestic life and manners, the Sanskrit epics are even more true and real than the Greek and Roman. In the delineation of women the Hindu poet throws aside all exaggerated colouring and draw from nature – Kaikeyei, Kausalya, Mandodari ... who are drawn from life. Sita, Draupadi and Damyanti engage our affections and our interest far more than Helen or Penelope ... Sanskrit epic poetry is unrivalled even by Greek epics ... There are indications in the Indian epics of a higher degree of civilization than that represented in the Homeric poems.

He wrote extensively on religious philosophies of India classifying them into "Vedism, Ritualistic Brahmanism, Philosophic Brahmanism, Mythological Brahmanism and Nomistic Brahmanism". He also wrote of Shavism, Vaishnavism, and Shaktism. Sir Monier was no less enthusiastic about Buddhism and says of Lord Buddha, "He always maintained that the only revelation he had received was an illumination from within due entirely to his own intuitions, assisted by his reasoning powers and by severe discipline protracted to countless previous births in every variety of bodily form."

The first public lecture on the election of Monier Williams to the Boden Chair was on the *Study of Sanskrit in Relation to the Missionary Work in India*. Monier Williams wrote the treatise but did not live to see it published. He wrote:

> The primary object of a Sanskrit dictionary should be to exhibit by a lucid etymological arrangement, the structure of a language which as most people know is not only the elder sister of Greek but the best guide to the structure of Greek as well as every other member of the Aryan or Indo-European family – a language in short which is the keystone of the science of comparative philology.

> The Aryan languages of which Sanskrit is the eldest sister and English one of the youngest proceeded from a common but nameless and unknown parent whose very home in Central Asia cannot be fixed into absolute certainty though the locality may conjecturally be placed somewhere near Bactria (Balkh) and Sogdonia or not far from Bokhara or the first course of the River Oxus.

Monier Williams believed that Balkh was once the chief ancient home of the Aryan civilization.

From this Center radiated as it were eight principal lines of speech, each taking its own course and radiating in its own way – namely

(1) Two Asiatic lines –
  (A) The Indian comprising Sanskrit, the very ancient Prakrits, including the Prakrits of the inscriptions, the Pali, the Buddhist Sacred Canon, the Ardha-Magadhi of the Jains, and the modern Prakrits or the vernacular languages of the Hindus such as Hindi, Marathi, Gujarati, Bengali, Oriya etc.

  (B) The Iranian comprising the Avesta language commonly called the Zend or old Persian or Akhaemenian, Pahlavi, modern Persian and in connection with these Armenian and Pushtu

(2) Six European lines -
  (a) Celtic (b) Hellenic (c) Teutonic (d) Italian (e) Slavonic (f) Lithuanian – each branching into various sub-lines as exhibited in the present languages of Europe.

It is this Asiatic and European ramification of the Aryan languages which has led to their being called Indo-European.

In regard in what may be thought to be a needless multiplication of indecent words and meanings, offensive to European notions of delicacy, I am sorry to say that they had to be inserted, because in very truth, Sanskrit like all Oriental languages abounds with words of that character and to such an extent that to have omitted them, would have been cut out a large percentage of the language. A story is told of a prudish lady who complimented Dr. Johnson of having omitted all bad words from his English dictionary whereupon he replied, 'Madam, it is true I have done so but I find that you have been looking for them.'

In extenuation it might be urged that in India the relationship between the sexes is regarded as a sacred mystery and is never held to be suggestive of improper or indecent ideas.

Doubtless in India from the greater exclusiveness of the educated few and the desire of a proud priesthood to keep the key of knowledge in their own possession, the language of the learned classes became so highly elaborated that it received the name 'Sanskrita' or 'perfectly constructed speech' both to denote its superiority over the common dialects (called in contra-distinction Prakrita) and its more exclusive dedication to literary and religious purposes.

> We are appalled by the length of some of India's literary productions as compared to those of European countries. For instance Virgil's *Aeneid* is said to consist of 9000 lines, Homer's *Iliad* of 12,000 lines and the *Odyssey* of 15,000 whereas the Sanskrit epic poem *Mahabharat* contains at least 200,000 lines without reckoning the supplement known as the *Harinama*. In some subjects, especially in the poetical descriptions of nature and domestic affection Indian works do not suffer in comparison with the best specimens of Greece and Rome, while in wisdom, depth and shrewdness of their moral apothegms, they are unrivalled.
>
> More than this the Hindus had made considerable advances in astronomy, algebra, arithmetic, botany and medicine, not to mention their superiority in grammar, long before these sciences were cultivated in the most ancient nations of Europe. Hence it has happened that I have been painfully reminded during the progress of this dictionary that a Sanskrit lexicographer ought to aim at a kind of quasi omniscience.
>
> For indeed I know full well that all who belong to the straightest of Hindu scholars will at once flatly deny that their divine Sanskrit can be exhibited to the eye in any other alphabetic dress than their own 'divine Nagari'? Na hi putam syad go kshiram/ sva dritan dritam'. Let not cow's milk be polluted by being put into a dog's skin.
>
> The Sanskrit language is indeed a master key to a knowledge of all Hindu vernaculars and should moreover be studied as a kind of linguistic bond of sympathy and fellow feeling between the inhabitants of the United Kingdom and their Indian subjects.

There is no superciliousness or patronization in Monier Williams' attitude to Sanskrit.

Monier Williams gives credit to Sir Charles Trevelyan regarding transliteration of Indian languages into Romanised letters. Many Oriental books published on a plan substantially agreeing with Sir William Jones' Indo-Romanic system have been published.

In the introduction to his translation of *Shakuntala* in January 1856, Sir Monier gives a comprehensive history of Sanskrit literature. He wrote: "Indeed, it has now been ascertained that the antiquity of some of the Sanskrit dramas thus brought to light, extends back to a still more remote period before the commencement of the Christian era."

> The earliest dramatic works in Sanskrit is the *Mrichhakatika* or *Toy-Cart* translated by Professor H.H. Wilson, is attributed to a regal author, King Sudraka whose reign is generally fixed in the second century BC, and it is not improbable that others, the names of which only have been preserved, may belong to a previous century. Considering that the nations of Europe can scarcely be said to have possessed a dramatic literature before the fourteenth or fifteenth century of the present era, the great age of the Hindu plays would have itself be a most interesting and attractive circumstance, even if their poetical merit were not of a very high order. But when the antiquity of these productions is added to their extreme beauty and excellence as literary compositions, and when we also take into account their value as representations of the early condition of Hindu society – which notwithstanding the lapse of two thousand years has in many particulars obeyed the law of unchangeableness ever stamped on the manners and customs of the East – we are led to wonder that the study of the Indian drama has not commended itself in a greater degree to the attention of Europeans, and especially of Englishmen. The English student at least is bound by considerations of duty, as well as curiosity, to make himself acquainted with a subject which illustrates and explains the condition of the millions of Hindus who owe allegiance to his own Sovereign and are governed by English laws.

In his Foreword to his translation of Kalidasa's *Shakuntala*, Sir Monier writes:

> Of all Indian dramatists and indeed of all Indian poets the most celebrated is Kalidasa, the writer of the present play. He comes next in date to the author of the 'Toy Cart'; and although little is known of the circumstances of his life, yet there is satisfactory evidence to prove that he lived in the time of King Vikramaditya-I whose capital was Ujjayni (now Oujein - a sacred and very ancient city) situated to the north east of Gujarat and who flourished in the middle of the century preceding the commencement of our era.
>
> From the absence of historical literature in India our knowledge of the State of Hindustan between the incursion of Alexander and the Mohammadan conquest is very slight. But it is ascertained with tolerable accuracy that after the invasion of the kingdoms of Bactria and Afghanistan, the Tartars or Scythians (called by the Hindus Sakas) overran the north-western provinces of India and retained possession of them till the reign of Vikramaditya. This great monarch succeeded in driving back the barbaric hordes beyond the Indus and so consolidated his empire that his dominion extended over

> the whole of northern Hindustan. His name is even now cherished among the Hindus with pride and affection and the date of his victory over the Scythians in 56 BC is the starting point of the Samvat era, from which they still continue to count. There is good authority for affirming that the reign of Vikramaditya I was equal in brilliancy to that of any monarch in any age or country. He was a liberal patron of science and literature and gave the most splendid encouragement to poets, philologists, astronomers and mathematicians. Nine illustrious men of genius adorned his court and were supported by his bounty. They were called the 'Nine Gems' or 'Navaratna': and Kalidasa is by general consent allowed to have been the brightest of the nine. To him (as to another celebrated Indian dramatist, Bhavabhuti, who flourished in the eighth century) only three plays are attributed; and of these the *Sakoontala* (here translated) has acquired the greatest celebrity. Of the other two the most celebrated, called *Vikramorvasi* has been excellently translated by Professor H.H. Wilson and will be found in his book *Hindu Theatre.*
>
> Indeed the popularity of this play with the natives of India exceeds that of any other dramatic and probably of any other poetical composition. But it is not in India alone that *Sakoontala* is known and admired. Its excellence is now recognized in every literary circle throughout the continent of Europe; and its beauties if not yet universally known and appreciated are at least acknowledged by many learned men in every country of the civilized world.

Monier Williams had written, "I pledged myself at some future time to present the English public with a free translation of the whole play. That pledge is here redeemed and the following pages contain the first English translation in prose and verse of the true and pure version of the most celebrated drama of the Shakespeare of India."

Monier Williams felt that a fresh translation of Shakuntala was needed ... "in which the bold and nervous phraseology of Kalidasa ... The text of my edition on the contrary represents the old and pure version of the drama and from that text the present translation has been made; while abundant notes have been added, sufficient to answer the exigencies of the non-Oriental scholar. Moreover the metrical portions of the play have for the first time been rendered into verse."

Monier Williams goes on to describe the poetical merit of *Sakoontala* which is "so universally admitted that any remarks on this head would be superfluous". He observes that the Fourth Act describes the departure of Sakoontala from the hermitage "contains the most obvious beauties; and that no one can read this act nor indeed any part of the play without being struck with the richness and elevation of its author's genius, the exuberance and glow of his fancy, his ardent love of the beautiful, his deep sympathy with Nature and Nature's loveliest scenes, his profound knowledge of the human heart, his delicate appreciation of his most refined feelings, his familiarity with its conflicting sentiments and emotions. But in proportion to the acknowledge, excellence of Kalidasa's composition, and in proportion to my own increasing admiration of its beauties, is the diffidence I feel lest I may have failed to infuse any of the poetry of the original into the present version. Translation of poetry must at the best resemble the process of pouring a highly volatile and evanescent spirit from one receptacle into another. The original fluid will always suffer a certain amount of waste and evaporation."

Monier Williams marvels at the skill of Kalidasa who lived before the Christian era. He praises the "dexterity with which the plot is arranged and conducted, the ingenuity with which the incidence are connected, the skill with which the characters are delineated and contrasted with each other, the boldness and felicity of the diction; would scarcely be unworthy of the great dramatist of modern times."

Monier Williams goes on to state that dramatic poetry is said to have been invented by the sage Bharata who lived at a very remote period of Indian history and was the author of a system of music. He traces the development of dramatic dialogue the art of theatrical representation during the Vikramaditya era. He states that as in Greece scenic entertainments in India took place at religious festivals and on solemn public occasions.

Kumar Sambhavu is another of Kalidasa's play translated by Monier Williams. It describes the events leading to the birth of Kumara (also called Kartikeya or Skanda), the son of Shiva and the god of war in the Hindu pantheon, born to bring about the defeat of the demon Taraka. He observes: "It would seem that the poet's intention was not realized. Though in some manuscripts it is in cantos it is generally agreed that the later cantos are spurious and that the genuine work of Kalidasa goes no further than the eighth canto stopping short of the actual birth."

The poem covers wooing of Shiva by Kama, the god of love, accompanied by Rati, a pilgrimage to the mountain hermitage of Shiva. Kama stretches his bow to shoot Shiva but Shiva catching sight of him reduces him to ashes with a ray from this third eye. This part also contains an exquisite description of spring coming to the forest. Here one is tempted to compare John Brough's translation with that of William Jones and Monier Williams and Aurobindo.

Like many great Oriental scholars, Sir Monier Williams believed that if British rule in India was to be just and enlightened then British attitudes to India would have to be fair and sympathetic. He writes in his book *Modern India* "above all let those who are preparing for an Indian career bear in mind that Sanskrit is the only source of life, health and vigour to all the spoken languages of the Hindus, the only repository of Hindu religious creeds, customs and observances".

Sir Monier Williams was a great admirer of India and a true friend of Indians. He wanted to see Indian civilization restored to its original vitality and to bring about greater understanding between India and the West.

63
Sir Edwin Arnold

Edwin Arnold was one of the greatest interpreters of the East to the West. By studying Indian philosophy and literature he was able to convey to Europe some of the intellectual and spiritual wealth of India. Indeed his attachment to India and admiration for her culture went beyond scholarly interest. With a poignant wistfulness he wrote in the book *With Sa'adi in the Garden*

Some that he dreamed the west and east would meet
On some far day, lay some fresh opened path,
In sisterly new truths and strove for that;
I think he did but find wisdom's wide stream
Nearest the fountain clearest, India's air
Softer and warmer than his native skies;
And liked the gentle speech, the grave reserve,
The piety and quiet of the land
Its old world manners and its reverent ways
And kind simplicity of Indian homes
And classic comeliness of Indian girls,
More than his proper people and tasks,
He was to blame but he loved India.

Arnold's fascination for Indian epics and legends is mirrored in another poem:

While on a light strung lyre, I sought to tell
Indian Sidhartha's wisdom; and the spell
Of Jaydev's deep verse; and proud deeds wrought
By Pandu princes ...
I tender lessons of Upanishads teach –
Secret of death and subtle soul of speech ...
The lofty glory of the song divine –
Arjuna's speech with Krishna –
Once more come and listen to the veena and the drum!

Come once more with me from our sombre skies
To hear great Sa'di's tuneful songs.

Edwin Arnold had a classical education at Kings School, Rochester, and then at the Universities of Oxford and London. He was an acknowledged poet at age of twenty when he won the Newdigate Prize for a poem, *Belshazzar's Feast*. Soon after he published *Poems Narrative and Lyrical*. He taught briefly in English schools and at the young age of twenty-four Arnold was appointed Principal of the Deccan College at Poona. His poem *Garden of Repose* reveals his growing enchantment with India and affection for his students. Along with his teaching career Arnold began studying Turkish and Persian.

In the turmoil and conflict of 1857 Arnold was one of the few Britons who continued to be sympathetic to India and advocated a liberal attitude towards India both in education and in governance. His balanced attitude and empathy won him the affection of Indians and the appreciation of the British Government. Arnold returned to England at the age of thirty and began to write for the *Daily Telegraph* in London. While journalism was his profession, his love was for Oriental intellectual heritage. He travelled widely in the East and studied Hinduism and Buddhism with great depth and understanding.

Today Edwin Arnold is remembered for his epic poem on the life of Lord Buddha – *The Light of Asia.* The story is told with passion and wisdom. The message of Buddhism, its ethical foundations, its simplicity and the drama of Buddha's renunciation come alive in this work. So great was the success of this epic poem that numerous translations in European and Asian languages appeared.

Like many Western scholars and men of letters, Arnold also was drawn to the power and beauty of the *Bhagavad Gita* which he translated as *The Song Celestial*. Many scholars have said that Arnold's translation of the *Bhagavad Gita* is the most poetic of all English translations. Take for instance one of the most famous utterances of Krishna at Kurukshetra:

Never the spirit was born; the spirit shall cease to be never
Never was time it was not; end and beginning are dreams!
Birthless and deathless and changeless remaineth the spirit forever;
Death hath not touched it at all, dead though the house of it seems!

Following in William Jones's footsteps Arnold translated his own version of Jayadev's *Gita Govinda,* which he describes with a sensual yet tender rapture –

Oh Radha, Radha! Take this soul that trembles,
In life's deep midnight, to thy golden house.

In his book of poems *Indian Idylls,* he describes episodes from the *Mahabharata* about the devoted wife Savitri and the *Story of Nala and Damayanti.* Like all Oriental scholars Arnold could not escape the enchantment of Kalidasa and translated several of his poems.

While eighteenth century Britons admired William Jones' hymns to 'pagan gods', nineteenth century Britain was less tolerant; his orthodox Christians compatriots criticized Arnold for his obvious admiration for Buddhism and Hinduism.

Persian legends and Mughal stories, especially the love story of Shah Jahan and Mumtaz, impelled him to write about the building of the Taj Mahal. Arnold wrote also poems on Japan and Egypt. He was particularly attracted to Japanese womanhood whom he described as "the most dutiful, the most self-denying, the most considerate and pleasing".

Arnold's prodigious literary work revealed to the West the literature and legends of Asia and brought them to the domain of the ordinary people. He pleaded for understanding and empathy between his own countrymen and those of the East.

But he knew that the dialogue of civilization is not a smooth one. In a powerful passage from his book on the administration of Lord Dalhousie he wrote,

> We are introducing in Indian an idea unknown to the East as it was unknown to Europe before commerce and the Italian cities thought it – the idea of popular rights and equality before an impartial and a written law. If in that mission we ourselves violate justice and let our ambition get before our duty we shall spoil our own work; which will else bring the circumference or civilization back to its starting point, and completing the round of human intercourse, repay to the East the heavy debt due to it from the West in religion, art, philosophy, language – in almost everything but the science of Government.

We hear the echoes of William Jones reverberating still.

64
Vincent Smith

Vincent Arthur Smith was one of the last great Orientalists who wrote on India's heritage. His knowledge of Indian history and art was vast and authoritative. His research was profound and erudite. He did for Indian art what Giorgio Vasari did for the art of the Italian renaissance.

Vincent Smith was born in Dublin in 1848 into a scholarly family. His father, a physician by profession, was also an amateur numismatist and archaeologist. His collection of coins were later donated to the British museum. Vincent Smith graduated from Trinity College, Dublin, with high honours. Shortly thereafter he obtained his Doctorate. In 1869 Smith sat for the Indian Civil Service (ICS) examinations and topped the list of successful candidates. His first posting was in what was then called United Provinces (present day Uttar Pradesh). He worked for a while in the Land Settlement Department and wrote a Manual for settlement officers. He served for some time as Magistrate-Collector and then became a District Judge. In 1898 he came Chief Secretary to the Government of United Provinces. By this time he had become deeply immersed in his scholarly pursuits and took premature retirement in order to devote himself entirely to his research and writing.

While attending to his bureaucratic duties he became fascinated by the art and architecture of India. On his official tours he collected material on various subjects and began to do research on them and for four decades he pursued his studies, wrote books and articles on numerous subjects.

Returning to England Vincent Smith settled down in Oxford where he joined as member of the academic staff in St. John's College. Thereafter he was appointed as Curator of the Indian Institution and literary adviser for Oriental publications. In view of his profound knowledge of India's heritage, Dr. Smith was elected a member of the Royal Asiatic Society and became its vice-president four years later. He worked with a number of eminent Orientalists – G.U. Pope the Tamil scholar, George Grierson, Director of the Linguistic Survey of India and J.F. Fleet the founder of scientific Sanskrit Epigraphy.

His first publication *Early History of India* was an innovation in that for the first time a British historian interpreted the history of India in a different light. It was indeed a far cry from James Mill's uninformed chronicle. Vincent Smith relied heavily on epigraphical evidence for the Asokan and Gupta periods as well as on the Greek historians and Chinese pilgrims as well as the Kashmiri Kalhana's *Rajatarangini.* He called his history "Stock Taking of Accumulated Stores of Knowledge". His knowledge of Sanskrit enabled him to throw light on the historical background of the Puranas.

Vincent Smith's next work – *History of Fine Art in India and Ceylon* – was published in 1911. This work has become a classic. Here again it was the first time an attempt was made to give a comprehensive survey of the entire spectrum of Indian art from the earliest period to the late nineteenth century, from the earliest architecture to Gandharan sculpture, Central Asian and Persian art, the Buddhist artistic tradition of Ceylon. Vincent Smith like H.G. Rawlinson believed that Tibet, Burma, Thailand, Java, Sumatra were all part of 'Further India' and included the art of Java and Tibet in this book. Vincent Smith was a great art historian of India and his books like Havell's are still used for reference by art students.

Vincent Smith was a prolific writer and contributed regularly to the *Indian Antiquary* on subjects ranging from the coins of the Gupta dynasty, the epigraphic inscriptions of Bodh Gaya, Tibetan connections with the Lichchavis, the coinage of the Chandelas of Madhya Pradesh, the Palas of Bengal. He discovered the works of an obscure Sanskrit playwright named Bhasa who was a predecessor of Kalidasa. The journal of the Bengal Asiatic Society received many of his articles as well. He was no less generous to the journal of the German Oriental Society for which he wrote a number of articles on the early Andhra dynasties, the Indo-Parthian rulers and the Sakas of North India. Working in the United Provinces aroused his interest in the history and architecture of

Bundelkhand. His study of coins and epigraphy enabled him to fix the dates for the ancient history of North India. He concentrated particularly on the achievement of the imperial Guptas who ruled India in the early centuries of the first millennium AD. From Bundelkhand he went to Kasia in Gorakphur district where he studied Buddhist heritage. There was a debate between Vincent Smith and Alexander Cunnigham, the Director General of Archaeology, whether Kasia was the same Kushinagar where Lord Buddha was said to have attained *parinirvana*. Smith wrote about the Jain *stupas* and the monuments of Mathura. His great work, *Asoka, the Buddhist Emperor of India,* was published in 1901 and formed the first of a series entitled *Rulers of India*. To write this he drew on the researches of Dr. Buhler's translations of Asoka inscriptions. Another remarkable biography was that of the Moghul Emperor Akbar. Vincent Smith brought a literary flair to the writing of history.

65

Aurel Stein – Explorer-Scholar-Translator

Professor Owen Lattimore, an eminent Central Asian traveller and historian, called Stein "the most prodigious combination of scholar, explorer, archaeologist and geographer of his generation". His archaeological explorations which took him twenty-five thousand miles through Chinese Turkestan made him famous and he has been called "the greatest explorer of Asia since Marco Polo". Stein was knighted by the British Government for his contributions to Central Asian studies, received honorary degrees from Oxford and Cambridge Universities and won the gold medal of the Royal Geographical Society.

Stein was in his own words, "an archaeological explorer". He wrote voluminously about his travels and he preferred to do his writing in the solitude of the high mountains. He translated the *Rajatarangini* for instance in his camp at the mountain meadow of Mohand Marg, 11,000 feet above the Kashmir Valley.

He was a bachelor and from what is known of him, of a formal and austere temperament. In build he did not conform to the tall, rangy, sinewy physique of the great explorers. He was small made – only five feet four inches in height. There is a photograph of him, outside his tent in the Taklamakhan desert, dressed in a felt hat, over-coat, wing collared shirt, neatly knotted tie and well-polished shoes with buttoned-down spats.

Stein was born of Jewish parents in Budapest in 1862 but was baptized a Christian because his parents believed that in the climate of those times, he would fare better. His adopted faith remained with him all his life and when in 1943, he was dying at the age of eighty-one in Afghanistan (from where he had been planning one last great Central Asian journey) he asked for a Church of England burial service.

Aurel Stein

From his schooldays to his grave, Stein was fascinated by the campaigns and travels of Alexander the Great. He was to spend much of his life trying to retrace the routes and pinpoint the battlefields which carried the Greeks, together with their art and learning, into Central Asia. Their art he was to pursue further, across the passes of the Karakoram and eastwards along the ancient Silk Road. Perhaps too like the Hungarian Orientalists, Csoma de Koros and Arminius Vambery before him, he was attracted subconsciously to Central Asia by the ancient belief that the Hungarians are descended from the Huns. Certainly he was influenced and inspired by these two great travellers.

After studying Oriental languages at the universities of Vienna and Liepzig and receiving his Ph.D from Tubingen at the age of twenty-one, he came to Britain, which was eventually to become his adopted country. He spent three years at Oxford and at the British Museum studying classical and Oriental archaeology and languages, but omitted Chinese – a gap in his linguistic armoury which was to cost him dear some twenty years later at the Caves of the Thousand Buddhas near Tun-huang.

When his mother died, he turned his back on Hungary for good moving to India where in 1888 at the age of twenty-six he joined the Indian Education Service at Lahore. There he became a friend of Rudyard Kipling's father who was curator of the 'wonder house', the museum of Gandhara, another Indian art expert immortalized in the novel *Kim*. From the elder Kipling Stein learned much about the iconography of India as well as all that was known at that time of the art of Buddhist Central Asia. From Lahore he made the first of his many forays into areas where no European had set foot before – a rapid archaeological survey of mysterious Buner while accompanying a punitive expedition to the north-west frontier region of India.

Despite the solitary life he was to lead, sometimes not seeing another European for a year or more at a time, Stein enjoyed warm friendships. These, of necessity had to be maintained over enormous distances by correspondence usually written at night in his tent by candle-light and conveyed across desert and mountain range by native mail carrier. Nevertheless his work always came first, whether he was writing up his field notes at the end of a long day's work in the desert or later preparing the monumental accounts of his expeditions at his isolated tented home in Kashmir.

Stein had the good fortune of gaining as an ally the most powerful man in India, the new Viceroy. In April 1899, when Lord Curzon was visiting Punjab, Stein was asked to conduct him around the Lahore Museum. In the course of their tour Stein explained to him the significance of Gandhara art, simultaneously seizing the opportunity of telling him of his plan to solve the mysteries of what lay beyond the Karakoram. Curzon, who had himself written a book on Central Asia, gave instructions that Stein should be given the necessary authorizations for his expeditions.

Stein set up camp on Mohand Marg, a grassy meadow eleven thousand feet above sea level, which was to be his home on and off for many years, and the launching point of all his expeditions.

Following in the tradition of William Jones, Stein translated Kalhana's great epic poem *Rajatarangini* into English. Kalhana lived in eleventh century Kashmir when it was a great Hindu kingdom. Memories of Kashmir's golden age, of Lalitaditya and Avantivarman were still fresh. It is due to *Rajatarangini* that the history of Kashmir is known. On this Aurel Stein comments, "The interest of Kalhana's *Rajatarangini* for Indian history generally lies in the fact that it represents a class of Sanskrit composition which comes nearest in character to the chronicles of medieval Europe and of the Islamic east together with the later Kashmir chronicles which continue Kalhana's narrative, it is practically the sole extant specimen of this class".

The *Rajatarangini* of Kalhana is accessible even to those who do not know Sanskrit largely because of the meticulous translation of this classic by Aurel Stein. On his first visit to Kashmir in 1888 he was impressed by Kalhana's chronicle which he called "our oldest and fullest record of Kashmir history". In between his heavy official duties and his scanty leisure at Lahore he did not have enough time to continuously work on the translation and it was only "by availing myself of two months period of special duty in extension of the summer vacations of 1895 and 1896 and 1898 that I was able to complete the translation of the chronicle". Stein did most of the work at his camp in the beautiful mountain meadow of Mohand Marg about which he wrote "almost the whole of Kashmir lies before me from the ice-capped peaks of northern range to the long snowy line of the Pirpanjal, a little world of its own enclosed by mighty mountain ramparts". It was at Mohand

Marg that on 18th May 1900 Aurel Stein completed his great translation of the *Rajatarangini.*

Aurel Stein in his introduction to the translation of the *Rajatarangini* says –

> It has often been said of the India of the Hindus that it possessed no history. The remark is true if we apply it to history as a science and art, such as classical culture in its noblest prose-works has bequeathed it to us. But it is manifestly wrong if by it is meant historical development or the materials for studying it. India has never known among its *sastras* the study of history such as Greece and Rome cultivated it or as modern Europe understands it. Yet the materials for such a study are equally at our disposal in India. They are contained not only in such original sources of information as inscriptions, coins and antiquarian remains generally; advancing research has also proved that written records of events or of traditions concerning them have by no means been wanting in ancient India.
>
> This is not the place to examine the causes which in India have prevented the growth of a historical literature in the western sense of the word. They are most closely connected with deep-rooted peculiarities of Indian thought and culture which have rendered the mind of the Indian scholar indifferent to the bare truths of historical facts and have effectively prevented it from arriving at the perception of historical development and change.
>
> It is a direct result of these causes that we find the great mass of what we must call records of Indian history, in departments of literature which to the student of European history would appear distant from the field of his research. Much of what popular tradition had retained of the events of an early past, has found its way, overgrown and interwoven with myths and legends into the Indian epics – the Puranas and the fable literature. The object to which we owe such records of traditional lore was didactic and religious but not historical.

Stein writes,

> Kalhana attributes to Asoka the foundation of Srinagari, the old capital which can be shown to have occupied a site in the close vicinity of the present Srinagar and to have left its name to the later Srinagar. Jalauka whom the traditions preserved by Kalhana represent as the son and successor of Asoka appears before us as the popular hero of many wonderful stories. He is represented as having cleared the land of oppressing Mlecchas and effected

> extensive conquests. He is supposed to have brought in settlers to Kashmir and established there for the first time a complete system of administration. Kalhana reproduces several stories which show the King to have figured traditionally as a fervent worshipper at the shrine of Shiva Vijayesvara and Nandisa. Also the mention of the Saint Avaddhuta as Jalauka's religious instructor shows the presence of Shaivite tradition. He saw in Asoka's son pre-eminently the pious Salva... it is impossible for us to indicate what historical elements if any there are in the Kashmirian tradition regarding Jalauka the name of this alleged son of Asoka cannot otherwise be traced in our available sources and the account given of his reign in the chronicle bears in its main part a manifestly legendary character.

From the notes of Aurel Stein at the end of his translation of the *Rajatarangini* –

On the Vitasta:

> The great river which is the recipient of the whole drainage of the country is now known to the Kashmiris by the name of Vyath. This modern designation is the direct Sanskrit derivation of the ancient Sanskrit Vitasta which we meet already among the river names of the Rigveda. The name Jhelum which is now borne by the Vitasta in its course through the Punjab is wholly unknown to the genuine usage of Kashmir.
>
> The river to which the name Vitasta or Vyath is properly applied is formed by the meeting of the several streams which drain the south eastern portion of the valley. This meeting takes place in the plain close to the present town of Anantnag or Islamabad.
>
> An ancient legend related at length in the Nilamata and reproduced by the author of Haracaritacintamani represents the Vitasta as a manifestation of Siva's consort Parvati after Kashmir had been created. Siva, at the request of the sage Kasyapa, prevailed upon the goddess to show herself in the land in the shape of a river, in order to purify its inhabitants from the sinful contact with *Pisacas* (demons). The goddess thereupon assumed the form of a river in the underworld and asked her consort to make an opening by which she might come to the surface. This he did by striking the ground near the habitation of the Nilanaga, with the point of his trident. Through the fissure thus made, which measured one *vitasti* or span, the river gushed forth, receiving on account of this original the name *Vitasta*.

> The spring basin where the goddess appeared is the famous Nilanag near the village of Vernag in the district of Anantnag. The streams which unite close to Anantnag and there from the true Vitasta river are the Sandran, the Bring, the Arpath and the Lidder. A short distance below the village of Khanabal (now part of the town of Anantnag), where the three streams hitherto mentioned unite their waters, are joined from the north by those of the Lidder. This river, the ancient Ledari receives a number of glacier-fed streams draining the high range towards the upper Sind Valley.

One of Stein's famous works is *Serindia,* a detailed report of explorations in Central Asia and Western China that he undertook during the years 1906 to 1908. This exploration was in continuation of an earlier one in Chinese Turkestan. In this exploration he had hope of recovering "from ruins long ago abandoned to the desert more relics of that ancient civilisation which their joint influences of Buddhist India, China and the Hellenized East had fostered in the scattered oases of those remote Central Asian passage lands".

Aurel Stein wanted the details of the ancient routes that had been the scene of interaction of civilisation between India, Western Asia and the Far East, an interchange through trade and religious missionaries which persisted despite the hazards of difficult terrain and political disorder caused by China's expansionist policy in Central Asia. The entire area for this extended between the Pamir mountains in the west to the Pacific in the east. This was the area that for more than a millennium was the meeting point of Chinese and Indian civilization. Stein's *Serindia* is a brilliant and unsurpassed report on this area. He makes some startling discoveries; excavations at sites buried by the sand at Domoko yielded huge quantities of antiques and manuscript remains written in Sanskrit, Chinese, Kharosthi, Kuthcean, Sogdian, Turkish, Manichaean, Khotanese and Tibetan. Manuscripts survived because they were made of wood. Also found were paintings, embroidered textiles that were given as offerings to Lord Buddha. These finds opened a new perspective of the cultural exchanges in this area.

Aurel Stein was one of the last of the line of intrepid, multi-faceted, erudite Oriental scholars-cum-explorers who braved inhospitable deserts and high mountain passes to explore the history of remote regions, to literally unearth their mysteries, and to demonstrate through their findings the constant interaction of ideas in art and religion as well as commerce that shaped the civilization of these places for several millennia.

The tradition of Indian studies that commenced under the inspiration and example of Sir William Jones and Warren Hastings came full circle with versatile scholars such as Aurel Stein. They combined in themselves many roles – teacher, judge, administrator, poet, translator, art critic, historian, archaeologist, epigraphist, and numismatist. Without this amplitude of talent it would not have been possible to address themselves to the many tasks demanded of them in their rediscovery and interpretation of Indian civilization. Most of them brought to their work minds that had a largeness of vision, horizons not obscured by prejudices, and an insatiable curiosity to learn about a civilization that had been long forgotten even by its legatees in the turmoil of a millennium.

It is to these great scholars that the people of India owe a debt of gratitude.

* * * * *

Bibliography

Arberry, A.J., *Asiatic Jones*. Longman, Green & Co., UK. 1946.

——, *Oriental Essays: Portrait of Seven Scholars*. George Allen & Unwin, UK. 1960.

Arnold, Edwin, *The Song Celestial*. Translation of the Bhagavad Gita (Reprint). 1985.

——, *Light of Asia* (Reprint). 1985.

Asiatick Researches or Transactions of the Society (1784) (Reprint). Oriental Publishers and Books, Bharat-Bharati, Varanasi. 1984.

Bagchee, Moni (compiler and editer), *Discourses and Essays of Sir William Jones*. Peoples Publishing House, Calcutta. 1960.

Balakrishnan, Purasu, *Glimpses of Kalidasa*. Bharatiya Vidya Bhavan, Bombay. 1970.

Basham, A.L., *The Wonder That Was India* (Reprint). Rupa Publishers, New Delhi.

Bearce, George D., *British Attitude to India*. Oxford University Press, UK. 1961.

Bishop, Isabella Bird, *Among the Tibetans*. Royal Geographic Society, 1894 (Reprint). Pilgrims Book Pvt. Ltd. 1999.

Bose, N.S., *The Indian Awakening and Bengal*. K.L. Mukhopadhyay, Kolkata. 1960.

Brassey Halhed, Nathaniel, *A Grammar of Bengali Language*. 1778 (Reprint). Ananda Publishers Pvt. Ltd., Calcutta. 1980.

Busteed, *Chronicle of Calcutta*. Calcutta Historical Society. 1916.

——, *Echoes of Old Calcutta*. Calcutta Historical Society. 1921.

Cannon, Garland, *Oriental Jones*. ICCR, New Delhi. 1964.

Chamberlain, M.E., *Britain and India – The Inter-action of Two Peoples*. David and Charles, Newton Abbot. 1974.

Chatterjee, Sir Atul and Sir Richard Burn, *British Contributions to Indian Studies*. British Council and Orient Longman. 1943.

Chaudhuri, Tapan Ray, *Europe Reconsidered*. Oxford University Press, India. 1988.

Clark, Kenneth, *Civilization*. Penguin Books, UK. 1969.

Cobban, A., *Edmund Burke and the Revolt Against the Eighteenth Century*. George Allen & Unwin, London. 1929.

Collis, Maurice, *British Merchants and Adventurers*. Collins Publishers, London. 1942.

Comfort Start, Nathan, *The Pursuit of Learning*. Harcourt Brace Publishers.

Dasgupta, J.N., *Bengal in the Sixteenth Century*. Vintage Books, India. 1989.

Dubois, Abbe J.A., *People of India and of their Institutions: Civil and Religious*. 1879 (Reprint). Asia Education Society, Madras. 1989.

Durant, Will, *Age of Faith*. Simon & Schuster, New York. 1936.

——, *Age of Reason*. Simon & Schuster, New York. 1943.

——, *Age of Napoleon*. Simon & Schuster, New York. 1976.

Firminger, Walter Kelly, *Genuine Memoirs of Asiaticus*. Calcutta Historical Society. 1790.

Fitzgerald, C.P., *China*. Cresset Press, UK. 1935.

Florinsky, M.I., *History of Russia*. Russian Academy of Sciences. 1935.

Garrat and Thomson, *Rise and Fulfilment of British Rule in India*. Macmillan & Co., UK.

George, T.G., *The Briton In India*.

Ghosh, A. (ed.), *History of Indian Archaeology*. Centenary Volume. 1961.

Gleig, E., *Memoirs of Warren Hastings* (Memoirs of Warren Hastings ... Including his correspondence with Sir John Shore, afterwards Lord Teignmouth). Calcutta. 1836.

Hastings, Warren, *Memoirs Relative to the State of India*. J. Murray of Fleet Street, London. 1786.

Hodcart, M.J.C., *Samuel Johnson and His Times*. B.T. Batsford Ltd. Publishers, UK. 1962.

Huntington, Samuel, *Clash of Civilization*. Journal of Foreign Afairs. 1993.

India A Hundred Years Ago. Bishop Heber's Memoirs. Longman, Green & Co. 1830.

Keith, Arthur Berriedale, *Constitutional History of India, 1600-1935*. Methuen & Co., London. 1969.

——, *History of Sanskrit Literature*. Oxford University Press, Delhi. 1973.

Kincaid, Denis, *Social Life in India 1608-1937*.

Krishnaswami, P.R., *Tom Munro Saheb*. Higginbothams, Madras. 1960.

Leifer, Walter, *India and the Germans*. Horst Edmar Vorlag, Germany & Shakuntala Publishing House, Bombay. 1971.

Lord Meston (ed.), *Modern India and the West – A Study of the Inter-action of their Civilizations*.

Lyall, Sir Alfred, *The Rise and Expansion of the British Dominion in India*. John Murray Publishers, UK. 1919.

——, *Asiatic Studies in Religion and Art*. John Murray Publishers, UK. 1923.

Malcolm, Sir John, *Political History of India*. Longman, Green & Co., London. 1820.
Marshall, P.J. (ed.), *The Writings and Speeches of Edmund Burke* (Volume V. India: Madras and Bengal – 1774-1785). Clarendon, Oxford. 1981.
Menon, V.P., *Integration of Indian States*. Orient Longman, Madras. 1995.
Mill, James, *The History of British India*. 1817 (Reprint). Associated Publishing House. 1972.
Mirsky, D.S., *Russia*. Cresset Press, UK. 1931.
Moore-Gilbert, B.J., *Kipling and Orientalism*. Croom Helm Publishers, UK. 1986.
Mosley, Leonard, *Curzon, the End of An Epoch*. Longman, Green & Co., UK. 1961.
Mukherjee, Hiren, *The Pilgrim-Scholar – Alexander Csoma de Koros*. Sterling Publishers, New Delhi. 1981.
Mukherjee, S.N., *Sir William Jones – A Study of British Attitudes to India*. Cambridge University Press. 1968.
Murray, H.J.R., *History of Chess*. Oxford University Press, Oxford. 1913.
Nikitin, Afanasy, *Travels Across the Seven Seas*. Moscow Publishing House. 1975.
O'Malley, L.S.S. (ed.), *Modern India and the West – A Study of the Interaction of Their Civilizations*. OUP, London. 1941.
Pachori, Satya S. (ed.), *Sir William Jones – A Reader*. Oxford University Press, UK. 1993.
Panikar, K.M., *Asia and Western Dominance*. George Allen & Unwin, UK. 1953.
Penderel Moon, *Warren Hastings and British India*, Hodder & Stoughton Pvt. Ltd. 1947.
Philips, C.H., *The East India Company*. Manchester University Press, Manchester. 1961.
Radhakrishnan, S., *Eastern Religions and Western Thoughts*. Oxford University Press. 1939.
Rawlinson, H.G., *Intercourses Between India and The Western World*. Rai Book Service, Bombay. 1925.
——, *India*. Cresset Press, UK. 1937.
Reynolds, Reginald, *The White Sahibs in India*. M. Secker & Warburg Pvt. Ltd., London. 1937.
Rhyn, Henne am, *Cultural History of the German People*. Horst Edmar Vorlag, Germany. 1885.
Riencourt, Amoury de, *The Soul of India*. Honeyglen, London. 1986.
Rocher, Rosane, *The Checkered Life of Nathaniel Brassey Halhed*. Motilal Benarsidass Publishers, New Delhi. 1983.
Said, Edward, *Orientalism*. Routledge & Kegan Pvt. Ltd. 1978.

Sansom, George, *Japan*. Cresset Press, UK. 1937.

Seeley, Sir J., *Expansion of England*. Macmillan & Co., UK. 1884.

Sen, Surendranath, *India through Chinese Eyes*. Madras University Press. 1956.

Sencourt, Robert, *India in English Literature*. 1920 (Reprint). Vintage Books, UK. 1980.

Sir William Jones – Commemoration Volume. Royal Asiatic Society of Bengal. 1948.

Smith, Vincent, *History of India*. OUP, Oxford. 1923.

Stokes, Eric, *The English Utilitarians and India*. Oxford University Press, UK. 1959.

Sutton, Jean, *Lords of The East – East India Company and its Ships*. Conway Maritime Press, UK. 1981.

Sylvester, D.W., *Clive in India*. Longman, Green & Co., UK. 1968.

Syme, R., *Colonial Elites* (Rome, Spain and the Americas). Oxford University Press, London. 1958.

Thompson, Edward John and G.T. Garratt, *Rise and Fulfilment of British Rule in India*. Macmillan & Co., London. 1934.

Toynbee, Arnold J., *A Study of History*. Vols. 1 & 2, Oxford University Press, UK. 1938.

——, *Civilization on Trial: The World and the West*. Meridian Books, New York. 1958.

Travels of Marco Polo, Folio Books, UK. 1970.

Trevelyan, George M., *Social Life in England in the Eighteenth Century*. Longman, Green & Co., UK. 1945.

Trevelyan, Lord, *The India We Left Behind*.

Trevelyan, Sir George Otto, *The Life and Letters of Lord Macaulay*. Longman, Green & Co., UK. 1923.

Watson, Ian Bruce, *Foundations of the British Empire* (Foundations for Empire: English Private Trade in India, 1659-1760), Vikas, New Delhi. 1980.

Wheeler, J. Talboys, *A History of English Settlements in India*. Vishal Publishers. 1972.

Williams, Monier, *Modern India and the Indians*. Oriental Publishers, Delhi. 1971.

Wint, Guy, *The British in Asia*. London. 1947.

Index